Text and Context

Essays on Translation & Interpreting in Honour of Ian Mason

Edited by

Mona Baker, Maeve Olohan and María Calzada Pérez

St. Jerome Publishing
Manchester, UK & Kinderhook (NY), USA

Published by
St. Jerome Publishing
2 Maple Road West, Brooklands
Manchester, M23 9HH, UK
Telephone +44 (0)161 973 9856
Fax +44 (0)161 905 3498
ken@stjeromepublishing.com
http://www.stjerome.co.uk

InTrans Publications
P. O. Box 467
Kinderhook, NY 12106, USA
Telephone (518) 758-1755
Fax (518) 758-6702

ISBN 978-1-905763-25-2 (pbk)

Printed and bound in Great Britain by
T. J. International Ltd, Padstow, Cornwall, UK

Typeset by
Delta Typesetters, Cairo, Egypt
Email: hilali1945@yahoo.co.uk

British Library Cataloguing in Publication Data
A catalogue record of this book is available from the British Library

Library of Congress Cataloging in Publication Data
Text and context : essays on translation & interpreting in honour of Ian Mason /
edited by Mona Baker, Maeve Olohan and María Calzada Pérez.
    p. cm.
 Includes bibliographical references and index.
 ISBN 978-1-905763-25-2 (pbk. : alk. paper)
1. Translating and interpreting. I. Baker, Mona. II. Olohan, Maeve. III. Calzada
Pérez, María.
 P306.2.T53 2010
 418'.02--dc22
                        2010006467

Text and Context
Essays on Translation and Interpreting in Honour of
Ian Mason

Edited by Mona Baker, Maeve Olohan and María Calzada Pérez

Ian Mason has been a towering presence in the now flourishing discipline of translation studies since its inception, and has produced some of the most influential and detailed analyses of translated text and interpreted interaction to date. The sophistication, dynamism and inclusiveness that have characterized his approach to all forms of mediation are the hallmarks of his legacy.

Text and Context celebrates Ian Mason's scholarship by bringing together fourteen innovative and original pieces of research by both young and established scholars, who examine different forms of translation and interpreting in a variety of cultural and geographical settings. In line with his own inclusive approach to the field, these contributions combine close textual analysis with keen attention to issues of power, modes of socialization, institutional culture, individual agency and ethical accountability. While paying tribute to one of the most innovative and influential scholars in the field, the volume offers novel insights into a variety of genres and practices and charts important new directions for the discipline.

Table of Contents

IV. The Impact of Translation & Interpreting in a Changing World

Introduction

"In Translation Studies … where the raw data are situated at the interface between two languages", Ian Mason argues in a recent publication, "it is impossible (or futile) to conduct analysis independently of cultural considerations, including perceptions of power, status, role, socio-textual practices, etc." (2009:55). This statement sums up one of the key contributions that Ian Mason has made to both translation and interpreting studies in the course of a distinguished career that has spanned several decades. His publications – including those written in collaboration with Basil Hatim – have repeatedly shown us that attempts to treat any form of mediation as culture-free, or to engage in dissecting the history of the discipline into a number of 'cultural' vs. other 'turns' or 'approaches', simply miss the point. Acknowledging the power of culture and the cultural workings of power, he has produced some of the most influential and detailed analyses of translations and instances of interpreted interaction to date. The sophistication, dynamism and inclusiveness that have characterized his approach to all forms of mediation are the hallmarks of his legacy. Not surprisingly, they have attracted many young (and not so young) scholars to draw extensively on his work over the years, and to see him as a role model and a source of continued inspiration. The many students who enjoyed the privilege of having him as doctoral supervisor now occupy key positions in Europe, Asia, the Middle East, Australia and elsewhere, and are setting the agenda for a new generation of scholars in the field.

Ian Mason's contribution spans a number of key areas, the most important of these being socially-situated textual analysis of translation and interpreting, informed by critical discourse analysis and pragmatics; dialogue interpreting, an area of research that has particularly been transformed by his pioneering publications; institutional translation; audiovisual translation; translation pedagogy; and research methodology. These themes are reflected in the articles that constitute this modest tribute to his scholarship.

The volume opens with a section on *Language Matters*. The two articles, by Wadensjö and Campbell *et al.*, focus on close linguistic analysis of specific textual features that have concrete implications for participants in any interaction, within and outside a pedagogical context. **Wadensjö** focuses on the interpreter's mediation of answers to yes/no questions in Swedish/Russian court trials. Her study sheds light on the conditions for producing expanded answers to yes/no questions in interpreter-mediated trials, and demonstrates that defendants are dependent on interpreters' active support in attempting to gain and secure conversational space. **Campbell *et al.*** explore another important and under-researched aspect of language patterning, namely sentence openings, as a feature of textual competence. The study compares the output of Arab students translating and interpreting into English as a second language with that of professional translators and interpreters and concludes with a set of recommendations for curriculum designers. The emphasis in designing curricula for translators should be on text- rather than sentence-based diagnosis and amelioration of problems with determiners. For consecutive interpreting, the emphasis should be on developing the student's capacity to build an argumentative plan, a content plan, and a sense of audience.

The next section, *Forms of Mediation*, consists of three articles that engage with the issue of the translator's presence in the text. **Hermans** attempts to distinguish between the mimetic nature of translation and the evaluative attitude, or modality, that informs it. Arguing that understanding the social functioning of translation requires us to focus on the translated text as it reaches its audience, without checking it against the original, he explores a number of concepts that allow us to detect and describe the nature of the translator's mediating role. These concepts are drawn primarily from Relevance Theory and Hallidayan linguistics. **Munday**'s analysis of aspects of the translator's intervention in the text is similarly informed by systemic functional linguistics. He revisits Hatim and Mason's static-dynamic continuum and links it to the concept of evaluation, and more specifically to recent work on appraisal theory, to investigate how translators feed in their ideological perspective to the text. Munday offers examples from a range of different genres to illustrate some of the ways in which the translator's attitude (realized as affect, judgement or appreciation) may be inscribed or invoked in the text. **Mossop** begins by redefining the notion of moves, applied by Ian Mason in the context of interpreting, as 'events' in the translator's mind, and more specifically as 'conscious mental acts'. Drawing a distinction between motivating, composing and transmitting utterances, he demonstrates that any move on the part of the translator (e.g. repairing an error in the original, writing a footnote), may be accompanied by a change of footing between the roles of Motivator and non-Motivator, and that the role of 'Motivator' can be described in terms of four types of reporting: Plain, Reconstructive, Summary and Fictive. Mossop finally uses a passage from Thucydides in English translation to revisit the traditional distinction between translation and adaptation.

In a pioneering article that appeared in the second edition of Lawrence Venuti's reader, Mason (2004:470) described "institutional approaches to translating" as "a neglected factor within the field of translation studies". The third and longest section of this volume, *Institutional Context and Individual Agency*, attempts to address this gap and to respond to his call for "the whole issue of institutional cultures of translating" to be subjected to "more systematic exploration, across a range of institutions and language pairs" (*ibid.*:481). It begins with two studies, by Beaton-Thome and Koskinen, which focus on different aspects of interpreting and translating for the European Union institutions. **Beaton-Thome** examines simultaneous interpreting between German and English in the European Parliament, focusing on the ideological significance of the first person plural *we* and the role it plays in the construction and negotiation of in- and out-group identities. One of the most significant findings of this study is that interpreted utterances reveal an intensified trend towards the use of the inclusive *we* to refer to *we, the parliamentary community* and *we, the EU*, at the expense of more peripheral identities such as the national, regional and political group. **Koskinen** looks at the new strategies and modes of communication currently being adopted by the European Commission to support participatory policies and enhance dialogic interaction with European citizens. She charts new developments on this front in order to determine who is invited to participate in the dialogue and to delineate the challenges and opportunities that the new communication strategies present for translators. Koskinen predicts that the trend towards multimedialization will become more evident in the future, not only in the European Union but across the field of institutional translation, and argues that this – together with the growing emphasis on English as *lingua franca* of the EU – poses a challenge for the recruitment and training of translators with new skills profiles.

The next article in this section moves us out of the European context to explore institutional translation in a very different cultural location and genre. **Kang**'s data consist of an article published in *Newsweek U.S. Domestic Edition* and its corresponding Korean article, published in *Newsweek Hankukpan*. Both are based on an interview of the then newly elected South Korean President Roh Moo Hyun. While the English article constructs an image of Roh as uncooperative and anti-American, the Korean version shifts the focus to issues of fact construction and *Newsweek Hankukpan*'s own commitment to convey Roh's views accurately. Lending credibility to and ensuring the acceptability of the target text by embedding and contextualizing the original text within the narrative framework of a translating institution, Kang argues, may not only involve aspects of giving, silencing, distorting and blending voice, but also evoking intertextual connections that may deviate from the typical source-target relationship.

The articles by Tipton and Maltby focus on institutional settings in which the conceptualization of the interpreter's role and the way the interpreter interacts with other participants have serious social and political consequences. **Tipton** examines trust as a potential norm of interaction and its impact on the relationship between the interpreter, the service provider and the service user. She argues that changes in social work practice and policy, and increased public scrutiny at both a general level (public perception) and a formal level (audit), have impacted on the practitioner's role in recent times and have served to question the traditional server-served relationship between the service provider and service user, with consequences for the interpreter. Based on focus-group work conducted in the Greater Manchester region, with participants from several social services, she concludes that a general degree of basic trust is still likely to exist between professionals, but that this has often been eroded and has led to particular compensation strategies being deployed to establish a degree of 'normalcy' as a backdrop against which the social work practitioner and interpreter can carry out their work. **Maltby** examines a related issue, that of impartiality and neutrality, in the context of codes of conduct as articulated in institutional interpreting policies. Drawing on Critical Discourse Analysis, he investigates the ways in which two voluntary sector organizations in the UK asylum context articulate notions of interpreter impartiality in their policies. His findings suggest that although they both position interpreters as impartial and neutral agents to greater or lesser extents, the policies of the two organizations are underpinned by particular institutional notions of impartiality that depart from normative models to allow client interests to remain of central concern. Both policies allow room for interpreters to offer advocacy and advice to clients in the daunting process of applying for asylum in the UK.

This tribute to Ian Mason appropriately ends with a section on *The Impact of Translation and Interpreting in a Changing World*, in recognition of the vision and insight with which he has steered the discipline for several decades, continually looking ahead and initiating new avenues of research that respond to social, intellectual and political developments as they begin to take shape.

All four articles in this section engage with forms of intervention that are characteristic of the global society in which we now live. The section starts with a historical study by **Cheung**, who argues that studying the past not only enhances our understanding of the past but also facilitates reflection on present realities. This includes the reality of a growing number of people who explicitly identify themselves as part of a community that is focused on effecting change. Cheung draws on this sense of 'activism' in her investigation of a number of translation initiatives undertaken during the late Qing period in China, and concludes that the larger the readership of a translation, the greater the scope for disseminating activist values, but also the less predictable the outcome of such dissemination. While Cheung ends with a call for today's activist translators to make better use of internet technology to attract more recruits, **Pérez González** demonstrates that translation is increasingly being appropriated by politically engaged individuals, without formal training in translation, in order to tamper with the dynamics of the global media marketplace and to promote their own narrative take on political events. His analysis retraces the process by which such fluid networks come into being by examining how a televised interview with Spain's former Prime Minister, José María Aznar López, conducted in English and broadcast on the BBC programme *Hardtalk*, came to be subtitled into Spanish and circulated on the internet by one such network. Pérez González argues that given their fluidity and lack of structure, we should speak of ad-hocracies rather than networks, the former term referring to groups of like-minded individuals who meet online and capitalize on the potential of networked communication to exploit their collective intelligence.

Moving from written and audiovisual translation to face-to-face interpreting, **Barsky** takes up the cause of illegal immigrants in the United States and argues for activism over machine-like fidelity on the part of interpreters, given the enormity of abuses in certain legal contexts. He uses examples from a large-scale research project to demonstrate the extent to which illegal immigrants are ill-served by the entire legal system, which treats them as 'guilty by virtue of being there'. He concludes that interpreters should be sensitized to the issues that confront immigrants and should drop the façade of 'impartiality' when they are faced with clear and obvious abuses of power. **Cronin**'s contribution finally concludes the volume with a wide-ranging discussion of translation and mobility in a globalized world. Eschewing what he describes as 'the beatific visions of universal understanding' often evoked in discussions of translation, he stresses that we must instead take the incomprehensibility of the other as our starting point. It is in this conflicted sense, he argues, that translation can provide a productive way of thinking about contemporary multilingual and multicultural societies. Ultimately, translation needs to be situated in what he calls 'a new *politics of introversion*' which seeks to expand possibilities, not reduce them, and which reconfigures fundamentals of space and time in the new century, with attendant socio-political and cultural consequences.

Ian Mason's scholarship – "engaged, solid, serious", as Barsky describes it in this volume – has provided inspiration for generations of researchers, including the present contributors and editors. But it is also for his personal integrity and modesty that he is held in such high esteem by those who have been privileged enough to know him firsthand. This collection celebrates both his scholarship and his personal qualities, and is offered as a tribute to an outstanding scholar, colleague and friend.

Mona Baker, Maeve Olohan and María Calzada Pérez
February 2010

References

Mason, Ian (2004) 'Text Parameters in Translation: Transitivity and Institutional Cultures', in Lawrence Venuti (ed.) *The Translation Studies Reader*, Second Edition, London & New York: Routledge, 470-81.
------ (2009) 'Role, Positioning and Discourse in Face-to-Face Interpreting', in Raquel de Pedro Ricoy, Isabelle Perez and Christine Wilson (eds) *Interpreting and Translating in Public Service Settings: Policy, Practice, Pedagogy*, Manchester: St. Jerome Publishing, 52-73.

I. Language Matters

On the Production and Elicitation of Expanded Answers to Yes/No Questions in Interpreter-mediated Trials[1]

CECILIA WADENSJÖ
Stockholm University, Sweden

Abstract. *This article offers a comparative analysis of sequences drawn from two interpreter-mediated (Swedish-Russian) court trials, documented in Sweden. In single-language trials, defendants' ability to gain conversational space to expand a minimal answer heavily depends on the immediate sanction of the legal questioners. In interpreter-mediated court proceedings, however, the analysis suggests that the ability of foreign-language speaking defendants to expand a narrative is relatively independent of the direct sanctions of the questioners. Overall, the analysis indicates that, similarly to the strategies used by defendants to produce answers, questioning strategies used by legal questioners tend to function somewhat differently in face-to-face interpreter-mediated court trials, compared to single-language trials. This, it is assumed, must be explained by a range of linguistic and pragmatic factors. Those explored in this paper include the potentially increased multifunctionality of conversational units in interpreter-mediated encounters, the various means by which foreign-language defendants attempt to project further talk, the restricted immediate access of the legal questioners to these means, and the various ways in which interpreters may deal with the ambiguity of spontaneous spoken discourse.*

In everyday life, court interpreting is often thought of as a purely ancillary activity. A number of detailed enquiries into this practice, however, have demonstrated its complex character and potentially unforeseen effects on the judicial process. Berk-Seligson (1990), for instance, demonstrates in a broad ethnographic study that interpreters are occasionally far from the unobtrusive figures court personnel may expect them to be. She further demonstrates through an experimental study that differences in the interpreter's performance may alter the way people (in this case, mock jurors) form an

[1] My thanks to members of the Talk-in-Interaction seminar series at Linköping University and to Mona Baker for valuable comments on earlier drafts of this article. Financial support from the Swedish Research Council (421-2003-1825) is also gratefully acknowledged.

impression of the trustworthiness and intelligence of testifying witnesses. Working with naturally occurring discourse data, Lee (2009) demonstrates how the ambiguous utterances of witnesses pose a major challenge to court interpreters. Hale (2004), too, draws attention to this issue, in addition to showing, among other things, that interpreters' renderings of questions can impinge on lawyers' questioning strategies. And law scholars such as Laster and Taylor (1994) and Roberts-Smith (2007) have expressed and reported concerns about interpreted court trials.

In interviews conducted by the current author, Swedish legal officials have complained that they find it difficult to use normal questioning strategies in interpreted court trials. Some argue that it is impossible to do so and express considerable frustration at this situation. In practice, of course, numerous interpreter-mediated court trials take place every day. Questions are indeed posed and answers are given via interpreters. It seems reasonable to suggest that if the courts assign well-trained interpreters to the task they can expect them to perform much more satisfactorily than non-trained individuals. Interpreters' education, however, does not automatically enhance court personnel's satisfaction with their performance in court. The interpreter-mediated hearing differs qualitatively from the single-language hearing. It seems plausible to suggest that both the elicitation and the production of answers are bound to function somewhat differently in a face-to-face, interpreter-mediated hearing, compared to a single-language trial. The inevitable period of suspension between question and answer, where the interpreter comes in, seems to bring some extraordinary conversational mechanism into play (Wadensjö 1997, 2008a). Taking as a starting point the mutual dependence among conversationalists in an encounter, this paper will examine Russian-speaking defendants' production of answers to legal questioners' yes/no questions in two Swedish court trials. More precisely, viewing language and mind dialogically (see, for example, Linell 2009) and adopting an interactionist analytical approach, it will explore the conditions for the defendants' expansion of minimal answers ('yes' or 'no') and the questioners' sanctioning (or otherwise) of such expansions.

1.   Expansions of minimal answers

A court hearing regularly starts with what in everyday language is usually called an open question, i.e. a question designed to elicit a relatively free narrative about a certain event. This narrative is then taken as a point of departure for more specific questions. In order to control the exchange and elicit precise answers, legal professionals typically formulate many of these as yes/no questions. This does not mean they always expect a simple 'yes' or 'no' as an answer. In fact, there is no such straightforward cause and effect relation between the type of question and the type of answer one might assume to be elicited at first glance. Already some thirty years ago, studies of courtroom proceedings (Atkinson and Drew 1979, Danet 1980, Adelswärd *et al.* 1987, among others) showed that witnesses typically do not confine their answers to 'yes' or 'no', but normally expand them as they see fit, when afforded the space to do so.

In a recent study of an Italian court case, Galatolo and Drew (2006) show that yes/no questions may implicitly invite more than a simple 'yes' or 'no', but that at the same time the question gives the questioner room to ignore or heed information that goes beyond the minimal answer. Galatolo and Drew (*ibid.*) further found that when a witness first produced a 'yes' or a 'no', their chance of getting a narrative expansion sanctioned was much better than when they did not. Being permitted to expand, they could provide answers that went far beyond the framework of the question. By expanding their answer to a yes/no question defendants can mitigate their subordinate position in court to some extent.

Narrative expansions clearly demand conversational space. Speakers normally need to actively secure this space, using verbal or prosodic means. In interpreter-mediated courtroom proceedings, conversational space is distributed in a non-conventional way. In principle, dialogue interpreters take or are allocated every second turn at talk, since they typically provide renditions of utterances more or less as they are produced. What may this atypical communicative pattern – which is nevertheless typical for interpreted face-to-face interaction – imply when it comes to defendants' chances of expanding a minimal answer and questioners' chances of inviting, permitting or not permitting expansions?

Galatolo and Drew (2006) distinguish between *expansion* of a "minimal answer, such as 'yes, they did', or 'yes, they told me' which remains within the framework of the question" (i.e. a yes/no question), and a *narrative expansion*, i.e. a type of expansion that "goes beyond what is minimally and explicitly requested by the question" (*ibid.*:663). In Galatolo and Drew's terms, a narrative expansion basically fulfils the function of further substantiating and sometimes also recontextualizing a given minimal answer. Narrative expansions are described as *defence practices* in which defendants typically engage while on trial (*ibid.*). Understanding this kind of discourse practice requires close analysis of recorded and transcribed discourse data.

2.   Analyzing interpreting as social interaction

Looking closely at sequences of interaction, this paper treats the interpreter-mediated courtroom hearing as a *situated system of activity* (Goffman 1961). The approach taken follows the basic assumption that through analyses of naturally occurring talk it is possible to gain knowledge of how conversationalists relate to each other and to the ongoing social activity. An important epistemic assumption is that knowledge generated through this kind of analysis is primarily demonstrated, not reported. In other words, the analysis aims to establish, not what people think or claim, but how they *display* their knowledge and understandings *in and by interaction*.

When monolingual speakers interact in a first language setting, it is taken for granted that they share knowledge of what is going on. In the case of foreign language interaction, it may not be clear from the outset in whose frame (or frames) a given encounter operates. However, as Wagner (1996) remarks, if participants in these settings are able to interact at some level of mutual understanding, it must be possible to analyze how they are doing this.

In interpreted encounters, two out of three participants as a rule have no or limited knowledge of another party's language and consequently would normally not be able to understand, without the interpreter's assistance, either what this party's talk is about, or how the shared event is managed and organized locally. As demonstrated in numerous empirical studies, when an interpreter is introduced in a face-to-face communicative situation the organizational format of interaction becomes fundamentally different from a dyadic, one-language situation (Apfelbaum 2004, Bolden 2000, Davidson 2002, Mason 2006, Roy 2000, Russell 2004, Valero Garcés 2002, Wadensjö 1998). Nevertheless, at some level, people involved in interpreter-mediated interaction arguably still share some knowledge of what is going on.

2.1   Analyzing questions in courtroom hearings

Individuals brought to trial must have their say. Yet, their right to talk during court proceedings is strictly regulated. More precisely, they may speak only when requested to do so. In order to make witnesses and defendants talk in institutionally relevant ways, legal officials use certain questioning strategies. Questions and answers constitute the basic sequential organization of talk towards which participants are oriented (Atkinson and Drew 1979).

The importance of questioning strategies is amply described in research on forensic linguistics and forensic psychology. In her pioneering study, Loftus (1979) found that variation in types of questions can have an impact on the answers they elicit, and that questions are systematically used as a means of control in the courtroom. In her study, it is more or less taken for granted that the meaning of a question is fixed, as it were, in its lexical units and syntactic form. A different, interactional, empirical approach would show that participants draw on these and on various other locally available resources in establishing the meaning of a question. In other words, the meanings of words and utterances are negotiable in social interaction.

In the present study, the concept of *adjacency pair* (Sacks *et al.* 1974) is considered relevant in examining questions and their function in talk. As the first part of an adjacency pair, a question sets the frame for an answer, just as a greeting sets the frame for another greeting. The communicative format of an interpreted encounter, however, seems to challenge this universal mechanism of human conversation. Clearly, a question plus a version of this question in another language followed by an answer and the interpretation of this answer constitute four conversational units – a structure that does not equate with an adjacency pair. Nevertheless, conversational conventions established in single-language interaction inevitably have an impact on the way talk is organized in practice in interpreter-mediated encounters (Mason 2006, Wadensjö 1998). Moreover, the physical presence of dialogue interpreters and their image as 'non-present' create what we could call a *communicative wiggle room* (Wadensjö 2008b; cf. Erickson 2001), which is uniquely available as a communicative resource in interpreter-mediated interaction.

3.   Data: communication in court

The trials drawn upon in this paper belong to a corpus of tape-recorded interpreter-mediated courtroom proceedings, collected for a research project conducted at Linköping University, Sweden. A Swedish criminal trial differs in several respects from its counterpart in other court systems. As elsewhere, a judge chairs the proceedings and other main legal actors include the prosecutor and – in some cases – the counsel for the defence. None of the legal professionals wear wigs or other symbolic garments, however, and hearings are carried out in a relatively informal way. There is no jury, but three or four lay judges sit at the front panel together with the judge and a clerk; the latter attends to issues of protocol. The proceedings are less adversarial than in courts in English-speaking countries. The judge is fairly active during the hearings and there is no pronounced difference between examination and cross-examination.

The data collection took place over a period of three months and involved observing and recording in three regional courts. The main data consists of 24 hours of tape recordings. These relate to 14 minor criminal offences, involving 24 Russian-speaking defendants and 14 interpreters, all authorized (working between Swedish and Russian).

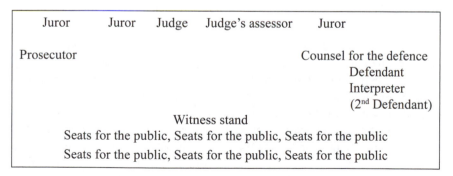

Figure 1. The courtroom set-up

I recorded the trials, using a small tape recorder and a microphone placed on the desk where the interpreter and the defendant were seated (see Figure 1).

The idea was to ensure that all talk, including what the interpreter was communicating in *chuchotage* (in Russian), should be captured on tape. As a result, I could hear, and subsequently transcribe, most of what the participants said in the encounters. In the transcripts below, talk in Swedish and talk in Russian are presented in two separate columns. It is worth noting that Swedish talk constitutes talk on the record, whereas talk in Russian may be heard as talk but may not necessarily be understood by members of the court.

3.1   Criminal court cases

Two examples will be contrasted in the following analysis. These are drawn from two hearings with Russian-speaking defendants who appeared in court cases concerning theft. The defendants deny guilt in both cases and are both found guilty of the charges held against them. In the present context, the interesting difference between the two trials is that one defendant produces numerous narrative expansions and the other none. This might be partly a consequence of one being generally more talkative than the other, but also, I would argue, it has to do with how participants, including the interpreter, orient to the frames of the event and to the production of requested minimal answers. The sequences below were selected to show how the defendants, the legal questioners and the interpreters may variously contribute to the occurrence and the non-occurrence of expanded answers.

  During the proceedings recorded for this project, most interpreters produced Swedish talk, i.e. talk for the court, in a louder voice than talk in Russian, which was aimed at the defendant sitting next to the interpreter on duty. The interpreter in Excerpt 1 however hardly altered the pitch of his voice at all, making his talk equally available for the two Russian-speaking defendants present in that case.

3.2   *"So to start with you intended to steal, but you changed your mind"*

The first excerpt is from a trial where two Russian-speaking individuals, a man and a woman, are accused of colluding in theft. The case concerns stealing cosmetics in a department store. The excerpt starts shortly after a witness, a department store detective, has stated that he observed the female defendant fill a plastic bag with mascara and then leave the shop with the bag in her hand, at the same time as the male defendant was distracting the salesperson at the front desk. Later, the witness reports, the woman came back into the shop and left the bag in question among a pile of clothes, but in legal terms, the theft had already been committed. The defendant is thus caught red-handed stealing, and the most important issue for the court is to consider whether the offence was intended and planned and, if so, by one or both defendants. The woman is heard first, and at the point of Excerpt 1, her hearing is coming to an end.

The counsel for the defence gives her one last chance to explain herself, asking her (in Swedish): 'How come you left a bag full of cosmetics among a pile of clothes'? The excerpt starts where she begins to answer the question.

Excerpt 1 (Case 4, Tape 6)[2]
C = Counsel for the defence (man), **D** = woman defendant, **I** = interpreter (man)

		Talk in Swedish		Talk in Russian
01			D	m potomu čto ja dumala::: *m because I thought:::*
02	I	för att jag har tänkt över. *because I have thought over.*		
03	C	[haa. [*right.*	D	[ja dumala. pust u menja budet ljubie [*I thought. let me have any other*
04			D	drugie nepriytnosti no tolko ne *troubles but just not*
05			D	svyzannye s kraszhej. vot *connected to theft. so that's*
06	I	[ja sa, det får gärna vara vilka [*I said, I may well meet with*	D	[i vse. [*all.*
07	I	obehag som helst, e:: som kan drabba *whatever trouble there is, e::*		
08	I	mig, bara de inte blir stöld. *it just mustn't be theft.*		
09	C	haa. *right.*		
10	I	(.hh)		
11		(0.5)		(0.5)
12	C	så från början så var du inställd på *so to start with you intended to*		
13	C	att du skulle stjäla, men men du *steal, but but you*		
14	C	ångrade dig. e de så, *changed your mind. is this how,*		

---

[2] A key to transcription conventions is given at the end of the paper.

15	C	[man ska förstå dej. *[one should understand you.*	I	[značit em e s načalo, vy xoteli *[that is em e to start with, you wanted*
16			I	varovat, no nakonets vy *to steal, but finally you*
17			I	peredumali. tak? *changed your mind. that's it?*
18	I	[JA. *[YES.*	D	da ja pe[redumala, *yes I cha[nged my mind,*
19		(.)		(.)
20	C	haa. innan du (.) la ifrån dig dom här *right. before you (.) put away these*		
21	C	sakerna. var du på något sätt *things. were you in some way*		
22	C	ute? ur affären. *outside? of the shop.*		

The counsel for the defence asks a yes/no question concerning the defendant's intentions (so to start with you intended to steal..., lines **C**:12–15). This question is rendered (**I**:15–17) and the defendant starts to confirm the suggestion (yes I changed, **D**:18). Right on 'changed', the interpreter comes in, rendering her answer as a distinct *JA* (YES) (**I**:18), with the effect, it appears, that the defendant's minimal expansion is silenced. The interpreter seems to have been oriented to the form of the question. Both the timing of *YES* and its finalized prosodic contour suggest to monolingual Swedish speakers present in the court that this is the complete answer. The impression communicated is that the defendant has no wish whatsoever to explain herself any further. A closer look at the sequence reveals *contextualization cues* (Gumperz 1982) in the defendant's earlier utterances that might support the interpreter's take-up of this one (**D**:18) as a plain 'yes'. For one thing, the defendant has just said: *vot i vse* (so that's all) (**D**:15–16). Secondly, she does not develop a narrative when, in principle, an empty slot is available for her to do so (lines 10–11). At the same time, other cues are present that could support the opposite interpretation. Excerpt 1 starts with the defendant's hesitant 'm because I thought:::' (**D**:01). The prolonged vowel is a typical means by which speakers project further talk. At the same time, it might also indicate an ongoing search for words. Dealing immediately with this ambiguous start, the interpreter anticipates a plausible completion and renders the start as 'because I have thought over' (**I**:02) (with a finalized prosodic contour). The interpreter's take-up is formulated in non-standard Swedish (and is translated into non-standard English here – a conventional expression would be *för jag hade tänkt över saken* – 'because I had thought it over'). The interpreter seems to be more attentive here to the form of the lawyer's question than to the form of the defendant's answer;

attention to the latter might have prevented a Russian-speaking counsel for the defence (who would have had unmediated access to the answer) from doing what the current one does.

On hearing this exchange, the counsel for the defence says *haa* (right) (**C**:03), which indicates that he takes the defendant's utterance as a statement of fact, rather than a search for words that he might have wanted to support. Instead, he poses a follow-up question which explicitly raises the issue of intentionality: 'so to start with you intended to steal, but but you changed your mind. is this how, one should understand you' (**C**:12–15). This question gives the interpreter reason to re-use his 'planted' 'thought over' (**I**:02) and an opportunity to guide the defendant towards confirming that this was indeed what she had meant to say (**D**:18), which she does.

Tacit coaching work such as that initiated by the interpreter here when rendering the defendant's open-ended start to an answer as a semantically more complete sentence (**D**:01 and **I**:02) can hardly be transparent to a person with no command of the foreign language. But in this case, the questioner might have been alert to the fact that the interpreter's rendition interrupted the defendant's talk. After all, he might have expected his question 'How come you left a bag full of cosmetics among a pile of clothes?' to elicit more of a free narrative.[3] He provides the defendant with two more opportunities to speak, asking two final questions. Notably, however, the first comes after a second fact-establishing *haa* (right) (**C**:20). Willingly or unwillingly, he thus helps to establish as a fact the current defendant's intention to steal. Lacking immediate access to her reply, the lawyer's opportunities for supporting a narrative expansion of the follow-up yes/no question, possibly shedding light on both defendants' behaviour in the shop, are significantly constrained.

The above instance of tacit coaching work makes evident the interpreter's need to convey an impression of himself as a person using others' words. His chief means of conveying this impression throughout the proceedings is to adopt a bland style, with a minimal degree of expressiveness. It is worth noting that the current defendant's testimony is quite emotional, partly lamenting. The interpreter in Excerpt 1 performs what might be called *relaying by displaying* (Wadensjö 1998:247), representing, rather than re-presenting the defendant's talk.

3.3   *"And your pal Kolya, where did he go? Do you know?"*

The second example is drawn from a case where a man is charged with stealing diesel from a truck. The prosecutor has read the charges, the defendant has pleaded not guilty and a witness who met the accused on the night of the

---

[3] According to the police report, she had said that the co-defendant in this case had forced her to steal the cosmetics against her will. During the trial she claimed that she didn't know anything at all about the man sitting on the other side of the interpreter.

event under scrutiny has told his story, which supports the accusation. The excerpt begins shortly after the prosecutor starts to focus on details mentioned in the defendant's account concerning what he was doing in the parking lot, where he was observed and the diesel was stolen that night. The defendant states that a certain Kolya had given him a lift to the area, that his girlfriend was living there and that he had planned to visit her. The prosecutor continues his questioning by asking about Kolya, who, the accused claims, is the owner of the car in which the police found the defendant's ID documents and plastic containers of the same kind as the one found in the parking lot, filled with stolen diesel.

Excerpt 2. (Case 12, Tape 22)
P = prosecutor (man), **D** = defendant (man), **I** = interpreter (woman)

		Talk in Swedish		**Talk in Russian**
01	P	å din kompis Kolja? va- vart tog *and your pal Kolya? w- where did*		
02	P	han vägen. vet? du det. *he go. do you* (sg.) *know?*		
03			I	a vash priyatel Kolya on kuda delsya. *and your pal Kolja where did he go.*
04			I	znaete? *do you* (pl.) *know?*
05			D	ne znaju. ja vot eto toszhe u:: divlyajus. *don't know. me like too I'm surprised.*
06			D	znaesch? ya toszhe xotel ego najti *you* (sg.) *know? I too wanted to find him*
07			D	da? ja toszhe sam ne naschel. *okay? I too myself didn't find.*
08	I	nä [°ja vet i°] *no* [°*I don't k-*°]	D	[>ubeszhal<] vidno da? on e::: [>*ran away*<] *seemingly 'kay? he e:::*
09			D	uvidel eto vse i ubeszhal, da? *saw all this and run away, okay?*
10	I	nä ja [vet inte var] *no I* [*don't know where*	D	[(esche)] (xxx)] esli on [*(also) (xxx)*] *if he had been*
11			D	voroval eto. da? *stealing this. okay?*

12	I	vart han tog vägen. vet inte. ja blev *where he went. don't know. I was*		
13	I	själv förvånad. han bara *surprised myself. he just*		
14	I	försvann liksom. jag ville ju få tag *disappeared as it were. I wanted to*		
15	I	i honom själv. men han fanns ju *get hold of him myself. but he*		
16	I	inte där. kanske såg han *wasn't there was he. perhaps he*		
17	I	allt den där å:: så bara gick iväg. *saw everything a::d then just left.*		
18	I	ja vet inte.= *I don't know.=*		
19			D	=esche elsi ya i tam voroval *=also if I also there had been stealing*
20			D	čego-nibud. da? tam desyat metra *something. 'kay? like ten metres*
21			D	rasstoyaniya ne sidel by tam u korpusa. *distance wouldn't sit there by the house.*
22			D	da? ubeszhal by ya toszhe uschel by *'kay?I would run away too run away*
23			D	otsjuda. da? *from here. 'kay?*
24	I	skulle ja skulle skull- de var jag *would I would wou- it be me*		
25	I	som stal de där, då skulle ja inte *who had stolen this, then I wouldn't*		
26	I	stanna där. å liksom bara tio meter *stay there and like be ten metres*		
27	I	bort å sen å satt mig där ner *away and then and sat down there*		
28	I	å väntat. då då skulle ja också:: *and waited. then then I too:: would*		
29	I	sprungit å:: gått iväg. *have run a::nd walked away.*		

The exchange transcribed in this excerpt ran very quickly, like the rest of the testimony in this case. The defendant takes the opportunity to talk when given a chance. At this point in time, he substantiates a denial that goes far beyond a simple 'no'. More precisely, he indicates that he shares the prosecutor's interest in Kolya's disappearance, rather than that he feels obliged to answer by declaring what he himself actually knew. Moreover, he hints at the possibility that Kolya might be to blame for the theft (**D**:08–11), whereas he, who did not run away from the crime scene, must not be blamed for anything (**D**:19–23).

In one of the studies I mentioned earlier, Galatolo and Drew (2006) identify different modalities used by witnesses to project further talk and to prevent the questioners from taking the turn immediately after a minimal answer. These are: *minimal answer plus prosodic and rhythmic devices* (such as *rising intonation* and *rush-through devices*), *minimal answer plus partial repetition of the question* and *minimal answer plus conjunction* (*ibid.*:673–75). All these devices seem to be at work here, co-deployed by the defendant and the interpreter.

Looking closely at how the narrative expansions were accomplished, we can see that the defendant starts by repeating part of the question (don't know) (**D**:05), denying knowledge of where Kolya went. The interpreter starts rendering the answer, but the defendant regains the turn, using what Schegloff (1982) calls a *rush-through device*. In other words, the defendant speaks the first words in a speeded-up tempo (>ran away<) (**D**:08), as indicated by the use of angle brackets. The interpreter starts again, but the defendant's *esche* (also) overlaps with her speech (**D**:10). The defendant's use of a conjunction here projects further talk. The same conjunction is used once more when the defendant starts talking again after the interpreter's first rendition (**D**:19).

Occupying the speaker position, the defendant uses typical means to maintain his turn at talk as he searches for words; for example, he produces prolonged vowels – *e::* (**D**:08) – and tags pronounced with a rising intonation – *znaesch?* (you know?) (**D**:06) and '*da?*' (here: okay?) (**D**:07, 08, 09, 11). It should be added that the defendant speaks a broken Russian with a heavy foreign accent. Hence, from his point of view, the tag questions may have additionally served as a means of checking that the interpreter did understand him. The grammatical form of 'you know?' (*tu*-form) (**D**:06) reveals an orientation towards one particular conversational partner.

The interpreter reflects the defendant's somewhat poor and uncertain (but wordy) style of speaking in her renditions, for instance, by using the conventional Swedish floor filler *liksom* (that is) twice (**I**:14, 26), spoken with a flat intonation, as well as twice using the particle *ju* (**I**:14, 15), conventionally used to downplay a claim. This indicates that the interpreter probably reads the defendant's 'you know?' and 'okay?' as stylistic features of talk, which she subsequently seeks to reflect in her renditions, but not necessarily as genuine requests for confirmation of understanding, at least not as requests addressed to the prosecutor. Using *ju* (that is) and a flat rather than rising intonation in rendering the defendant's style also implies that, for the monolingual Swedish speakers in court, the interpreter does not appear to be directly addressed. Her renditions thus downplay her need to mark her own speaking as speech on another's behalf. Her style of *relaying by replaying* (Wadensjö 1998:247) assumes that the court treats her as an impartial participant.

Interestingly, the defendant does not provide a minimal 'yes' or 'no' even once, but when the interpreter starts to interpret the defendant's negative reply, an initial minimal *nä* (no) is heard (**I**:08), together with part of the question, before her voice fades away (**I**:08). Another minimal *nä* (no) introduces the interpreter's next attempt (**I**:10). The court thus immediately hears the expected minimal answer, which tends to make questioners more willing to sanction narrative expansion, according to Galatolo and Drew (2006). As Galatolo and Drew also point out, in providing a minimal answer when required to do so, a defendant avoids giving the impression that he or she is trying to avoid answering the question. As a result of the 'communicative wiggle room' in interpreter-mediated talk (Wadensjö 2008b), the same inserted *nä*-tokens (**I**:08 and 10) may also encourage further talk on the part of the defendant, just as feedback tokens from a conversational partner would normally do.

In conclusion, for the defendant the question constituted an opportunity to influence the choice of topic to be discussed, an aspect of court proceedings that is ordinarily and in principle controlled by those who pose the questions. The defendant obtained the floor and occupied it for quite some time, adding information that was not explicitly asked for. The prosecutor made no effort to compete with him for the floor. In the case of interpreter-mediated exchanges, when talk in the foreign language is not accessible to the questioners they may find it difficult to identify a relevant slot – in conversation analysis terminology a *transition relevance place* (Sacks *et al.* 1974) – for rejecting a defendant's ongoing expansion. In this case, the prosecutor later followed up on the defendant's expanded narrative. Hence the defendant did succeed in influencing the meaning that emerged from the question-answer sequence. In the end, what he said might not have been very relevant for the decision of the court, but he managed to mitigate to some extent the subordinate position he occupied as defendant.

4. Concluding discussion

The interpreters in the examples explored in this article were both authorized (in Swedish-Russian interpreting). Their relatively high qualifications do not, it seems, mitigate the limitations on the production and elicitation of talk in interpreter-mediated encounters identified in the above analysis. In a bilingual court trial, the primary participants' control of the interaction is necessarily somewhat restricted due to their lack of shared linguistic competence. This suggests that participants' awareness of and ability to understand conversational units produced in the exchange varies – more so, I would argue, than in single-language trials. For instance, in Excerpt 1 above, the legal questioner, a counsel for the defence, provides minimal feedback, which in principle allows space for a defendant to say something more on the current topic. In the exchange, however, these tokens appear as fact-establishing units, coming as they do after the interpreter's renditions, which are delivered in a quick and categorical style. Instead of eliciting a narrative from the defendant, the counsel for the defence helps to bring the topic to an end. In Excerpt 2, two of the interpreter's attempts to start interpreting potentially function both as minimal responses – normally used to accomplish a transition to a narrative expansion – and as feedback tokens – devices normally used to encourage the current speaker to go on talking. In both functions, the units pave the way for a narrative expansion on the part of the defendant.

The defendant in Excerpt 2 thus produces a narrative expansion, but without first producing minimal responses ('no' in this case), which normally precede narrative expansions. The defendant in Excerpt 1 does not produce an expanded narrative, either in response to an open question or to a yes/no question.

When I started to compare the two interpreted sequences, I intuitively felt that the second interpreter did a much better job than the first. The interpreter in Excerpt 2 appears to have avoided competing with the defendant for the floor, despite his tendency to produce rather long stretches of talk. The interpreter in Excerpt 1 seems to have outmanoeuvred the defendant in securing space for his own renditions.

Clearly, however, the different outcomes of the two exchanges are partly the result of the fact that the defendants apply different means to project further talk. When the counsel for the defence provides the defendant in Excerpt 1with an opportunity to explain her intentions in relation to the charges against her, she starts talking hesitantly, seeking – but failing – to occupy the floor by means of a prolonged vowel in mid-sentence.

In contrast to the female defendant in Excerpt 1, the male defendant in Excerpt 2 is very talkative, notwithstanding the fact that his talk involves quite a few ambiguities. He speaks in broken Russian, with a heavy foreign accent. Nevertheless, as the analysis demonstrates, he uses several pragmatic devices for projecting further talk. Apart from prolonged vowels and tag questions, his expansion involves minimal answer plus partial repetition of the question, minimal answer plus a rush-through device and minimal answer plus a conjunction. These devices – the latter co-produced with the interpreter – prove much more successful than the softly spoken prolonged vowel deployed by the female defendant in Excerpt 1.

Moreover, when the interpreter in Excerpt 1 presents the female defendant with the questioner's understanding of her interrupted answer, she confirms the interpreter's anticipated completion of it as correct. More precisely, she says: 'yes, I changed my mind'. The interpreter does not render this minimal expansion of the answer. Instead, he displays its content, quickly providing a distinct 'yes'. To my mind, the interpreter in Excerpt 1 thus demonstrates that he is oriented towards matching the form of the question at that point, towards getting the defendant to confirm that he (the interpreter) was correct in anticipating what she had just meant to say and towards securing space for his rendition of that confirmation. As Lee (2009) has demonstrated, the ambiguous speech of witnesses poses a serious challenge in court interpreting. The interpreter in Excerpt 1 handles this by taking responsibility for disambiguating the defendant's vague message rather than reflecting its ambiguity in his renditions. The consequences in this case offer us some food for thought. In Excerpt 1, the questioner's efforts to provide the defendant with opportunities to explain her behaviour in the department store, where she had been seen walking out of the shop with a bag full of stolen cosmetics, and to explain why she pleads not guilty, merely result in a confirmation of her intention to steal.

The interpreter in Excerpt 2 also seems to have been oriented towards making her renditions match the framing of the yes/no question. At the same time, however, she is clearly oriented towards re-presenting at least some of the vagueness of the defendant's answer in her rendition. It is worth noting that in Excerpt 1 the female defendant is responsive to the interpreter's tacit coaching and does not compete with him for the floor, whereas in Excerpt 2, the co-production of the pragmatic devices that secure space for the male defendant is a result of his competing with the interpreter for the floor.

The interpreter in Excerpt 2 adapts to the defendant's pace and style of talking. Her sense of timing her renditions is reminiscent of the manner of a musician who adds variations on existing themes. At the same time, her performance resembles a staging of the defendant's talk. She is confident, one might assume, that the court sees her as someone who uses others' words. The style she adopts could be classified as relaying by replaying, as defined in Wadensjö (1998:246-48). This manner of interpreting undoubtedly matches the talkative defendant's communicative style. In Excerpt 1, the interpreter's style of talking is bland, even somewhat officious. This is his way of conveying an impression of himself as a narrator of others' words. This way of relaying by displaying' (ibid.) seems considerably less suitable to the silent defendant's communicative style.

In their study of a single-language, Italian court trial, Galatolo and Drew concluded that the particular structure of expanded answers "allows witnesses to respect the constraints imposed by the form and, at the same time, to gain a conversational space in which they can exert a partial control over the information" (2006:688). The analysis offered in this article provides some details about the conditions for producing expanded answers when defendants and questioners talk in different languages, via interpreters, in face-to-face interaction. It has shown that the specific organization of turn-taking and turn-allocation in interpreter-mediated trials can indeed influence defendants' chances of expanding minimal answers to yes/no questions. Treating the interpreter-mediated trial as a situated system of activity, the study demonstrates that defendants are dependent on interpreters' active support in attempting to gain and secure conversational space and are relatively independent of the immediate sanctions of the legal questioners. More generally, the study suggests that both questioning and answering strategies are bound to function somewhat differently in face-to-face interpreter-mediated court trials compared to single-language ones. The analysis has suggested several reasons for this difference, and has discussed some of the significant implications of viewing interpreted events as interaction – or, as Mason (2001) puts it, as *triadic exchanges.*

Transcription conventions

text in italics	my English translation of talk originally spoken in Swedish or Russian
square bracket [	overlap of talk
colon :	a prolonged vowel
dot .	terminating intonation
comma ,	continuing intonation
question mark ?	questioning intonation
number within round brackets	duration of a silent pause, in seconds
single dot within round brackets (.)	a micropause
hyphen -	sudden cut-off of the current sound
equals sign =	one turn immediately following the one before
text in angle brackets	uttered in a speeded-up tempo
text in uppercase	uttered in a raised volume

References

Adelswärd, Viveka, Karin Aronsson, Linda Jönsson and Per Linell (1987) 'The Unequal Distribution of Interactional Space: Dominance and Control in Courtroom Interaction', *Text* 7(4): 313-46.

Apfelbaum, Birgit (2004) *Gesprächsdynamik in Dolmetsch-Interaktionen: Eine empirische Untersuchung von Situationen internationaler Fachkommunikation unter besonderer Berücksichtigung der Arbeitssprachen Deutsch, Englisch, Französisch und Spanisch*, Radolfzell, Germany: Verlag für Gesprächsforschung.

Atkinson, M. John and Paul Drew (eds) (1979) *Order in Court*, London: McMillan.

Berk-Seligson, Susan (1990) *The Bilingual Courtroom: Court Interpreters in the Judicial Process*, Chicago: The University of Chicago Press.

Bolden, Galina B. (2000) 'Towards Understanding Practices of Medical Interpreting: Interpreters' Involvement in History Taking', *Discourse Studies* 2(4): 387-419.

Danet, Brenda (1980) 'Language in Legal Process', *Law and Society Review* 14(3): 445-564.

Davidson, Brad (2002) 'A Model for the Construction of Conversational Common Ground in Interpreted Discourse', *Journal of Pragmatics* 34(9): 1273-300.

Erickson, Frederick (2001) 'Co-membership and Wiggle Room: Some Implications of the Study of Talk for the Development of Social Theory', in Nikolas Coupland, Srikant Sarangi and Christopher N. Candlin (eds) *Sociolinguistics and Social Theory*, London & New York: Longman, 152-81.

Galatolo, Renata and Paul Drew (2006) 'Narrative Expansion as Defensive Practices in Courtroom Testimony', *Text & Talk* 26(6): 661-98.

Goffman, Erving (1961) *Encounters: Two Studies in the Sociology of Interaction*, Indianapolis & New York: The Bobbs-Merrill Company.

Gumperz, John, J. (1982) *Discourse Strategies*, Cambridge: Cambridge University Press.

Hale, Sandra B. (2004) *The Discourse of Court Interpreting*, Amsterdam & Philadelphia: John Benjamins.

Laster Kathy and Veronica Taylor (1994) *Interpreters in the Legal System*, Leichhardt, NSW, Australia: The Federation Press.

Lee, Jieun (2009) 'Interpreting Inexplicit Language during Courtroom Examination', *Applied Linguistics* 30(1): 93-114.

Linell, Per (2009) *Rethinking Language, Mind, and the World Dialogically*, Charlotte, NC: Information Age Publishing.

Loftus, Elisabeth F. (1979) *Eyewitness Testimony*, Cambridge, MA: Harvard University Press.

Mason, Ian (2001) 'Introduction', in Ian Mason (ed.) *Triadic Exchanges,* Manchester: St Jerome Publishing, i-vi.

Mason, Ian (2006) 'On Mutual Accessibility of Contextual Assumptions in Dialogue Interpreting', *Journal of Pragmatics* 38(3): 359-73.

Roberts-Smith, Len (2007) 'Forensic Linguistics', paper presented at the international conference *Critical Link 5*, Paramatta, Australia, April 2007.

Roy, Cynthia B. (2000) *Interpreting as a Discourse Process*, New York & Oxford: Oxford University Press.

Russell, Sonja (2004) 'Three's a Crowd: Shifting Dynamics in the Interpreted Interview', in Janet Cotterill (ed.) *Language in the Legal Process*, New York: Palgrave Macmillan, 111-26.

Sacks, Harvey, Emmanuel A. Schegloff and Gail Jefferson (1974) 'A Simplest Systematics for the Organization of Turn-taking for Conversation', *Language* 50(4): 696-735.

Schegloff, Emmanuel, A. (1982) 'Discourse as an Interactional Achievement:

Some Uses of 'uh uh' and Other Things that Come between Sentences', in Deborah Tannen (ed.) *Georgetown University Round Table on Language and Linguistics 1981. Analyzing Discourse: Text and Talk,* Washington, DC: Georgetown University Press, pp. 71-93.

Valero Garcés, Carmen (2002) 'Interaction and Conversational Constrictions in the Relationships Between Suppliers of Services and Immigrant Users', *Pragmatics* 12(4): 469-96.

Wadensjö, Cecilia (1997) 'Recycled Information as a Questioning Strategy – Pitfalls in Interpreter-Mediated Talk' in Silvana E. Carr, Roda Roberts, Aileen Dufour and Dini Steyn (eds) *The Critical Link: Interpreting in the Community.* Amsterdam & Philadelphia: John Benjamins, 35-52.

------ (1998) *Interpreting as Interaction*, London & New York: Longman.

------ (2008a) 'The Shaping of Gorbachev: On Framing in an Interpreter-Mediated Talk-Show Interview', *Text & Talk* 28(1): 119–46.

------ (2008b) 'In and Off the Show: Co-constructing 'Invisibility' in an Interpreter-Mediated Talk Show Interview', *META* 53(1): 184-203.

Wagner, Johannes (1996) 'Diversity and Continuity in Conversation Analysis', *Journal of Pragmatics* 26(2): 215-35.

Information Structure Management and Textual Competence in Translation and Interpreting

Sentence Openings in Translation from Arabic into English as a Second Language

STUART CAMPBELL
University of Western Sydney, Australia

ALI ALDAHESH
Australian National University

ALYA' AL-RUBAI'I
Duhok University, Iraq

RAYMOND CHAKHACHIRO
University of Western Sydney, Australia

BERTA WAKIM
University of Western Sydney, Australia

Abstract. *Information structure management is a key aspect of textual competence in translation and interpreting; a high degree of competence is marked by the ability to sequence elements in such a way that the target text looks stylistically authentic while maintaining the integrity of the information structure of the source text. The difficulty is accentuated when working into a second language, and where the source and target languages are structurally disparate. This study focuses on one aspect of information structure management, namely how Arabic speakers tackle sentence openings in translating and interpreting into English. Three student and three professional translators/interpreters were asked to generate output in three different production modes: fast translation, consecutive interpreting, and scaffolded speech, the latter providing baseline interlanguage output. Types of sentence openings were found to be markedly different in fast translation*

*and consecutive interpreting, and to an extent between novices
and experts. The findings are consistent with the predictions of the
Translation-Interpreting Continuum (Campbell and Wakim 2007),
a processing model which predicts that various translation and
interpreting production modes rely on different kinds of mental
representation, and that competence levels are distinguished by
degree of automatization. Implications for curriculum design and
assessment are discussed.*

T he research reported here aims to throw light on an acknowledged
problem in translation research and interpreter/translator education,
namely that it can be very difficult for interpreters and translators to
produce texts that are stylistically authentic. The roots of the work go back
to foundational publications such as Hatim and Mason (1990) that linked
translation to aspects of discourse analysis, including the study of the information structure of texts. Part of producing stylistically authentic translations is
managing information structure, "which links word-order rules to discourse
structuring rules, that is, to the rules that control progress in discourse"
(Doherty 2002:21). In many cases "translations have to be reordered … if
they are to achieve contextual appropriateness and meet optimal processing
conditions in the target language" (*ibid.*). For translators working into a second language, there is the extra burden of mapping information relationships
onto a target language in which their discourse competence is more limited
than in the source language. For example, although an interpreter or translator might be capable of constructing English cleft sentences like *It is politics
that fascinates me*, competence of a higher order is required to deploy such
a sentence in a translation – rather than a simple active sentence like *Politics
fascinates me* or a passive sentence like *I am fascinated by politics* – so that
the relationships among *politics*, *fascinates* and *I/me* are optimally equivalent
to the relationships among the counterparts in the original. This paper reports
on one aspect of a broader project designed to explore information structure
management among native speakers of Arabic and Chinese translating into
English. The present study focuses on Arabic–English translation and interpreting, with specific attention to sentence openings. Besides broadening our
understanding of translation competence, this empirical study has the potential
to make a practical contribution to improving the teaching and assessment of
translation and interpreting.

The research questions of the broader project in which this study is embedded are:

- What are the major difficulties in managing information structure in
interpreting and translating into L2 English?
- To what extent do specific source languages influence the management

of information structure in L2 English interpreting and translation?

- To what extent are difficulties in managing information structure in L2 English interpreting and translation a function of the type of production mode, i.e. written translation versus oral interpreting, consecutive versus simultaneous interpreting, etc.?
- What light do the findings throw on the psycholinguistic processes underpinning translation competence?
- What practical implications are there for interpreter and translator education?

The research reported here narrows the scope to Arabic-to-L2/English translation, and specifically the investigation of sentence openings. The limitations of the study are chiefly methodological in that the data are difficult to collect in large quantities because of the fatigue factor in translation and in interpreting. Another limitation is that we have controlled for text type by deriving the experimental materials from press releases, so that our findings may not be fully generalizable to other contexts. Finally, the findings here clearly relate only to subjects working into English as a second language.

1.   Theoretical underpinnings

The theoretical underpinnings of this study lie in the areas of textual and discourse competence in interpreting and translation, decision making in interpreting and translation, interpreting and translation into English as a Second Language, information structure in translation, translation research methodology, and the psycholinguistics of interpreting and translation.

We begin with a few words about directionality. The practice of translating and interpreting into English as a second language is an inevitable consequence of globalization (Adab 2005, Campbell 2005, Rogers 2005). Given the shortage of native speakers of English who are competent in interpreting and translating from typologically distant languages such as Arabic, a large proportion of translators and interpreters work, and will continue to work, into L2 English. This throws into prominence the importance of acquiring higher order L2 skills of textual and discourse competence. In countries like Australia, where translation into English – mainly in the areas of police investigative work, personal documents, press monitoring and back translations – is carried out on the whole by non-native speakers of English, "the need for reliability and the concomitant *accountability* attached to the performance of the translator" (Rogers 2005:229) are a key factor.

Translation and interpreting competence in this context must be of the textual and discourse pragmatic type; any translator – whether working into a first or a second language – should "know how to make the sentence play a role within a sequence that is eventually part of a well-formed text, discourse and genre" (Hatim 1997:223). The same goes for interpreting; court interpreters, for example, must ensure a smooth "pragmatic reconstruction of the message" (Hale 2004:239). This message reconstruction aspect of translation competence will involve knowing when and if "surface equivalence [must be] sacrificed in the interests of grammaticality and optimal processing conditions" (Doherty 2002:25-26). The interpreter is an apt example of the "special category of communicator" (Hatim and Mason 1997:2) whose textual and "discursive" competence is reflected "not in the translation of individual items but in the clues these provide to an overall textual strategy and the way this may inform translators' decisions" (*ibid.*:13). Decisions at textual level include issues of transitivity and thematic choice, of backgrounding and foregrounding (*ibid.*).

Textual and discourse competence is also explored in Campbell (1998) in the teaching and learning context. Campbell's approach is methodologically oriented, and one of the major aims of the author is to apply his model of translation competence in the "[d]esign of individualized teaching and learning strategies" (*ibid.*:167). Unlike Hatim (1997), Hatim and Mason (1990, 1997), and Hale (2004), whose focus is on the communicative aspect of textual and discourse competence, Campbell's approach is focused on translation competence into the second language as "a very special variety of second language proficiency" (Campbell 1998:58), with a major emphasis on the developmental aspect of translation competence. If learning to translate into a second language is indeed a special kind of language acquisition, how are the higher order skills of information structure acquired, and how can the principles of acquisition be used to guide curriculum design and the development of assessment tools?

Sentence openings were chosen as an object of study because of their critical status in the unfolding of the translated text. In information structure theory, sentence openings are most frequently associated with Theme, an element that has a "Janus-faced quality of operating as an information organiser simultaneously at the levels of sentence syntax and text progression" (Mauranen 1999:63); at the opening of each sentence in a text the novice translator must call on high order skills to make decisions that shape not only the sentence at hand but the unfolding text. Indeed, information theory recognizes three different but interacting aspects of Theme: a syntactic aspect associated with "the starting point of the clause", an informational aspect associated with Givenness, and a semantic aspect more often associated with the term Topic, which entails "a relationship of 'aboutness' with the rest of the message" (Gómez-González 1997:148).[1]

For Arabic to English translators, the basic word order differences – VSO

---

[1] See Gerzymisch-Arbogast *et al.* (2006) for an approach that proposes theme/rheme as a concept that overlaps with coherence and isotopy; the three concepts "account for and make transparent" the "information structure", "the sense constitution" and "the meaning set-up", respectively (*ibid.*:357).

versus SVO – especially compound the difficulty for translators; Modern Standard Arabic sentences do not routinely begin with nominal subjects. In her discussion of German and English, Doherty proposes that sentence openings are parametrized, i.e. "the grammatical parameters that determine the profile of a language determine the conditions for processing linguistic expressions in that language, too" (2002:22). For example, the parameter of configurationality differentiates sentence openings in English and German. As a less configurational language (i.e. one with more flexible word order), German subjects "are not bound to a special position" (*ibid.*:24), while in English sentences tend to begin with subjects; for each language a different set of grammatical options is available as a new sentence is built upon the informational relations in the preceding text. A similar argument for parametrized sentence openings can be made for Arabic and English; the verb-first parameter for Arabic conflicts with the subject-first parameter for English, where syntactic subjecthood and 'aboutness' are conflated in a nominal element; these different grammatical parameters determine the way that discourse is processed with respect to the role of sentence openings.

European translation scholars working with bilingual corpora have displayed a keen interest in how information structure is managed in translation – especially with regard to sentence openings – drawing on theoretical insights from both Prague School and Hallidayan scholarship. Rogers (2006) studied sentence openings in the English translation of a German investment report and found that the thematic perspective of the original German was mostly maintained by way of restructuring techniques. Loosely defining sentence opening as "the initial field of the sentence, in most cases up to and including the main verb", Hasselgård (1997:3) studied declarative sentences in translations from English to Norwegian and from Norwegian to English, and found that word order was closely maintained when the target language allowed it. Preservation of the original information structure was observed in Mauranen's (1999) study of existential sentences in a parallel corpus of English and Finnish texts, which identifies a number of translation strategies such as "maintaining the original information structure" (*ibid.*:67), making changes but "maintain[ing] the main focus of the original" (*ibid.*:68), and "chang[ing] the information structure" (*ibid.*:69). Mauranen's study draws on the Hallidayan notion of the topical theme optionally preceded by textual and interpersonal elements. Her model for handling English and Finnish themes has a similar bipartite organization of an "orienting theme" and a "topical theme", where the topical theme for English is typically the subject, but for Finnish may be some other preverbal nominal (*ibid.*:62). Hasselgård (2000) explicitly explores multiple themes in translation, working closely within the Hallidayan notion of the topical theme with preceding interpersonal or textual elements. The study works with English to Norwegian and Norwegian to English translations of fictional texts, as well as translations into German of several of the English texts. As in Mauranen's study, information structure is largely found to be preserved in translation, with topical theme being preserved "with great regularity ... even when the syntactic structure of the source and the target language makes this difficult" (*ibid.*:32). The Hallidayan notion of multiple theme also underpins the study reported in Hasselgård (2004), which explores the kinds of "transitivity roles that are selected as topical Theme" in English and Norwegian sentence pairs, as well as "the kinds of textual and interpersonal elements that may occur as part of a multiple Theme" (*ibid.*:188). The data set – 1200 translated sentences randomly selected from eight texts in a corpus – unequivocally locates this study in lexicogrammar rather than in discourse. Gundel (2002) tackles a special kind of sentence opening in her study of the "discourse distribution of cleft sentences in English and Norwegian". Working within a Praguian framework, her analysis of cleft sentences in the translation of a Norwegian novel into English explores the interplay between topic and focus. Using the three aspects of Theme previously mentioned as a frame of reference, we can consider Gundel's analysis to be within the Givenness and 'aboutness' domains; indeed a central issue in the study is distinguishing between referential and relational givenness in order to show how topic and focus may or may not coincide in cleft sentences. Gundel's discourse orientation is evident in her findings, i.e. that Norwegian more consistently maps information structure onto syntactic structure, while English employs clefts primarily as a stylistic device (*ibid.*:15). Mauranen (1999) does not restrict herself to the syntactic or starting points aspect of Theme; she also explores the discourse functions of *there* sentences, finding that they relate mainly to "the marking of junctures in texts" (*ibid.*:82). More broadly, invoking Daneš (1974), Mauranen states that "the theme is principally responsible for establishing the mutual relevance of adjacent sentences in text" (*ibid.*:64), a notion that is central to the research reported here. To summarize, sentence openings, more technically termed Theme or Topic, have interested translation scholars from the points of view of their internal structure, their discourse functions, and the preservation of information structure in translation.

Where our study differs from those discussed above is in its understanding of translation *per se*. All of the translation data used in the studies mentioned so far are dislocated from the translators who produced them, so that any conclusions about the preservation of information structure are essentially observations about similarities and differences between sets of data, not about the process of translation or translators in action. The basis for the claim in Hasselgård (2004:187) that "translators tend to preserve the topical Theme of the original in the great majority of cases" is that something about the behaviour of translators can be inferred by examining data from a random sample of translated sentences from several different works. In fact we would claim that using data like this can show that translations, rather than translators, preserve Topical theme; it does not offer insights into the how and why of translator behaviour. If, as Gómez-González (1997:135) maintains, there is a consensus that "*Theme/Topic* should be described within some kind of *functionalist* framework", should this kind of research not require "an active engagement with communicative materials" (Beaugrande 1992:34)? To take two awkward issues that might arise when we examine translators in action, Gómez-González points to the difficulty of identifying themes in unplanned discourse (*ibid.*:138); how planned are translators' early drafts, and might they not reveal more about the translation process than final polished versions? And in relation to Givenness, how new is new? Wouldn't the "fictional dividing point [between old and new information] ... be constantly transcended by mental processing?" (Beaugrande 2002:21)?

The data problem we have outlined in the preceding paragraph was one of the key motivations for the development of the Translation-Interpreting Continuum (Campbell and Wakim 2007). The Continuum (see Figure 1) describes various modes of interpreting and translation production (e.g. fast translation,[2] consecutive interpreting) in terms of psycholinguistic notions. In essence it proposes that the different modes vary in their degree of attention switching (Klin *et al.* 2004, Sanford 1990, Sanford and Garrod 1981, Christoffels and de Groot 2005, Paradis 1994), automatized processing (Gile 1995, Dechert 1987, Paradis 2004), word order variation (Levelt 1981, 1989), and retention or decay of the source text (Christoffels and de Groot 2005, Isham 1994). The data used in the studies discussed above by Hasselgård, Mauranen and Gundel would be classified in the Continuum as "Slow translation", a mode that is characterized by (a) slow attention switching (e.g. compared to sight translation), (b) a low degree of automaticity, (c) high potential for word order variation, and (d) high potential for decay of source text formal structures. In brief, while we may learn a lot about the differences between the abstract linguistic systems of two languages, we can learn much less about how individual translators process sentence openings from this kind of data.

Instead, the present study uses fast translation and consecutive interpreting data, on the basis that these modes will provide insights into the mental processes underpinning sentence openings. The Continuum predicts that sentence openings in fast translation will be shaped by the source text material in the mental representation, given that the source text is being constantly referred to. In consecutive interpreting, the absence of source text material immediately to hand (i.e. because it cannot be wholly retained in memory) will motivate sentence openings that are less influenced by the source text material. The Continuum also predicts that the degree of automatization will distinguish novice and expert performance with respect to sentence openings. In short, this study sets the empirical investigation of cross-linguistic information structure management in a psycholinguistic context using a methodological framework that requires research questions to be matched with appropriate data.

---

[2] With fast translation, subjects translate against the clock and are not allowed to postedit. The problem of defining fast translation is discussed in Campbell and Wakim (2007).

		Production modes				
		Slow translation	Fast translation	Sight translation	Simultaneous interpreting	Consecutive interpreting
Elements of mental representation	Attention switching	slow ⟵————————————————————⟶ fast				
	Automaticity as transcoding	low ⟵————————————————————⟶ high				
	Potential for word order variation	high ⟵————————————————————⟶ low				
	Retention/ decay of ST formal structure	high ⟵————————————————————⟶ low				

Figure 1: Translation-Interpreting Continuum (Campbell and Wakim 2007)

Our study also draws on the literature on decision making in translation. Indeed decision making and choice making have been recognized as a rich vein of investigation in studies of interpreting and translation (Setton 1999, Tirkkonen-Condit 2005, Wilss 1994, 1996). Wilss (1996) draws on the broader field of decision making theory in an attempt to explain the special complexity of decision making in translation, unlike earlier research on decision making which was based on "discovering the optimal strategy of an undertaking by gradually filtering out alternative, less efficient strategies" (*ibid.*:177). Wilss (1994, 1996) understands decision making in translation as a complex behavioural process based on "an interplay between the translator's cognitive system, the translator's knowledge bases, the task specification, and ... "the problem space", i.e., the leeway a translator has in solving a problem by applying decision-making procedures" (Wilss 1996:191). Decisions are made on two levels: (1) the macrocontextual level, where decisions are about text type, style or register, and (2) the microcontextual level, where decisions are about "textual coherence ... semantic complexity, intricate text strategies (rhetorical strategies), theme/rheme distribution", among others (*ibid.*:176). Sentence opening choices seem to operate at both levels of strategy; we will see later that our experimental subjects make quite different kinds of macrotextual and microtextual decisions in translation as opposed to interpreting.

Tirkonnen-Condit's (2005) experimental studies on expertise and monitoring in translation throw some light on the ways in which experts develop these skills: "[o]n the whole, experts have been found to invest decision-making effort strategically instead of wasting it on irrelevant details" (*ibid.*:407). Setton (1999:278) notes that highly skilled interpreters have a "mental phrase book" that allows an easy rendition of source text discourse into the target language without having recourse to extensive problem solving and decision-making strategies. On the other hand, in cases where a direct mapping of the source text onto the target text structure would have "satisfied the equivalence criterion", simultaneous interpreters opted for a different word order than in the source text (*ibid.*:161-63). Despite the complexity of making decisions in translation or interpreting, it seems that by acquiring higher textual skills combined with proper practice, translators are able to "develop cognitively simplifying decision-making heuristics" (Wilss 1996:189); through trial and error, decision-making strategies are learnt and become automatized.

Sentence openings, then, involve decisions made at critical points in the unfolding of a target text; they may syntactically anchor the evolving sentence, they look backwards at what has been translated so far and point forwards to what will be translated, and they may signal what information is shared between writer and audience. To what extent can this decision making be plausibly captured and described? We turn here to Choice Network Analysis. CNA is a method proposed by Campbell (1998) for constructing models of the mental processing underlying translation, and elaborated in Campbell (2000a, 2000b) and Campbell and Hale (1999). It uses target text evidence from samples of subjects to model the mental processes of a hypothetical population. CNA allows the combination of psycholinguistics, cross-linguistic data, cognition, and text linguistics to be investigated within the same framework (Campbell 2000a:29). It is utilized later in this paper to model decisions about sentence openings in consecutive interpreting and scaffolded speech, i.e. speech that a subject composes using written prompts.

The subjects under investigation here are Arabic speakers working from Modern Standard Arabic[3] (MSA) into English, and we supply a brief contrastive discussion of sentence openings in English and MSA as a backdrop to discussions about subjects' motivations for particular choices and to broach the question of whether acquisition of textual and discourse competence follows universal principles or is influenced in language-specific ways.[4] From a contrastive standpoint, MSA and English seem to share a similar range of choices of sentence openings. However, there are two special cases where sentence openings in MSA are constrained. The first is the very frequent use of the conjunction *wa* (and) to begin a sentence. Holes (1995:217) describes *wa* as "both a textual- as well as a sentence-connective" which can be used to begin every sentence in a simple narrative except the first; its function is "to simply mark the next episode in the report" (*ibid.*). See also Chakhachiro's (2005) more translation-focused view of the function of *wa*. The second case, as mentioned earlier in our discussion of parametrized processing, is

---

[3] Modern Standard Arabic refers here to the written variety of Arabic used across the Arab World, as opposed to the spoken dialects of Arabic that are acquired as the mother tongue.

[4] Examples of contrastive studies of language pairs in translation studies are Malmkjaer (1998) for Danish/English, Ebeling (1998) for Norwegian/English, and Campbell and Hale (1999) for Arabic/English and Spanish/English.

that in MSA writers and speakers can make a choice between verb or subject as a starting point, depending on whether the sentence is "event-oriented" or "entity-oriented" (Holes 1995:205).

Holes links Givenness and Newness with definiteness and indefiniteness respectively, so that "what is already 'known' from the previous text or context (and is usually grammatically definite) precedes what is 'new' (and is usually indefinite)" (*ibid.*:203). He calls this the "definite-first" principle (*ibid.*:206). While English and MSA share a general tendency for given information to precede new information, they differ in the extent to which this principle interacts with syntax. In MSA, given information generally precedes new information *regardless* of whether the given information is grammatical subject or object; in English the sentence initial position of subject generally overrides the information structure principle.

Just as English employs the device of End-weight to present the Comment in a position where uncertainty is eliminated for the Addressee (Östman and Virtanen 1999), MSA respects the same principle; and, as Holes says, this "reinforces the 'definite first' principle" (Holes 1995:206). In cases of conflict between the End-weight and the definite first principle, it is the definite first principle that usually wins in Arabic.

The principal similarities and differences in information structure pertaining to sentence openings between English and Arabic are summarized in Table 1.

	English	MSA
Syntax	n/a	Sentences often begin with *wa*
	Subject-initial is the unmarked word order	Verb-initial or subject initial depending on orientation
Givenness	Given information generally precedes new information *as long as* the given information is grammatical subject	Given information generally precedes new information *regardless* of whether the given information is grammatical subject or object
'aboutness'	Heavy items follow light items	
	n/a	Definite-first principle overrides principle that heavy items follow light items.

Table 1: Principal similarities and differences in information structure between English and MSA pertaining to sentence openings

In summary then, a study of the choice of sentence openings in Arabic-to-L2/English translation and interpreting seems warranted as a test bench for a number of specific research questions:

- What sentence opening choices are made by translators and interpreters working into L2 English?
- To what extent are these choices common to both translation and interpreting?
- What role does L1 contribute to sentence opening choices?
- What are the psycholinguistic drivers of sentence opening choice?
- How can the teaching and assessment of interpreting and translation be improved through a better knowledge of how to open sentences?

2. Methodology

The subjects of the empirical study were: three non-native speakers of English of Arabic-speaking background enrolled in an undergraduate or postgraduate programme in Interpreting and Translation, and three trained professionals, accredited as Interpreters and/or Translators by the National Accreditation Authority for Translators and Interpreters, who were non-native speakers of English of Arabic-speaking background. The subjects were identified as AS1 (Arabic Student 1), AS2, AS3, and AP1 (Arabic Professional 1), AP2, AP3.

The materials comprised a fast translation test and a consecutive interpreting test, intended to elicit production mode differences. There was also a scaffolded speech test to provide baseline interlanguage data not directly influenced by a source text in another language. The tests were constructed as follows:

- Two Arabic texts for fast translation into English.[5] These texts were based on texts that were themselves published translations of two World Health Organization English texts labelled here as *Bangkok* and *Locusts*. In preparing these materials we began by identifying a 300-word passage of each English original. We then identified the counterpart passages in the Arabic and had them revised by native speakers to amend elements that were obviously translationese.
- An Arabic speech for use as source text for consecutive interpreting into English. To prepare this text we identified an additional part of the *Bangkok* text that would stand as a coherent passage, broke it into six key information chunks, and asked an Arabic native speaker to turn the six chunks into a speech, respecting the order of the key chunks but rearranging them internally if need be.
- A set of ten written talking points in English based on the whole *Bangkok* text. These were used as the scaffold for the scaffolded speech test.

The test materials were sequenced to optimize results, as shown in Table 2.

---

[5] The Arabic text *Bangkok* can be found in the Appendix at the end of this article.

Materials	Rationale
Fast translation – *Bangkok*	n/a
Consecutive interpreting – *Bangkok*	Placed after the fast translation test so that the subjects have some general familiarity with the topic.
Fast translation – *Locusts*	Intended to destroy memory traces of the English and Arabic texts of *Bangkok*
Scaffolded speech – *Bangkok*	Best chance of the target text being based on the meaning of the scaffold points, uninfluenced by the Arabic and English texts that they have previously been exposed to.

Table 2: Sequence of test materials

Subjects were asked to attend on-campus sessions. They undertook the fast translation by handwriting on custom stationery, which incorporated an ethics statement. Each target text by each subject was transcribed and cross checked by two analysts in Microsoft Word and saved as text files. Marking up of the texts was also undertaken and cross checked by two analysts; transcription conventions are detailed later in this article. Interpreting and speech data were recorded on audio tape, transcribed in Microsoft Word and the tape recordings wiped. No identifying data were collected. Student subjects were remunerated by way of book vouchers. Professional subjects were paid a fee equivalent to 0.5 days' work.

The subjects were given the following instructions for fast translation:

- We would like you to translate this passage into English very quickly, but as accurately as you can. We will allow up to thirty minutes. We don't want you to use dictionaries or any other aids. If you make a mistake, cross it out and keep translating. Don't use liquid paper. We don't want you to read the text first all the way through before you start translating; just start translating as soon as we tell you to. We only want one version, so don't make a rough version first and rewrite it. When you have finished, don't go back and revise the translation; just stop work and quietly leave the room. If you are still working after thirty minutes we will stop you. I'll repeat those instructions. Does anyone have any questions? Please start writing now.

These were the instructions for consecutive interpreting:

- We are going to ask you to interpret a passage into English of about three hundred words on the same topic as the translation you did earlier, that is health promotion. We will read the passage aloud just once at the speed of a formal speech to an audience. We won't repeat the passage. You may take notes as you listen. When the reading has finished we will give a break of fifteen seconds, and then you will render the speech into English. We will tape record your rendition. If you make a mistake or get mixed up, just try to keep going until you have interpreted as much as you can. I'll repeat those instructions. Do you have any questions? Please start interpreting now.

The subjects were given the following instructions for scaffolded speech:

- We want you to make a short speech in English – maybe two to three minutes in length. The speech is going to be on the topic of the Bangkok health promotion conference, which you are now familiar with. We are going to give you some talking points for your speech. Use them as the main points, but feel free to be creative; if you can't remember all the details of the Bangkok conference, you can make them up. Here are the talking points. We are going to give you three minutes to compose the speech in your head. Please don't write anything down. When the three minutes are up we will ask you to make the speech and we will record it. Please start your speech now.

3. Findings

Here we present an analysis of sentence openings in fast translation, and in consecutive interpreting and scaffolded speech. We include discussion of how the data were processed, followed by analysis of selected examples and presentation of tentative explanatory models.

3.1 *Sentence openings in fast translation*

The fast translation data were aligned by subject and broken into main clauses as far as could be determined. We follow Hasselgård (1997) in loosely and atheoretically defining sentence openings as all the material occurring in a main clause up to and including the main verb. A fragment of marked up target text data by a professional subject is shown in Figure 2. In this fragment, [SENTOP **The conference was hosted**] indicates a sentence opening, and [DEL Ministry] indicates that *Ministry* was written by the subject and deleted.

There was a good match of target text sentences with source text sentences, the only deviation being where some subjects broke a long sentence into two, thereby supplying an extra opening. The differences in sentence openings are set out below. Note that we deal only with the first six; not all subjects completed the translation, and there were insufficient data to deal with the last three sentence openings.

[SENTOP **The conference was hosted**] by the World Health Organisation and the Thai [DEL Ministry] Health Ministry.
[SENTOP **The convention** [DEL deals with] **points out**] to the major challenges [DEL as well as the steps] as well as as the procedures and obligations required in order to deal with health issues in the age of globalisation by including all the relevant [DEL and active] parties who play a main role in providing health services.
[SENTOP **The convention highlights**] [DEL the] world health issues which are changing and [DEL ?] the challenges [DEL facing] [DEL which] including the double burden caused by the common diseases and chronic illnesses which are on the rise.
[SENTOP **These include**] heart attacks, strokes, cancer and diabetes.

Figure 2: A fragment of marked up fast translation data

Sentence 1

Source text gloss: *confirmed today the participants in the Sixth Conference for Health Promotion the new Bangkok Charter for Health Promotion,*

Sentence openings:

(1) AS1: *Participent[6] have confirmed today the sixth conference for enhancing health at the new bound in Ban[DEL g]cok.*
(2) AS2: *The participates in sixth conference to enhance the health convention adapted*
(3) AS3: *The participants of The six conference [DEL to] for enhancing Health[7]*
(4) AP1: *Participants in the Sixth Conference for Better Health adopted*
(5) AP2: *Participants [INS in the third conference [DEL to] [INS for health promotion] [DEL health]] have adopted*
(6) AP3: *part[DELi]icipants in the 6 conference have agreed*

> Summary: All subjects, with the exception of AS1, began Sentence 1 with *participants* and some version of *in the Sixth Conference for Health Promotion. The* was inconsistently supplied. Subject AS1 failed to identify the whole of the grammatical subject, moving the defining material into the grammatical object position: *Participent have confirmed today the sixth conference for enhancing health at the new bound in Ban[DEL g]cok.*

---

[6] Note that misspellings are preserved in the transcriptions.
[7] AS3 did not supply a main verb.

Sentence 2

Source text gloss: *and had hosted this conference all of the World Health Organization and the Thailand Ministry of Public Health.*

Sentence openings:

(7) AS1: *The [DEL ?]Internation Health Organization and T[DEL?]iland Health Ministry have sponsored*

(8) AS2: *The Bankong [INS new] conference hosted*

(9) AS3: *The conference held by*

(10) AP1: *The conference was hosted by*

(11) AP2: *Both World Health Organisation and the Thai Ministry for Public Health have hosted*

(12) AP3: *this conference has been received by*

> Summary: Subjects were split between using a passive sentence that maintained *conference* in the initial position (AS2, AS3, AP1, AP3), or an active sentence that maintained the syntactic relations of the source text (AS1, AP2). There was inconsistency in the use of determiners.

Sentence 3

Source text gloss: *and defines this Charter the major challenges and likewise the necessary procedures and commitments to deal with the health concepts in the era of globalization by way of the participation of the many of the effective parties and supporters of the issue who have a basic role in the field of providing health to all.*

Sentence openings:

(13) AS1: *and [DEL ??] it determinds*

(14) AS2: *This convention [DEL outlined] highlights*

(15) AS3: *This Treaty try to point out*

(16) AP1: *The convention [DEL deals with] points out*

(17) AP2: *Th[DEL is]e convention identifies*

(18) AP3: *this agreement has set out*

> Summary: One subject began with *and it*. All others began with some translation of *Charter*, i.e. *convention, treaty* or *agreement*, again with inconsistent use of determiners, and evidence from AP2's editing of attention to the choice of determiner.

Sentence 4

Source text gloss: *and casts this Charter light on the course of world health (that is) opening to change and on the challenges thrown before the realization of the desired goals including the dual burden (that is) beginning to develop which forms it all of the common and chronic diseases which include the heart diseases and the strokes and the cancer and the diabetes.*

Sentence openings:

(19) AS1: *This agreement highlights ... These diseases[DEL include] are*
(20) AS2: *This convention sheds light on ...Also the conventions[DEL out][DEL hi] highlights*
(21) AS3: *This conference bring to the light ...The concept of this issue to achieve*
(22) AP1: *The convention highlights ... These include*
(23) AP2: *The convention focuses on*
(24) AP3: *this agreement cast a light on ... This includes*

Summary: All subjects began with some translation of *Charter*, i.e. *convention*, *treaty* or *agreement*, again with inconsistent use of determiners. Five of the six subjects broke the segment into two, but varied in where they made the break.

Sentence 5

Source text gloss: *there is a need also to address the health effects of globalization and its impact, such as the gaps (that are) beginning to widen and the growth of cities in a rapid way and the deterioration of the environment*

Sentence openings:

(25) AS1: *Also [DEL there is a need] discussing and [DEL modifying] [INS modifying] healthy factors [DEL for] of globalization is demanded*
(26) AS2: *There is a need to discuss*
(27) AS3: *In addition, There is [DEL a] need to study*
(28) AP1: *There is also a need to address*
(29) AP2: *[DEL These] globalisation impact on health needs also to be addressed and controlled*
(30) AP3: *We have to take into account as well*

Summary: There was a good deal of variation in translations of this opening. A major difference was between maintaining an existential sentence (AS2, AS3, AP1) or producing a de-existentialized version (AS1, AP2, AP3). AP2 and AS1 did this by making the source text *to address the health effects of globalization and its impact* into the grammatical subject of an obligation verb; AS1's editing reveals his/her indecision. AP3 paraphrases *there is a need* to *we have to*, leaving the obligation element to the left and thus more effectively maintaining the information structure than AS1 and AP3.

Sentence 6

Source text gloss: *and is considered the Bangkok Charter a new direction in the field of health promotion, and that by way of the call for the pursuit of balanced policies and for investment and the establishment of partnership relationships between the governments and the international organizations and the civil society and the private sector to work for the sake of fulfilling four main commitments which follow: Ensuring the place of health promotion at heart of the agenda of the world development actions, and making it one of the essential institutional responsibilities standing on the shoulder of the govern-ments and one of the good practices and one of the fields which concentrate on it the government initiatives and the initiatives if civil society.*

Sentence openings:

(31) AS1: *Bangok agreement is considered*
(32) AS2: *Bankong conventions is considered*
(33) AS3: *The conference is ... This move can be achieved*
(34) AP1: The Bangkok [DEL c][INS C]onvention is considered
(35) AP2: *[DEL The] Bangkok convention is considered [INS to be] to be*
(36) AP3: *Bangkok agreement is considered to be*

Summary: All subjects began with some version of *the Bangkok Charter*, with inconsistent determiner use and indecision on the part of AP2. Subject AS3 broke the sentence into two.

This analysis reveals a number of key sentence opening strategies used by the group of subjects as a whole:

A. OMITTING *WA* (AND)

Four of the Arabic segments began with the conjunctive particle *wa* (and). The fact that only subject AS1 translated sentence-initial *wa* in one instance strongly suggests that omission of *wa* is automatized.

B. LOCATING THE FIRST NOUN PHRASE IN THE SOURCE TEXT TO CREATE A THEME

The default strategy in finding a noun phrase for the target text theme posi-tion seems to be to locate the first noun phrase in the Arabic segment, as all subjects did in Sentences 1 and 6. In Sentence 2, two subjects (AS1 and AP2) used for the opening noun phrase a version of *the World Health Organization and the Thailand Ministry of Public Health*, which is the second noun phrase in the source text. The remaining four all began with the first noun phrase in the source text; two made reasonable passive sentences with a version of *conference* as the subject, and two created ungrammatical sentences – perhaps passive was their intention – with a version of *conference* in the subject position. In Sentence 5 the default strategy was harder to apply, possibly because of the large amount of semantically colourless material in *there is a need also to address* before the occurrence of the first noun phrase that coheres with prior segments.

C. USING DETERMINERS COHESIVELY

Determiners[8] are used by subjects with varying degrees of correctness, and with varying degrees of cohesive effect. In Sentence 1 above, for example, subject AS1 clearly has not acquired the determiner system to a level of automaticity where he/she can use it correctly under stress; Subject AS2 is in a similar position; Subject AP2 uses the English determiner system accurately, and is able to choose the option of omitting *the* before *participants* where it is followed by a defining prepositional phrase.

We cannot, however, consider determiners in the target texts without reference to those in the source text: In Sentences 2, 3 and 4, source text *conference* and *Charter* are preceded by an Arabic deictic pronoun *this*, which if translated faithfully conveys excessive focus in English. If we examine the instances where subjects have used a definite article rather than a deictic of some kind (see Table 3), a pattern begins to emerge suggesting the ability of subjects AP2 and AP3 to recognize the need to downplay the focus. AP2's *both* suggests a further layer of sophistication in his/her use of the determiner system in English.

	AS1	AS2	AS3	AP1	AP2	AP3
Sentence 2	n/a	*The*	*the*	*the*	*both*	this
Sentence 3	n/a	This	this	*the*	*the*	this
Sentence 4	this	This	this	*the*	*the*	this

Table 3. Downplaying of focus by replacing a deictic

D. BREAKING UP LONG SENTENCES

Finally, some subjects broke large sentences up and created extra openings, seen especially in Sentence 4 above. Subjects AS2 and AS3 seemed to have picked the break point fairly randomly, using *also* and *the concept of this issue* as new openings to try to maintain cohesion with the first part of the long source sentence. Subjects AS1, AP1 and AP3 used the subordinate clauses *including the dual burden ...* and *which includes the heart diseases and the*

---

[8] We use the term loosely to include deictics and quantifiers.

strokes and the cancer and the diabetes as the break points.

To summarize, this analysis permits a glimpse of the components of competence underlying sentence openings in fast translation in the context under consideration. These seem to be:

- Automatized translation-specific competencies such as omitting *wa* as a sentence connective
- Automatized second language competencies such as the use of determiners
- Executing the default strategy of using the first meaningful noun phrase in the source text as the grammatical subject; and strategically deploying grammatical alternatives when that noun phrase competes with other material for subjecthood
- Strategically downplaying the focusing effect of source text deictics
- Strategically breaking up large sentences and supplying new cohesive sentence openings.

3.2 Sentence openings in consecutive interpreting and scaffolded speech

The consecutive and scaffolded data sets were each aligned by subject and broken into sentences, but with much looser boundaries than in fast translation, where target text sentences could be easily aligned with source text sentences. Sentences were identified principally by agreement between two analysts using prosodic and functional criteria: did the prosody indicate that the speaker had finished a single semantically coherent message? Identifying sentence openings in consecutive interpreting and scaffolded speech was a very different task from the generally grammatical and largely atheoretical approach we used in fast translation. Speaking to an immediate audience, the interpreting and scaffolded speech subjects had to strike a balance between generating a coherent text and interacting with the listener; non-linguistic utterances, hesitations and corrections abounded.

Theories of information structure point to various ways of understanding the role of these messy sentence openings. The Hallidayan notion of multiple Theme used by Hasselgård, i.e. a topical theme that may be preceded by textual or interpersonal elements (Hasselgård 2004:188), can be appropriated and adapted to account for some of these openings. For example, in the bolded part of a scaffolded speech opening such as

(37) AS1.7: *[..]* ***so*** *[...] [nlu]* ***I*** *would remine I would like to remind you [.] guys*

the first *I* equates to the topical theme, and the preceding *so* is a textual element that provides a cohesive link with the previous segment.

Similarly, in the bolded part of this scaffolded speech opening in (38), while *we* equates to the topical theme, *actually* seems to have an interpersonal function of suasion.

(38) AS1.5: *[nlu]* **actually we** *have faced [.] [nlu] many tr many problems*

And in this consecutive interpreting opening in (39), while the subject is clearly struggling to find a meaningful topical theme with *all these factors [..] [nlu] in addition to [.] certain other factors*, the preceding *OK*[9] seems to function as an interpersonal element that asks the listener to bear with the subject while he/she collects their thoughts.

(39) AP2.8: *OK [.] all these factors [..] [nlu] in addition to [.] certain other factors [.] [nlu] come into play*

On the other hand, there are topical themes in the data that in themselves have an interpersonal or textual role. In this scaffolded speech opening the entire bolded component, anchored by the topical theme *I*, is intended to engage the listener's attention:

(40) AP1.2: *[...]* **I'll start by first giving you an idea** *[.] about why we're here in this conference [.] in Bangkok*

And in (41) the whole of the bolded component, with its false starts and corrections, equates to a topical theme but at the same time plays a textual role by providing a cohesive link to the preceding sentence.

(41) AP3.12: **[..] [nlu] all those issues all those factors combined together** **[.] [nlu] they** *may*

At this point, we enlist the help of Praguian theory, and in particular the "more text oriented conception of 'theme'" (Beaugrande 2002:30). In such a conception, as Beaugrande explains, following Daneš (1974), a rheme normally becomes the theme of the following sentence, with variations to account for themes that are repeated, omitted or partially developed. For our scaffolded speech and consecutive interpreting data, a text-oriented conception of theme supplements the Hallidayan idea of multiple themes in providing an understanding of these sentence openings.

Before we propose a model to handle these sentence openings, we need to deal with the numerous salutations and other non-topical interpersonal elements that occur in sentence openings, for example this piece of scaffolded speech data:

---

[9] See Gardner (1994) for the various functions of *OK* in conversation.

(42) AS3.1: ***Ladies and gentleman*** *[..]* ***you are welcome*** *[..] for our conference*

The bolded element is clearly interactional in function, as might be the entire sentence, and *you* seems to be no more than part of a formulaic utterance; it has no topicality. If the sentence is 'about' anything at all, it is the *conference*, which represents information already known to the listener and thus plays a textual role in helping to scaffold the discourse.

    While the opening in (42) seems to have both interpersonal and textual functions, in the case of (43), a consecutive interpreting example, the utterance has a solely interpersonal role.

(43) AP2.1: *good evening ladies and gentlemen . gentlemen[eos]*

    In what follows, we attempt to outline a model for analyzing sentence openings in consecutive interpreting and scaffolded speech. The fact that subjects were speaking to an immediate audience, unlike in the fast translation context, strongly calls for an analysis that accounts for the interpersonal and textual functions of sentence openings, and downplays the syntactic make up of these openings. The relative messiness of the data also argues against a syntactic orientation, and furthermore suggests a very loose definition of 'sentence'; as we have stated, our working definition was that the prosody should indicate that the speaker had finished a single semantically coherent message, so that for instance (43) would qualify as a sentence. The analysis, then, posits two main sentence opening strategies: some openings, e.g. greetings, are interactional in that they serve to establish or maintain interaction between speaker and audience. Others are textual, in that they serve to progress the discourse by way of cohesive devices. In the examples in the following section we have provided the whole sentence, and bolded the opening elements that are functionally textual or interpersonal.

A. TEXTUAL OPENINGS

Textual openings are further subdivided into those that:

- Link to a previous sentence by a conjunction, deictic pronoun, or some other device, i.e. by way of grammatical cohesion.[10] Examples are:

(44) AP1.11: ***these things*** *interact with other habits such as [.] [nlu]*

---

[10] We acknowledge the suggestion of one of the anonymous referees to equate the three types of links described here as examples of grammatical cohesion, lexical cohesion and cohesion through inference.

smoking [.] drinking alcohol [.] they how active a person is [eos][11]

(45) AP1.12: *[.] [nlu]* **and** *[nlu] [nlu] [nlu] the [...] [nlu] and [nlu] us being here today [.] [nlu] by by being here today [.] we hope that we [nlu] come out with [nlu] a [nlu] [..] [nlu] [...] a way to promote [.] and encourage people [.] to [nlu] minimize [nlu] health problems by following certain [nlu] [..] [nlu] [...] practices [eos]*

The links to previous sentences may be made with a limited or varied range of devices, e.g. *and ... and ... and* versus *however .. nonetheless ... also.*

- Link by way of a word or phrase to a word or phrase in a previous sentence, i.e. lexical cohesion, e.g.

(46) AS2.11: *[..] [nlu]* **the Thai campaign** *[.] aimed at [.] how to gather all [nlu] [..] all [...] all participant [nlu] and make final aim [.] what they going to do next and [.] how to fund for the programs and enterprises that [.] aiming to [eos]*

(47) AS2.12: *[...] [nlu]* **other Thai campaigns** *[.] [nlu] it is [nlu] conducting like educational [..] campaign [nlu] promotion all health issues [.] important issues [eos]*

Word/phrase links may be to the last sentence, or they might chain to the last sentence by repeating a lexical link, or they might jump several sentences.

- Link to a concept implied but not explicitly mentioned previously in the text, i.e. cohesion by inference, e.g.

(48) AP3.1: *[nlu]* **this [nlu] the world organization** *[.] [nlu] has [.] introduced the sixth global [nlu] World Health Organization [.] [nlu] in in Thailand [eos]*

(49) AS2.7: *[..] [nlu]* **a number of issued** *[.] discussed in conference [.] like [.] what other aspect that [..] has [.] affect on health public health [.] or health [eos]*

B. CHOICES AVAILABLE TO THE SUBJECTS

This analysis reveals a clear set of choices available to the subjects, modelled with a Choice Network as shown in Figure 3.

---

[11] Note that these data were tagged for pauses, e.g. [.], non-linguistic utterances such as *mmm* and *aah* [nlu], and end of sentence [eos].

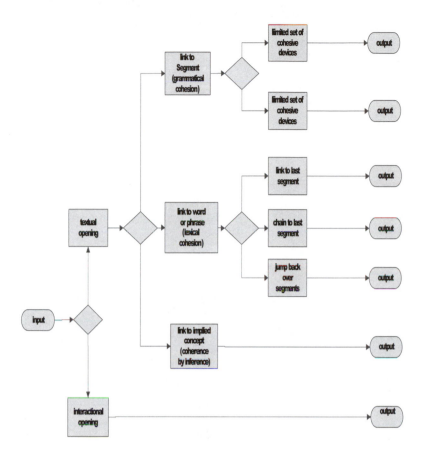

Figure 3. Choice Network of sentence openings in consecutive interpreting and scaffolded speech

C. INDIVIDUAL DIFFERENCES AMONG SUBJECTS

The performance of individual subjects can be shown graphically with a sentence opening flow diagram (see Figure 4).

In Figure 4, the spine of circles and rectangles represents sentences, with the solid arrows showing the progression of the discourse. Circular sentences have interactional openings, and rectangular sentences have textual openings. The axis above the spine represents links between sentences; the axis below the spine represents links between words *within* sentences. The bottom axis (only present in the consecutive diagram for this subject) represents links to implied concepts, indicated by the downward pointing box. This example demonstrates that while subject AS3 uses a simple paratactic strategy in scaffolded speech, a richer range of strategies is employed in consecutive interpreting.

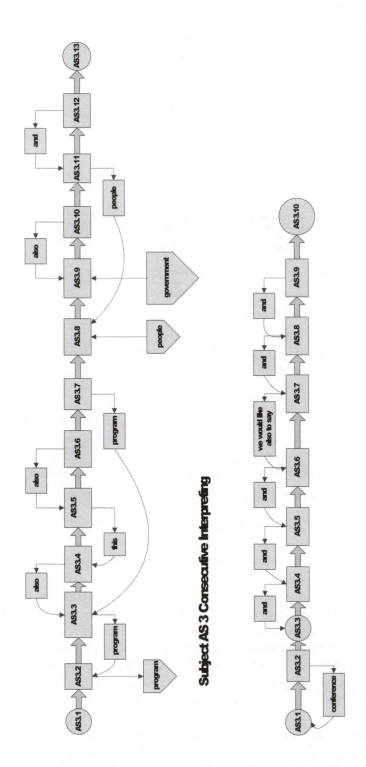

Figure 4. Sentence opening flow diagram for consecutive interpreting and scaffolded speech

D. GROUP DIFFERENCES

A statistical analysis was carried out (see Table 4) to discern differences in performance between students and professionals, and between consecutive interpreting and scaffolded speech.

Bearing in mind the limitations of a quantitative analysis using a small amount of data and relatively contestable categories, we suggest the following possible trends:

- *Interactional vs. textual openings.* Over the whole group of subjects, the proportion of textual and interactional openings is uniform, i.e. there is no difference between consecutive and scaffolded, or between students and professionals. However, there are marked differences among individuals: For example, AS2 barely used interactional openings in consecutive or scaffolded, while AP3 used no interactional openings at all in scaffolded speech.

- *Links to sentences.* Over the whole group of subjects, scaffolded speech contained more links to sentences on average than did consecutive. The dominance of links to sentences was shown in all subjects individually, except in AP3, in whom the consecutive and scaffolded contained about the same proportion. In scaffolded there was a smaller range of cohesive devices than in consecutive, i.e. all but one subject had a higher type/token ratio of cohesive devices in consecutive. Over consecutive and scaffolded, students tended to link to sentences more frequently than professionals.

- *Links to words.* Over the whole group of subjects, scaffolded speech contained fewer links to words than did consecutive. Professionals tended to link to words more frequently than students in both consecutive and scaffolded, and they were more likely to jump sentences. In consecutive, both students and professionals jumped sentences more frequently than in scaffolded speech.

- *Links to implied concepts.* There were no overall differences in the extent to which subjects linked to implied concepts. However, there were marked individual differences, e.g. AS1 never linked to implied concepts, but AS2 did so frequently in consecutive and scaffolded.

4.   Discussion

Scaffolded speech represents the unmarked interlanguage of the subjects, i.e. it is formulated without explicit input from a second language. In all subjects,

	consecutive students & professionals	scaffolded students & professionals	consecutive & scaffolded students	consecutive & scaffolded professionals
textual openings as % of total openings	83.07	79.99	79.82	83.24
interactional openings as % of total openings	16.93	20.01	20.18	16.76
total openings	100.00 (6 examples)	100.00 (6 examples)	100.00 (6 examples)	100.00 (6 examples)
link to sentence (grammatical cohesion) as % of total textual openings	42.60	69.58	61.02	51.16
link to word (textual cohesion) as % of total textual openings	37.90	14.07	21.74	30.24
link to implied concept (cohesion through inference) as % of total textual openings	19.49	16.35	17.24	18.60
total textual openings	100.00 (6 examples)	100.00 (6 examples)	100.00 (6 examples)	100.00 (6 examples)
type/token ratio of sentence connectives	0.68	0.51	0.62	0.58
link to last sentence as % of total link to word	55.00	75.00	76.00	50.00
chain to last sentence as % of total link to word	5.56	12.50	0.00	16.67
jump sentences as % of total link to word	39.44	12.50	24.00	33.33
total links to word	100.00 (6 examples)	100.00 (4 examples)	100.00 (5 examples)	100.00 (5 examples)

Table 4: Differences in performance between students and professionals, and between consecutive interpreting and scaffolded speech

Note: Mean scores are expressed as a percentage, except for type/token ratio. Percentage scores are followed by the number of examples, where 6 represents the full data set; where some subjects made no links to words, the data set has fewer than 6 examples.

there was little or no possibility of matching their discourse to the sentences of the scaffold, suggesting that it was authentically spontaneous monolingual speech. The paratactic nature of much of the scaffolded speech suggests that it was only loosely planned, and that the evolving mental representation of the discourse was largely conceptual rather than containing formal features of a text. Individual differences in the interlanguage system of theme choices were evident, with some employing a richer range of openings than simple parataxis.

Sentence opening choices in fast translation were closely linked to the source text. In terms of automaticity, there were clear differences among subjects, with most able to consistently omit *wa* (and), and only some able to use the English determiner system accurately. There was evidence of varying capacity to act strategically, e.g. in deploying alternatives to the default strategy of using the first meaningful noun phrase in the source text as the topical theme, softening the focusing effect of source text deictics, and breaking up large sentences. These strategic capacities operate beyond the boundaries of the sentence, suggesting that subjects differ in the richness of their mental representation of the task at hand with respect to information structure; for example, those who strategically soften the focusing effect of deictics must have in their evolving mental representation a mapping of the relative information prominence of key concepts.

In consecutive interpreting, the discourse was more strongly planned than in scaffolded speech. Consecutive was less paratactic, with subjects using words in prior sentences as 'hooks' to get them to the next sentence. This suggests that the evolving mental representation of the discourse includes formal features of the prior sentence or sentences of the text; professionals, with their higher rate of sentence jumps, seem to have a richer mental representation in this respect. Where parataxis was found in consecutive, the richer variety of cohesive devices than in scaffolded suggests a higher awareness of argumentative structure; we suggest that the mental representation includes an evolving 'map' of the argument, which would be more detailed in those subjects with more varied connectives. Individual differences in the proportion of interactional themes suggest another element of the evolving mental representation, i.e. a consciousness of the listeners' expectations. For example, in AP3 there appeared to be little sense of an audience, while AS1 had a rich sense of who he/she was talking to.

What we suggest for consecutive interpreting is that our subjects construct an evolving mental representation that includes (a) an argumentative plan based largely on the textual themes of the source text, and (b) a content plan based largely on the semantics of the source text, and (c) a sense of audience based largely on the interactional themes of the source text.

We conclude by revisiting the research questions posed earlier:

What sentence opening choices are made by translators and interpreters working into L2 English?
In fast translation, sentence opening choices are driven fundamentally by default strategies that generate openings based on material in the source text, and are moderated by the individual's interlanguage capacity to deploy more or less sophisticated strategies. In consecutive interpreting, there are two main drivers of choice, i.e. maintaining an interaction with the audience and maintaining textual cohesion. There is variation in the sophistication of cohesive links, which appears to be driven by interlanguage capacity and working memory capacity.

To what extent are these choices common to both translation and interpreting?
There is little or no commonality in the way that sentence opening choices are made in fast translation and consecutive interpreting; the immediate presence of the source text in fast translation and its absence in consecutive interpreting is the key differentiating factor. However, choices in interlanguage capacity affect the success or otherwise of choices in both production modes.

What role does L1 contribute to sentence opening choices?
In fast translation, L1 plays a role in that subjects are forced to make a choice when confronted with an MSA grammatical object that precedes the grammatical subject. Interestingly, there seems to be evidence of automatized strategies to deal with differences between L1 and L2, e.g. the omission of *wa*. We may hypothesize that different L1 factors will be found with other language pairs.

What are the psycholinguistic drivers of sentence opening choice?
For both fast translation and consecutive interpreting, there is evidence of differences in the evolving mental representation of the task. In fast translation, the mental representation retains some of the source text, and may include a mapping of the relative information prominence of key concepts to allow the deployment of alternatives to default strategies, and of determiners and deictics. The mental representation for consecutive interpreting retains some of the previously generated target text, and may include an argumentative plan, a content plan, and a sense of audience. In fast translation there is evidence of automatized processes such as *wa* omission and the basic use of determiners. While it is axiomatic that consecutive interpreting must entail automatized processing, e.g. as a function of monolingual production, there is no evidence of automatized processes specific to consecutive interpreting. These conclusions are based only on the evidence to hand and are not, of course, exhaustive.

How can the teaching and assessment of interpreting and translation be improved through a better knowledge of sentence opening choices?

This study provides clear pointers about how the teaching and assessment of interpreting and translation may be improved. Curriculum design for translation can clearly benefit from focused work on diagnosis and amelioration of problems with determiners, with special attention to very fast error-free execution in a text-based rather than sentence-based framework; we have much to learn from the "focus on form" movement in Second Language Acquisition research (Long 1988, 1991). Also warranted is work to help students rapidly identify matches between MSA grammatical subjects and English topical themes. For consecutive interpreting, a key element of curriculum design should be the development of the capacity to build an argumentative plan, a content plan, and a sense of audience. Profiling of translation performance can be sharpened by an analysis of sentence opening choice. For example, in Table 5 we have used three of our analytical measures as indicators of components of the evolving mental representation. Figures in bold indicate scores higher than the mean, allowing us to suggest a profiling of our subjects: professionals AP1 and AP2 and student AS2 have superior argument and content plans; student AS2 might have sacrificed sense of audience for argument and content. Student AS1 may be propping up a weak argument and content plan with interaction. We would strongly argue that profiling of this kind be developed as a diagnostic tool and a means of intervention at the group and individual level, or as part of a screening process.

	AS1	*AS2*	*AS3*	*AP1*	*AP2*	*AP3*	*mean*
Argument plan (type/token of cohesive devices)	0.50	**1.00**	0.50	**1.00**	**0.67**	0.43	0.68
Content plan (links to words as % of textual themes)	16.67	**41.67**	36.36	**60.00**	**54.55**	18.18	37.90
Sense of audience (interactional themes as % of themes)	**25.00**	7.69	15.38	16.67	**21.43**	15.38	16.93

Table 5. Profiling of subjects' consecutive interpreting performance

This study has focused on the importance of one aspect of information structure management and the potential for sound empirical research allied with a cross-disciplinary theoretical approach to generate practical outcomes for interpreter and translator education. We invite scholars to test our findings by extending and replicating the study.

References

Adab, Beverly (2005) 'Translating into a Second Language: Can We? Should We?', in Gunilla M. Anderman and Margaret Rogers (eds) *In and Out of English: For Better, for Worse,* Buffalo: Multilingual Matters, 227-41.

Beaugrande, Robert de (2002) 'The Heritage of Functional Sentence Perspective from the Standpoint of Text Linguistics {1}'. Available at http://beaugrande. com/LinguisticaPragiensa.htm (last accessed 22 July 2009).

Campbell, Stuart (1998) *Translation into the Second Language*, London: Longman.

------ (1999) 'A Cognitive Approach to Source Text Difficulty in Translation', *Target* 11(1): 33-63.

------ (2000a) 'Choice Network Analysis in Translation Research', in Maeve Olohan (ed.) *Intercultural Faultlines: Research Models in Translation Studies I: Textual and Cognitive Aspects*, Manchester, UK & Northampton, MA.: St. Jerome Publishing, 29-42.

------ (2000b) 'Critical Structures in the Evaluation of Translations from Arabic into English as a Second Language', *The Translator* 6(2): 211-29.

------ (2005) 'English Translation and Linguistic Hegemony in the Global Era', in Gunilla M. Anderman and Margaret Rogers (eds) *In and Out of English: For Better, for Worse*, Buffalo: Multilingual Matters, 27-38.

Campbell, Stuart and Berta Wakim (2007) 'Methodological Questions about Translation Research: A Model to Underpin Research into the Mental Processes of Translation', *Target* 19(1): 1-19.

Campbell, Stuart and Sandra Hale (1999) 'What Makes a Text Difficult to Translate?', *Proceedings of the 1998 ALAA Congress*. Available at http://www. latrobe.edu.au/alaa/proceed/camphale.html (last accessed 22 July 2009).

Chakhachiro, Raymond (2005) 'Revision for Quality', *Perspectives* 13(3): 225:38.

Christoffels, Ingrid K. and Annette M. B. de Groot (2005) 'Simultaneous Interpreting: A Cognitive Perspective', in Annette M. B. de Groot and Judith F. Kroll (eds) *Handbook of Bilingualism: Psycholinguistic Approaches*, New York: Oxford University Press, 454-79.

Daneš, František (1974) 'Functional Sentence Perspective and the Organisation of the Text', in František Daneš (ed.) *Papers on Functional Sentence Perspective*, The Hague: Mouton, 106-28.

Dechert, Hans. W. (1987) 'Analysing Language Processing through Verbal Protocol', in Claus Færch and Gabriele Kasper (eds) *Introspection in Second Language Research,* Clevedon, Avon: Multilingual Matters, 96-112.

Doherty, Monika (2002) *Language Processing in Discourse: A Key to Felicitous Translation*, London: Routledge.

Ebeling, Jarle (1998) 'Contrastive Linguistics, Translation, and Parallel Corpora', *Meta* 43(4): 602-15.

Gardner, Rod (1994) 'Conversation Analysis: Some Thoughts on Its Applicability to Applied Linguistics', in Rod Gardner (ed.) *Spoken Interaction Studies in Australia. Australian Review of Applied Linguistics*, Series S (11): 97-118.

Gerzymisch-Arbogast, Heidrun, Jan Kunold and Dorothee Rothfuß-Bastian (2006)

'Coherence, Theme/Rheme/Isotopy: Complementary Concepts in Text and Translation', in Carmen Heine, Klaus Schubert and Heidrun Gerzymisch-Arbogast (eds) *Text and Translation: Theory and Methodology of Translation*, Tübingen: Gunter Narr, 349-70.

Gile, Daniel (1995) *Basic Concepts and Models for Interpreter and Translator Training*, Amsterdam & Philadelphia: John Benjamins.

Gómez-González, María Ángeles (1997) 'On Theme, Topic and Givenness: The State of the Art', *Moenia* 3: 135-55.

Gundel, Jeanette (2002) 'Information Structure and the Use of Cleft Sentences in English and Norwegian', in Hilde Hasselgård, Stig Johansson, Bergljot Behrens and Cathrine Fabricius-Hansen (eds) *Information Structure in a Cross-linguistic Perspective*, Amsterdam & New York: Rodopi, 113-28.

Hale, Sandra Beatriz (2004) *The Discourse of Court Interpreting: Discourse ractices of the Law, the Witness, and the Interpreter*, Amsterdam & Philadelphia: John Benjamins.

Hasselgård, Hilde (1997) 'Sentence Openings in English and Norwegian', in Magnus Ljung (ed.) *Corpus Based Studies in English. Papers from the Seventeenth International Conference on English Language Research on Computerized Corpora (ICAME 17)*, Amsterdam & Atlanta, GA: Rodopi, 3-20.

------ (2000) 'English Multiple Themes in Translation', *Copenhagen Studies in Language: CEBAL* (25): 11-38.

------ (2004) 'Thematic Choice in English and Norwegian', *Functions of Language* 11(2): 187-212.

Hatim, Basil (1997) *Communication across Cultures: Translation Theory and Contrastive Text Linguistics*, Exeter, Devon: University of Exeter Press.

Hatim, Basil and Ian Mason (1990) *Discourse and the Translator*, London: Longman.

Hatim, Basil and Ian Mason (1997) *The Translator as Communicator*, London: Routledge.

Holes, Clive (1995) *Modern Arabic: Structures, Functions, and Varieties*, London: Longman.

Isham, William P. (1994) 'Memory for Sentence Form after Simultaneous Interpretation: Evidence both for and against Deverbalization', in Sylvie Lambert and Barbara Moser-Mercer (eds) *Bridging the Gap: Empirical Research in Simultaneous Interpretation*, Amsterdam: John Benjamins, 191-211.

Klin, Celia M., Kristin M. Weingartner, Alexandria E. Guzman and William H. Levine (2004) 'Readers' Sensitivity to Linguistic Cues in Narratives: How Salience Influences Anaphor Resolution', *Memory & Cognition* 32(3): 511-22.

Levelt, Willem J. M. (1981) 'The Speaker's Linearization Problem', *Philosophical Transactions of the Royal Society, London [Series B]* 295: 305-15.

------ (1989) *Speaking: From Intention to Articulation*, Cambridge, Massachusetts: The Massachusetts Institute of Technology Press.

Long, Michael H. (1988) 'Instructed Interlanguage Development', in Leslie M. Beebe (ed.) *Issues in Second Language Acquisition: Multiple Perspectives*, New York: Newbury House Publishers, 115-41.

------ (1991) 'Focus on Form: A Design Feature in Language Teaching Methodology', in Kees de Bot, Ralph B. Ginsberg and Claire Kramsch (eds) *Foreign Language Research in Cross-Cultural Perspective*, Amsterdam, The Netherlands: John Benjamins, 39-52.

Malmkjær, Kirsten (1998) 'Love Thy Neighbour: Will Parallel Corpora Endear Linguists to Translators?', *Meta* 43(4): 534-41.

Mauranen, Anna (1999) 'What Sort of Theme Is *there*?' A Translational Perspective', *Languages in Contrast* 2(1): 57-85.

Östman, Jan-Ola and Tuija Virtanen (1999) 'Theme, Comment, and Newness as Figures in Information Structuring', in Karen Van Hoek, Andrej A. Kibrik and Leonard G. M. Noordman (eds) *Discourse Studies in Cognitive Linguistics: Selected Papers from the Fifth International Cognitive Linguistics Conference, Amsterdam, July 1997*, Amsterdam: John Benjamins, 91-110.

Paradis, Michel (1994) 'Toward a Neurolinguistic Theory of Simultaneous Translation: The Framework', *International Journal of Psycholinguistics* 10(3): 319-35.

------ (2004) *A Neurolinguistic Theory of Bilingualism*, Amsterdam & Philadelphia: John Benjamins.

Rogers, Margaret (2005) 'Native Versus Non-native Speaker Competence in German English Translation: A Case Study', in Gunilla M. Anderman and Margaret Rogers (eds) *In and Out of English: For Better, for Worse*, Buffalo: Multilingual Matters, 256-74.

------ (2006) 'Structuring Information in English. A Specialist Translation Perspective on Sentence Beginnings', *The Translator* 12(1): 29-64.

Sanford, Anthony J. (1990) 'On the Nature of Text Driven Inference', in David A. Balota, Giovanni B. Flores D'Arcais and Keith Rayner (eds) *Comprehension Processes in Reading,* Hillsdale, New Jersey: Laurence Erlbaum, 515-35.

Sanford, Anthony J. and Simon C. Garrod (1981) *Understanding Written Language: Explorations of Comprehension beyond the Sentence*, Chichester & New York: Wiley.

Setton, Robin (1999) *Simultaneous Interpretation: A Cognitive-pragmatic Analysis,* Amsterdam & Philadelphia: John Benjamins.

Tirkkonen-Condit, Sonja (2005) 'The Monitor Model Revisited: Evidence from Process Research', *Meta* 50(2): 405-14.

Wilss, Wolfram (1994) 'A Framework for Decision-making in Translation', *Target* 6(2): 131-50.

------ (1996) *Knowledge and Skills in Translator Behaviour*, Amsterdam & Philadelphia: John Benjamins.

Appendix: *Bangkok* Arabic Source Text for Fast Translation

اعتمد اليوم المشاركون في المؤتمر السادس لتعزيز الصحة ميثاق بانكوك الجديد لتعزيز الصحة، وقد استضافت هذا المؤتمر كل من منظمة الصحة العالمية ووزارة الصحة العامة التايلندية. ويحدّد هذا الميثاق التحديات الكبرى وكذلك الإجراءات والالتزامات الواجبة لمعالجة المفاهيم الصحية في عصر العولمة عن طريق إشراك العديد من الأطراف الفاعلة وأصحاب الشأن الذين لهم دور أساسي في مجال توفير الصحة للجميع.

ويسلط هذا الميثاق الضوء على سياق الصحة العالمية الآخذ في التغيّر وعلى التحديات المطروحة أمام تحقيق الغايات المنشودة، بما في ذلك العبء المزدوج الآخذ في التنامي الذي تشكله كل من الأمراض السارية والأمراض المزمنة، التي تشمل الأمراض القلبية والسكتة الدماغية والسرطان والسكري. وهناك حاجة أيضاً إلى تناول الآثار الصحية للعولمة وضبطها، مثل التفاوتات الآخذة في الاتساع ونمو المدن بشكل سريع وتدهور البيئة.

ويعتبر ميثاق بانكوك توجهاً جديداً في مجال تعزيز الصحة، وذلك عن طريق الدعوة إلى انتهاج سياسات متسقة وإلى الاستثمار وإقامة علاقات شراكة بين الحكومات والمنظمات الدولية والمجتمع المدني والقطاع الخاص للعمل من أجل الوفاء بأربعة التزامات أساسية تشمل ما يلي: الحرص على وضع مسألة تعزيز الصحة في صميم جدول الأعمال الإنمائي العالمي، وجعلها إحدى المسؤوليات المؤسساتية الجوهرية الواقعة على عاتق الحكومات وإحدى الممارسات الجيدة، وأحد المجالات التي تركز عليها المبادرات المجتمعية ومبادرات المجتمع المدني.

وفي خطابه الافتتاحي أمام المؤتمر قال الدكتور جونغ- ووك لي، المدير العام لمنظمة الصحة العالمية، "إنّ ميثاق بانكوك لتعزيز الصحة سيكون الهيكلية المشتركة بين العديد من المنظمات والمجموعات والأفراد في بلدان كثيرة، إذ يحثّ هذا الميثاق جميع أصحاب الشأن على التعاون في إطار شراكة عالمية من أجل الوفاء بالالتزامات والاضطلاع بالاستراتيجيات الواردة فيه. ويمكن للإجراءات التي يتخذونها على ضوئه أن تحسّن، بشكل جذري، الآفاق الصحية في مجتمعات وبلدان العالم".

Adapted from http://www.who.int/mediacentre/news/releases/2005/pr34/ar/
index.html, accessed 22 July 2009.

II. Forms of Mediation

The Translator as Evaluator

THEO HERMANS
University College London, UK

Abstract. *This essay explores approaches and concepts that enable us to capture the translator's presence in translated texts. One approach consists in contextualizing the individual form each translation assumes, as translators position themselves through the display of a particular mode of representation seen against the possibility of alternative modes . Other approaches are designed to tease out translators' attitudes as conveyed in actual translations or their paratexts. If, following relevance theory, we construe translation as echoic discourse, we can identify the translator's attitude by gauging the difference between what is said and what is implied in the translated discourse. Modality, too, is concerned with the speaker's attitude towards and appraisal of what is being said. A focus on modality allows investigation, not just of the translator's value judgements about the discourse being rendered, but also of the rapport with the audience which is established in the process.*

How often do we consciously read translations together with their originals? Not very often. Except when, as teachers or students or researchers, we are comparing one with the other, the engagement with a translation alongside its original must be a relatively rare and fleeting occurrence, restricted, by and large, to scanning bilingual notices and signs, official documents, subtitles and surtitles, the occasional bilingual edition of a text and, beyond written translation, some interpreting situations. In the majority of cases we have recourse to a translation because we have no or only imperfect access to the original, physically or cognitively. Bearing this in mind, it is surprising that discussions of the role of the translator as communicator routinely draw on the comparison between a translation and its original. For most readers the original is not, or not readily, accessible. In what follows, therefore, I will take a different line. It seems to me that, if we are to understand the social functioning of translation better, we need to pay attention to the translated discourse as it reaches its audience. This means concentrating on the translation by itself and resisting the urge to check it against the original. To this end I will propose some approaches and concepts that allow us to detect and describe the way translators act out their mediating role in the presentation of their translations. Recourse to the original is strictly optional. Recourse to other translations however is a factor. True, relatively few readers consult and compare different translations of the same original, but they can do so if they wish and, more importantly, our expectations of what translation is and does are shaped by the translations we have encountered in the past.

As a starting point, let me stress that I am concerned with texts that function as translations. So-called covert translations, provided they are so comprehensively covert that nothing leads us to assume they are translations, are not translations in this functional sense. I also take it for granted that a translation cannot be equivalent to its original. A translation that *is* equivalent to its original, that is recognized as equivalent and functions as such, ceases to be a translation and becomes a version on a par with the original, one version among other versions of the same work (Hermans 2007:1-25). The relevance of this point is that, if a translation is elevated to the rank of an equivalent version and consequently ceases to be a translation, there can no longer be a translator either. It follows, conversely, that for as long as a translation is recognized and functions as a translation, a translator's discursive position is necessarily inscribed in it. As a communication separate from the original and speaking about this original to an audience, a translation must have a speaking subject. Of course, translators may strive to create an illusion of equivalence, and a convincing illusion requires projecting a disembodied or at least anonymous translator (Pym 1992:51-52), but this merely means that the translator is playing hard to get or hard to spot. Even if translators make themselves so thin that we remain unaware of their presence or see right through them, they are still there. It is a matter of devising the methodological means to capture their positioning. It seems to me that we can tease out the presence of a translator in a translated text in a number of ways.

1.   Display

Translations represent originals. In order to bring about the resemblance that, as a rule, enables translations to speak for their source texts, translators re-enact – or, as Cecilia Wadensjö (1998:247) puts it, they 'replay' – those originals, indeed they may do this so adroitly that we almost take the re-enactment for the original, in which case we largely forget about the translator's speaking self for the duration of the performance. But Wadensjö usefully contrasts 'replay' with 'display'. Whereas 'replay' indicates the relation between translation and original, 'display' draws attention, self-referentially, to the particular character of the replay or re-enactment, to the choice of this or that mode of representation that the translation exhibits, in contrast to other modes that could also have been chosen. Display holds the translation's particular mode of representation up for inspection, as it were, and signals that it could have been different. In other words, what Wadensjö calls 'display' flaunts the manner of representation that an individual translation exhibits, against the backdrop of possible alternatives. The information value of the display consists in the difference between the actual and the possible, the choices that were made and the choices that could have been made but were not. It does not matter whether the choices made amount to an idiosyncratic or a subversive or an ostentatious or an entirely conventional translation style. In each case a given, concrete form gains relief by being set against its other side, that which it could have been but has remained potential.

The distinction between display and replay allows us to discern the translator in the form of the very positioning that the individual choices taken together add up to. Even in the case of a translation striving for the illusion of equivalence, the choice for anonymity and transparency is not part of the replay but of the display. The translation keys its particular re-enactment in a certain manner, and this keying is not itself part of the re-enactment.

Translations are part of the historical continuum of culture. If the difference between what is and what might have been provides a clue to the way translators position themselves, it will pay to look for intertextual links that tie different translations of the same original together. Assuming that different translations of the same original are likely to have at least some elements in common, if only at the level of propositional content, their similarity supplies a shared element against which to gauge their differences and hence their individual signatures.

Here is a particularly blatant, literary example. In the second book of Virgil's *Aeneid*, Aeneas tells of the destruction of Troy and the killing of the Trojan king Priam, whose body was unceremoniously dumped outside the city. This is how John Dryden's 1697 translation of the *Aeneid* describes the corpse:

> On the bleak shore now lies th'abandoned king,
> A headless carcass, and a nameless thing. (Andrews 1968:55)

To the second of these two lines Dryden added a marginal note: "This whole line is taken from Sir John Denham" (Davis 2008:39). Indeed, in 1656, in *The Destruction of Troy*, his celebrated translation of a large part of the second book of the *Aeneid*, John Denham had:

> On the cold earth lies th'unregarded King,
> A headless Carkass, and a nameless Thing. (Davis 2008:36)

Modern popular editions of Dryden's *Aeneid* (like Andrews 1968, from which I quoted above) usually omit the marginal note. However, for those – admittedly now very few – readers who are aware of the borrowing, the reference, and with it the homage that Dryden pays to Denham, are there. The homage expresses respect and perhaps a degree of affinity. The affinity may well have been ideological as well as purely translative, but only the latter aspect is of interest to me here. I would like to see it as the thin but visible end of a large wedge.

The marginal note obviously highlights an intertextual connection. While it acknowledges Dryden's inability to improve on Denham in this particular line, it also suggests that, in all the other lines of his *Aeneid*, Dryden's approach to translating Virgil differs from Denham's and leads to different results, beginning with the no more than partial overlap between his own and Denham's version in the line immediately preceding the verbatim repetition. The homage to Denham occurs in a translation that knows exactly how and where – and presumably why – it differs from Denham's.

There is more. We can read Dryden's adoption of Denham's line as signalling a comment by a translator about translation. It is a comment about the open-ended possibility of and the need for differential renderings, tempered by the occasional admission that a predecessor in this or that particular instance has hit the nail on the head and may as well be imitated when he cannot be emulated. Dryden's reference to Denham therefore concerns the felicity, the appropriateness and perhaps the relevance of certain ways of representing, in English, Virgil's Latin. To that extent the verbal echo with which Dryden salutes Denham points well beyond the latter's achievement towards prevailing ways of rendering, in English or languages like English, Virgil's *Aeneid* or texts like it, and perhaps other texts. Dryden has read other translations of Virgil besides Denham's, and he has read translations of other classics; his *Aeneid* bears the traces of that study.

In this way we can reach into the generic, architextual dimension that lies behind the particular intertextual reference. The move from the intertextual to the architextual allows us to recognize the verbal echo not just as connecting two individual texts but as translation speaking about translating as such. The echo, that is, amounts to a comment about translation produced in the act of translating. Dryden's marginal comment identifying the echo only makes explicit what is already there in the translation itself, in the very choice of its words combining into its specific signature, a signature it displays especially effectively at the point where it brushes against Denham's version.

The evidence may be rather less obvious than a direct verbal echo, and we may need more circumstantial data to appreciate its significance. Thomas Hobbes's translations of the *Iliad* and *Odyssey* appeared in the 1670s. They were, in George Steiner's words, "the work of a philosopher in his mid-eighties, with no poetic talent" (1996:65); Dryden observed likewise that Hobbes studied poetry "as he did Mathematics, when it was too late" (Kinley 1958:1448). Both translations employ rhyme. This does not seem unusual, since every English translator of Homer, from Arthur Hall in the 16th century to John Ogilby just ten years before Hobbes, had done so. But by the time Ogilby and Hobbes were translating, something had changed. The English Civil War had happened (1641-1651) and, as a result, rhyme was no longer what it had been. It had become political. In the preface to *Paradise Lost* (1668), John Milton, a republican, famously associated rhyme with "bondage" and regarded "neglect of rhyme" as "ancient liberty recovered". Andrew Marvell, another republican, praised Milton's use of blank verse. Dryden, on the other hand, a monarchist like Ogilby and Hobbes, used rhyme; in the essay *Of Dramatick Poesie* of 1668 he recommended rhyme as the medium for poetry at court and dismissed blank verse as "too low for a Poem". To Milton's chagrin, Dryden even sought permission to turn *Paradise Lost* into a rhyming play (Nelson 2008:xxxi-xxxii). In other words, even the apparently innocent and purely literary choice of verse form here signals an added value that invests the translation not just with an emphatic medium but with topical relevance and meaning beyond the representational and translative. Through the use of rhyme versus blank verse, translators position themselves in a political landscape, and this positioning takes place irrespective of the role of the translation as re-enactment of an original.

Hobbes's versions of Homer are decidedly unpoetic, not just because Hobbes had no poetic talent and came to poetry when it was too late but also because, as a political philosopher, he was intensely suspicious of poetic orna-ment and rhetoric. Rhetoric and poetic fancy, for Hobbes, lacked discretion and hence could not teach people to think rationally. In his translation Hobbes consistently portrayed Homer's heroes as dignified rather than brutish; he tamed Homer's language and bridled his verse. The books came out in small, inexpensive, unadorned editions without notes (Nelson 2008:xxxvi-xxxix, lv). In all these ways the translations manifest an emphatic display of form and style and a wayward relation with existing translations; all these choices reveal the translator's agenda, which becomes visible in and through all aspects of the text, down to the size and quality of the paper it is printed on.

The conclusion must be that, apart from the way a translation speaks about another text by re-enacting or 'replaying' it, translation also speaks about itself in the sheer display of its distinctive mode of re-enactment or replay. But the distinctiveness of that mode only shows itself when it is contextualized by means of an intertextual web of contrasts and parallels. The display, as the relief given to a specific mode of representation in the context of past and current alternatives, positions the translator in the translation.

2.   Reporting

Following relevance theory and a host of other approaches, we can construe translation as a form of reported speech, that is, as a form of quoting.[1] Quoting,

---

[1] It may well be that casting translation as a form of reported discourse, and developing that idea with reference to particular characteristics of reported discourse, is language-specific, in that distinctions and inferences are being made which assume the structure of English or a similar language. I am not in a position to gauge how different the picture may look when viewed through radically different languages. With thanks to Hans Vermeer, who reminded me of this drastic limitation of the model.

in turn, can be viewed, with Herbert Clark and Richard Gerrig (1990), as an instance of demonstration, a mimetic re-enactment rather than a diegetic verbal account of an event. The value of Clark and Gerrig in the context of translation is twofold. First, they regard translation as a valid instance of quotation and therefore of demonstration. Secondly, they stress that demonstrations are not wholly mimetic but retain a diegetic margin, partly because re-enactments are necessarily selective and partly because they invariably occur in the context of a reporting discourse.

Since a reported discourse is normally embedded in a reporting clause, the latter frames the words being reported. In the case of translation, the reporting clause can be elaborate and comprise various liminary and other paratexts, from the announcement on a title page that the text which follows is a translation, to all manner of translator's prefaces, footnotes, epilogues and asides. The reporting clause can be minimal, for instance the barest mention of the translator's name in the colophon of a printed book. It may not even take the form of an explicit statement, and may have to be inferred on the basis of contextual information leading to the assumption that something is translated. It can even be spurious, as in the case of pseudotranslations. If the reporting clause is entirely absent, that is, if there is no detectable trace of one and no reason to infer or suspect one, it does not make much sense to speak of a translation; fully covert translations or cases of undetected plagiarism would be illustrations of this state of affairs. Linguistically, they would represent instances of free direct discourse. Socially and functionally speaking, such texts only become translations when they are unmasked as being translations, even though genetically they were translations all along.

Reported discourse comes in a range of different types, from direct and free direct discourse to various kinds of indirect discourse. Kristiina Taivalkoski-Shilov (2006:54) has usefully mapped this continuum. It stretches from a paraliptic résumé, in which a translator informs the reader or listener of the existence of someone else's words but then omits them, via summary and gist translation, to the kind of indirect and free indirect speech one occasionally hears from amateur interpreters ("she's saying her uncle doesn't live here any more"), until reaching the direct speech typical of most standard translations.

As one moves along this scale and its gradations, several shifts in the relation between the reporting and the reported speech occur. Indirect discourse means the reported utterance remains syntactically dependent on the reporting discourse ("He says he can't make it"), whereas direct discourse is syntactically autonomous and hence involves a marked switch in grammatical person and vantage point from the reporting to the reported speaker ("He says: 'I can't make it!'"). Direct discourse implies a more mimetic mode of representation of the anterior utterance than indirect discourse, in which the diegetic presence of the reporter remains more in evidence, especially with respect to word choice and register. But it is important to remember that, however mimetic the reported discourse, the translator's diegetic presence in it is never zero. This is because, firstly, even verbatim quotation remains selective; secondly, reported speech, however mimetic, is embedded in a diegetic reporting speech; and thirdly, especially in the case of translation, there must be an agent who is responsible for the choice of manifestly different words in the new language. The translator's diegetic voice presents, frames and accompanies the mimetic report. Unless we are dealing with totally covert translations or with undetected plagiarism, the re-enunciation of an anterior discourse has to be announced and performed, even if the announcement is not explicitly stated and needs to be inferred, as is common, for instance, in international news reporting. The point about construing translation as a form of quoting is that, apart from the replay or reporting of another person's words, this model makes room for the reporting frame, a space in which translators speak in their own name about what it is they are transmitting.

As speakers who report a pre-existing utterance in another language, translators convey attitudes through and along with the translated discourse they offer up to their readers. The attitudes conveyed are a significant aspect of the social role of translation, as they contribute to affirming, modifying or questioning the values held by the individuals or communities the translator is addressing. This is why it is of methodological importance to devise ways of identifying these attitudes. To my knowledge, at least two conceptual tools are available to assist with this task. One is called echoic speech, the other modality.

3.   Echo

Ever since Gutt (1991) it has been possible to view translation as a type of interpretive utterance, relevance theory's term for reported discourse. If we want to treat the translator's attitude as part of the reporting, we may view translation more specifically as an instance of what relevance theory calls echoic speech. An echoic utterance is an interpretive utterance which derives its relevance from the attitude which the speaker signals with regard to the represented discourse.[2] The belief which the speaker indicates regarding the represented utterance may be associative or dissociative; in other words, it may be supportive, empathetic and respectful or it may be disapproving, distancing,

---

[2] Let me take this opportunity to correct an error in my *Conference of the Tongues* (Hermans 2007). An echoic utterance is an interpretive utterance which conveys an attitude, but this attitude is not necessarily dissociative. In my book I suggested that it was (2007:77). Fortunately, the error does not affect the argument in the book. Ironic speech, which the relevant chapter is concerned with, is that variety of echoic speech which conveys a dissociative attitude towards the speech being echoed. With thanks to Xosé Rosales Sequeiros, who pointed out the error within days of the book appearing in print.

sceptical or mocking (Sperber and Wilson 2004:621-22). The belief or attitude does not have to be linguistically encoded; it may have to be inferred from paralinguistic signals (Noh 2000:94).

When echoic discourse is dissociative, we can speak of irony as relevance theory understands it. Irony operates when something is said which evokes something else that is left unspoken and a sceptical, mocking or critical attitude is conveyed in the process. The weather is awful, someone looks out of the window and exclaims: "Beautiful day!". The difference between the said and the unsaid, and the dissociative attitude attached to this difference, forms an essential part of the ironic utterance. In the case of translation, a preface critical of some or indeed all aspects of an original will mean that the translation itself must be read from a double perspective, with an eye both to what the words ostensibly say and to what needs to be understood additionally as secondary meanings on the basis of the reservations expressed in the preface. A supportive preface, too, resonates within the actual translation. Since the preface frames the translation, it does not directly interfere with its performance but still affects the reader's or hearer's perception of this performance because the evaluative attitude is carried over from the framing to the framed speech. Piling an unspoken discourse on top of a reported discourse means two speaking positions are brought into play, one which pretends to duly translate and one which knows better and communicates its supportive or sceptical or dismissive stance towards the message being translated. The absence of a preface need not mean the absence of an attitude, as the audience is most likely to project standard expectations on the translation.

Translator irony can work without the explicit distancing signal of a preface. The concluding lines of John Denham's *The Destruction of Troy* of 1656, as quoted earlier, can serve as an illustration: "On the cold earth lies th'unregarded King,/ A headless Carkass, and a nameless Thing". The words achieve more than their status as a discourse representing Virgil's Latin. They can be read both as a plain translation and as a political comment, but in this latter case they amount to a subtle, veiled comment made from a relatively safe position, which would allow the translator to deny, if the need arose, that anything more than a plain translation was at stake. As Paul Davis (2008) and others have pointed out, the episode describing Priam's dead body did not occur in Denham's 1636 manuscript of his translation. We cannot be certain that the lines reflect Denham's horror at the execution of Charles I in 1648, but it is generally assumed that they do, especially as in the 1656 version these are the concluding lines of the poem, which now ends on a stark note of desacralization (Davis 2008:36). The presence of so poignant an image which leaves the poem suspended is a matter of display, and fuels interpretive speculation. Whether or not Denham actually intended to do more than merely translate Virgil's lines is not the issue. Irony can be in the eye of the beholder; it does not depend exclusively on the speaker's intention. That is what enables modern critics to speculate that in these lines Denham was saying more than he was saying, and that contemporary readers may well have interpreted the lines in this way. The point here is not so much the fact that Denham makes a political statement, but that, in translating, he appears to be commenting also on the potential of Virgil's Latin to be relevant to the translator's place and time. The comment is less than explicit, for good political reasons, given Denham's circumstances at the time. It is precisely the echoic nature of translation that allows someone like Denham to exploit the ambiguity of saying one thing and leaving the reader guessing whether more is being implied.

4.   Modulation

Reported speech is necessarily echoic to some extent, however small. There cannot be a total absence of attitude in a reporting speaker and, by implication, in a translator. The attitude can be indifferent or neutral, even though the decision to be neutral is not itself a neutral decision, and thus conveys an evaluative attitude towards the attitude that is being adopted.

Linguistically, the expression of an attitude concerning the propositions one is uttering is ranged under modality. Modality covers what M.A.K. Halliday calls the interpersonal metafunction of language; it is the component that "represents the speaker's intrusion into the speech situation" by expressing the speaker's attitudes, judgements and expectations (Halliday 2002:199); in so doing it defines the role speakers assign to themselves as well as the role they assign to the audience that is being addressed. In other words, apart from signalling a speaker's perspective on the communicative exchange, modality also assigns and acts out social roles (*ibid.*:206).

It has become standard to distinguish, with Paul Simpson (1993:47-48), three kinds of modality: deontic, boulomaic and epistemic. Epistemic modality expresses the speaker's relative certainty regarding the truth or probability of the proposition being uttered, and need not concern us here. Deontic and boulomaic modality are, however, of relevance. They are closely related; whereas deontic modality expresses obligation, boulomaic modality expresses inclination.

Halliday uses a slightly different terminology from Simpson. He speaks of 'modalization' where Simpson has epistemic modality, and groups under 'modulation' the two kinds that Simpson distinguishes as deontic and boulomaic modality (Halliday 1994:356-58). However, within 'modulation' Halliday makes a distinction between active and passive modulation. The former refers to an ability or willingness presented as intrinsic to the actor, the latter indicates a compulsion or permission extrinsic to the actor (Halliday 1970:341). Halliday's active modulation corresponds to Simpson's boulomaic modality, and passive modulation resembles deontic modality. Terminology aside, the distinction itself is of relevance to the study of translation. In the one case, translators may build a rapport with their audience by signalling a personal commitment or desire to translate in a certain way or with certain personal reservations, or to offer a certain text in translation in the first place; in the other case, translators may appeal to a shared understanding of the nature of translation or the translator's responsibility.

Examples of both types of modality are not hard to find. The late-medieval translator of *Der vrouwen heimelijcheit* (The hidden secret of women), a gynaecological tract translated into Dutch via French from a Latin source in the 14th century, explains in his prefatory verses that he has omitted a good part of the section on terminating unwanted pregnancies because abortion is a sin, but, he adds, he did not want to omit the offending section entirely because he worried that he might be regarded as an incompetent or ignorant translator: "Yet I have disclosed it somewhat / So nobody will be able to say / I do not know or understand it" ("Doch hebbics wat ontbonden,/ Dat nie-men en derf orconden / Dat ics niet en versta no ne weet"; Besamusca and Sonnemans 1999:90).

The statement shows a dual and contradictory pull, with both a moral and a professional aspect. The moral no (do not disseminate knowledge about sinful practices) meets a professional yes (translate accurately and in full), and the result is a compromise (translate but abridge troubling passages). I am inclined to read the translator's statement as expressing, in Halliday's terms, active modulation, in that it presents the translator's stance as resulting from his own decision and inclination, without invoking an extrinsic power that obliges him to act as he does. In this sense Halliday is right to stress that modality defines both the speaker and the speaker's perception of his audience. As regards the actual translation, the reader who goes on to peruse the text will need to bear in mind that the section on terminating unwanted pregnancies carries the translator's disapproving judgement in its every word. This is what makes the translation, in relevance theory terms, ironic. The translator is giving us the gist of the original but is at the same time signalling moral reservations about what it says. His diegetic presence in the mimetic representation stems from the fact that we know we are being presented with an abridged version and we know the considerations that led to the abridgement. Both as regards his moral stance and his perception of his professional task the translator is aware of the values that are alive among his contemporary audience, and his positioning helps to secure those values. At the same time, he asks for his audience's understanding of his predicament as a translator, and their appreciation of his problem also pervades the reading. In all these ways the translator's positioning is a matter of appraisal (Hunston and Thompson 2000, Martin and White 2005). He evaluates the discourse being translated and his own responsibility towards it. This evaluation reverberates through the translation and builds a rapport with the audience.

Thomas Carlyle, in the preface to his 1824 English translation of Goethe's novel *Wilhelm Meister*, observes: "to follow the original in all the variations of its style, has been my constant endeavour. In many points, both literary and moral, I could have wished devoutly that he had not written as he has done, but to alter anything was not in my commission". Just two sentences later, however, he adds: "Accordingly, except a few phrases and sentences, not in all amounting to a page, which I have dropped as evidently unfit for the English taste, I have studied to present the work exactly as it stands in German" (Frank 2004:1572).

Here the translator claims he let his professional instinct prevail over his stylistic and moral misgivings ("to alter anything was not in my commission") but he has nevertheless omitted the odd passage deemed "evidently unfit for the English taste". The reference to the translator's commission characterizes Carlyle's stance as one of passive modulation, even though his particular interpretation of it (how much modulation or how little, and what kind) may be a matter of a historical translation poetics. The translator anticipates the audience's approval of his decision to cut the original here and there and, to that extent, he appeals to shared values. A faint whiff of irony will hang over the actual translation, for the reader will have to guess exactly where Carlyle decided to drop or alter something, and where he says one thing when something else, but something presumably less tasteful, could have been said in its place. Here, too, both the preface and the actual translation engage in social bonding by seeking to secure shared values recognized as 'our' values, in contrast with foreign mores. In addition, an allegedly common notion of what translation entails is being perpetuated by means of both statement and performance.

Let me end with an altogether different example, which stretches some of the points I have been making. The nineteenth-century Dutch poet J.J.L. Ten Kate (1819-89), a deeply religious man, was a prolific and eagerly 'christian-izing' translator. He translated almost exclusively religious authors, and even then he occasionally adapted them to intensify or highlight their Christian message. He was aware of the new scientific ideas about geological time and evolution that were causing widespread consternation and controversy in intel-lectual circles. His own epic poem *The Creation* (*De schepping*, 1866) sought to reconcile those revolutionary theories with the biblical creation story, and came down firmly on the side of what we now call creationism. The poem presented the seven biblical days of creation as corresponding to successive geological periods, and argued in a seven-page footnote that science and the Bible concurred in dating the first emergence of man as having happened around six thousand years ago (Ten Kate 1866:307-13).

Not all the scientists agreed. In an article published in a general periodical a year after Ten Kate's poem, the Dutch palaeontologist T.C. Winkler (1822-79) called *The Creation* "stupid" and "a slap in the face of science" (Winkler 1867:45, 25, Hegeman 1970:279). Winkler, trained as a medical doctor and the curator of a geological and palaeontological museum in Haarlem, took a very different view of the earth's history. A few years earlier, on 7 July 1861, Winkler had sent a copy of one of his own articles, on fish fossils, to Charles Darwin, together with his Dutch translation of *The Origin of Species*. In the covering letter, written in French, Winkler explained that the gift was a token of his great respect for Darwin's scientific work ("je désire vivement vous témoigner ... le respect que m'inspirent vos travaux scientifiques", Winkler 1861). Winkler wrote appreciatively about Darwin in cultural journals, and also translated scientists other than Darwin, including the geologists Charles Lyell (*Principles of Geology*, 1830) and David Page (*Philosophy of Geology*, 1864). In this way he was affiliated with other Dutch scientist-translators like Herman Hartogh Heijs van Zouteveen (1808-78), who translated most of Darwin's other works, including a version of *The Descent of Man* which appeared in 1872, simultaneously with the English original (Van Baren 1912, 1924, Hegeman 1970).

The point of the example is this: both Ten Kate and Winkler translated writers they sympathized with, and they both wrote and translated against one another. They actually clashed only once, in the few brief words quoted above, not over translation but over Ten Kate's creation poem and its Christian fundamentalism. But even though Ten Kate's numerous renderings of Christian authors and Winkler's translations of scientists like Darwin, Lyell and Page have no immediate point of contact, we can read each translator's choice of what and how to translate, and consequently each translator's entire career, as pitched against the other. Each translator expressed affinity with the authors they translated, and through their translations they strengthened the particular body of ideas they identified with. They almost certainly acted out of a combination of personal conviction and a sense of professional duty, collapsing Halliday's active and passive modulation into one. But the modality underpinning their work is obvious; it involves inclination and obligation, and a pervasive epistemic doubt about the ideas being propagated through the other's translations.

They found themselves in opposite camps in a battle of ideas. Each man's sympathy for one side meant scepticism or hostility towards the other, and each one of their translation choices bears this out. The values they sought to secure through their translations point well beyond the world of translation to one of the defining intellectual conflicts of the age, the clash between religion and science. But this very much larger stake only becomes visible when we have a way of revealing the translator's agenda, that is, when we are able to distinguish between the mimetic nature of translation and the evaluative attitude, or modality, that informs it.

References

Andrews, Clarence (ed.) (1968) *Virgil's Aeneid. Translation by John Dryden*, New York: Airmont.

Besamusca, Bart and Gerard Sonnemans (eds) (1999) *De crumen diet volc niet eten en mochte. Nederlandse beschouwingen over vertalen tot 1550* (The

Crumbs the People Were Not Meant to Eat. Dutch Discourses on Translation until 1500), 's-Gravenhage: Stichting Bibliographia Neerlandica.

Clark, Herbert and Richard Gerrig (1990) 'Quotations as Demonstrations', *Language* 66: 764-805.

Davis, Paul (2008) *Translation and the Poet's Life. The Ethics of Translating in English Culture, 1646-1726*, Oxford: Oxford University Press.

Frank, Armin Paul (2004) 'Main Concepts of Translating: Transformations during the Enlightenment and Romantic Periods in France, Great Britain, and the German Countries', in Harald Kittel, Armin Paul Frank, Norbert Greiner, Theo Hermans, Werner Koller, José Lambert and Fritz Paul (eds.) *Übersetzung Translation Traduction*, Berlin & New York: Walter de Gruyter, 1531-609.

Gutt, Ernst-August (1991) *Translation and Relevance. Cognition and Context,* Oxford: Blackwell

Halliday, M.A.K. (1970) 'Functional Diversity in Language, as Seen from a Consideration of Modality and Mood in English', *Foundations of Language* 6(3): 322-61.

------ (1994) *An Introduction to Functional Grammar*, second edition, London: Edward Arnold.

------ (2002) *On Grammar*, London & New York: Continuum.

Hegeman, J.G. (1970) 'Darwin en onze voorouders. Nederlandse reacties op de evolutieleer 1860-75, Een terreinverkenning' (Darwin and Our Ancestors. Dutch Responses to the Theory of Evolution 1860-75. An Exploration), *Bijdragen en mededelingen betreffende de geschiedenis der Nederlanden* (Studies and Contributions Concerning the History of the Low Countries) 85: 261-314.

Hermans, Theo (2007) *The Conference of the Tongues,* Manchester: St Jerome Publishing.

Hunston, Susan and Geoff Thompson (eds.) (2000) *Evaluation in Text. Authorial Stance and the Construction of Discourse*, Oxford: Oxford University Press.

Kinley, James (ed.) (1958) *The Poems of John Dryden*, 4 vols, Oxford: Oxford University Press.

Martin, James R. and Peter R.R. White (2005) *The Language of Evaluation. Appraisal in English*, Basingstoke & New York: Palgrave Macmillan.

Nelson, Eric (ed.) (2008) *Thomas Hobbes. Translations of Homer*, Oxford: Clarendon.

Noh, Eun-Ju (2000) *Metarepresentation. A Relevance-Theory Approach*, Amsterdam & Philadelphia: John Benjamins.

Pym, Anthony (1992) *Translation and Text Transfer. An Essay on the Principles of Intercultural Communication,* Frankfurt: Peter Lang.

Simpson, Paul (1993) *Language, Ideology and Point of View*, London & New York: Routledge.

Sperber, Dan and Deirdre Wilson (2004) 'Relevance Theory', in Laurence Horn and Gregory Ward (eds.) *The Handbook of Pragmatics*, Oxford: Blackwell, 607-32.

Steiner, George (ed.) (1996) *Homer in English*, London: Penguin.

Taivalkoski-Shilov, Kristiina (2006) *La tierce main. Le discours rapporté dans les traductions françaises de Fielding au XVIIIe siècle* (The Third Hand. Reported Speech in French Translations of Fielding in the 18th Century), Arras: Artois Presses Université.

Ten Kate, Jan Jakob Lodewijk (1866) *De schepping* (The Creation), Utrecht: Kemink.

Van Baren, J. (1912) 'Hartogh Heijs van Zouteveen, Hermanus', *Nieuw Nederlandsch biografisch woordenboek* (New Dutch Biographical Dictionary), Vol. 2, Leiden: Sijthoff, 545-47..

------ (1924) 'Winkler, T.C.', *Nieuw Nederlandsch biografisch woordenboek* (New Dutch Biographical Dictionary), Vol. 6, Leiden: Sijthoff, 1313-14.

Wadensjö, Cecilia (1998) *Interpreting as Interaction*, London & New York: Longman.

Winkler, Tiberius Cornelius (1861) Letter 3202 [to Charles Darwin]. Available at http://www.darwinproject.ac.uk/darwinletters/calendar/entry-3202.html (accessed 10 June 2009).

------ (1867) 'De leer van Darwin' (Darwin's Theory), *De Gids* (The Guide) 31(4): 22-70.

Evaluation and Intervention in Translation[1]

JEREMY MUNDAY
University of Leeds, UK

Abstract. *This paper focuses on the translator's mediation, or intervention, from the perspective of Halliday's (1984, 1995) interpersonal function and drawing on Hatim and Mason's (1997) notions of 'mediation' and the 'static-dynamic' cline of language use. Recent work from systemic functional linguistics on authorial evaluation and appraisal is examined, notably Martin and White's (2005) study of appraisal in English. In doing so, the aim is to investigate the relevance for translation studies of such a model drawn from monolingual English work. It is argued that, for a translator, evaluation – and mediation or intervention – is to be found at 'critical points' that may not coincide with prominent evaluation in appraisal theory. Examples analyzed from tourist texts and the translation of a Borges short story and Barack Obama's political manifestos suggest that such critical points may be those that require a high degree of interpretation from the translator because of the use of 'invoked' (less explicit) attitudinal markers, because of ST ambiguity or fuzziness, or because of a lack of an obvious target language equivalent. The paper concludes by advancing a possible explanation through Martin and White's notion of 'reaction', evaluative interpretations being dependent on the different readings to which a text may be subjected.*

The work of Ian Mason and Basil Hatim (Hatim and Mason 1990, 1997) has been crucial for developing a Hallidayan, systemic functional framework within translation studies (see also House 1981, 1997, Bell 1991, Baker 1992, Teich 1999, Steiner and Yallop 2001, amongst others).

---

[1] Earlier versions of this article were presented as papers at the First international conference for Language for Specific Purposes and Translation-Studies Oriented Text Analysis, El-Jadida, Morocco, May 2008, at the University of Bergen, Norway, October 2008 and at a workshop at the Graduate Academy, Tripoli, Libya, November 2008. My thanks go to the organizers and sponsors for their invitations and to the audiences for their interesting comments and suggestions. I also acknowledge the kind support of a British Academy Overseas conference grant and from the Faculty of Arts, University of Leeds, allowing me to present a concise version of this finished article at the third conference of IATIS (International Association of Translation and Intercultural Studies), Melbourne, Australia, July 2009.

From an initial register analysis perspective, analyzing realizations of idea-tional, interpersonal and textual functions in source and target texts, Hatim and Mason's work has broadened to consider a wide range of linguistic and pragmatic factors. They have importantly brought out the role of the translator as a communicator and focused on translation as a form of 'mediation', defined as "the extent to which translators intervene in the transfer process, feeding their own knowledge and beliefs into their processing of a text" (Hatim and Mason 1997:147). In later text analysis work, Ian Mason looked, amongst other things, at the importance of transitivity patterns in institutional texts (Mason 2004) and of deixis as an interactive feature in literary texts (Mason and Serban 2003).

This paper acknowledges the value of these contributions, but the main interest will be in the way that the translator's mediation, or intervention, may be analyzed through Halliday's interpersonal function, which is key to the writer-reader relationship. Most importantly, the paper will discuss the potential for developing such analysis by incorporating more recent systemic functional work on authorial evaluation, known as appraisal theory (Martin and White 2005), which, until now, has been relatively overlooked by transla-tion theorists.

The starting point of this paper will be the systemic functional framework which underpins much of the text and discourse analysis undertaken by Ha-tim and Mason. More particularly, their central concept of the static-dynamic continuum in translational mediation will be examined, especially in as far as it relates to the key notion of writer-reader relationship.

1.   The static and dynamic in text analysis

Hatim and Mason's vanguard publication, *Discourse and the Translator*, set out "to relate an integrated account of discourse processes to the practical concerns of the translator" (Hatim and Mason 1990:xi). But it was much more than that: it was perhaps the most influential of the texts which approached translation studies from a discourse analysis perspective, at a time when Hallidayan-inspired register and discourse analysis was coming into vogue. This seminal model of language as 'social semiotic' (Halliday 1978) operates as an interlinked system of selections at different levels (discourse, genre, register, semantics, lexicogrammar), each of which has 'meaning potential'. In a text, it is the selections of lexis and grammar (the 'lexicogrammatical' choices) that contribute to producing functional meaning, categorized by Hal-liday (Halliday 1984, 1995; Halliday and Matthiessen 2004) into ideational, interpersonal and textual functions. Different lexicogrammatical features tend to correspond to each function: subject-specific lexis and transitivity patterns for the ideational; mood and modality for the interpersonal; cohesion and thematic structure for the textual. Crucially, the system centres attention on the function of these choices in the specific situational and sociocultural contexts in which they occur. This is what Hatim and Mason apply in *The Translator as Communicator* (1997), where they speak about mediation through translation in the context of potential ideological distortion of a source text discourse. For this, their definition of ideology (*ibid.*:144), drawn from the work of Paul Simpson (1993:5), is based upon "the taken-for-granted assumptions, beliefs and value-systems which are shared collectively by social groups", yet at the same time acknowledging that the individual (translator/interpreter) does have some control over the process.

Hatim and Mason (*ibid.*:153-59) discuss the now well-known example of an English translation of a history text about the indigenous peoples of Mexico (by the Mexican historian Miguel León Portilla), published in the *Unesco Courier* and earlier studied by Mason himself (Mason 1994/2010). They analyze the ideological shifts which occur in the translation according to 'lexical choice', 'cohesion' and 'transitivity' and which lead to the erasure of some important elements of the indigenous culture. Thus, for example, under 'cohesion', they note that the key concept of oral *memoria*, which occurs five times in the source, is diluted and re-perspectivized through a European lens into *history, knowledge of the past* and in one case omitted altogether, with the term *memory* only being used twice. The semantic field of 'effort' is similarly distorted: *esfuerzos* (efforts) becomes *obstinate determination; épocas de gran creatividad* (epochs of great creativity) is downplayed to *bursts of creativity*, and so on. But it is the general category of 'lexical choices' where the most obvious distortions are to be found: the Mexicans' *sabios* (wise men) are translated into the less rational *diviners* and the *hombre indígena* (indigenous man) himself becomes *pre-Columbian civilization*. In this way, the translator exerts "maximal mediation" (*ibid.*:153), "interven[ing] in the transfer process, feeding their own knowledge and beliefs into their processing of a text" (*ibid.*:147).

The relation of the term 'mediation' to the more assertive and evaluative 'intervention' has since been pursued elsewhere (e.g. the papers in Munday 2007) and related to other contexts. Ian Mason's own later work has included important studies on what in essence are the effects of translator intervention as expressed in shifts in deixis in literary texts rendered into Romanian (Mason and Serban 2003) and shifts in the transitivity selections in institutional settings (Mason 2004). In the latter, Mason examines a corpus of articles from the *Unesco Courier* and from European Parliament speeches, making the important and commonsense point that, while "individual shifts may be individually significant and provide some clues to translators' approaches to their task", it is what he calls the "concatenation" of shifts which may establish a trend and cause a shift in discourse, such as an intensification of the discourse of blame in French translations of a Spanish MEP's speech criticizing the United Kingdom for their response to Bovine Spongiform Encephalopathy (Mason 2004:478-81).

Such concentration on *patterns* of shifts, rather than individual instances, reduces the obstacle of the crucial question of interpretation; while, for example, ideational choices of language (e.g. transitivity choices or nominalizations) may generally serve to constitute a perspective on experience, they do not absolutely determine them and do not fully constrict the possible interpretations the reader might bring to the text (cf. Fairclough 1992:75, Widdowson 2004:96). Indeed, from a very early point Hatim and Mason (e.g. 1990:11) have emphasized the importance for the translator of maintaining as far as is possible in the target text the range of interpretations in the source, of not constraining the reader by imposing a reading. Here they are considering what they term the 'static-dynamic' continuum of language, a concept they develop in their later work, where they relate it to reader expectations and norms, according to the textual parameters of cohesion, coherence, situationality, intentionality, intertextuality and informativity (Hatim and Mason 1997:28). 'Static' texts are described as "expectation-fulfilling" and "norm-confirming", while 'dynamic' texts are "expectation-defying" and "norm-flouting". This is clearly and explicitly related to the concept of 'markedness' (see also Hatim 2004), referring to the expected frequency or informativity of the linguistic feature; thus, for example, VS order in modern English is generally 'marked' (that is, infrequent and hence potentially more informative). A marked term is more 'dynamic' since it defies reader expectations, which may be genre-linked; the use of the English conjunction *and* in a first position in a sentence is generally discouraged by teachers, for instance, yet it is likely to be less marked as a feature of traditional fairy tales, some older translations of the Bible, and in transcriptions of oral language.

When considering the implications of markedness and the static-dynamic continuum for translators, Hatim and Mason suggest that it is the dynamic use of language in the source text that poses more problems precisely because it potentially carries more weight (1997:30-31). Thus, the idiolectal and dialectal use of language (Cockney accent, marked tags such as *he ain't*, etc.) by the flower-girl in Shaw's *Pygmalion* is indicative of her social position, but this use gradually changes to a more standard form in the course of the play. Different translations deal in different ways with the dynamic, marked form: the Catalan uses a low social dialect, the Arabic chooses Egyptian dialect, the French prefers a standard form of the language, each producing different emphases in the translations.

This is given by Hatim and Mason (*ibid.*:97-110) as an example of tenor analysis, since it pertains to the interpersonal function of language and the relationship between speaker and receiver. Yet there is another aspect of the interpersonal function which, though relatively underdeveloped by Halliday, who focuses mainly on mood and modality (Thompson and Hunston 2000:4), is perhaps even more important for the construction of the writer-reader relationship and for investigating how the writer and, by projection, the translator, feed in their ideological perspective to the text. This is the crucial concept of evaluation, investigated by systemic functionalists as the system of 'appraisal'.

2. The concept of evaluation

It should be emphasized that there are various different theoretical terms in use for the concept we are investigating. These are, notably, 'stance' (Biber and Finegan 1989, Conrad and Biber 2000), 'appraisal' (Martin 2000, Martin and White 2005) and 'evaluation' (Hunston and Thompson 2000). In their introduction to the latter volume, Thompson and Hunston *(ibid.:*5) opt for the general term 'evaluation' and the subordinate term 'stance', since for them "evaluation is a broad cover term for the expression of the speaker or writer's stance towards, viewpoint on, or feelings about the entities or propositions that he or she is talking about". Irrespective of the specific term used, they make some generally important points regarding the phenomenon, outlining the three main functions of evaluation as follows:

1. To express the speaker's or writer's opinion, and in doing so to reflect the value system of that person and their community. With its emphasis on shared value systems, this is clearly linked to what is often termed 'ideology' (see above); yet the inclusion of the person's value system allows for the individual input of the text producer or, in our case, the translator.
2. To construct and maintain relations between the writer and reader (or speaker and hearer). This may have a goal of persuading or manipulating, where evaluation makes the author's point less easily challenged (Thompson and Hunston 2000:8) or directly or indirectly evaluates the truth or certainty of a statement (see also Fairclough 2003:171).
3. To organize the discourse (Thompson and Hunston 2000:6, 10-12). This relates to those conceptualizations of evaluation, such as Labov's famous sociolinguistic study of the narrative structure of natural storytelling among Blacks in New York (Labov 1972), which explicitly comment on and signal the important points in the discourse.

While the general functions of evaluation are giving opinion, constructing writer-reader relationships based on truth values and giving immediate feedback on discourse, the question remains, and is posed by Thompson and Hunston *(ibid.:*13), as to how evaluation is to be recognized. The system of 'appraisal' developed by Martin and White (2005) within a Hallidayan framework of interpersonal meaning may provide a solution.[2]

---

[2] Martin and White's (2005) is the most detailed analysis, but amongst the many other sources are also Martin (2000), Macken-Horarik and Martin (2003), White (2002, 2005) and Bednarek (2006).

3.   The system of appraisal

The definition of the appraisal system given by Martin and White (2005:164) is "the global potential of the language for making evaluative meanings, e.g. for activating positive/negative viewpoints, graduating force/focus, negotiating intersubjective stance". Appraisal is one of three constituent 'discourse-semantic' elements of interpersonal meaning, in the register variable of tenor. The others are the systems of 'negotiation' and 'involvement':

1.   Tenor – **Negotiation**, through speech function and exchange, such as mood and tagging
2.   Power/status – **Appraisal**, through engagement, affect, judgement, appreciation and graduation
3.   Solidarity – **Involvement**, through naming, technicality, abstraction, anti-language, and swearing. (Martin and White 2005:35)

Here 'tenor' is to be considered as a superordinate category, with the sub-categories of 'power/status' relating primarily to appraisal, and 'solidarity' to involvement. In this schema, Hatim and Mason's analysis of the flower-girl speech (above) would be seen as referring to certain features of negotiation (e.g. tagging) and involvement (slang and dialect), which locates the speech, and hence the character, in a relationship of gradually increasing proximity to the values of standard English and the society which that represents. As an aside, we should note (with Martin and White 2005:34) that solidarity through involvement is partly created through the technical and specialized lexis of the group. While for sociolinguists this could mean the non-standard anti-language of a social gang, or the group-specific argot of the likeminded engaged in, for example, texting, video-gaming, or whatever other activity, for translation theorists it clearly also relates to the use of subject-specific technical language, the language for specific purposes that is central to most translators' business.[3] Similarly, other features of involvement, such as taboo language, have, from other perspectives, already been problems noted in audiovisual translation, dialogue interpreting, etc. (see, for example, Chiaro 2008).

However, the main focus in this paper is on that part of interpersonal semantics which has thus far been relatively overlooked in translation studies: the specific form of appraisal which is predominantly concerned with the lexicalization of evaluation. Table 1 sets out its main features.

---

[3] Although not discussed further in this paper, it is worth pointing out, as do Martin and White, the overlap between the ideational and interpersonal here; technical lexis is a primary constructive element of the ideational or experiential world (the activity that is occurring) as well as helping to form a bond of solidarity between its participants.

Domain of appraisal	Feature	Value
Attitude	Affect	Through feelings and emotional reactions
	Judgement	Of ethics, behaviour
	Appreciation	Of things, phenomena, reactions
Graduation	Force	Raise Lower
	Focus	Sharpen Soften
Engagement	Monogloss	Contraction
	Heterogloss	Expansion

Table 1. Appraisal resources (adapted from Martin and White 2005:38)

This article concentrates mainly on attitude since it is, in many ways, the most basic form of evaluation, most archetypally realized through attitudinally loaded adjectives or, to use Halliday's terms, "evaluative epithets" (Halliday 1994:184) or "interpersonal epithets" (Halliday and Matthiessen 2004:318). As can be seen in Table 1, Martin and White describe three types of attitude. Examples of typical realizations are as follows:

(1) **affect**, related to feelings and emotional reactions: *happy, sad, horrified*, etc.
(2) **judgement**, of behaviour, ethics, capacity, tenacity, etc.: *wrong, right, stingy, skilful, cautious, brave, insightful*, etc.
(3) **appreciation**, the evaluation of phenomena and processes, including aesthetics, taste, worth: *beautiful, pleasant, brilliant, tedious, creative, authentic*, etc.

Importantly, the basis for affect is essentially personal and the response it envisages is emotional; by contrast, judgement and appreciation, although they will vary according to the individual, presuppose shared community values which may even be institutionalized (Martin and White 2005:57). Our evaluations are strongly linked to the values instilled in us by the educational, legal, cultural and other institutions in which we are formed. Cross-culturally, education and legal frameworks and values differ. Thus, what is ethical, 'right', expected and accepted behaviour also varies. Likewise, variation is to be expected in the criteria for aesthetic and other evaluation, which, whether it concerns a modern style of building in an historic setting, a style of fiction or a clothing fashion, is largely socially instilled but partly individual.

3.1   Attitude inscribed and invoked

The most obvious expression of attitude is by "direct inscription" (Martin and White 2005:61), through openly evaluative epithets. Typical are promotional texts of various types (e.g. conventional advertising, tourist brochures, product brochures), such as Example 1:

> **Example 1** *TimeOut/HSBC Miniguide to London*, Spring 2009
> London is cosmopolitan, trendy and exciting: a truly wonderful place
> to visit. The city combines old-fashioned charm and cutting-edge
> fashion. Quiet courtesy and a great deal of fun.

Positive inscribed affect and appreciation is evident and intense: *cosmopolitan, trendy, exciting, wonderful, cutting-edge, quiet*; the nouns *charm, fashion, courtesy* and *fun* are similarly positive. However, here one should note the cultural and institutional basis of this attitude; these are positive because the audience envisaged is one that tends to be attracted to London precisely because of some or all of these qualities, and the predominant cultural frame of the city prides itself on them. Individuals, of course, may have a more negative appreciation of some of these qualities. For example, *trendy* and *cutting-edge fashion* are not appealing to the author of this article. However, the point that Martin and White make[4] is that there is a general infusion of inscriptions of attitude which have a more general effect on evaluation throughout a text:

> [T]he prosodic nature of the realisation of interpersonal meanings such
> as attitude means that inscriptions tend to colour more of a text than
> their local grammatical environment circumscribes. The inscriptions
> act as sign-posts, in other words, telling us how to read the ideational
> selections that surround them. (*ibid.*:63)

This is also attested by Bednarek's study of evaluation in media discourse, where she stresses how the local or global "evaluative prosody" of a text may influence the evaluation of otherwise neutral terms (2006:209).

In many ways, the very point of Example 1 is to communicate positive appreciation to as many readers as possible, to convey that London, with its huge variety and contrasts, offers something that appeals to everyone. For a translator approaching this text, and given a similar communicative purpose to that of the source text (e.g. a target text available to tourists at ports of entry to London), the goal most probably would be to reproduce the positive appreciation in the target text. In the case of the above, we may hypothesize that reproducing this inscribed appreciation should not be an overly problematic task, unless there is some value that would not be positively appreciated by

---

[4] See also the brief comment in Halliday and Matthiessen (2004:319).

the target culture audience.

This communicative, 'something for everyone' purpose is made more explicit in the continuation of the text:

> **Example 2** *TimeOut/HSBC Miniguide to London*, Spring 2009
> All of these characteristics will be revealed as you wander from museum to gallery, down Victorian arcades and busy streets, across vast parks and along cobbled streets. The contrasts are endless: next to every historical sight, there's a skyscraper gleaming with the wealth of modern life. Discovering these contrasts is one of the city's great pleasures.

Space prohibits detailed discussion here, but it is easy to see the continued inscribed appreciation of *vast, gleaming, wealth, modern* and *great pleasures*. Positive attitude is conveyed very strongly by verbal processes (*gleaming,* and to a lesser extent *wander*), showing that attitude may be transmitted by various parts of speech, something which we shall return to in 3.2 below. Collocation also plays an important role: *vast* has a positive value here because of its collocation with *park* in the genre of a tourist text. Numerous other examples can be found in similar texts, such as the description in Example 3 of a Paris *quartier*, taken from the online English particulars of a property company:

> **Example 3** *The Apartment Service Worldwide*,
> http://www.apartmentservice.com/search/France/Paris/property1551
> (accessed 27 April 2009)
> An authentic, unspoilt district, with open-air markets, streets full of shops, traditional restaurants and boulevards lined with magnificent, early 20th century buildings. And, what's more, it's surrounded by **vast parks**, where you can forget all about the city and stroll for hours listening to the birds.

Not only is the attitude of the whole hugely positive; here, the second sentence, and especially the final clause (*where....birds*), explicitly presents the reason for the positive value of *vast parks* and makes it very difficult for the reader to disagree.

Sometimes, however, the evaluation is less evident; in Martin and White's terms, it is 'invoked',[5] i.e. an 'attitudinal token' (White 2006) may cause a positive reaction not because of its inherently positive attitudinal qualities but because it triggers a latent contextual connection which needs to be recognized and responded to by the reader. In Example 2, positive appreciation is invoked by *Victorian arcades* and *cobbled streets*, not because the epithets

---

[5] The alternative term 'evoked' is also used by some appraisal theorists, for example Bednarek (2006:38, Fn6).

Victorian and *cobbled* are inherently positive nor even inherently evaluative, but because in their collocations and in this communicative context they have a semiotic role in representing what institutionally are perceived to be positive traditional values dating from the 19th century. This creates a coherence projected by the use of the similarly invoked *old-fashioned* in Example 1. The specific connotation will vary according to the reader; possibilities are authenticity and quality of life, the quality of traditional products, seemingly a world away from the frenzy and potentially exploitative nature of the modern capital (represented by the gleaming skyscraper), but in fact co-existing with and complementing it.

That such invokedness lies beneath the surface and is, at least to a degree, subjective is a potential problem for the translator, who needs to both identify the intended evaluation and reproduce it appropriately in the target text, in a new context of culture which may not apply the same value to the entities, for example where *Victorian* may negatively connote out-dated, restricted or an oppressive empire and where *cobbled streets* denote dirty factories or the revolutionary stones of Mai '68.

Martin and White (2005:206) make the important point that invokedness, by its implicitness or lack of specificity, plays a key role in "facilitat[ing] if not encourag[ing]" a variety of reader response. It is a locus of negotiation of meaning, the reader having a freedom of action that is shared by the translator as reader. The interesting question for us to research is how far the translator retains this invokedness, and thus possible variety of response, or restricts and controls response by inscription. In the context of evaluation and appraisal, inscription, (that is, the elimination of invokedness), is potentially a special kind of explicitation since it presents an evaluative interpretation and encourages, if not forces, an evaluative reaction in the readership.

To illustrate this, let us consider Example 4, from a well-known Borges short story. The main character, Emma Zunz, gazes out of the window of a tram in Buenos Aires, on her way to avenge her father and in the immediate aftermath of having sex with an unknown sailor, a stratagem she has devised as part of her plan to escape punishment for killing the man she holds responsible for her father's death. She is relieved to see that the action has not 'contaminated' the rest of the city:

> **Example 4** *Jorge Luis Borges 'Emma Zunz'*
> Viajó por barrios *decrecientes* y *opacos*, viéndolos y olvidándolos en el acto, y se apeó en una de las bocacalles de Warnes.
> [She travelled through *decreasing* and *opaque* neighbourhoods, seeing them and forgetting them at once, and alighted on one of the side-streets of Warnes.]

The interest is in the evaluative epithets *decrecientes* (decreasing) and *opacos* (opaque). These are relatively unspecific in the Spanish: does *decrecientes* refer to the visual image of distance, or does it have some invoked negative appreciation of decline? And how should *opacos* be rendered, particularly given that in literary translation many translators may prefer to avoid Latinate calques in English? The published translations in English illustrate this very dilemma for the translators. Donald Yates (Borges 1962) opts for *diminishing* and *opaque*: inscribing negative appreciation in the former, but retaining a freedom of response with the latter calque. The revision by Andrew Hurley (Borges 1998) preferred *shrinking* and *gloomy*, both of which are generally negative: *gloomy* inscribes a more precise value to *opacos*; *shrinking* is perhaps less negative than *diminishing*, although it begs the question 'shrinking from what/whom?' and may have a 'semantic association' (Hoey 2005) with *fear*. Interestingly, although in the source language and text words such as *decrecientes* and *opacos* (or *Victorian* and *cobbled* in Example 2) may not be strongly evaluative (or at least the value is invoked), in a translation context the translator may have to interpret their value. In an experiment reported in Munday (forthcoming), 15 MA student translations of extracts of the story were analyzed. Considerable variation of evaluative items was found in the translations of the above epithets, particularly *decrecientes*. This is illustrated in Tables 2 and 3.

Decrecientes	*dwindling* (4 instances), *diminishing* (3), *declining* (2), *deprived* (1), *ever-decreasing* (1), *fading* (1), *increasingly distant* (1), *run-down* (1), *waned* (1)

Table 2. Translations of decrecientes *amongst 15 subjects*

Opacos	*dull* (5), *gloomy* (5), *opaque* (2), *dark* (1), *lifeless* (1), Ø (1)

Table 3. Translations of opacos *amongst 15 subjects*

The translations of *decrecientes* all show some degree of negative appreciation. This includes instances of 'high degree' negativity, either of the state of the neighbourhoods (*declining, deprived, run-down*) or of appearance and location (*ever-decreasing, increasingly distant*). There are other 'lower degree' realizations (*dwindling, diminishing, fading*) that reflect these two interpretations even if they are less intense. The translations of *opacos* show a smaller yet still significant range of instantiation: from *gloomy* to *dark, dull, opaque* and the metaphorical interpretation *lifeless*.

What these translations show is that, certainly in the case of these two epithets, the scope for variation in interpretation is great. They have attitude-rich potential which is brought to light particularly sensitively in translation, especially where multiple translations allow comparison of individual reader-translator's reactions to the words. This seems to be a new perspective on

Hatim and Mason's static-dynamic continuum. While Hatim and Mason were particularly concerned with the dynamic function of markedness, and its challenge to the translator, attitude-rich potential may be located in source text words that seem to invite or demand interpretation, for reasons which include invoked rather than inscribed attitude, inherent fuzziness, lack of obvious target language equivalent, perceived lack of suitability of the 'obvious' literal translation, etc. These are the 'critical points' of a text where evaluation in translation is most likely to vary significantly by degree. In a literary text, the interpretation might be based on the translator's overall understanding of the structure and voice of the narrative; in a non-fiction text, the interpretation may be informed by values encouraged by society, institution and/or individual.

3.2   Appraisal meanings as an integrated complex

Although, for reasons of space, my focus has been very much on what Martin and White call 'attitude', it is important to be aware that the whole discourse semantic system of appraisal (see Table 1) integrates other domains such as 'graduation' (Martin and White 2005:135-54), which can vary in 'force', based on intensity (e.g. ***extremely*** *unwise*, ***great*** *pleasure*, ***increasingly*** *distant*) or 'focus', based on prototypicality (e.g. *a **true** gentleman, an apology **of sorts**)*, 'softening' or 'sharpening' the evaluation. The other domain is 'engagement', crucial for the degree of freedom of response allowed to the reader, for the solidarity which the writer presumes or constructs with the envisaged reader (*ibid.*:95). Engagement draws on the Bakthinian concepts of 'monogloss' and 'heterogloss' (Martin 2004:276); monogloss constricts response, for example with categorical assertions or reporting verbs (e.g. *demonstrate, show*) that do not allow for easy disagreement, while heterogloss is 'dialogically expansive' by acknowledging the possibility of alternative viewpoints, responses and/or truth values (e.g. the reporting verb *claim*, modal particles such as *almost, nearly*, and modal adjuncts and auxiliaries – *possibly, should*, etc.) (Martin and White 2005:97-104). These are resources for thus "writ[ing] the reader into the text" and for establishing the relationship and alignment of solidarity between writer and reader (*ibid.*:95).

It is also important to be aware that these various elements of the appraisal system (attitude, graduation and engagement) are said to operate not individually but in conjunction, "as elements in integrated complexes of meaning" (*ibid.:*159) with an overall rhetorical purpose. So, for example, a very evaluative text that seeks to convince the reader of what is the writer's opinion, such as Examples 1 and 2, may adopt a monoglossic, categorical style with 'upscaled' attitudinal evaluation (the obvious evaluative epithets) together with intensification through force, insisting lexicogrammatically in a fashion that resembles shouting in phonological terms (*ibid.*:227). In political texts, this kind of rhetoric may be particularly significant. Take Example 5, from the English original of *Latino Blueprint for Change*, a document produced by the

Barack Obama US presidential election campaign to outline policies relevant
to the US's Latino population of over 40 million:

> **Example 5** (Obama '08 2008a:49)
> *Moral Leadership*
> Obama's faith shapes his values, as it does for millions of Americans.
> As he said in a recent speech on faith and politics:
> ...[O]ur values should express themselves not just through our churches
> or synagogues, temples or mosques; they should express themselves
> through our government. Because whether it's poverty or racism, the
> uninsured or the unemployed, war or peace, the challenges we face to-
> day are not simply technical problems in search of the perfect ten-point
> plan. They are moral problems, rooted in both societal indifference and
> individual callousness – in the imperfections of man.

Solidarity is produced by the repeated use of the pronouns *our* and *we*, The
deontic modality of *should express themselves* is an explicit statement of
judgement. Negated modal adjuncts (*not just, not simply*) reject softening
of force and prepare the culmination of the continuation of the speech The
categorical assertions of the challenges faced restrict the reader's response
(are 'monoglossic'). The rhythm of the couplets of negative evaluation is
reinforced phonologically at key points (*the **un**insured and the **un**employed*).
The sharpening of focus of ***perfect** ten-point plan*, the intensified metaphor
of *rooted in* and the lexicalization of judgement of *callousness* all contribute
to the construction of a discourse centred on judgement (especially on ethical
behaviour) that performs the function of convincing the listener of the severity
of the challenges and therefore the truth of the solution proposed by Obama.

Our interest is in how much of such evaluative discourse is likely to alter
in translation. In the absence of censorship or motivated ideological distortion
– though they provide juicy material for analysis, they are not generally the
norm[6] – changes to such sensitive speeches of politically prominent figures
are likely to be far more subtle. The Spanish translation of Example 5 (see
Example 6 below), produced by the Obama campaign team and directed at
the Latino population themselves, demonstrates a generally literal translation
strategy:

> **Example 6** (Obama '08 2008b:57)
> *Liderazgo moral*
> La fe de Obama informa sus valores, como ocurre con millones de
> estadounidenses. Como dijo en un reciente discurso sobre la fe y la
> política:

---

[6] Note, however, that Obama's inaugural address, interpreted live on TV, was apparently
cut by the state-controlled Chinese Central Television when he mentioned the struggle
against and defeat of communism. Official Chinese translations also omitted some of these
references (Bristow 2009).

Nuestros valores deben expresarse no sólo a través de nuestras igle-
sias o sinagogas, templos o mezquitas; deben expresarse a través de
nuestro gobierno. Porque se trate de la miseria o el racismo, los no
asegurados o los desempleados, la guerra o la paz, los desafíos que
afrontamos hoy no son sencillamente problemas técnicos en busca de
un plan de diez puntos. Son problemas morales, que tienen su origen
en la indiferencia de la sociedad y la insensibilidad del individuo, en
las imperfecciones del hombre.

The overall evaluative style of the text and the moral judgement of behaviour
have been maintained. Obvious shifts are few, but still noteworthy:

- the force of the phonological repetition of the ST prefix 'un' (the uninsured
  or the unemployed) is lost (*los no asegurados o los desempleados*)
- the sharpened focus of the judgement *perfect ten-point plan* is softened
  by omission
- the conceptual metaphor *moral problems rooted in* is altered to the less
  emphatic *tienen su origen en* (have their origin in)
- the strongly lexicalized judgement of the noun in *individual callousness*
  becomes the much lower degree *insensibilidad del individuo* (insensitiv-
  ity of the individual)

In this example, therefore, the overall negative evaluation of the challenges
has been somewhat 'downscaled', particularly in the second and fourth instances above. This last, *insensibilidad* for *callousness* is the most striking
since it reduces the strength of the problem and hence urgency for action.
Why it should have been downscaled is unclear, but perhaps it has something
to do with the concern to avoid offending the target reader by the use of a
more strongly attitudinal noun such as *crueldad* (cruelty). In this respect, it is
interesting to compare what Channell (2000:55) suggests in her discussion of
evaluative language treatment in dictionaries and of the preoccupation with
negative items; she posits that this may be because "the social consequences of
an error with a negative item are much greater than those arising from misuse
of a positive item". Similarly, in cases such as Example 6, it may not be excessive to suggest that the translator is wary of reproducing strongly negative
attitude in a sensitive communicative situation where the target text is going
to be taken as the words of the presidential candidate himself. The potential
consequences of 'getting it wrong', of overstating the negativity and offending the reader (who may possibly read him or herself into the 'individual' of
the text), would be outweighed by the alternative of a softer, less intense and
aggressive selection.

4.   Concluding remarks — tactical, resistant and compliant readings

Of course, the act of reading and interpretation of evaluative meaning in a
text will vary from individual to individual; this phenomenon of reading and

interpretation is what Martin and White (2005:206) refer to as 'reaction'. It is of special import for translation since the reading supplied by the translator will strongly condition the reaction of the target text reader. In this respect, consideration of the three kinds of reading – tactical, resistant, compliant – described by Martin and White (*ibid.*) may be particularly applicable in translation:

> By a tactical reading we refer to a typically partial and interested reading which aims to deploy a text for social purposes other than those it has naturalized; resistant readings oppose the reading position naturalized by the co-selection of meanings in a text, while compliant readings subscribe to it.

These readings may have little to do with the original purpose of the text; thus, a tactical reading could be provided by a language theorist like myself who selects a text to analyze for a new purpose, and a resistant reading rejects the argumentation of the writer. Translation is clearly an example of a text that is produced for a new communicative purpose, or at least that is normally directed at an audience different from that envisaged by the source. It will therefore be tactical, since the translator's reading, and interpretation, will be part of the preparation and production of the target text. It will be predominantly 'resistant' if it seeks to overturn the ideology of the source, as with Ralph Mannheim's translations of Hitler's *Mein Kampf*, where footnotes were added to point out the illogicality of the ideas (see Hermans 2007). It will most likely seek to be compliant if the translator's view of the task is to reproduce the source 'faithfully' no matter whether he or she is in agreement with the source or not.

However, I would suggest that these translator-reading positions may be adopted with reference to the overall 'evaluative style' of the text (which Martin and White (2005) sub-analyze into *key* and *stance*), whether it be the overwhelmingly positive evaluation of the London promotional material, the narrative point of view of the Borges text or the negative evaluation of the challenges of the Obama text. What seems to me most interesting for future research is the possibility that it is the evaluation at certain sensitive or 'critical' points in a text that is most crucial for translation: these critical points include the recognition and reproduction of invoked translation that may be culturally located (e.g. *cobbled streets*); the downscaling of strongly lexicalized judgement of negative behaviour when the risk of overstatement may be deemed to be too high (e.g. *callousness*); and the potential, indeed the requirement, for a translator to draw out specific evaluation from an ambiguous or fuzzy term that does not have a ready target-language equivalent (e.g. *decrecientes*). It is at these critical points, which will vary according to text and genre, that the dynamic cline of language is activated through the translator's interpretation in the target text. Here, 'dynamic' would entail a shift from Hatim and Mason's 'expectation-defying' elements in the source to the choices in the target text which are triggered and rendered consciously or unconsciously, prompted by shared social values in the target culture and the translator's own individual evaluations.

References

Baker, Mona (1992) *In Other Words: A Textbook on Translation*, London & New York: Routledge.

Bednarek, Monica (2006) *Evaluation in Media Discourse: Analysis of a Newspaper Corpus*, London: Continuum.

Bell, Roger (1991) *Translation and Translating: Theory and Practice*, Harlow: Longman.

Biber, Douglas and E. Finegan (1989) 'Adverbial Stance Types in English', *Discourse Processes* 11(1): 1-34.

Borges, Jorge Luis (1962) *Labyrinths: Selected Stories and Other Writings*, trans. Donald Yates and James E. Irby, New Directions: New York.

----- (1998) *Collected Fictions*, trans. Andrew Hurley, New York & London: Penguin.

Bristow, Michael (2009) 'Obama Speech Censored in China', *BBC News*, 21 January. Available at http://news.bbc.co.uk/1/hi/7841580.stm (accessed 15 January 2010).

Channell, Joanna (2000) 'Corpus Analysis of Evaluative Lexis', in Susan Hunston and Geoff Thompson (eds) *Evaluation in Text: Authorial Stance and the Construction of Discourse*, Oxford: Oxford University Press, 37-55.

Chiaro, Delia (2008) 'Issues in Audiovisual Translation', in Jeremy Munday (ed.) *The Routledge Companion to Translation Studies*, London & New York: Routledge, 141-65.

Conrad, Susan and Douglas Biber (2000) 'Adverbial Marking of Stance in Speech and Writing', in Susan Hunston and Geoff Thompson (eds) *Evaluation in Text: Authorial Stance and the Construction of Discourse*, Oxford: Oxford University Press, 56-73.

Fairclough, Norman (1992) *Discourse and Social Change*, Cambridge: Polity Press.

----- (2003) *Analysing Discourse: Textual Analysis for Social Research*, London & New York: Routledge.

Halliday, Michael (1978) *Language as Social Semiotic: The Social Interpretation of Language and Meaning*, London: Arnold.

----- (1985) *An Introduction to Functional Grammar*, first edition, London: Arnold.

----- (1994) *An Introduction to Functional Grammar*, second edition, London: Arnold.

Halliday, Michael and Christopher Matthiessen (2004) *An Introduction to Functional Grammar*, third edition, London: Arnold.

Hatim, Basil (2004) 'The Translation of Style: Linguistic Markedness and Textual

Evaluativeness', *Journal of Applied Linguistics* 1(3): 229-46.

Hatim, Basil and Ian Mason (1990) *Discourse and the Translator*, Harlow: Longman.

----- (1997) *The Translator as Communicator*, London & New York: Routledge.

Hermans, Theo (2007) *The Conference of the Tongues*, Manchester: St Jerome Publishing.

Hoey, Michael (2005) *Lexical Priming: A New Theory of Language*, London & New York: Routledge.

House, Juliane (1981) *A Model for Translation Quality Assessment*, Tübingen: Gunter Narr.

----- (1997) *Translation Quality Assessment: A Model Revisited*, Tübingen: Gunter Narr.

Hunston, Susan (2000) 'Evaluation and the Planes of Discourse: Status and Value in Persuasive Texts', in Susan Hunston and Geoff Thompson (eds) *Evaluation in Text: Authorial Stance and the Construction of Discourse*, Oxford: Oxford University Press, 176-207.

Hunston, Susan and Geoff Thompson (2000) (eds) *Evaluation in Text: Authorial Stance and the Construction of Discourse*, Oxford: Oxford University Press.

Labov, William (1972) 'Some Further Steps in Narrative Analysis', *The Journal of Narrative and Life History* 7(1-4): 395-415.

Macken-Horarik, Mary and James R. Martin (2003) *Negotiating Heteroglossia: Social Perspectives on Evaluation*, special issue of *Text* 23(2).

Martin, James R. (2000) 'Beyond Exchange: APPRAISAL Systems in English', in Susan Hunston & Geoff Thompson (eds) *Evaluation in Text: Authorial Stance and the Construction of Discourse*, Oxford: Oxford University Press, 142-75.

------ (2004) 'Sense and Sensibility: Texturing Evaluation', in Joseph Foley (ed.) *Language, Education and Discourse: Functional Approaches*, London: Continuum, 270-304.

Martin, James R. and Peter R.R. White (2005) *The Language of Evaluation: Appraisal in English*, Basingstoke: Palgrave MacMillan.

Mason, Ian (1994/2010) 'Discourse, Ideology and Translation', in Robert de Beaugrande, Abdullah Shunnaq and Mohamed Helmy Heliel (eds) *Language, Discourse and Translation in the West and Middle East*, Amsterdam & Philadelphia, John Benjamins, 23-34. Reprinted, with new postscript, in Mona Baker (ed.) *Critical Readings in Translation Studies*, London & New York: Routledge, 83-95.

Mason, Ian (2004) 'Text Parameters in Translation: Transitivity and Institutional Cultures', in Lawrence Venuti (ed.) *The Translation Studies Reader*, second edition, London & New York: Routledge, 470-81.

------ and Adriana Serban (2003) 'Deixis as an Interactive Feature in Literary Translations from Romanian into English', *Target* 15(2): 269-94.

Munday, Jeremy (2004) 'A Comparative Analysis of Evaluation in Spanish and English World Cup Reports', *Revista Canaria de Estudios Ingleses* 49 (November): 117-33.

----- (ed.) (2007) *Translation as Intervention*, London: Continuum.

----- (forthcoming) *Translation and Evaluation: Critical Points in Translator Decision-making*, London & New York: Routledge.

Obama'08 (2008a) *Latino Blueprint for Change: Barack Obama's plan for America*. Available at *obama.3cdn.net/0d94ca010d1549effb_ttm6i26ne.pdf (accessed 12 January 2010)*.

----- (2008b) *Proyecto latino para el cambio: El plan de Barack Obama para Estados Unidos*. Available at *obama.3cdn.net/f3fe74c297f597139d_e4m6i2awh. pdf (accessed 12 January 2010)*.

Simpson, Paul (1993) *Language, Ideology and Point of View*, London & New York : Routledge.

Steiner, Erich and Colin Yallop (eds) (2001) *Exploring Translation and Multilingual Text Production: Beyond Content*, Berlin & New York: Mouton de Gruyter.

Teich, Elke (2003) *Cross-Linguistic Variation in System and Text: A Methodology for the Investigation of Translations and Comparable Texts*, Berlin & New York: Mouton de Gruyter.

Thompson, Geoff and Susan Hunston (2000) 'Evaluation: An Introduction', in Susan Hunston and Geoff Thompson (eds) *Evaluation in Text: Authorial Stance and the Construction of Discourse*, Oxford: Oxford University Press, 1-27.

White, Peter R.R. (2002) 'Appraisal – The Language of Evaluation and Stance', in Jef Verschueren, Jan-Ola Östman, Jan Blommaert and Chris Bulcaen (eds) *The Handbook of Pragmatics*, Amsterdam & Philadelphia: John Benjamins, 1-27.

----- (2005) 'The Appraisal Website'. Available at www.grammatics.com/ Appraisal/ (accessed 15 January 2010).

----- (2006) 'Evaluative Semantics and Ideological Positioning in Journalistic Discourse: A New Framework for Analysis', in Inger Lassen, Jeanne Strunck and Torben Vestergaard (eds) *Mediating Ideology in Text and Image*, Amsterdam & Philadelphia: John Benjamins, 37-67.

Widdowson, Henry G. (2004) *Text, Context, and Pretext: Critical Issues in Discourse Analysis*, Oxford: Wiley-Blackwell.

Translating What Might Have Been Written

BRIAN MOSSOP
York University School of Translation, Canada

Abstract. *Starting from Mason's idea of a dialogue interpreter making various 'moves', such as 'repairing miscommunication', the article looks at the production of written translations in terms of switching among various ways of producing language. Translators may report all and only what they see as the meaning of the source text, or they may report what they think the source writer should have written (they correct errors) or might have written (they add or subtract material). In the latter case, they become the 'motivator' behind the ideas expressed in the translation, but they may be either 'loyal' motivators (adding or subtracting in the spirit of the source as they see it) or 'disloyal' motivators (engaging in their own writing project). A reworking of the traditional distinction between translating and adapting is proposed, and a passage from the historian Thucydides is analyzed to shed light on the distinction between what someone wrote and what they might have written.*

Ian Mason describes an interesting case of dialogue interpreting: at an immigration interview, a Polish speaker utters words which grammatically mean 'I have the passport at my place', but it appears from context that she means that the passport is at 'his place'. The interpreter says *his place*, thus conveying what the woman means, or as Mason nicely puts it, translating "what might have been said but was not" (2006:116).[1]

Written source texts similarly contain wordings that fail to convey what the author appears to mean. A text about highway construction states that there is a need for:

Augmentation de la résistance à la fissuration au gel par des sols supports   gélifs
Increase   of resistance to   frost cracking   through soils supporting frost-prone

The text seems to say that the contractors building the road should reduce frost cracking by placing frost-susceptible soil under the asphalt. But surely

---

[1] In Mason (2006), it is not clear whether this phrase means 'what the interpreter might have said' or 'what the woman might have said'. Mason (personal communication) is quite sure he intended the former, but, he says, "it applies equally to the source text … part of the translator/interpreter's expertise lies in judging the significance of what is said in the source text in the light of what else might have been said but was not". In this article, the phrase means 'what might have been said by the source'.

the negative prefix *non-* is missing before *gélifs*: the idea must be to use soils that are *not* susceptible to freezing. The translator proceeds on the basis of 'what might have been written'.[2]

Such correcting work is part of a broader phenomenon that may be called 'cleaning up the source text'. Non-literary translators very frequently have to deal with texts written by people who have no time or motivation to edit what they have written, or simply never learned to write well. These texts typically have confusing inter-sentence connections, ambiguous syntactic structures and other features that make the meaning unclear. Translators may engage in a mental clean up of the text, and then work from this cleaned up version, with the result that the intent shines through in the target language wording much better than it did in the source text.

The cleaning up process can be discussed from various points of view. There is the mental process involved in *interpreting* problematic passages (see Mossop 1995). Then there is the practical question of the extent to which translators *ought* to clean up source texts, and the norms that differ-ent translating institutions might follow in this respect. Finally, there is the *function* of cleaning up: in the example of the immigration interview, Mason says that the interpreter's goal was to make sure that the immigrant's story contained no self-contradiction, as it would if the immigration official were to hear that the passport was at the woman's house. To accomplish this goal, the interpreter made what Mason (2006:116) calls the 'move' of 'repairing miscommunication' (what I am calling 'cleaning up'). This notion of 'moves' is a recurrent one in Mason's writings of the past few years, and I have found it to be highly evocative. In this article, my aim is to identify and character-ize several different moves which in various ways involve translating 'what might have been written'.

There is a very important difference between moves in dialogue interpreting (as Mason describes them) and moves in the translation of written documents. The former are essentially social in nature – the interpreter is interacting with other human beings who are physically present. In written translation, however, the moves take place in the mind. Certainly written translation has social causes and social effects. However, this social aspect does not manifest itself at the moment when the translation is being composed, for the simple reason that no one other than the translator is present. There may be another translator in the next cubicle working on another chunk of the same text, and occasionally

---

[2] A check with the source text writer confirmed the absence of *non-*. However authors are not always available, and translators do make such corrections without confirmation. They may of course err. A text in the field of naval architecture states that the "water used to cool the ship's machinery must be heated". Why heat water that is used for cooling, one might wonder. In fact, the text makes perfect sense: in winter, the cooling water may freeze and must therefore be heated sufficiently to keep it above the freezing point. A translator who undertook a 'correction' here would land in hot water! Such a translator would nonetheless be working from beliefs about 'what might have been written'.

there may be telephone or email discussion about the text with the source text writer or the client, but for the most part, the interaction with authors, clients and readers is imagined. Unlike a dialogue interpreter, the translator is not responding to actions by other parties as the translation proceeds. Indeed, much of the time the translator is not even thinking about the other parties involved – an impossibility for the dialogue interpreter, who is in their immediate presence. A translation scholar may see a vast network of social forces of all kinds (sociolinguistic, economic, political, ideological) at work when comparing a passage of the source text with its *completed and received* translation, but in this article, I am interested solely in what translators *think they are doing at the moment of selecting a particular target language wording.*

Moves will thus be seen as events within the translator's mind. They are further to be understood as conscious mental acts that are distinct from mere *happenings.* Suppose a translator fails to notice a careless ambiguity in the source writer's wording and simply translates on the basis of the one meaning which happens to come to mind, and suppose this happens to be the meaning which makes sense in context. The translator is not then engaged in repairing a potential miscommunication, for there is no conscious identification of a problem in the source text wording, followed by action to repair that problem.

1.   The translator changes footing

Ian Mason has suggested that concepts first used in the study of dialogue interpreting may also be applicable to written translation (2004:89-90), and in this regard he has specifically referred to the ideas of sociologist Erving Goffman (1981). Following up on this suggestion, we can characterize what a translator is doing when 'cleaning up' or making other moves by drawing on Goffman's notion, as developed by linguist Stephen Levinson (1988), that being a 'speaker' can mean several different things. Someone who speaks (or writes) may be playing one, two or all three of the following roles:

- Motivating the utterance; that is, supplying the ideas to which the words attest[3]

---

[3] I have used my own terms for the three roles, drawing to some extent on Levinson. The translation studies literature contains several different interpretations of Goffman's three-way distinction between 'principal' (Motivator), 'author' (Composer) and 'animator' (Transmitter). Goffman, whose definitions tend to be suggestive rather than rigorous, defines 'principal' variously as "the party to whose position, stand and belief the words attest" (1979:226); "someone who has selected the sentiments that are being expressed … someone whose beliefs have been told, someone who is committed to what the words say" *(ibid.:*144). Now, unlike conversation (Goffman's interest), writing is usually institutional in nature. When employees write on behalf of their employers, they may well have "selected the sentiments" but they may not at all be personally "committed to what the words say". To resolve this issue, the employer might be called the 'ultimate Motivator', but for our present purposes such a distinction is not necessary.

- Composing the utterance; that is, formulating the sequence of words
- Transmitting the utterance; that is, speaking the wording aloud or writing it out.

Goffman was thinking of conversation, and so it is not surprising that Wadensjö (1992/1998) drew on Goffman in order to conceptualize the kind of translation which is most like conversation, namely dialogue interpreting. She wanted to account for what happens when, for example, a dialogue interpreter stops translating and speaks on her own behalf to one of the other parties in order to clarify some point. An interpreter who makes such a move changes 'footing' (as Goffman termed it), from being a non-motivating Composer/ Transmitter to being a Motivator as well. Translators change footing when, for example, they write a note in which they address readers on their own behalf.

In sum, translators may at any time make a move (e.g. repair a miscommunication, write a footnote). A move is a switch from one kind of language production to another. This switch may be accompanied by a change of footing between the roles of Motivator and non-Motivator.

2.   Motivation: a matter of degree?

Here is an interesting question: who is the Motivator when a translator starts to engage in what I have called 'cleaning up'? The answer in both of the examples discussed so far seems clear: the Motivator is the speaker/writer of the source text. The translators have not expressed their own ideas; they have not changed footing from being Composer/ Transmitters. But consider the following less clear cut example, a passage of purple prose from the description of a plant in the catalogue of a garden supply company which is being translated for distribution to potential customers:

> The varied colours and textures of their foliages and swaying flower spikes offer a colourful and restive scene which can rival any field of golden wheat or waving green oats.

The translator identifies the word *restive* as problematic. She suspects the writer does not know the standard dictionary meaning of this word, which is 'impatient, restless'. If this were poetry, she might translate as if the intended meaning were indeed 'restless', but since it is not poetry, she seeks a meaning which makes sense to her. Suppose she immediately thinks it obvious that 'restful' was intended, and without any more ado translates accordingly. The case is then on a par with the 'frost-susceptible soil' example. The translator has cleaned up the source text, but she has not become the Motivator.

Now suppose instead that the translator considers not one but several possibilities: the catalogue writer meant 'restful'; or he meant 'festive' but his finger hit the nearby 'r' key instead of the 'f' key by mistake; or he first thought of 'restful' and then of 'festive', or even thought of festiveness as restful, and ended up writing a word which contained a bit of each – *rest-ive*. The translator decides that she has some freedom of action here, since this passage does not convey any information that is vital to clients ordering seeds for their gardens. She picks 'restful' and translates accordingly. Certainly *colourful and restful scene* is something which 'might have been written', but the translator is now aware that she is in part substituting her own thoughts ('maybe the writer did mean 'festive' – it goes with 'colourful' – but I like the picture of a restful scene'). Has the translator changed footing to become a Motivator for the translation of this one word?

Here are two further possibilities for our translator. First, she might subtract whatever concept is expressed by *restive* and translate by omission (i.e. as if the source text were *a colourful scene*). Second, she might subtract whatever concept is expressed by *restive* and then add a thought of her own which is not her interpretation of *restive*. Let's say she translates as if the source text read *colourful and inviting scene*. Perhaps she personally likes the idea of walking into a bed of tall flowers. Or perhaps she picks this word because she knows that in the target culture, people like to walk through tall flowers rather than just view them from a distance, and thus target language readers will be more likely to buy the seeds if they think the effect will be 'inviting'. In the former case, she is expressing her own thoughts about gardens; in the latter, she is engaged in cultural tailoring. She seems to have become the Motivator herself, whether on her own behalf or on behalf of the translation commissioner's goal of inducing target language readers to buy seeds.

We now have several different cases. In interpreting the source text wording *colourful and restive*, the translator (1) picks 'restless' as the meaning, treating the passage as poetry; (2) picks *restful* without further thought; (3) picks 'restful' after weighing it against 'festive'; (4) omits whatever meaning is conveyed by *restive*; (5) replaces *restive* with *inviting* to tailor the text to the target culture; (6) replaces *restive* with *inviting* to express the translator's own thoughts about gardens. There is a sense in which any of the wordings corresponding to (2)-(6) (*colourful and restful, colourful and festive, colourful,* and *colourful and inviting*) 'might have been written' by the author of the garden catalogue. How should this situation be analyzed? I see two possibilities.

First, we could replace a binary notion of the Motivator (the translator either is or is not the Motivator in any particular instance) by a cline from less to more 'motivatorness'. In our examples, the degree of motivatorness attributable to the translator increases as we move from (1) to (6). However, I am not very partial to cline solutions in theoretical work. While some see such solutions as reflecting the richness of reality, I see them as giving up too easily. I shall therefore pursue the second possibility, that is, attempt to characterize the Motivator role in a way that preserves it as a binary concept.

3.   The translator reports

I shall now work toward a conception of Motivator that is suited to one particular kind of speech and writing, namely reporting the discourse of others,
of which translation is a particular instance. To begin with, it will be useful to
locate translators more precisely within the Motivator/Composer/Transmit-
ter system. This triad of roles can be used to identify various categories of
speaker or writer, the following examples being based loosely on Levinson
(1988:171):

- An Author is anyone who is simultaneously Motivator, Composer and
  Transmitter.
- A Relayer, such as a news reader or a dubbing actor, is a Transmitter but
  not a Motivator or Composer.
- A Formulator, such as a newswriter or playwright, is a Motivator and
  Composer, but not a Transmitter.
- A Spokesman, such as a lawyer representing a client in court, a ghost-
  writer or a politician's speechwriter, is a Composer and Transmitter but
  not a Motivator.
- A Sponsor, such as a movie star who hires a ghostwriter to prepare an
  autobiography, is a Motivator but not a Composer or Transmitter.

As an initial approximation, one might identify translators as Spokespersons. However they differ in one crucial way from the examples given
above: lawyers, ghostwriters and speechwriters do not start from a source text.
They listen to their clients, and perhaps record their words or obtain some
written documentation from them, but their work does not consist in reporting these materials. A rapporteur at a conference is a Spokesperson who does
of course report, but in the form of a summary, picking out key ideas from a
discussion and conveying them either from memory or aided by notes, and
in no particular order, often hours after hearing the source ideas expressed.
Translators, by contrast, typically include more or less all the ideas in the
source text, down to small details, and more or less in the order they appear
in the source. Furthermore, and most importantly, translators are rapporteurs
who work directly from a source text, which is generally visible on the screen
in front of them, or propped up next to the screen on a sheet of paper. There
is thus a very intimate spatial and temporal relationship between reading
source and writing report. It's read-write-read-write. The source of ideas is
constantly available to the translator in full detail, and its separateness from
the translator's own ideas is manifest at all times through the visible presence
of the source text.[4]

---

[4] When the source text is on paper, its ongoing existence as separate from the translation
is particularly visible. When the source is on a screen, it may be in a separate column or a
separate window, but sometimes it gradually disappears as the translator types over it.

As they report the source discourse in the manner just described, translators use a variety of grammatically distinct forms, as exemplified below:

Engineer: Je recommande l'emploi de sols gélifs.

Translator/interpreter:
(1) "I think it's best to use soil that won't freeze", she's saying.
(2) She says it's best to use soil that won't freeze.
(3) "I recommend using soil that won't freeze", said engineer Marie Lévesque, speaking in French.
(4) Engineer Marie Lévesque said that she always uses non-frost-susceptible soils.
(5) I recommend the use of non-frost-susceptible soils.

Form (1) might be used in voiceover translation by a television journalist; here the engineer would be heard speaking in French in the background. Form (2) might be used by a dialogue interpreter, especially one who is not a professional (professionals are trained to use form (5) most of the time). Forms (3) and (4) might be used by a print journalist writing a story on highway construction in cold climates. Form (5) is the form normally used in written translation of entire texts: no quotation marks, and direct rather than indirect reporting (the pronoun *I* stands for the engineer, not the translator, whereas in the indirect reporting of (4), the journalist is the speaking subject, and the engineer becomes *she*).

The vast scholarly literature on reported discourse, whether in fiction or non-fiction, is almost entirely concerned with forms such as (1)-(4), which all feature some sort of embedding of the reported material in a larger discourse. Embedding has the effect of signalling which party is to be taken as the Motivator of which words. Thus in (3), the journalist writing a story about highway construction indicates that he is changing footing and setting aside his role as Motivator. The quotational phrase *said engineer Marie Lévesque* together with the quotation marks signal that the engineer is to be taken as the Motivator of *I recommend ... freeze*, though the journalist/translator continues to be the Composer of the English words (as is made explicit in this case by the phrase *speaking in French*). In (4), the journalist signals, through the grammatical structure of indirect reported discourse, that he is the Motivator of the entire sentence. Here the reader is to understand *she always uses ... soils* as the journalist's interpretation, that is, the reader is explicitly called upon through the grammatical form to realize that the report may be mixed with the journalist's own ideas, even to the extent of being mistaken or incomplete. Indeed the journalist does seem to have engaged in such mixing in (4): he assumes that Marie Lévesque herself uses non-frost-susceptible soil, rather than merely recommending it.

Forms (1) to (4) differ radically from (5), the standard form for written translation, in that (5) has no embedding of the reported material in a larger discourse. There is no attribution to a prior writer and no overt indication that the prior text was in another language. The reader may in fact never realize that (5) is a translation (i.e. that it is reported discourse).[5] And even readers who do realize it will probably never become aware of the cleaning up the translator has performed by including the negative expression *non-frost-susceptible*. Only those who check the translation against the source text will be so aware, but such checking is not common among final users of translations. For the purposes of this article, awareness by readers is irrelevant; I am solely concerned with the viewpoint of the translator, who is definitely reporting a prior text, and cleaning it up, whether the final readers know it or not.

Unlike in (1)-(4), there is no signalling of the Motivator in (5). There are no words through which the translator presents the reported material, and thus *the translator does not explicitly promise the reader, through the form of the sentence*, that he is either conveying the engineer's ideas – as in (3) – or conveying his own understanding of the engineer's ideas, possibly mixed with his own – as in (4). Of course, even in (3), the promise implied by the grammatical form – that the engineer spoke words whose meaning is conveyed by the material between quotation marks – may not be kept. Nothing (aside from professional standards, which are not under consideration here) prevents the translator from adding to or subtracting from the engineer's message while using the direct speech of (3), just as nothing prevents him from conveying all and only the engineer's message (no addition or subtraction) while using the indirect speech of (4).

Form (5) is likewise compatible with either approach to reporting: add/subtract meaning, or give all+only the meaning of the source. Still, form (5) does *encourage* all+only reporting because the translator has to use the first-person pronoun *I* to mean someone else. This reminds the translator that someone else's ideas are being expressed, as does a factor already mentioned: the immediate presence of the source text in front of the translator's eyes. The easy availability of the source also helps achieve all+only reporting by reducing reliance on memory, whereas in oral translation good intentions (to convey the meaning of the source) may be foiled by memory limitations.

Summing up, the act of reporting discourse in form (5), the standard form of written translation, is compatible with the translator either being or not being the Motivator. In the next section, I distinguish various possibilities.

---

[5] There may of course be various indicators of translation, such as unintended translation-ese, intentional literalness, the words "translated by ...", translators' footnotes, and so on. Readers may or may not attend to these, and thus may or may not be aware of the fact of translation, and such awareness may vary from moment to moment as they read.

4. Four kinds of reporting

Let us now return to our garden catalogue text and recall four of the possibilities considered earlier. The translator works as if the source reads:

> The varied colours and textures of their foliages and swaying flower spikes offer a
> **A** colourful and restive
> **B** colourful and restful
> **C** colourful
> **D** colourful and inviting
> scene which can rival any field of golden wheat or waving green oats.

Here are some terms for the moves that the translator can make while writing a wording in the target language for each of these four cases:

A In this case, we'll say that the translator is engaging in Plain Reporting: she now tries to convey all[6] and only the meaning she attributes to the source wording *colourful and restive*.

B Here we'll say that after the word *and*, the translator switches from Plain to Reconstructive Reporting: she tries to convey all+only the meaning she attributes to the source after repairing any wording that strikes her as not representing the intention of the writer, in this case the word *restive*. This is what I earlier called 'cleaning up' and what Mason calls 'miscommunication repair'.

C After the word *colourful*, the translator switches from Plain to what I shall call Summary Reporting: she conveys only meaning which she attributes to the source, but not all of the meaning.

D After the word *and*, the translator switches from Plain Reporting to Fictive Reporting – fictive because there is no corresponding source text. She replaces whatever she thinks *restive* means by her own message, or a message she is conveying on behalf of the commissioner.

---

[6] The word *all* should not be taken too literally. The translator may decide, for example, to ignore a minor bit of meaning because, given the lexical and syntactic resources of the target language, it would be hard to capture both that bit and the rest of the meaning without writing a very awkward sentence. Such a decision must be distinguished from a decision to subtract meaning. Subtracting, like adding, has to do with tailoring translations to the perceived needs of readers, the wishes of the commissioner, or even the translator's own writing project. There are also cases where aspects of meaning are left out because of semiotic considerations: the translation is being fitted to music, or to the small space allotted for subtitles. A more precise definition of subtracting is not necessary for our present purposes.

(Alternatively, she adds her own message without replacement, translating as if the source were ... *offer a colourful, restive and inviting
scene*....)

The concept of Motivator can now be defined in terms of these four types of
reporting: the translator is the Motivator of a passage in the translation *unless*
she is engaging in some combination of Plain and Reconstructive Reporting.
Thus in A and B, the translator is not the Motivator anywhere; in C and D the
translator switches from not being Motivator to being Motivator. There are
no degrees of 'motivatorness', only switching back and forth between types
of reporting.

Now, some may be tempted to think that whenever anyone says or writes
anything, they put a little of themselves into it, and that this is particularly the
case in translation, since the ideas of the source are being processed through
the mind of the translator, which is in some sense in 'dialogue' with the
source and must inevitably analyze and interpret it. This is perhaps what leads
Petrilli to say that translation is actually "indirect discourse masked as direct
discourse" (2003:22); that is, we are really listening to the interpreting voice
of the translator even though formally, the first-person pronoun represents
the source-text writer. Hermans (2007:65ff) arrives at a very similar position, though he puts matters the other way round: "translation can be viewed
as direct speech mixed with elements of indirect speech" (*ibid.*); it is direct
but "animated by the translator's vision and to a significant extent under the
translator's control" (*ibid.*:75). In such a view of things, a reporter who is
Composing (as translators inevitably do when reporting a text that is written
in another language) is automatically a Motivator at the same time. However,
as I see it, the unavoidable contribution of any reporter is simply a general
background fact of all communication. It does not prevent us from distinguishing cases where the translator *intends* to convey all+only someone else's ideas
(i.e. the translator is *not* the Motivator) from cases where the translator intends
something else. What counts is the intention, not the limitations on success
which are inherent in the nature of communication.

Intent is what underlies the above definitions of the four types of reporting.
A translator is engaged in Plain Reporting if she *intends* to convey all and only
the various meanings she finds in the source. Whether a panel of revisers thinks,
after the fact, that she has correctly interpreted the source, and succeeded in
conveying that interpretation, is a completely separate matter.

The criterion of intent makes it easy to distinguish implicitation from
omission, and explicitation from addition. If the translator believes that her
translation leaves implicit an element of meaning that is explicit in the source
text, then the translator is engaging in Plain Reporting. If however she intends
to leave out an element of meaning so that it is not recoverable, then it is
omission, and the translator is engaging in Summary Reporting. Similarly,
if the translator believes that a certain element of meaning is implied in the

source text and she is now going to make that element explicit, then she is explicitating (Plain Reporting); if she does not think this element is implied in the source, then she is adding (Fictive Reporting).[7]

5.   An astronomer does some Fictive Reporting

Consider this passage from the 1966 book *Intelligent Life in the Universe*, which the publisher describes as a translation, extension and revision of Russian astronomer I.S. Shklovskii's *Vselennaja, Zhizn', Razum* (universe, life, intelligence):

> Let us now discuss the anticipated character of radio ∇ or optical laser Δ signals which we might receive from another civilization. Von Hoerner has suggested the nature of the signals would be determined ultimately by (a) the purpose they are to serve; and (b) the most economical transmission channel. There are three general types of signals which we might anticipate: (1) local broadcast, that is, radiation due to local communications on a planet such as from domestic television transmitters. ∇ Eavesdropping on such calls is, under some circumstances, feasible; Δ (2) long distance calls, that is, specifically directed radio contact between two particular civilizations; (3) announcement signals, that is, signals transmitted for the purpose of attracting the attention of any civilization which has not yet been contacted. (Shklovskii and Sagan 1966:421)

In his introduction to the English translation, the American astronomer Carl Sagan writes:

> I wrote to Shklovskii, asking him if we might translate it into English. Shklovskii readily consented, and invited me to add additional material as I saw fit. As the translation proceeded, in the capable hands of Paula Fern, I found myself unable to resist the temptation to annotate the text, clarify concepts for the scientific layman, comment at length, and introduce new material .... I have sent much of the entirely new

---

[7] One could look at any type of shift in terms of the four types of reporting. For example, what about translating metaphorical by non-metaphorical language? If the translator sees the metaphor as superfluous (thinks non-metaphorical language would make no difference within the context of the source-language readers), then using non-metaphorical language in the target language is Plain, not Summary Reporting; nothing has been omitted as far as the translator is concerned, and the translator is not the Motivator. However, if the translator does see the metaphor as significant within the context of the source-language readers, then a switch to non-metaphorical language in the target language is Summarizing (the cognitive content of the metaphor has been preserved, but not the vehicle). The translator becomes the Motivator.

material to Shklovskii for his comment, and he has sent much new material to me for inclusion ... Consequently, there are places in the present work where Shklovskii and I alternate sentences, or even occasionally insert clauses into each other's sentences. Shklovskii and I agree on almost all the substantive issues of this book, but to avoid the possibility of attribution to Shklovskii of a view which he does not hold, I have adopted the following strategem: Sentences or paragraphs which appeared either in the Russian edition of this book, or in additions provided by Shklovskii, are presented in ordinary type. Annotations, additions and discussions of my devising are surrounded by the symbols ∇ and Δ, the first preceding and the second following my contribution. In those cases where Shklovskii uses the word 'we', as in 'we believe' or 'we feel', this generally represents a sentiment shared by both of us. (*ibid.*:vii-viii)

For the sake of argument, let us overlook the fact that there are two different writers here – Fern and Sagan. Instead, imagine them as two personalities of a single writer, with the Sagan personality writing the material between triangles, and the Fern personality the rest. How does the Fern personality report the source text? Here is the Russian source for the first sentence of the above passage with a gloss in English:

В такой обстановке представляет интерес обсудить харахтер
in such situation   there is   interest   discuss   nature
ожидаемых радиосигналов. (Shklovskii 1962:203)
of anticipated radio signals

Fern's translation reads:

Let us now discuss the anticipated character of radio signals which we might receive from another civilization.

As can be seen, Fern's translation is not close. For one thing, it contains a lengthy explicitation: *which we might receive from another civilization* expresses an idea implicit in the Russian book as a whole, which is precisely about the existence of intelligent life elsewhere in the universe and the possibility of communicating with it. Furthermore, *anticipated* modifies *character* whereas the Russian word it translates modifies the Russian word for *radio signals*; and the introductory phrase has been adjusted to *let us now* (that is because the English book does not follow the chapter divisions of the Russian: this passage starts a chapter in the English, whereas in the Russian it does not). Despite these changes, Fern does appear to be engaged in Plain Reporting throughout; while we cannot enter her mind, none of the changes seem to be ones that seek to add or subtract meaning.

Very different is the sentence between triangles (*Eavesdropping on such calls ... feasible*), which does seek to add meaning (we know this because Sagan has told us so in his introduction). The writer's Sagan personality is engaged in Fictive Reporting. The inverted triangles function as a sort of anti-quotation mark; they specifically indicate that the passage they surround is one that does not correspond to anything said or implied in the source text. On the other hand, the triangle-marked passages do appear to be in line with Shklovksii's thought, judging from the comments in Sagan's introduction. Sagan has not, he tells us, written anything he believes to be incompatible with Shklovskii's views. He is a Motivator, but a 'loyal' one. The situation might be compared to what happens when a ghostwriter imagines her subject expressing certain ideas, and then has the subject approve what she has written. Let us look more closely at this important question of compatibility.

6. What might, what should, and what would not have been written

In both Reconstructive and Fictive Reporting, translators write words they believe to be compatible with the source. In Reconstruction, the source text appears to call out for rewording, and this is done on the basis of some combination of logic, textual evidence and subject-matter knowledge. In our highway text, the translator believes there is good reason to translate as if the source had *non-gélifs* instead of *gélifs*. We could say that in such Reconstructive Reporting, the translator is trying to decide not so much 'what *might*' as 'what *should*' have been written in the source text.

In Fictive Reporting, on the other hand, the wording used as a basis for translation is merely plausible; in the garden catalogue text, *inviting* is a word that *might* have been in the source, so the translator believes. The distinction between Reconstructive and Fictive rests on the translator's belief. Reporting is Reconstructive if the translator believes that the source writer would agree that there is an error of some sort in the source text. Reporting is Fictive if the translator believes the added wording to be in line with the motivation behind the source text, that is, believes the source writer would approve (or at least not disapprove) of the addition if asked, in the way Shklovskii was asked by Sagan. With Summary Reporting, the translator must similarly believe that even though the omitted material will not be recoverable by the reader, the resulting 'summary' will not mislead the reader about the motivation of the source writer. *Not just anything goes in Fictive and Summary Reporting; not just anything 'might have been written'.*

It is thus quite possible for a reporter to add and subtract meaning without being 'disloyal'. Indeed, I want to say that if translators cease to believe that what they are writing is compatible with the source, then they are no longer engaged in Reporting of any kind. At that point in the text where they begin to add or subtract material 'disloyally', I will say that they switch from Reporting to Adapting. They are then working from a wording which, they believe, *would not* have been written by the author of the source. They become 'disloyal' Motivators.

An example: translators used to omit or replace references to homosexuality in English translations of the Greek and Roman classics. A man's male lover would become a female lover in translation, or there would be wholesale deletions of 'offending' passages. A translation critic might approve or disapprove of such a change (perhaps disapprove as a manifestation of homophobia, or approve as necessary to ensure sales or avoid legal action). Here, however, I am using Adapting quite neutrally. I have placed the word 'disloyal' in inverted commas to indicate that Adapting is not inherently a bad thing. Of course, if a text that includes Adapting is presented to readers as a complete and accurate translation, then the publisher is lying, but as long as such outright deception is absent, Adapting is simply a manifestation of a writing project that differs from Reporting.

The Adapting writer's attitude to the source may be "I don't believe my source would have written this" or alternatively "I don't care whether my source would have written this". We might think again here of the translator who rendered *colourful and restive scene* as if it were *colourful and inviting scene*. Perhaps she knows that the commissioner only cares about accuracy for the passages of the catalogue that convey technical information such as the names of plant varieties or the instructions for placing an order. But in passages such as the one under consideration, loyalty is not a consideration and she lets her fancy reign. If she does not believe or does not care whether *inviting* is compatible with the intent of the source text, then she is Adapting rather than engaging in Fictive Reporting.

In using the term Adapting, I am modifying this traditional concept. Adapting is traditionally a matter of adding and subtracting to tailor a text to the time, place and culture of the target readers regardless of what the source text says, and perhaps also to reflect what the adapter wishes to convey. However, Carl Sagan's preface to the Shklovskii translation suggests an important distinction within the general category of additions and subtractions: those which the translator believes to be compatible with the source, and those where compatibility is not a consideration.

This conception of loyalty is very different from the traditional servile conception of their role that is common among non-literary translators. In that conception, even obvious corrections must be checked with source authors, while additions/subtractions are completely out of the question, and the matter of their compatibility with the source does not even arise. In other words, what I am calling Reconstructive and especially Fictive Reporting is traditionally lumped indiscriminately with the act I am calling Adapting.

I want to suggest eliminating the traditional distinction between *translating* and adapting, where translating is restricted to all+only reporting (perhaps with some explicitations/implicitations and certain unavoidable adjustments to the new readership); anything else, in the traditional view, is adapting. I propose instead a distinction between *reporting* and adapting. Reporting is 'loyally' conveying the meaning of a prior text; it is a broad notion that includes Plain, Reconstructive and, most importantly, Fictive Reporting. Adapting is then restricted to 'disloyal' rewriting of an existing text. The distinction between the two kinds of writing – reporting and adapting – lies not in whether meaning has been added/subtracted, but in the fundamentally different attitude of the translator toward the source. As to the label society attaches to the reporter/ adapter or to the output of the reporting/adapting, this will vary: a person who engages in reporting only, or reporting plus some adapting, or even pure adapting, may be labelled a 'translator' or not; the product may be labelled a 'translation' or something else.

It is true that additions/subtractions thought by the translator to be in the spirit of the source might be rejected by its author if they were to come to the latter's attention, but as I explained earlier, I am concerned here only with the translator's intent. Intent is a vital consideration for anyone who wants to understand how written translation works because, as already mentioned, no one but the translator is present when translations are composed. I suspect that in the solitude of their offices, many non-literary translators quietly go beyond Plain or even Reconstructive Reporting and switch to Fictive Reporting while avoiding any Adapting, and on other occasions they indulge in Adapting as well.

7.   A historian on Fictive Reporting and Adapting

Further investigation of Fictive Reporting and Adapting might draw on writings in literary studies and philosophy concerning the topic of verisimilitude. Also of interest might be research on the intersection between history and fiction, and in this regard I shall conclude with a brief discussion of a statement by a famous historian. In the late 5th century BCE, Thucydides briefly commented on how he had gone about reporting speeches for his history of the Peloponnesian War, which contains 141 addresses in either direct or indirect discourse, some by noted historical figures such as Pericles and Alcibiades. The passage below comes just after a section where Thucydides has specifically been contrasting his own approach to history with that of previous writers whose compositions are, he says, "attractive at truth's expense,[8] the subjects they treat of being out of the reach of evidence, and time having robbed most of them of historical value by enthroning them in the region of legend".

---

[8] 'belles infidèles' avant la lettre!

With reference to the speeches in this history, some were delivered
before the war began, others while it was going on; some I heard
myself, others I got from various quarters; it was in all cases difficult
to carry them word for word in one's memory, so my habit has been
to *make the speakers say what was in my opinion demanded of them*
by the various occasions, of course adhering as closely as possible to
the general sense of what they really said. (Book I, chapter 22, section
1, trans. Richard Crawley, in Strassler 1996:15, my italics)

The italicized passage has given rise to a vast amount of commentary by
classicists.[9] There are several different understandings – and thus several different translations – of what Thucydides meant, centring on the two Ancient
Greek expressions *ta deonta* (translated by Crawley as "what was demanded")
and *te ksympasa gnome* (translated as "the general sense"). Some commentators have seen a contradiction here and others not:

Does not Thucydides admit to contrary agendas: contrivance ("to make
the speakers say what was in my opinion demanded of them") and
historical exactitude ("adhering as closely as possible to the general
sense of what they really said")? ... [but] ... Apparently, Thucydides
is envisioning two very different circumstances for setting down
speeches in his history: well-known addresses in which he was more
or less able to find out what was really said, and other instances in
which something probably was spoken, but went unrecorded or was
forgotten. The latter orations had to be reconstructed more or less according to Thucydides' own particular historical sense of what was
likely, appropriate, and necessary. (Hanson 1996:xvi)

Rusten (1989:11ff) actually translates the passage in accordance with
this view:

I have written the speeches more or less as it seemed to me the individuals would have said what had to be said about the respective
situations, although I have kept as closely as possible to the general
content of speeches which were actually delivered.

In this view, some of the speeches are dramatizations by Thucydides, who then
writes in the way he thinks the individuals would have said what needed to be
said on that occasion. Ste Croix (1972:11) has a related interpretation: instead

---

[9] The classicists' debate is not about transcription. "What they really said" must surely
be taken as a reference not to the precise sequence of words but to the detailed meaning
of whatever words were uttered – the particular arguments the speakers put forward.
Thucydides all but admits that the speeches are not word-for-word transcripts. Emily
Greenwood says that little is known about the practicalities of recording in Thucydidean
Athens (2006:65).

of distinguishing different speeches, he distinguishes different passages of each speech. He suggests that *te ksympasa gnome* has to be given a restrictive reading as 'main thesis'. So in passages that express the main thesis of an orator, Thucydides is claiming truth; in other passages, the words he is putting into the mouths of the characters are ones which are merely appropriate to the occasion. Of course "we can seldom be sure that we know how extensive the *ksympasa gnome* is, and therefore we may often not be able to decide how much of a speech represents what was actually said, and how much is the historian's own formulation of the issues" (*ibid.*). In the terms I have used, the former would be Plain/Reconstructive Reporting, the latter either Fictive Reporting or Adapting.

Greenwood (2006:64) suggests that while *ta deonta* can be taken to mean 'what was required' in the estimation of the historical figures whose speeches are being reported, given the circumstances and the audience as they spoke, it could also be taken to mean what was required in the estimation of Thucydides himself, given the circumstances under which he was addressing *his* readers and telling them what the historical figures said. Applying this distinction to translation, the former interpretation concerns the relationship between the source text writer and that writer's audience; the latter concerns the relationship between the translator and *the translator's* audience. Now, as Ste Croix says (1972:12), "what seemed to Thucydides the most appropriate sentiments on a given occasion might be very different from those which would have seemed appropriate to most people – including the actual speaker and his audience". Thus in those passages which express *ta deonta* rather than *te ksympasa gnome*, Thucydides may have been engaging in either Fictive Reporting or Adapting, depending on whether he believed that the words he was putting into their mouths were or were not compatible with the speakers' own views.

8. The translator's view

Table 1 summarizes the five[10] moves that have been discussed in this article.

---

[10] This is not a complete list of moves. In a book now in preparation entitled *Standing Behind the Translator*, I discuss some twenty moves the translator may make. A move that has been used for censorship purposes is Copying of source-language wording directly into the translation: Hermans (2007:60) gives an amusing example of an early twentieth-century English translation of Boccaccio where an 'obscene' passage is simply left in Italian. Copying is also used when translating texts that contain metalinguistic passages (a judge's decision that discusses the source-language wording of the law). More commonly, Copying is used with proper names. For example, in translating French texts from Quebec into English, I might Copy 'Université de Montréal' or use Plain Reporting and write 'University of Montreal'. At the moment I start Copying, I stop being a Composer/Transmitter and become a simple Transmitter. One might argue, however, that I also become a Motivator, because of the added ideological significance of retaining the French name of the university (see Mossop 2007). Another move in which translators become simple

Move	Translator is motivator	Translator conveys	Translator gives all+only the meaning of the source text
Plain Reporting	NO	What *was* written	YES (possibly with explicitation or implicitation)
Reconstructive Reporting	NO	What *should* have been written	YES after correcting the source
Fictive Reporting	YES	What *might* have been written	NO – adds, but in spirit of ST
Summary Reporting	YES	What *might* have been written	NO – subtracts, but in spirit of ST
Adapting	YES	What *would* NOT have been written	NO – adds or subtracts, and not in spirit of ST

Table 1. Characterization of five translator moves

Translating can be described from the translator's viewpoint as a sequence of moves, with the translator switching from one way of producing language to another. In some moves, the translator becomes the Motivator, in others not.

It is not hard to imagine the translator setting down a wording of which any of the following could be true:

(i)   Here I was simply reconstructing the author's intent, and was therefore not the Motivator.

(ii) Here I was adding, so I was the Motivator, but I think that what I wrote was compatible with the source

(iii) Here I was simply writing what I wanted to say or what my client wanted me to say even though it is not compatible with the source.

Only the reporting translator can say which of these actually happened. Consequently the schema presented here cannot be used for text analysis by an observer. However, that is not a drawback in my view. There is a tendency in

---

Transmitters is Cutting & Pasting, where an existing target-language wording is pasted into the translation (perhaps a passage from an old translation). With Cutting & Pasting, as well as Copying, the question of whether translators are conveying all+only the meaning of the source becomes a matter of revision: they may rewrite a Copied or Pasted passage so that it reflects all+only their interpretation of the source text, or adopt a Fictive, Summarizing or Adapting approach instead.

translation studies to always look at matters from the viewpoint of a translation teacher or a reviser or a translation scholar, rather than that of the translator. But what the scholar sees as an omission may have been seen by the translator as implicitation or as reconstruction (removing what he believes to be a redundancy perhaps). And what the reviser sees as disloyal addition may really be Fictive Reporting: the translator may have believed that he was conveying 'what might have been written'.

References

Goffman, Erving (1981) *Forms of Talk*, Philadelphia: University of Pennsylvania Press.

Greenwood, Elizabeth (2006) *Thucydides and the Shaping of History*, London: Duckworth.

Hanson, Victor (1996) 'Introduction', in Robert Strassler *The Landmark Thucydides*, New York: The Free Press.

Hermans, Theo (2007) *The Conference of the Tongues*, Manchester: St Jerome.

Levinson, Stephen (1988) 'Putting Linguistics on a Proper Footing: Explorations in Goffman's Concepts of Participation', in Paul Drew and Anthony Wootton (eds) *Erving Goffman: Exploring the Interaction Order*, Boston: Northeastern University Press, 161-227.

Mason, Ian (2004) 'Conduits, Mediators, Spokespersons: Investigating Translator/ interpreter Behaviour', in Christina Schäffner (ed.) *Translation Research and Interpreting Research*, Clevedon & Buffalo: Multilingual Matters, 88-97.

------ (2006) 'Ostension, Inference and Response: Analysing Participant Moves in Community Interpreting Dialogues', *Linguistica Antverpiensia* NS 5: 103-20.

Mossop, Brian (1995) 'Understanding Poorly Written Source Texts', *Terminology Update* 28(2): 4-21. Available at http://www.btb.termiumplus.gc.ca/tpv2guides/ guides/favart/index-eng.html?lang=eng&lettr=indx_autr28&page=81#zz28 (last accessed 15 January 2010).

------ (2007) 'Reader Reaction and Workplace Habits in the Translation of French Proper Names in Canada', *Meta* 52(2): 202-14

Petrilli, Susan (2003) 'Translation and Semiosis. Introduction', in Susan Petrilli (ed.) *Translation Translation*, Amsterdam & New York: Rodopi, 17-37.

Rusten, Jeffrey (1989) *The Peloponnesian War Book II*, Cambridge & New York: Cambridge University Press.

Shklovskii, Iosif Samuilovich (1962) *Vselennaja, Zhizn', Razum*, Moscow: Akademia Nauk SSSR.

------ and Carl Sagan (1966) *Intelligent Life in the Universe*, San Francisco: Holden-Day.

Ste Croix, Geoffrey Ernest Maurice de (1972) *The Origins of the Peloponnesian War*, London: Duckworth.

Strassler, Robert (1996) *The Landmark Thucydides*, New York: The Free Press.

Wadensjö, Cecilia (1992/1998) *Interpreting as Interaction*, London & New York: Longman.

III. Institutional Context & Individual Agency

Negotiating Identities in the European Parliament

The Role of Simultaneous Interpreting

MORVEN BEATON-THOME
University of Manchester, UK

Abstract. *This article investigates the role of simultaneous interpreting (SI) in the European Parliament, focusing on the effect SI has on identity construction and negotiation via detailed comparative analysis of the use of the first person plural 'we'. Data from a case study on the potential resettlement of Guantánamo Bay detainees in EU member states is explored using the concepts of in-group and out-group identities to establish interpreter positioning and stance. Descriptive analysis is conducted in three categories: stable 'we' group reference in both ST and TT; ST/TT shifts in 'we' reference; and the introduction of 'we' reference in the TT where no identifiable trigger exists in the ST. Findings suggest that a trend could be established in the simultaneous interpretations towards intensified use of the inclusive* we *to refer to* we, the parliamentary community *and* we, the EU, *at the expense of more peripheral identities such as the national, regional and political group. This points towards a tendency of SI to strengthen the dominant institutional presence, ideology and identity and weaken or fail to represent the full complexity of the 'traffic in voices' (Bakhtin 1981) and heteroglot identities present in such an institution.*

As the largest employer of translators and conference interpreters worldwide (Directorate General for Interpretation website), the European Union (EU) provides rich data for an investigation of translation and interpreting in an institutional setting. The European Parliament (EP), with its special status as the only democratically elected body within the EU, is a forum in which the ideological significance of multilingual communication and transparency of proceedings in all official languages is particularly salient. Consequently, translators and interpreters would appear to be central to the functioning of the Parliament and, by extension, the political institution of the EU as a whole. However, despite this seemingly pivotal role, translators and interpreters have been accorded little attention in the extensive critical discourse-based studies into the ideological importance of multilingualism for the EU that are currently available (see Wodak 2007 for a comprehensive overview), or anthropological and political investigations into the institution (see Koskinen 2008:63-64). Indeed, in translation studies itself, relatively few researchers have devoted attention to the ideological significance of written translation or conference interpreting in the EU. In focusing on the ideological significance of transitivity patterns in a corpus of written translations of EP plenary sessions (Calzada Pérez 1997, 2007, Mason 2003/2004), detailed ethnographic study of translation in the European Commission, including text and discourse analysis of various texts in the drafting process of institutional translations (Koskinen 2008), and the effect of simultaneous interpreting on heteroglossic discourse in a corpus of EP plenary debates (Beaton 2007a, 2007b), these researchers share a concern with broader sociological and institutional issues and their manifestation in tangible discoursal and textual properties. This combined approach is also pursued in this article, which responds to Mason's plea that "the need to relate the sociology and politics of translation to actual translation behaviour – as evidenced in the textual moves translators make – has never been greater" (Mason, in Preface to Calzada Pérez 2007:XV).

Despite historical explorations of the ideological implications of the provision of simultaneous interpreting in other multilingual institutions such as the Nuremburg trials (Gaiba 1998) and the South African Truth and Reconciliation Commission (Wallmach 2002), the few available studies on interpreting in the EU context have focused on exploring the interpretation of institutional terms (Marrone 1998), specific organizational and cultural constraints of the institution itself (Marzocchi 1998), describing and establishing interpreting norms and their didactic application in the EU institutional context (Vuorikoski 2004), directionality (Monti *et al.* 2005) or investigating the role of repeated formulaic phrases in EU discourse (Henriksen 2007). In contrast, institutional public service and legal interpreting settings have attracted increased interest in ideological questions such as the appropriation of power in the asylum context (Blommaert 2001, Inghilleri 2007, Maltby 2008, Maryns 2006), role distribution and participant status in police interviews (Wadensjö 1998) and mental health settings (Bot 2005), or politeness and the exercise of control through discursive features of interpreted utterances in the courtroom (Berk-Seligson 1990, Hale 2004). Such settings provide rich data on interaction that challenges the traditional view of the interpreter as a mere conduit (Reddy 1999), a view which still pervades much discourse on professional conference interpreting and has only recently been convincingly challenged in conference interpreting research (Diriker 2004).

Building on my earlier research on the ideological significance of simultaneous interpreting provision in the European Parliament (Beaton 2007a, 2007b), this article will focus on the effect of SI on the construction and negotiation of the identities of Members of the European Parliament (MEPs) in the English and German language versions of 'heteroglossic' (Bakhtin 1981) discourse in the EP. In particular, I will focus on the ideological significance of the first person plural *we* and the role it plays in the construction and negotiation of 'in- and out-group identities'. For the purposes of this article, the term 'ideology' will be used "in the neutral sense of a world view, a largely unconscious theory of the way the world works accepted as common sense" (Fowler 1985:65), with 'common sense' understood as "the implicit social knowledge that group members take for granted in their everyday social practices" (van Dijk 1998:102).[1] Examples of German-to-English and English-to-German SI will be drawn from a case study of a debate in the plenary part-session[2] on the potential resettlement of Guantánamo Bay detainees in European Union member states.

1.   Personal pronoun use in institutional interpreting

Research on the negotiation of identity in interpreted interactions as evident in pronominal use has predominantly focused on the relationship between the choice of first or third person in interpreters' utterances and participant perception of interpreter role (Bot 2005, Bührig & Meyer 2003, Wadensjö 1998), or on forms of address in languages which differentiate between formal and informal second person pronouns (T/V distinction) (Angermeyer 2005, Berk-Seligson 1990, Krouglov 1999). Shifts in the use of forms of address have also been conceptualized as shifts between formal and informal registers (Hale 1997, Krouglov 1999). In these studies of authentic data, both shifts and inconsistent use of pronouns have been found to occur in all categories. Instances of inconsistent use of the first person singular *I* were also identified in Diriker's (2004) corpus-based study of conference interpreters, which showed clear evidence of the use of at least four different types of *I*, indicating that interpreter identity is more fluid and hybrid than meta-discoursal evidence would suggest. Rather than dismissing these findings as evidence of insufficient professional training, this data can be approached in qualitative terms and individual extracts analyzed according to the effect the change has on the continuation of the interaction and on interpreters' construction of their identities and the identities of other participants. This 'take-up' (Mason 2006:365) approach could potentially provide data on how interpreters position themselves as individuals and/or as a group within the institution.

In contrast to previous studies, the present study focuses exclusively on simultaneous interpreting in which two to three professional interpreters per

---

[1] For a more detailed discussion of the concept of ideology, see Beaton (2007a, 2007b).

[2] The European Parliament plenary sessions are held in Strasbourg on a monthly basis. Each of these, known as a 'part-session', lasts four days (from Monday to Thursday). Parliament also meets in Brussels six times a year for two days (Wednesday and Thursday). Each part-session is divided into daily sittings. See http://www.europarl.europa.eu/activities/plenary/staticDisplay.do?language=EN&id=2100.

booth interpret interventions from multiple speakers into the language of that booth for an audience consisting of MEPs at the Parliament and a number of external groups listening to the debate, either present at the debate or listening remotely to live or archived web streaming. The repercussions for the negotiation of individual speaker identity and the ideological potential for interpreters to influence perception of the identity of individual MEPs in the debate as a whole are particularly salient in this context. If interpreter influence is viewed as a continuum, we could situate, at one pole, varying interpreter personal style (van Besien and Meuleman 2008) and, at the other end of the continuum, the observed tendency of interpreters in the one booth to gravitate towards a similar style in which all speakers are interpreted in an "increasingly formulaic and thus progressively uniform" manner (Henriksen 2007:17). In ideological terms, drawing on Bakhtin (1981:273), these two tendencies have been previously categorized as "centrifugal (heteroglossic)" and "centripetal (unitary) forces", respectively (Beaton 2007a:273). These Bakhtinian terms will also be employed in the analysis offered in this article.

2.   Categorizing personal pronoun use in political debate

If cohesion is understood as "the ways in which the components of the surface text, i.e. the actual words we hear or see, are mutually connected within a sequence" (Beaugrande and Dressler 1981:3), the personal pronoun *we* can be categorized as a type of 'pro-form', with pro-forms defined as "economical, short words empty of their own particular content, which can stand in the surface text in place of more determinate, content-activating expressions" (*ibid.*:60). Pro-forms are used to refer *anaphorically* and less frequently *cataphorically* to nouns or noun phrases used elsewhere in the text. According to this approach, the pro-form is a "long range cohesive device" (*ibid.*:80). This type of easily recoverable anaphoric *we* reference is present in the debate under analysis here, as in the following example from Graham Watson, British MEP and Chairman of the Alliance of Liberals and Democrats for Europe in the European Parliament (ALDE), where the *we* at the start of the second sentence refers anaphorically to *Europe* in the first sentence:

> But Europe cannot stand back, shrug its shoulders and say that these things are for America alone to sort out. We lack the open debate and the collective change of will which American democracy allows.

However, the overwhelming majority of *we* references in the debate cannot be recovered by investigation of textual co-reference alone. In Halliday and Hasan's terms, this form of *we* reference is not cohesive but "exophoric" (1976:33), meaning that it is a situational rather than textual reference. Halliday and Hasan then proceed to exclude first and second person personal pronoun use from a study of cohesion, stating that

> it is only the anaphoric type of reference that is relevant to cohesion, since it provides a link with a preceding portion of the text. When we talk of the cohesive function of personal reference, therefore, it is particularly the third person forms that we have in mind. (Halliday and Hasan 1976:51)

The analysis offered here will therefore distinguish between cohesive *we* reference in the form of anaphoric and cataphoric co-reference and *we* reference in the form of exophoric reference. It is particularly this latter use of *we* to refer to agents outside the text that is of significance in a study of positioning, where it is exactly the lack of a determinate textual referent that is significant in the construction and negotiation of identities. Given that this is particularly salient in the case of the use of *we*, study of interpreter response to such indeterminate pronoun use, particularly in the 'on-line' simultaneous mode, is of special interest. Indeed, such exophoric *we* reference is part of a system of self- and other references which are "key to the reconstruction and negotiation of identities and social roles, and to the definition of the co partici-pants' interpersonal relationships, where they may signify intimacy, distance, or social hierarchy" (Bull and Fetzer 2006:3-4). As such, it is highly salient in terms of ideology, as pronominal choice can often indicate speaker positioning, distancing and stance on a particular issue. In the rhetoric of "othering", "expres-sions that are the most revealing of the boundaries separating Self and Other are inclusive and exclusive pronouns and possessives such as we and they, us and them and our and theirs" (Riggins 1997:8). The concepts of the Self and the Other, identification and distance, are also mirrored in positive "in-group positioning" and negative "out-group positioning" in van Dijk's (1998:267) ideological square. It is these concepts of in- and out-group identities that I will draw on in this discussion.

Given the indeterminate use of *we* reference outlined above, developing categories of reference for the current analysis proved problematic. The distinc-tion drawn in communicative grammar (Leech and Svartvik 1975/1994:58) between hearer "inclusive *we*" (Let's go to the dance tonight, shall we?) and hearer "exclusive *we*" (We've all enjoyed meeting you) is often employed in analyses of this type. This distinction is useful in indicating a general posi-tion, but it does not account for all the subtleties of *we* reference. It is not the focus of this article to discuss these subtleties in detail (cf. Mühlhäusler and Harré 1990:168-78 for a detailed functional analysis); nevertheless, further *we* distinctions need to be made for the analysis to proceed. In what follows, I will therefore draw on a modified version of Íñigo-Mora's (2004) categor-ization of *we* groups in British parliamentary discourse. Her categorization distinguishes between four distinct groups: (1) *exclusive* (I + my political group), (2) *inclusive* (I + you), (3) *parliamentary community* (I + parliamen-tary community), and (4) *generic* (I + all British people) (*ibid.*:49). As this categorization was developed for the British Parliamentary setting, the four

categories do not correspond to the groups in this study and require modifi-
cation and refinement. Therefore, adjusted to the EP context, the boundaries
of the exclusive and generic categories – (1) and (4) in Íñigo-Mora's scheme
– need to be redrawn to distinguish between the following: (a) exclusive (I
+ my group – not necessarily political), and (b) generic (I + all people). Indeed, building on this distinction, I would argue that there is also a need to
view the four categories in a more hierarchical manner, focusing on the two
broad categories of (1) exclusive *we* and (2) inclusive *we* and referring to *we,
the parliamentary community* as a subcategory of (1) exclusive *we*, and the
generic *we* as a subcategory of (2) inclusive *we*. The resulting categorization
is thus as follows:

(1) exclusive *we* (I + my political community, including *we, the parliamen-
     tary community*)
(2) inclusive *we* (I + you, including generic *we*, which may refer to I + all
     people, or normally I + all Europeans in this context)

3.   Data selection and analysis

The debate from 3 February 2009 on the potential resettlement of Guantánamo
Bay detainees in European Union member states was selected as data for the
case study as it proved to be an adversarial debate in which in- and out-group
identities were continually negotiated.

The English version of the debate, which consisted of video recordings of
all English original language interventions and English simultaneous interpretations of all non-English original language interventions, was downloaded as
a .mov file playable in Windows Media Player (European Parliament Media
Library website). Despite repeated attempts, it proved impossible to download
the German version of the debate in the same manner. However, the German
version, like all other language versions, was accessible via the EP internet
site. Therefore, the analysis of the German simultaneous interpretations was
carried out directly from the internet site. Transcripts were also made of all
German and English interventions and their respective interpretations to ensure that a written copy of the data was available should the German version
no longer be accessible on the site. In the examples quoted, the interpreter is
indicated by the insertion of the letter 'I', followed by 'E' for English or 'D'
for German, followed by a number that identifies the respective interpreter.
For example, 'IE3' denotes an interpretation from English interpreter number
three. This is then followed by the surname of the original speaker. Thus, an
example from an English interpretation of the German MEP Cem Özdemir
provided by English interpreter three would be accompanied by the reference
'IE3_Özdemir'.

Source text analysis of *we* reference was followed by independent target
text analysis of the same phenomenon to ensure that *we* references in the TT

that were not triggered by similar references in the ST were also picked up. Comparative analysis was then carried out to determine how *we* group reference was interpreted from German to English and vice-versa.

The total duration of the entire debate is one hour and fifty-seven minutes. The interventions analyzed consist of all original English and original German interventions and their interpretations into German and English, respectively; these interventions constituted the majority of the total debate. A total of three English interpreters (two male, one female) and two German interpreters (both female) were included in the data.[3] Given that the analysis that follows is based on one case study only, the findings cannot be treated as representative of simultaneous interpreted parliamentary debate in the EP as a whole and would have to be tested on a larger, more representative corpus before any broader claims can be made. In addition, this study is limited to the analysis of the English and German language versions of the interpreted debate, and its findings may therefore not be representative of other language versions.

In-group positioning of both MEPs and interpreters could potentially be explored by investigating a number of textual and discoursal characteristics such as the use of *transitivity* (Calzada Pérez 1997, 2007), discourse markers such as *hedges* (Hale 2004), lexical labelling (Beaton-Thome, forthcoming), or more global argumentative strategies such as the use of *disclaimers*, *storytelling* or the use of *rhetorical figures* (see van Dijk 1997:42 for a discussion of the ideological salience of such devices in monolingual parliamentary debate). Although these aspects may be touched on in the analysis, the following discussion will concentrate on the use of the first person plural pronoun *we* and the insight it provides into the construction and negotiation of in-group identity.

Before results of comparative ST/TT analysis are discussed, an outline of *we* use in both German and English language versions of the debate will first be briefly presented, using the *we* groups discussed above. For ease of reference, when examples are quoted, the ST is first presented in full, followed by the TT. A close backtranslation into English is provided in square brackets for all German language utterances.

In analysis of the German STs, it emerged that German MEPs employed both categories of inclusive and exclusive *we*, but made greater use of the latter. *We* was frequently used to refer to *we, the parliamentary community*, predominantly as a form of exclusive *we*, as in "Wir haben die Verpflichtung, die europäischen Bürgerinnen und Bürger vor potenziellen Terroristen zu schützen" [We have the duty to protect European citizens from potential terrorists], where the we group of *we, the parliamentary community* is distinct from the category of European citizens. The generic inclusive *we*, as in "Wir

---

[3] Official permission to analyze interpreter output was not sought, given that the debates and their interpreted versions are in the public domain. Anonymity of all interpreters is guaranteed by this procedure.

müssen deutlich machen" [we need to make clear], was used surprisingly infrequently in the original German interventions. There was also evidence in individual interventions of *we-shift* or use of the *wandering we* (Petersoo 2007:429), defined as "not a single type of 'we', but rather a particular usage that can be traced only within a paragraph or whole article" (*ibid.*). The shift generally tended to occur from the exophoric inclusive *we* to the specific exclusive *we* and back again. The ideological implications of such multiple voices and the complexity of identity construction and negotiation via this wandering *we* will be discussed in detail in the comparative analysis. Although both categories of inclusive and exclusive *we* were also found in original English language interventions, these interventions were characterized by a far higher frequency of use of the generic inclusive *we*, compared to original German language interventions. The exclusive *we* was used far less frequently in comparison, although the wandering *we* – from the inclusive to the exclusive *we* – was employed by several English-speaking MEPs for rhetorical and ideological effect.

In the following sections, detailed comparative analysis of three types of *we* group use in the ST and TT will be presented. Section 3.1 addresses the ideological significance of stable *we* group use in both ST and TT, followed by discussion of ST/TT shifts in *we* group reference in section 3.2. The concluding section, section 3.3, investigates the high number of occurrences of inclusive *we* group reference in the TT which had no equivalent trigger in the ST and discusses the potential ideological consequences of this finding.

3.1   No ST/TT shift in *we group use*

Before moving on to discuss ideologically salient shifts in the use of *we*, it is important to mention which *we* group identities remained unchanged in the simultaneous interpretation. It is not only the investigation of shifts, but also the investigation of what in-group identities are maintained that can offer insight into the ideological significance of SI in identity negotiation.

Use of the exophoric exclusive *we* to refer to an indeterminate Western or European in-group – as opposed to the out-group of Guantánamo detainees, the subject of the debate – was prevalent in the original German interventions. This *we* group reference was maintained throughout in the English interpretation, suggesting that, ideologically, this dichotomy of *we, the community of values* and *they who violate such values* is relatively stable for both the speaker and the interpreter. In Example 1, the speaker is Martin Schulz, German MEP and Chairman of the Socialist Group in the European Parliament (PES).

Example 1 (IE3_Schulz)

> **ST.** Die Überlegenheit, die wir für uns gegenüber der Philosophie von
> Terroristen beanspruchen, hat etwas damit zu tun, dass wir sagen: Wir

gestehen auch demjenigen seine fundamentalen Rechte zu, der sie seinerseits durch seine Aktionen anderen vorenthalten will.
[The superiority that we claim for ourselves over the philosophy of terrorists has something to do with (the fact) that we say: we also allow that person his fundamental rights who wants to deny others those rights via his actions]

TT. and this is something that we say...we say...we are superior to terrorists' philosophy and that's because of these values. We say these are fundamental rights and we allow them the fundamental rights which they take away from others. That...that demonstrates our superiority.

In this use of exclusive *we*, Schulz clearly delineates between an in-group (*we*) and an out-group (*terrorists*), as well as an in-group (*we*) and a member of an out-group (*that person*). Such positioning is ideologically salient as it typifies the dichotomy of inclusion and exclusion (Foucault 1981) that is central to the creation of group identity. In addition, the indeterminate use of the exophoric exclusive *we* is of interest here as it could potentially refer to a whole number of in-groups (such as *we, the West*; *we, the Europeans in general*; *we, the EU*; *we, the EP*). This is also a syntactically complex German utterance which makes extensive use of anaphoric pronominal reference. The co-referents are determinate in the original German utterance due to gender and case markings of the terms *demjenigen* (that person, masculine in the dative case and hence indirect object) and the definite article *der* (who, masculine in the nominative case and hence in subject position). Despite this determinate reference, such syntactical structures are difficult to process during the linear activity of SI due to the effort needed to recover the co-referents. This is a good example of the "trade-off" in the use of pro-forms, where "compactness might become so extreme that no savings in effort are attained after all, because energy is drained away reconstructing things" (Beaugrande and Dressler 1981:80). Although Beaugrande and Dressler were discussing the effort required by the listener or reader in reconstructing such co-reference, such insights are equally relevant to the simultaneous interpreter in their role as listener. In the simultaneous interpretation, the interpreter completely restructures the utterance by avoiding the syntactically difficult surface structure of the original while maintaining the clear *us* and *them* identities of the ST. In order to do this, significant cognitive effort would normally be required. In this case I would argue that this *us* and *them* dichotomy is so stable that it provided a general ideological frame of reference which enabled this syntactically difficult utterance to be disambiguated.

This consistency is also maintained with the second out-group created in the German language interventions via the use of the exclusive *we*. In this case, European citizens are allocated out-group status. These in- and out-group identities are maintained in the English simultaneous interpretation, as

Example 2 demonstrates. The speaker here is Hartmut Nassauer, German MEP and Vice-Chairman of the Group of the European People's Party (Christian Democrats) and European Democrats (EPP-ED).

Example 2 (IE1_Nassauer)

> **ST.** Wir haben die Verpflichtung, die europäischen Bürgerinnen und Bürger vor potenziellen Terroristen zu schützen
> [We have the duty to protect the European citizens from potential terrorists]

> **TT.** These people are potential terrorists and we have a duty to protect Europe's citizens from potential…terrorists

In this example, Nassauer uses the exclusive *we* as a distancing strategy and draws on the image of MEPs as representatives of EU citizens, rather than positioning himself as a European citizen himself. This positioning allows him to identify himself as part of the institution of the EP (*we, the parliamentary community*) and quite probably of the EU as a whole, and is replicated in the English interpretation. It is ideologically salient in terms of the democratic role of the EP within the institution of the EU as a whole, and this saliency is maintained in the interpretation.

Further, in the English interventions, in contrast to the German interventions, there is extensive use of the exophoric inclusive *we* which is maintained in the German interpretations. This is found particularly in the interventions by Alexandr Vondra, Czech President in Office of Council, as can be seen in example 3.

Example 3 (ID2_Vondra)

> **ST.** As we are all aware, during his first days in office President Obama in fact made three decisions.

> **TT.** Aber…wir wissen ja alle…in den ersten Tagen im Amt hat Präsident Obama diese drei Entscheidungen gefällt
> [But….we all know (of course)…in the first days in office President Obama made these three decisions]

This use of the inclusive *we* is widespread in political rhetoric and serves to strengthen the feeling of solidarity and sense of common knowledge of a particular community – in this case, most probably *we, the parliamentary community*. It is particularly prevalent in Vondra's concluding statement, in which he seeks to establish consensus both in the Parliament, across the political spectrum, and between the Council, Commission and Parliament. This identifying use of the inclusive *we* is reproduced here, as in the other four cases of its use, as *wir alle* [we all], despite *wir alle* not having been used at all in any of the German language interventions. A possible explanation is that the choice reflects the significance of the situational setting in SI, suggesting that interpreters view themselves as belonging to the institution of the EP and appear to identify themselves as active participants in the plenary part-session. Further research on how interpreters view their status in the EP, possibly depending on whether they are permanent staff interpreters or freelance auxiliary interpreters, would have to be conducted to substantiate this very tentative suggestion.

Later in this same intervention, Vondra continues his use of the exophoric exclusive *we*, as in Example 4.

Example 4 (ID2_Vondra)

> **ST.** We believe that these decisions, taken together with the decision to close Guantánamo, which I have already mentioned, will further strengthen cooperation with the US in countering terrorism.
>
> **TT.** Wir glauben, dass diese Entscheidung im Einklang mit der Entscheidung zur Schließung von Guantánamo, von mir bereits erwähnt, die Zusammenarbeit mit den USA im Kampf gegen den Terrorismus weiter stärken werden.
> [We believe that this decision, together with the decision to close Guantánamo which has already been mentioned by me, will further strengthen cooperation with the USA in the fight against terrorism]

Although the same type of *we* is used here, the exophoric referent is different, as Vondra is clearly referring to the Council which he represents in this debate (at this point the Parliament had not yet voted on the issue). This is an example of the use of the wandering *we* (Petersoo 2007:429) and appears typical for this particular speaker, whose use of the inclusive *we* 'wanders' from the generic inclusive *we* to the specific inclusive *we* of *we, the Council* and back again throughout his intervention. This could be interpreted as evidence of Vondra's attempt to construct and indeed negotiate his identity both as part of the larger European Union community (inclusive generic *we*), and as the representative of the Council (specific inclusive *we*). The German interpretation replicates this shift, indicating that the negotiation of multiple (institutional) identities has been identified.

3.2   ST/TT shift in we *group use*

In contrast to the absence of shifts in the use of inclusive *we* in interpreting from English into German, in interpreting from German into English the inclusive *we* seems to undergo a shift in terms of ideological positioning. In example 5, the speaker is Elmar Brok, German MEP and member of the Group of the European People's Party (Christian Democrats) and European Democrats (EPP-ED).

Example 5 (IE1_Brok)

> **ST.** Wir haben sehr deutlich gemacht, dass die Einrichtung von Guantánamo einen Bruch internationalen Rechts darstellt und dass dies auch ein Verstoß gegen die Menschenrechte ist
> [We made very clear that the institution of Guantánamo breaches international law and that this is also a violation of human rights]
>
> **TT.** I've been to Guantánamo together with a colleague and my view is that this eh was a breach of international law…this eh camp

In this example, the generic *we* is used as part of a formulaic phrase in German, *deutlich machen* [to make clear], which occurs twice in this particular short intervention. The phrase *wir müssen sehen* [we have to see] also occurs twice in the same intervention. These formulaic phrases appear to be part of the idiolect of this particular speaker, as noted in previous data (cf. corpus data in Beaton 2007b). This form of inclusive generic *we* is used in political argumentation to establish statements and points of view as facts, rather than as claims made by a certain speaker. In this particular example, the claim that can be 'clearly' made in the original is one in which a group states that the camp was in breach of international law. In the English interpretation, in contrast, this becomes a personal opinion, thus differentiating the individual view (of MEP Brok) from that of the colleague he refers to or indeed the wider Parliament. Ideologically, the result is a softening of the legitimacy of the claim made and a weakening of the inclusive *we* group created by the original intervention.

In the English ST, two particular uses of *we* to indicate MEP positioning appear to undergo a shift in the German simultaneous interpretation. One such instance involves the use of the wandering *we* by non-institutional representatives. A second involves the use of *we, the European Parliament*.

Example 6 demonstrates the use of the wandering *we* in the English interventions; the speaker is Graham Watson, British MEP and Chairman of the Alliance of Liberals and Democrats for Europe in the European Parliament (ALDE).

Example 6 (ID1_Watson)

> **ST.** But Europe cannot stand back, shrug its shoulders and say that these things are for America alone to sort out. We lack the open debate

and the collective change of will which American democracy allows...
So the challenge of Guantánamo, the problem posed by 245 suspects
floating outwith the justice system, is not an issue for America alone.
It is a conundrum we must solve together.

TT. Aber Europa kann sich auch nicht zurücklehnen und sagen
„das ist jetzt ja das amerikanische Problem – das müssen die selber
lösen"...Wir brauchen hier den entsprechenden positiven Willen...
Und...das...jetzt...diese Gefangenen nicht im luftleeren Raum bleiben
können, ist nicht nur Aufgabe der Amerikaner – das ist ein Problem,
was wir gemeinsam lösen müssen.
[But Europe cannot just sit back and say "(of course) that is now an
American problem – they have to solve it themselves"...we need the
relevant positive will... and...that...now these prisoners cannot
stay in a vacuum (this) is not just the task of the Americans – that is a
problem that we must solve together.]

In the original English intervention in Example 6, the first use of *we* is
anaphoric and exclusive, referring back to *Europe* and othering *America*. The
speaker then shifts in the final sentence to the inclusive *we*, which appears
to refer to both *America* and *Europe*. This is key to Watson's argumentation
strategy, in which he first creates two distinct groups of *us* and *them* before
bringing them together in the use of the solidarity pronoun, the inclusive *we*.
It provides clear evidence that the inclusive and exclusive *we* are not static
and clearly delineated categories and appears to support Fairclough's view that
in political discourse there is a "constant ambivalence and slippage between
exclusive and inclusive 'we'" (Fairclough 2000:35). In the German interpretation, in contrast, this juxtaposition of the two camps is diluted in the first
sentence with reference to Europe as a noun in subject position and America
reduced to an adjective in object position in the phrase *das amerikanische
Problem* [the American problem]. Reference to America is then completely
omitted in the second sentence of the interpretation, which erases all further
reference to the latter of the two groups constructed by the speaker. Although
on the surface level, *wir* [we] in the very general phrase *Wir brauchen hier
den entsprechenden positiven Willen* [we need the relevant positive will] could
potentially be viewed as an anaphoric reference to *Europe*, it is more likely to
be interpreted as a shift towards the inclusive generic *we* (i.e. to 'I + all people).
Indeed *man* [one] could have been used in this phrase with the same effect.
Therefore, I would argue that the *wir* [we] in the statement is inclusive and fails
to replicate the parallel construction of the Self and Other that is present in the
first part of the original via use of the exclusive *we*. The second occurrence of
wir [we] in the interpretation is also inclusive. In the German interpretation,
the shift towards the wandering *we* is significantly diluted and the positioning
and identity construction involved in moving from the specific to the general is

not replicated. It could then be argued that, in this particular instance, the dual positioning of the speaker as a European and part of a transatlantic partnership is not conveyed to the same extent in the German interpretation.

Specific group identity is also created via the use of *we* in the English interventions. This can be seen in Example 7, where the speaker is again Graham Watson.

Example 7 (ID1_Watson)

> **ST.** Many of us have criticized America in the past for its failure to work with others. We were right to do so, but our help may now be sought and we would be wrong to say 'no'

> **TT.** Wir haben unsere Stimme erhoben…wir waren richtig. Jetzt appelliert man an uns und es wäre falsch, nein zu sagen
> [We raised our voices…we were right. Now one appeals to us and it would be wrong to say no]

In this example, Watson, in his role as Chairman of the ALDE group, is making the point that *many of us* but not 'all of us' have criticized America in the past. In doing so, he is constructing an in-group by identifying himself and his political group with the *many of us* while distancing that group from the *we* of the Parliament as a whole. In turn, the subsequent instances of *we* and *our* refer back to the *many*, not to Parliament as a whole. This creation of an in-group within a group is lost in the interpretation, where the inclusive *we* referring to *we, the Parliament* replaces the specific *we* group of those who criticized America in the past. This is ideologically significant since the voice of those who criticized America in the past, a voice activated via the specification of the in-group within the *we* group in the English intervention, is silenced in the German interpretation.

3.3   Shifts from zero to we *reference*

By far the largest category of shifts that have an impact on ideological positioning involves the introduction of *we* reference in the simultaneous interpretations where it does not exist in the original interventions. These shifts fall into a number of categories. First, there is a shift from the use of a definite noun or noun phrase such as *The European Union* to inclusive *we* reference. This is the most frequent shift observed in the data. Second, there is an occasional shift from the use of the out-group marker *they* in the original intervention to use of the inclusive *we*. Although not prevalent throughout the debate, this type of shift seems ideologically salient and thus worthy of discussion. Third, a shift from a passive to an active construction employing the inclusive *we* could also be observed.

One of the most interesting shifts observed in the debate involved the replacement of a definite group such as *The Presidency, Ministers, The European Union* with inclusive *we*. Multiple shifts of this type can be seen in Example 8, from Alexandr Vondra's initial intervention.

Example 8 (ID1_Vondra)

> **ST.** I therefore believe that you have welcomed, as has the Council, President Obama's decision to close Guantánamo within a year. The Presidency expressed this sentiment through a statement which was issued shortly after President Obama signed the Executive Orders. The ministers unequivocally welcomed this decision at the last General and External Affairs Council meeting, as you probably know.

> **TT.** Wir haben eine Erklärung abgegeben...Wir begrüßen also diese Entscheidung wie auch die letzten Außen...die Außenminister, die es beim letzten Außenrat getan haben
> [We issued a statement...We welcome the decision as well as the last external...the foreign ministers who did it (welcomed the decision) at the last External Affairs Council]

In the original English utterance, two active agents are explicitly named (the Presidency and the Ministers ... at the last General and External Affairs Council meeting). A distinction is thus explicitly made between the Czech Presidency, which Vondra represents, and the ministers attending the General and External Council meeting (usually the Foreign Ministers of the respective member states). The German interpretation introduces two shifts, from the noun phrases to the inclusive *we* form, which in both cases can be understood as referring anaphorically to the Council (and in the second case, anaphorically to the first occurrence of *we*). In the interpretation, both instances of *we* can thus be understood to refer to the Council, with the foreign ministers added in as a second active agent. This has the ideological effect of backgrounding[4] the active role of the Czech Presidency and foregrounding the institutional role of the Council.

Another interesting shift from definite reference to the inclusive *we* occurs in relation to regional identity, as in example 9. The speaker is Wolfgang Kreissl-Dörfler, German MEP and member of the Socialist Group in the European Parliament (PES).

---

[4] I refer here to the textual device of foregrounding/backgrounding discussed in Fairclough (1992:59). In the current study (as in Beaton 2007a), foregrounding/backgrounding refers to the change of weighting of certain terms in the TT when compared to the ST. Items which feature more frequently in the TT than in the ST are 'foregrounded' in the interpretation, whereas those which feature less frequently in the TT than in the ST are 'backgrounded'.

Example 9 (IE3_Kreissl-Dörfler)

> **ST.** München beziehungsweise die dort lebenden Uiguren wären zum
> Beispiel bereit, diese Uiguren aufzunehmen, sie zu unterstützen, sie
> auch zu betreuen, damit sie ihre traumatischen Erlebnisse verarbeiten
> können.
> [Munich or the Uighurs that live there would, for example, be prepared
> to take these Uighurs in, to support them, to look after them, so that
> they can process their traumatic experiences]
>
> **TT.** But we should be ready for example to have the Uighurs from
> China, they've been through traumatic conditions and we should be
> able to help heal them…so why not the same here too?

The regional Bavarian identity of Kreissl-Dörfler, expressed via the
explicit agent of Munich and further qualified by *beziehungsweise die dort
lebenden Uiguren* [or the Uighurs that live there], is important in framing his
criticism of the Bavarian Home Secretary with respect to his stance towards
Guantánamo, later in the same intervention. This regional identity is omitted
and replaced by the exophoric inclusive *we*, probably referring to *we, the EU*.
As a result, the function of the EP plenary session as a forum in which German party political differences are being played out is blurred. In subsequent
criticism in this intervention, Kreissl-Dörfler voices concern at the reaction
of Joachim Hermann, the Bavarian Home Secretary and representative of
the Bavarian Christian Socialist Union (CSU),[5] to the potential transfer of
former Guantánamo detainees to Germany. That criticism is almost completely
omitted in the German simultaneous interpretation. Together with the shift in
example 9, it arguably results in one layer of the identity of Kreissl-Dörfler
as an MEP being lost, namely his Bavarian, regional identity. On the other
hand, it could also be argued that Kreissl-Dörfler's intervention was primarily
directed, not at the multilingual general audience of the EP, but at the German-
speaking MEPs in general and those from Germany in particular, perhaps even
more specifically at those from the EPP-DE political group who share the
same domestic political persuasion as the Bavarian Home Secretary, namely
members of the German Christian Democratic Party (CDU) such as Hartmut
Nassauer. Thus the interpreter's failure to convey the layers of 'voices' in the
MEP's intervention could be seen as part of a process (albeit subconscious)
of selecting only what is deemed 'relevant' to the multilingual context of the
Parliament itself. The ideological effect, however, is that the heteroglossic
nature of the EP as a forum for the negotiation of these competing identities
is downplayed and the institutional voice, the dominant institutional ideology,
is strengthened.

There are further, interesting occurrences of identity shift resulting from

---

[5] Sister party of the larger German Christian Democratic Union (CDU).

the introduction of *we* reference in the TT where it is not used in the ST. Example 10, from Alexander Vondra's first intervention in the debate, demonstrates an interesting shift from *they* to *wir* [we].

Example 10 (ID1_Vondra)

> **ST.** Ministers at last week's Council discussed ways in which the member states might be able to offer practical assistance to the US and, in particular, whether they might accept former detainees.
>
> **TT.** Die Frage ist natürlich, sind wir bereit ehemalige Häftlinge zu übernehmen?
> [The question is of course, are we prepared to take on former detainees?]

In the English intervention, the pronoun *they* is used to refer anaphorically to EU member states. The question is therefore posed from the point of view of the ministers (at last week's Council), who, in the above sentence at least, are viewed as distinct from the member states. The member states are thus allocated out-group status and are othered. In the German simultaneous interpretation there is a shift in perspective when the *they* reference to the member states in the original is replaced with the exophoric inclusive *we*. This shift in identification transforms a Council question about the member states into a question that *we, the member states, the EU* have to ask of ourselves. As a result, the distinction in the English intervention between the Council and the member states is lost and the signalling of multiple identities weakened. Ideologically, there appears to be an identification on the part of the interpreter with the member states and the EU as a whole, with a consequent shift from out-group to in-group use.

There are also several instances where the passive voice is replaced by an active structure featuring *we* in the simultaneous interpretation. The extract in Example 11 is from Alexandr Vondra's intervention.

Example 11 (ID1_Vondra)

> **ST.** However, it was agreed last week that a common political response would be desirable and that the possibility of coordinated European action could be explored further.
>
> **TT.** Aber letzte Woche haben wir gesagt, dass es natürlich wünschenswert wäre, eine gemeinschaftlich politische Antwort zu finden und, dass wir uns überlegen können, wie wir handeln wollen.
> [But last week we said that it would of course be desirable to find a common political answer and that we could think about how we want to act]

The exact referent of the *we* used in the interpretation is unclear from the context, but it may be understood to refer to the EU as an institution. There is therefore stronger identification with the agent of the decisions, statements and actions in the interpretation than in the original utterance. There could be many reasons for a shift of this type occurring in simultaneous interpreting from English into German. One potential reason is the high formality of the German passive and the difficulty of formulating it in this context. Another trigger for a shift of this type could be the spontaneity of the simultaneous interpretation as opposed to the original intervention, which would have been written to be read by a non-native speaker. This example in particular features a tendency towards oralization of the text, evidenced in the use of the active rather than the passive and the use of the particle *natürlich* [of course], which is more prevalent in oral discourse. Irrespective of the reasons, the ideological effect of this shift is ultimately a strengthening of interpreter identification with the institution of the EU as a whole.

5.   Conclusions

Investigating the details and impact of interpreter choices does not imply that the multilingual versions produced by interpreters are unreliable or unprofessional, but it does raise questions about the nature of interpreting practice and it contests the "the commonly held assumption…that translations simply are the source text – in a different code" (Mason, in Preface to Calzada Pérez 2007:XV). The findings of this descriptive study may help us address some of these questions productively.

Some instances of *we* use appeared relatively stable and were found to undergo little or no change during interpretation. These can be split into two major categories. First, the ideologically salient opposition of in- and out-groups via the use of the exclusive *we* is maintained in interpretation from German into English. The fact that these in- and out-groups were maintained in simultaneous interpretation from German into English, sometimes despite highly complex syntactic structures and the cognitive processing involved in recovering anaphoric reference, indicates fairly stable ideological frames of reference for both the MEPs and interpreters. Second, use of the exophoric inclusive *we* and of the wandering *we* by an institutional representative in English interventions appears to have been maintained in the German simultaneous interpretations. This again could be interpreted as signalling awareness of ideological markers and potential ideological identification with the institution of the EU on the part of the interpreters. Both of these categories of *we* use indicate that certain aspects of the ideological salience of *we* positioning on the part of MEPs appear to be recognized and reproduced by interpreters in both the English and German booths.

Some instances of *we* use were found to undergo shifts in the simultaneous interpretations. In German into English simultaneous interpretation, exophoric inclusive *wir* [we] was replaced with *I*, resulting in an ideologically salient shift in the inclusiveness and validity of the claim made, as well as evidence of interpreter influence on the negotiation of MEP identity. In the reverse direction, from English into German, there appears to be a difference in the degree of ideological salience for the interpreter in the use of the wandering *we* by institutional and non-institutional representatives. Unlike the wandering *we* of the institutional representative, which is identified and replicated in the interpretation, the rhetorical force of the wandering *we* used by the non-institutional representative is weakened in the simultaneous interpretation.

Perhaps the most significant finding in terms of ideological positioning is that, on a significant number of occasions, the use of *we* in both the English and German TTs is not triggered by a similar use in the relevant STs. Rather, such use, predominantly of the inclusive *we*, is independently introduced in the TT. This use of inclusive *we* falls into three distinct categories. First, definite noun or noun phrase reference to particular bodies and institutions is replaced by the inclusive *we*. Ideologically, this appears to strengthen the speakers' (and interpreters') identification with the institution of the EP and the EU as a whole and position them as part of this institution, at the expense of regional and minority identities. Second, the out-group marker *they* is occasionally replaced by the inclusive *we*. This signals explicit ideological positioning of the interpreter as part of the institution. Third, an observed tendency to replace passive constructions with active constructions using the inclusive *we* suggests a strategy of oralization of written texts on the part of the interpreters. This mode shift is ideologically salient since the inclusive *we* introduced in the simultaneous interpretation enhances ideological identification with the institution on the part of the speaker and the interpreters.

This study has thus revealed a trend in the simultaneous interpretations of interventions in this particular debate towards intensified use of the inclusive *we* to refer to *we, the parliamentary community* and *we, the EU*, at the expense of more peripheral identities such as the national, regional and political group. This points towards a tendency of SI to strengthen the dominant institutional presence, ideology and identity and weaken or fail to represent the full complexity of the 'traffic in voices' (Bakhtin 1981) and heteroglot identities that characterize such an institution.

Ideological identification with the institution, as manifest in extensive use of the inclusive *we*, could potentially point towards interpreter identification with that institution. The findings of the current study support those of earlier research, which suggested that the provision of simultaneous interpreting in multilingual institutions such as the EP is in itself ideologically significant (Beaton 2007a, 2007b). Further research is needed to establish whether this strengthening of ideologically centripetal forces can be conceptualized in terms of the co-optation of interpreters by the institutions that employ them.[6] Ideally,

---

[6] See Inghilleri (2007:208) for discussion of this concept in the context of the UK asylum system.

future research should aim to triangulate results of text and discourse analysis of a larger corpus with ethnographic research into the interplay between the way interpreters conceptualize their own identities and the effect of simultaneous interpretation on the portrayal and perception of MEPs' identities in the European Parliament.

References

Angermeyer, Philipp S. (2005) 'Who Is "You"?', *Target* 17(2): 203-26.

Bakhtin, Mikhail M. (1981) *The Dialogic Imagination: Four Essays*, edited by Michael Holquist; trans. Caryl Emerson and Michael Holquist, Austin & London: University of Texas Press.

Beaton, Morven (2007a) 'Interpreted Ideologies in Institutional Discourse. The Case of the European Parliament', *The Translator* 13(2): 271-96.

------ (2007b) *Intertextuality and Ideology in Interpreter-mediated Communication: The Case of the European Parliament*, unpublished PhD thesis, Edinburgh: Heriot-Watt University.

Beaton-Thome, Morven (forthcoming) 'Interpreting Europe', unpublished manuscript.

de Beaugrande, Robert and Wolfgang U. Dressler (1981) *Introduction to Text Linguistics*, London & New York: Longman.

Berk-Seligson, Susan (1990) *The Bilingual Courtroom: Court Interpreters in the Judicial Process*, Chicago: University of Chicago Press.

Blommaert, Jan (2001) 'Investigating Narrative Inequality: Analyzing African Asylum Seekers' Stories in Belgium', *Discourse & Society* 12(4): 413-49.

Bot, Hanneke (2005) 'Dialogue Interpreting as a Specific Case of Reported Speech', *Interpreting* 7(2): 237-61.

Bührig, Kristin and Bernd Meyer (2003) 'Die dritte Person: Der Gebrauch von Pronomina in gedolmetscheten Aufklärungsgesprächen' (The Third Person: The use of pronouns in interpreted diagnostic interviews), *Zeitschrift für Angewandte Linguistik* (Journal for Applied Linguistics) 38: 5-35.

Bull, Peter and Anita Fetzer (2006) 'Who Are We and Who Are You? The Strategic Use of Forms of Address in Political Interviews', *Text and Talk* 26(1): 3-37.

Calzada Pérez, María (1997) *Transitivity in Translation. The Interdependence of Texture and Context. A Contrastive Study of Original and Translated Speeches in English and Spanish from the European Parliament*, unpublished PhD Thesis, Edinburgh: Heriot-Watt University.

------ (2007) *Transitivity in Translating. The Interdependence of Texture and Context*, Berne: Peter Lang.

Directorate General for Interpretation website. Available at: http://scic.ec.europa.eu/europa/jcms/j_8/home (last accessed 18 January 2010).

Diriker, Ebru (2004) *De-/Re-Contextualising Conference Interpreting: The Interpreter in the Ivory Tower?*, Amsterdam & Philadelphia: John Benjamins.

European Parliament Multimedia Library: http://www.europarl.europa.eu/eplive/archive/default_en.htm (last accessed 18 January 2010).

Fairclough, Norman (1992) *Discourse and Social Change*, Cambridge: Polity Press.

------ (2000) 'Discourse, Social Theory and Social Research: The Discourse of Welfare Reform', *Journal of Sociolinguistics* 4(2): 163-95.

Foucault, Michel (1981) 'The Order of Discourse', trans. Ian McLeod, in Robert Young (ed.) *Untying the Text: A Post-Structuralist Reader*, Boston, London & Henley: Routledge & Kegan Paul, 48-78.

Fowler, Roger (1985) 'Power', in Teun A. van Dijk (ed.) *Handbook of Discourse Analysis*, London: Academic Press, 61-82.

Gaiba, Francesca (1998) *The Origins of Simultaneous Interpretation: The Nuremburg Trial*, Toronto: University of Toronto Press.

Hale, Sandra (1997) 'The Treatment of Register Variation in Court Interpreting', *The Translator* 3(1): 39-54.

------ (2004) *The Discourse of Court Interpreting*, Amsterdam & Philadelphia: John Benjamins.

Halliday, Michael A. K. and Ruqaiya Hasan (1976) *Cohesion in English*, London: Longman.

Henriksen, Line (2007) 'The Song in the Booth. Formulaic Interpreting and Oral Textualisation', *Interpreting* 9(1): 1-20.

Inghilleri, Moira (2007) 'National Sovereignty versus Universal Rights: Interpreting Justice in a Global Context', *Social Semiotics* 17(2): 195-212.

Íñigo-Mora, Isabel (2004) 'On the Use of the Personal Pronoun We in Communities', *Journal of Language and Politics* 3(1): 27-52.

Koskinen, Kaisa (2008) *Translating Institutions: An Ethnographic Approach*, Manchester: St. Jerome Publishing.

Krouglov, Alexander (1999) 'Police Interpreting. Politeness and Sociocultural Context', *The Translator* 5(2): 285-302.

Leech, Geoffrey and Jan Svartvik (1975/1994) *A Communicative Grammar of English*, London: Longman, second edition.

Mason, Ian (2004) 'Text Parameters in Translation. Transitivity and beyond', in Lawrence Venuti (ed.) *The Translation Studies Reader*, second edition, London & New York: Routledge, 470-81.

------ (2006) 'On Mutual Accessibility of Contextual Assumptions in Dialogue Interpreting', *Journal of Pragmatics* 38(3): 359-73.

Maltby, Matthew (2008) *Interpreting Policy in Asylum Applications in the UK*, unpublished PhD thesis, Manchester: The University of Manchester.

Marrone, Stefano (1998) 'Is It Possible to Translate Institutional Terms? A Pragmatic Approach', *The Interpreters' Newsletter* 3: 72-4.

Maryns, Katrijn (2006) *The Asylum Speaker: Language in the Belgian Asylum Procedure*, Manchester: St Jerome Publishing.

Marzocchi, Carlo (1998) 'The Case for an Institution-specific Component in Interpreting Research', *The Interpreters' Newsletter* 8: 51-73.

Monti, Cristina, Claudio Bendazzoli, Annalisa Sandrelli and Mariachiara Russo (2005) 'Studying Directionality in Simultaneous Interpreting through an Electronic Corpus: EPIC (European Parliament Interpreting Corpus)', *Meta*

50(4*) CD-ROM*. Available at: http://id.erudit.org/iderudit/019850ar (accessed 18 January 2010).

Mühlhäusler, Peter and Rom Harré (1990) *Pronouns and People: The Linguistic Construction of Social and Personal Identity*, Oxford: Basil Blackwell.

Petersoo, Pille (2007) 'What does "We" Mean? National Deixis in the Media', *Journal of Language and Politics* 6(3): 419-36.

Reddy, Michael J. (1979) 'The Conduit Metaphor – A Case of Frame Conflict in our Language about Language', in Andrew Ortony (ed.) *Metaphor and Thought*, Cambridge: Cambridge University Press, 284-97.

Riggins, Stephen H. (1997) 'The Rhetoric of Othering', in Stephen H. Riggins (ed.) *The Language and Politics of Exclusion: Others in Discourse*, Thousand Oaks, CA: Sage, 1-30.

van Besien, Fred and Chris Meuleman (2008) 'Style Differences among Simultaneous Interpreters', *The Translator* 14(1): 135-55.

van Dijk, Teun A. (1997) 'Political Discourse and Racism. Describing Others in Western Parliaments', in Stephen H. Riggins (ed.) *The Language and Politics of Exclusion: Others in Discourse*, Thousand Oaks, CA: Sage, 31-64.

------ (1998) *Ideology: A Multidisciplinary Approach*, London & Thousand Oaks: Sage.

Vuorikoski, Anna-Riitta (2004) *A Voice of Its Citizens or a Modern Tower of Babel? The Quality of Interpreting as a Function of Political Rhetoric in the European Parliament*, unpublished PhD thesis, Tampere: Acta Universitatis Tamperensis 317.

Wadensjö, Cecilia (1998) *Interpreting as Interaction*, London: Longman.

Wallmach, Kim (2002) '"Seizing the Surge of Language by Its Soft, Bare Skull": Simultaneous Interpreting, the Truth Commission and "Country of My Skull"', *Current Writing* 14(2): 64-82.

Wodak, Ruth (2007) '"Doing Europe": The Discursive Construction of European Identities', in Richard C. M. Mole (ed.) *Discursive Constructions of Identity in European Politics*, London: Palgrave Macmillan, 70-94.

On EU Communication 2.0
Using Social Media to Attain Affective Citizenship

KAISA KOSKINEN
University of Tampere, Finland

> *Communicating Europe is now a primary task for the EU.*
> Margot Wallström, Vice-President of the European Commission
> and Commissioner for Institutional Relations and Communica-
> tion (2005-2009)

Abstract. *In recent years the European Union institutions have put considerable emphasis on communicating their message to their European constituencies. To achieve the aim of creating affective European citizenship they have introduced new methods and tools for improved interaction. This article offers an overview of these new communication methods, focusing on the use of social media tools (blogs, EUtube) and other web-based communication. These methods are analyzed within a framework provided by audience design, and their impact on institutional translation practices in the European Commission is discussed.*

In recent years, the European Union institutions, most notably the European Commission, have focused on ways and modes of communicating with European citizens. A number of related documents have been published (see, for example, European Commission 2007) and several initiatives have been introduced. The newly drafted and implemented communication strategies involve novel departures from earlier principles and methods. The most notable changes are, firstly, the extent to which the EU is present and visible on the Internet, and, secondly, the new methods for establishing both participatory policies and dialogic interaction with the various constituencies. In this article I will chart these new developments from the perspectives of e-participation, social media and active and affective citizenship, to determine who is invited to participate in the dialogue and to delineate the kinds of challenges and opportunities which the new communication strategies present for the translators working for the European Commission.

The new communication strategies are a product of a rethinking of the type of governing that has been practised across the various levels and institutions of administration. Governance has been defined as a *relationship* between institutions and citizens (discussed in more detail below), and communication can thus be seen as an integral part of governance, since communication is involved in both constructing and maintaining that relationship. When communicating, the partners in this relationship, i.e. the European Commission and the European citizens, construct images and concepts of both themselves and the other partners. On the one hand, each participant communicates their understanding of the social role they are assuming in the dialogue and presents a particular image of their social identity and their social framing of the particular situation (Bora and Hausendorf 2006:35-36). On the other hand, the communicating partners also project particular images of their intended audiences, and they orient their style according to the communication partner, either gearing it towards that of their intended audience, in order to express solidarity or intimacy with them, or introducing stylistic deviation, to express distance (Bell 2001:141). By looking at these stylistic orientations, we can make assumptions about the intended audiences. The taxonomy of audiences, developed by Bell (1984) and introduced in translation studies by Ian Mason (2000), is as follows:

- Addressees – listeners whose presence is known, who are ratified participants in the exchange and who are directly addressed;
- Auditors – listeners who are not directly addressed, but who are known and ratified;
- Overhearers – known but non-ratified listeners who are not addressed;
- Eavesdroppers – non-ratified listeners of whom the speaker is unaware.

Not all audience members are equally important; the taxonomy presents a cline of diminishing status and importance, i.e. the addressees will exert more influence on the text producer than the auditors who, in turn, are more influential than the overhearers (Mason 2000:4). For their part, eavesdroppers, by definition, cannot affect the message. Bell also introduced a fifth group, that of referees. This is a high-status audience, one that the text producer tries to identify with and impress, even when addressing another audience (Bell 2001:163). In this paper I analyze the new communication methods employed by the European Commission from the point of view of social positioning and audience design; my aim in doing so is to ascertain what kinds of social roles and framings are being constructed and what levels of intimacy and affectivity are being employed.

1.   Governance and e-participation

One of the buzzwords for the contemporary Internet culture is 'Web 2.0'. This term is used to refer to web applications which focus on creativity and social networking (e.g. SecondLife, Facebook), the sharing of user-generated content (e.g. Youtube, blogs), interactive collaboration and participation in the production of content (e.g. wikis). Web 2.0 may thus be regarded as peer-to-peer media (Häyhtiö and Rinne 2008:17). Parallel to these developments in Internet cultures, governing institutions have been designing ways of increasing participation on the part of their citizens. The term 'governance', as opposed to classic 'government', has been coined to reflect the aims of enlarging civic participation beyond the traditional procedures of representative democracy by mobilizing citizens' cognitive and moral resources (Magnette 2003; cf. European Commission 2001). Governance has been described as "a relationship between any governmental institution and other social actors communicating with these institutions and with each other, i.e. citizens" (Bora and Hausendorf 2006:28). In other words, governance is fundamentally about interaction and dialogue, and citizens therefore play a crucial role in its success.

'Governance 2.0' is therefore a term used to highlight strategies for e-participation and the introduction of various web-based communication strategies. This trend, made possible by increased digitization and the continued development of information and communication technology, is visible at all levels of governance, from the local level (e.g. community online forums) to the national level (e-voting, online discussion with decision makers, etc.) and also in intergovernmental and transnational institutions such as the European Union (for more on e-participation and e-governance, see Molinari 2008).

One of the trendsetters for the new governance strategies was the Organization for Economic Co-operation and Development (OECD). In 1998, its proposed Multilateral Agreement on Investment (to establish a framework for investment liberalization and investor protection) failed after serious confrontations with various civil society organizations. This failure led to a period of reassessment which resulted in a new policy of greater participatory and dialogic interaction with civil society and a new communication strategy based on transparency, openness, dialogue and participation (OECD 2001). In many ways, this resembles the process around the new EU Treaty proposed a few years later; the referendums in the Netherlands and France in 2005, in which people showed their lack of support for the new constitution, sent the EU spiralling into a crisis of legitimacy. During the 'period of reflection', the communication strategies were revised, and a Plan D "for democracy, dialogue and debate" was drafted (European Commission 2005b, 2006; see also Koskinen 2008a:64-67). The idea of e-government was not new to the European Union; the 1990s had already seen the launching of a number of initiatives to increase the use of information technology in various administrative processes. That earlier approach had, however, been largely managerial in its style (Chadwick and May 2003:290-92), whereas Plan D was decisively participatory in its rhetoric. The core values of communication promoted by Plan D and its follow-up documents are openness and transparency, active citizenship and a strategy of 'going local'. These values and their practical implementation will be discussed in more detail below.

Similar to Plan D, the OECD has also promoted the spread of web-based participatory strategies of government as tools for engaging citizens and for enhancing trust and legitimacy:

> ICT can help build trust by enabling citizen engagement in the policy process, promoting open and accountable government and helping to prevent corruption. Furthermore … e-government can help an individual's voice be heard in the mass debate. (OECD 2003:12-13)

However, a fundamental difference exists between two modes of e-participation: *administrational e-democracy* and *actionism* (Häyhtiö and Rinne 2008:14). The initiatives of various governing institutions are based on a perceived lack of participation by the people (e.g. a low voter turnout in elections); to solve the problem of this democratic deficit, these institutions have set up forums and methods to engage citizens. On these administrational forums the institutions set the agenda, the framework and the deadlines for participation, but are often disappointed by the lack of forum activity on the part of citizens. At the same time, however, many people actively take part in political processes set up and created by themselves, often with the support of the Internet. In addition to the e-activities of traditional NGOs, active political involvement by citizens can also be witnessed in actions which include privately initiated online petitions and support or pressure groups, SMS alerts for protest action, activist peer-to-peer discussion forums and Facebook hate groups. In this way, citizens find channels for action which are beyond the control of governing administrations. A core distinction is therefore made between activity *by* the people and activity *for* the people (*ibid.*:12). In contrast to Web 2.0, this 'Governance 2.0' is not peer-to-peer, but administration-to-people. As noted, there may be little active involvement by citizens on institutional sites; similarly, actionist forums do not often welcome official contributions (on the challenges of creating a dialogue between the institution and the people, see also Koskinen 2008b).

2.   Active and affective citizenship

2.1   Active citizenship

Documents relating to the new EU communication strategy place particular emphasis on the concept of active citizenship. The participatory models of governance presuppose and require partners who are willing to play the roles designed for them. It is interesting to read these documents from the point of view of interpersonal relations. In *Communicating Europe in Partnership* (European Commission 2007), for example, an entire chapter is devoted to 'Empowering Citizens'. This chapter opens with a description of the needs of European citizens: they "feel that it is important to be informed", "want to know more about their rights as citizens" and "think that available information on the

EU is useful and interesting", but also "insufficient" (*ibid*.:6). Additionally, "there is a desire for a more open debate" (*ibid*.). The rest of the chapter, however, is about the Commission "developing", "launching", "targeting", "taking stock", "involving the citizens", "communicating", "managing networks" and "stepping up the activities of the public and civil society". Consequently, the 'active' citizens are seen as the target of institutional activities, not as partners in dialogic interaction.[1] This is typical of administrative texts; the institution assumes the role of a 'star player' (Koskinen 2008a:144-45). This social positioning also introduces a top-down element that does not fit too easily with the ideas of sharing, collaboration and the democratic generation of content that are inherent in the metaphor of 'Web 2.0'.

The institutional discourse on active citizenship is indeed a mixture of empowerment and paternalism. The background factors, including problems in Treaty ratification and less-than-optimal voter turnout in previous European Parliament elections, are explicitly addressed in the documents, as demonstrated by the following statement:

> Today, more than ever, the debate on Europe must be taken beyond the institutions to its citizens. This was emphasized by the 2007 June European Council which underlined the crucial importance of reinforcing communication with the European citizens, providing full and comprehensive information on the European Union and involving them in a permanent dialogue. This will be particularly important during the Reform Treaty ratification process and as we approach the 2009 European elections. (European Commission 2007:3)

It is thus made clear that the aim of the new communication strategies is to provide "full and comprehensive information" so that the citizens-cum-voters will 'do the right thing' (cf. Kantola 2003:209).

The rhetoric of European citizenship employed by the European Union institutions stresses the active role of citizens; to take the discussion further, it is first necessary to consider what is meant by citizenship in the European context.

2.2 Three dimensions of citizenship

Institutional attention has tended to focus on the 'active' dimension of the concept of 'active citizenship' but has devoted much less discussion to the notion of 'citizenship' itself. However, an analysis of that concept, both in general

---

[1] The term 'partnership' in the title of the document is not to be understood as a partnership between the EU and its citizens; it refers instead to a partnership between the various EU institutions. This partnership has also been formalized in a joint declaration (European Parliament 2009).

and in the EU context, can provide insights into the successes and failures of 'communicating Europe'. Citizenship is a contested concept that has been widely discussed in the academic literature (Bora and Hausendorf 2006:26). One way of analyzing the different aspects of citizenship is to perceive it as being composed of three distinct dimensions: formal, instrumental and affective. No polity can survive in the long run without establishing and maintaining a durable link between these three facets of citizenship (Jones 2001).

Formal citizenship consists of a set of legal provisions endowing individuals with a formal membership of a polity and defining the rights and duties involved. Formal citizenship grants the members various rights, such as the right to information and the right to participation, voice and standing (Bora and Hausendorf 2006:40). It can also legislate in areas such as domicile registration, taxation, schooling or voting. In the case of European citizenship this formal dimension of citizenship is not optimally developed. As an illustration, Article 8 of the Maastricht Treaty (1992) stipulates that "[e]very person holding the nationality of a Member State shall be a citizen of the Union". It follows that the right to define formal European citizenship is conferred on the national authorities, putting European citizenship firmly in a secondary position with respect to national citizenship. Likewise, it follows that formal European citizenship is beyond the reach of anyone who, for one reason or another, has not obtained citizenship in the member state in which they reside.[2] To combine the notion of formal citizenship with the taxonomy of audience, this means that some subgroups of the potential audience for the communication efforts intended to enhance European citizenship are, from the outset, assigned the role of overhearer, as they lack the legal ratification to become addressees.

The *instrumental* dimension of *citizenship* concerns the "instrumental purposes that the polity fulfils to its members" (Jones 2001:145). The provision of security, material benefits and other public goods can be measured in very pragmatic terms but, on a more fundamental level, instrumental citizenship provides a test for the legitimacy of the polity: "the putative 'citizens' must be persuaded that these are viable public goods, are best supplied by the polity in question, and have a reasonable chance of being supplied in practice by that polity" (*ibid.*:147). The core message of 'communicating Europe' seems to be directed at this challenge, i.e. trying to convince the 'putative' citizens of both the viability of the public goods and of the role of the European Union in supplying them. However, the supranational (rather than truly transnational) nature of European citizenship may be a serious obstacle if the intended audience remains unimpressed by what it adds to the rights and benefits they already enjoy on the basis of their national citizenship.

---

[2] The notion of denizenship opens up interesting avenues in this respect (see Atickan 2006, Cronin 2008).

In contrast, instrumental citizenship is crucially important for the development of the third dimension: *affective citizenship*. Affection and loyalty towards a polity grow and develop through sustained provision of the valued forms of institutional citizenship (*ibid.*:145). In many ways, these three dimensions of citizenship can be seen as developmental stages; formal citizenship is the basis for instrumental citizenship which, in turn, can foster the development of affective citizenship. Affective citizenship is "the bedrock upon which the polity rests and upon which it has to call when it is confronted by serious challenges and potentially costly decisions and courses of action" (*ibid.*). The EU documents emphasize active citizenship but it may well be that affective citizenship is the goal the document writers have in mind. One can also argue that it is, in many ways, a challenge for the European Union to cultivate this third stage of citizenship. While audience design starts from the idea of the communicator designing the audience they have in mind and wish to address, affective citizenship in a sense turns this around; affection makes you *wish to be addressed* or *accept* the role of the addressee, creating a dialogic or sympathetic relationship or bond.

3. Affectivity in communicating Europe

3.1 Barriers to affectivity

For a number of reasons, affectivity is not a straightforward issue for the European Union institutions. First, the sheer geographic distance of the institutions from the location of most Europeans may be seen by some as creating an alienating distance: 'Brussels bureaucrats' sit in their glass-walled palaces in their own world, far removed from us, and we only see glimpses of them on the news. Second, the hierarchies of power and the enormous difference in size between a multifaceted and complex supranational institution and local citizens create tension, even when institutions do their utmost to operate dialogically and democratically; the communicating partners are simply not on equal footing.

Third, there are a number of issues related to linguistic differences and language policies in the European Union, the most crucial being the ever more widespread use of English in the EU institutions. According to a recent survey, 44% of people living in the European Union speak only their mother tongue (Eurobarometer 2006:8-10). Monolingualism varies across the Member States (from 1% in Luxembourg to over 60% in the UK and Ireland) and the trend is declining, from 47% in 2001 (*ibid.*). Nonetheless, this means that nearly half of all European citizens (and more than half of the population in six EU countries) can only be addressed if the message is drafted in their own language; for messages drafted in other languages they cannot even be eavesdroppers, let alone addressees. It is also evident that the demographic profile of this monolingual group is rather distinct from the multilingual Europeans at the other end of the continuum. These are described in the same survey as being young, well educated and from a multilingual background, i.e. they live in a different EU country from the one in which they were born or from which their parents come. Their status as students or professionals often requires the use of foreign languages and they are motivated to learn (Eurobarometer 2006:10).

Importantly, language is also a strong identity marker (Bell 2001:160) and the affective aspects of using one's own language versus a foreign one are thus potentially significant. It is an age-old adage that if you are selling something you need to speak the customers' language. Multilingualism, and the equal status of all official languages, is also a cornerstone of the EU's language policy. The new communication strategies, some of which seem to prioritize English, will be discussed in more detail in the next subsection. However, from the point of view of audience design, this policy opens up interesting questions concerning the preferred audiences to be targeted. The addressees might perhaps fit the profile presented above (and they are also assumed to have ICT skills and access to computers). In the Eurobarometer survey, English is by far the most commonly studied and most widely spoken foreign language, and it is also the language that the respondents considered to be the most useful to them. For the younger generations who have grown up with videogames, MTV and Internet English, English may well be less foreign than other foreign languages, and their attitude towards using English may be different from that of previous generations. They may be positively predisposed towards English, and may regard the confident use of English as giving them membership of an international elite (for a similar attitude towards non-translated English advertisements in post-communist Hungary, see Cronin 2003:97). If the European Commission is trying to reach this young audience, then tapping into the affective elements of English in the repertoire of the young may be a clever policy. But is it also a step towards an English-only, or 'English-mainly' Europe?

3.2   Virtual affinity?

To overcome the barriers of affectivity discussed above, the European Commission is relying heavily on computer-mediated communication; consequently, the various modes and methods of e-communication, as well as the use of social media tools, play a growing role in its communication strategies. The web presence of the European Commission is extensive, and the Europa portal (http://ec.europa.eu) is a gateway to almost everything the Commission produces – if one can manage to navigate through the masses of sites and archives. The framework documents for the new communication strategies stress the need for European citizens to acquire more knowledge and information (see section 2.1 above). The Europa portal can be perceived as a celebration of transparency, but its unmanageable size also reminds us of the view that, like lying, secrecy and propaganda, information overload is also a tool of manipulation (Goodin 1980). As Michael Cronin observes, information overload is a common feature of late modernity: "we may be producing (and translating) larger and larger quantities of information but we may not quite know what to do with it" (2003:65).

3.2.1 Blogging

The potentially most directly engaging (and engaged) form of addressing lay audiences presently being used by the European Commission is blogging. The Swedish commissioner with responsibility for communication, Margot Wallström, was the first commissioner to set up her own blog, in 2005. Blogging activity has increased so that, by August 2009, there were ten commissioners and seven members of European Representations writing blogs on the Commission pages (http://blogs.ec.europa.eu/). In the commissioners' blogs English dominates (with some entries mainly in French). Although readers appear to have the option to choose different language versions, the blog entries of only one commissioner (Vladimír Špidla) actually appear in four different languages; on other blogs the apparent multilingualism applies only to the interface and not to the blog content. In contrast, the representations' bloggers use local languages. This indicates a division of labour in audience design; the commissioners seem to be mainly targeting a pan-European audience (well versed in English), whereas the representations' bloggers address more local constituencies and, through their linguistic choice, delimit the number of overhearers and eavesdroppers.

These blogs do not adhere to any uniform 'EU layout' or visual image; even login systems, terms of use and other policies vary. Blogging is clearly not a highly regulated activity in the Commission. Lack of regulation is in tune with the personalized ethos of blogs, but it is perhaps slightly unexpected for an institution that has tended to control its outreach activities. The style, content and levels of personal engagement of the writers vary considerably. The blogs also appear under different titles; in addition to *Blog* they are called *Diary*, *Theme of the Week* and *Latest News*. The different names also indicate a varied attitude towards interaction: *Latest News* implies little expectation of the addressees responding. The commissioners generally receive zero to ten replies for their blog articles, and some do not even include a response mechanism (a feature often considered an essential element of blogs). At least one of the blogs has house rules that explicitly rule out responding to comments: "This blog intends to provide a forum for discussion and as a general rule there will be no direct response to the issues raised by contributors" (Stavros Dimas' blog).

Margot Wallström's blog seems to have secured a steadier readership than the others, and features the liveliest debate (postings typically receiving 20-60 replies, sometimes even more than 150). It is, however, not quite a dialogue between the Commission and interested addressees, since Wallström (or even the impersonal moderator) rarely responds to the messages posted on the site. However, frequent visitors often discuss issues amongst themselves, responding to each others' postings.

In some responses to blog entries people ask for comments from the commissioner or representative or complain about not having received any for their prior postings, but these requests and complaints also remain unanswered. The Commission strategy is also different from, for example, newspapers inviting regular readers to establish their blogs on sites managed by the papers; there are no user-generated blogs on the EU sites.

Blogging is an interesting new medium for institutional communication and, since it is inherently personalized, it has tremendous potential for affective communication. For this reason, the commissioners' blogs merit analysis. For closer scrutiny I selected the most recent entries, at the time of writing, from the blogs of three commissioners: Margot Wallström (Vice President of the European Commission and Commissioner for Institutional Relations and Communication) because of her pioneering role in this context; Mariann Fischer Boel (European Commissioner for Agriculture and Rural Development) because of the centrality of agriculture in EU politics; and Meglena Kuneva (European Commissioner for Consumer Affairs) because I assumed that consumer issues might be of general interest. Analysis of even this small data set indicates clearly the versatility of this genre within the European Commission.

Meglena Kuneva's blog is the newest of the three (started 30 September 2008). It is fairly plain in its design, and the blog entries are text-based. The selected entry ('Consumer policy is on the right track', 6 July 2009) has few explicit addressees; the readers are not directly addressed at all. The role of the writer is also distant. Although the 'I' is explicit (I attended, I delivered, I had a talk with, our objective), it is the institutionalized 'I' of the commissioner who speaks, not Kuneva in a personal capacity. This is clearly deliberate; the entry discusses a report on consumer tactics, and the topic would have easily allowed for either a personal note or a direct appeal to the readers to contemplate their own consumer habits. This rather distant and non-personalized style is reciprocated in the four responses to the entry, all written in English. They are addressed to "Dear Commissioner Kuneva" (making us other readers overhearers) and, rather than responding to the entry as such, they contain general praise or criticism: "Thanks for your very important work, It is proud of yours to take a decision to stay to the end of mandate [sic]" and, finally, "You are a very good puppet, dear commissioner".

Mariann Fischer Boel's blog was started on 15 January 2007. Its visual appeal relies heavily on photos; each entry is accompanied by a related photo. In contrast to Kuneva's *I*-centred entry, Fischer Boel's entry ('Dairy sector: keeping the ship steady but straight', 22 July 2009) opens with a statement expressing concern for a group of stakeholders: "The EU's dairy farmers feel like they're sailing through a storm right now". The blog continues to emphasize that "it's real people who are feeling the pain" and then to assert that "EU heads of state and government are very concerned, as am I". The feeling of immediacy and concern is tangible, and the 'I' is affective rather than institutional. The personal involvement is further reinforced at the end of the entry: "I'm 100 % committed to doing just that" (notice the colloquial style). There is also a direct address to the readers: "Do have a look at the paper". This 'you', i.e. the addressee, is not the dairy farmers but anyone interested in agricultural policy, but it is clear that the dairy farmers are also a ratified readership, i.e. the auditors for the entry. There are three responses to this entry, two in German and one in English. They are similar to the ones sent to Kuneva in that they address the commissioner in a very polite way (*Sehr geehrte Frau Fischer Boel*) but they are different in terms of content, since they directly discuss the topic of the entry.

Margot Wallström's first blog entry was published on 13 January 2005. This blog is in many ways more fully developed than the others. The very first entry included comments on the 2005 tsunami in South East Asia, on fado music and on how she had gained weight over Christmas. Other commissioners tend to stick to topics related to their field of responsibility, but Wallström continues to cover a wide range of issues, from daily news to her personal interests and pastimes and even more personal commentaries. This versatility enhances the blog and helps keep a wide readership interested.

The selected entry ('Climate justice', 24 June 2009) is a formal and factual piece on the concept of climate justice, based on a meeting on the topic in Åre, Sweden on that particular day. From the point of view of audience design, the entry contains few clues, apart from an inclusive 'we' in "So how do we manage climate change and achieve climate justice". The six responses are therefore rather striking in their tone (there are only six, and one commentator points out that this lack of response may be an indication of the topic being too boring). In contrast to the polite messages addressed to the other commissioners, these either have no address at all and go straight to the point, or address Wallström on a first name basis: "Margot, don't bore us with you [sic] climate hysteria". The tone is more or less hostile in all six: "You've left your public behind, Mrs W", or, "Listen up, cerebrally challenged commissioner – Go away totalitarian antidemocratic regime. Make yourself extremely scarce. Go away now". Now this may seem harsh but can, in fact, be interpreted as a normal state of affairs, due to the longer life span, regular readership and engaged blogging style of this blog compared to those of many other commissioners. This kind of dialogue is to be expected between a representative of a big institution and a section of avid internet users. The lack of it on other blogs makes one suspect that they are either not read at all or that a (too) strict moderator constantly removes messages from the site. If the aim of blogging is to enhance affective involvement, Wallström's blog seems to be succeeding.

The majority of the responses are, in spite of their occasionally aggressive style, constructive in intent. The first response to this entry is a case in point. It is not addressed to Wallström at all but to anyone who is interested in reading more and taking action on the issue: "Do you want to get involved in the process". Wallström remains an auditor whose presence is tacitly acknowledged and who is given indirect advice on how to better inform the citizens: "So here is the White Paper of the Commission the Commissioner finds too difficult for you to read" [link to the document]. The comments rarely discuss language policy, but this entry interestingly contrasts white papers and blogging:

> It [the White Paper] is available in all languages of the member states. Because most EU documents get translated. Just the blog posts of a Commissioner are not translated because these communications is not so important, just directed to citizens.

3.2.2   Audiovisualization of EU communication

One mode of communication recently employed by the EU is clearly targeted at the young generation, and it is based on the idea of reaching out to them where they already are, in this case on YouTube, a popular participatory site for sharing and viewing video clips. The European Union has set up their own 'EUtube' (http://www.youtube.com/EUtube) where new video clips on the various policies of the EU are regularly posted. Many of these video clips are best described as infotainment or promotional material.

The EUtube site is trilingual (English, German and French) but the amount of material on the English site far exceeds that of the other two languages. The role of language is, however, reduced by the more dominant role of sounds and images; some of the video clips include words only in their title, and they play entirely on visual effects such as cartoons and music. The viewings vary: 'Film lovers will love this', the collected lovemaking scenes from European films promoting EU support for filmmakers, has been viewed more than seven million times, whereas clips offering basic information on the European Union may have been viewed a few hundred times.[3] EUtube is entirely unresearched, but it raises new questions about the role of multimedia and the power of visual images in institutional communication. EUtube is directly addressed to young viewers; these recent communication methods indicate that the young may

---

[3] The viewings for each video clip are given on the site.

function as a referee group for the European Commission. In EUtube, this crucially important audience is addressed by messages posted on the forum and by mimicking their preferred means of expression.

EUtube is only one example of the growing trend of using audiovisual media in administration. The same trend can also be seen in the blogs; many of them use visual elements, and Viviane Reding, the Commissioner responsible for Information Society and Media, bases her blog entirely on video clips. The European Commission has also taken steps towards using European radio and television networks to put forward its messages (see European Commission 2008). The idea is to support and sponsor programmes adapted and reused by local broadcasters. The European Commission itself is not, to my knowledge, currently broadcasting TV programmes, either on commercial channels or on the Internet, but the European Parliament offers subtitled news and interviews as well as interpreted live transmissions from the Parliament (among other things) on its multimedia site (see http://www.europarltv.europa.eu/). It would be interesting to examine the figures for these initiatives to see how many of the intended addressees are actually aware of these messages.

3.2.3 Localization

These e-communication strategies are based on computer-mediated communication and on a virtual presence that is predominantly English. At the same time, the communication policy documents also offered opportunities for the development of strategies for crossing geographic barriers and reaching out to local audiences. To this end, translators were placed in local representations in the Member States with the explicit task of localizing press releases, adapting and selecting them according to local needs (this activity and its institutional background are described in more detail in Koskinen 2009). While some translators had been seconded to local representations before, the role of these local 'antennae' had been controversial. This new strategy thus deviates both from the previous policy of employing translators in Brussels and Luxembourg and, even more significantly, from the ideal and the ideology of delivering the same message to all citizens in all official languages. Obviously, translators have always targeted their translations to a particular linguistic subgroup, but they had never before been given explicit permission to take this into account in drafting their translations. The localized press releases produced by the localizer-translator team in Helsinki, for instance, are targeted primarily at Finnish journalists (addressees), but are also available for other interested Finnish or Swedish-speaking readers[4] (auditors), as well as web surfers (overhearers).

---

[4] Even Finland and Sweden do not necessarily have the same press releases nor the same localized format.

4.   Institutional translation 2.0

If governance shifts to a 2.0 mode, it follows that institutional translation will also need to make a similar shift. The participatory model of governance cannot function without both effective and affective communication; in a multilingual context the same requirements need to be extended to translating as well. Creating affinity and affection through translation is a challenge. Institutional text production has traditionally focused on administrative and legal genres, meticulously drafted and translated but rather heavy to read. The more a text gets reworked by writers or by translators, the more institutionalized its language tends to become (Koskinen 2008a:141; for similar findings in institutional interpreting see Beaton 2007). To achieve the required levels of affectivity, institutional translation 2.0 will need to fight against this tendency and to strive towards a more engaging tenor and style, as well as clarity and readability.[5] In brief, new genres will require new translation strategies.

The emphasis on multimodal web-based communication requires new translator competences for those working for the European Union. In addition to the 'localized' translators, the DGT has set up a specialized web translation unit that concentrates on editing, translating and transediting (i.e. editing while translating) web pages. With the ever-rising number of these pages, it is increasingly evident that the DGT needs more experts in multimedia translation, with skills in information design, localization and online documentation, as well as expertise in combining verbal, visual and audio material. The European Parliament already employs subtitlers, and this trend of multimedialization will become more evident in the future, not only in the European Union, but across the field of institutional translation.

These new skills profiles create challenges for recruitment and training. The DGT has taken an active role in training by introducing the concept of a European Master's in Translation (EMT) that is now being established as a European quality label, and a network of translator training institutions.[6] However, in its present format the EMT model is too narrow and too traditional to accommodate the challenges posed by governance 2.0. The competences expected from the graduates, and the model curriculum, offer little if any support for working with social media and only pay lip-service to audiovisual translation. In addition to the technical skills of using web-based communication tools and combining audio and visual elements (e.g. subtitling for institutional purposes), the translators need enhanced skills on drafting affective and personalized messages. The EMT is work in progress, and it is perhaps to be expected that its first release is a 1.0 model, but if institutional

---

[5] On the thorny issue of readability versus institutionalization, see Koskinen (2008a:147-50).
[6] More information is available on the EMT website: http://ec.europa.eu/dgs/translation/external_relations/universities/master_en.htm.

translation is to meet the new and forthcoming challenges, the training of translators (and their continuing professional development) will need to be geared to an 'EMT 2.0' model.

Institutional translation also faces questions concerning its overall role. One crucial question will be the role of multilingualism in the face of the growing emphasis on English. English is by far the most important source language for translation in the European Commission, and is the *lingua franca* of the everyday workings of the institutions. Translators in all other units translate predominantly from English, and the DGT has also given up the once sacred principle of translating into the mother tongue only and is now actively encouraging a two-way translation policy (Lönnroth 2005). Coupled with the recent difficulties in recruiting translators into English, the DGT seems to embody what Cronin (2003:60) has identified as the dual translation burden for those who do not speak the dominant language in our increasingly English-speaking, "neo-Babelian" world: they, or rather we, will both need to translate ourselves into English and translate from English into other languages. In the light of the examples of new communication strategies discussed above, the burden is, however, often carried by the communicating partners themselves. For instance, the commissioners who blog in English and most of those who comment on their blogs do not have English as their first language. A massive translation project is underway, but one in which EU translators are not taking part.

Technological advances and *lingua franca* solutions do not, however, eliminate cultural distance. Participatory politics call for an increased emphasis on affectivity, thus bringing to the fore the need to address people in their own languages. In a multilingual setting such as the European Union, the role of translators is crucial in achieving this aim. In recent years, the DGT has indeed strengthened its political and institutional status. However, the growing emphasis on affectivity also makes it evident that all translations are not equally successful in reaching their target audience. The framework of audience design is based on the idea that language is always tailored for a particular audience. Governance 2.0 requires particular kinds of translations, i.e. translations that actively try to engage their readers. In order to produce those translations, translators will need to be given a certain amount of leeway in their strategies and choices. And translators in turn will need to accept and adapt to this new agency and the new competences it requires.

5. Challenges of 2.0

The contemporary scene of institutional communication and translation is rapidly evolving, and the new directions and communication strategies are opening exciting new vistas which are rather removed from a stereotyped bureaucratic image of institutional text production. The new landscape poses many challenges to those involved. Firstly, there are a number of institutional challenges. Affectivity and activity are largely ungovernable, and one cannot force emotions or actions on citizens. Pushing too hard may produce a counter-effect; the line between promotional material and propaganda is a fine one, and largely in the eye of the beholder. In some of the new models described above, the risk of an adverse reaction is great. For example, while many find the video clip on lovemaking scenes refreshing, others may be offended by the explicit sexual content. And since popular support is crucial to the institutions, the stakes are high.

Secondly, there are also political challenges. The greatest of these is deciding who is to be addressed, and who is to be invited to participate. Civic participation is always limited, and passive participation is known to be more prevalent at the supranational level (Magnette 2003). But, in addition to the challenge of securing and holding the attention of European citizens, the communication strategies seem to be creating additional blockages for some potential subgroups. Besides subscribing to a particular ideology, to become an addressee one needs to have a particular legal status as well as specific linguistic, communication and computer skills. One could argue that, in order to qualify as an 'active citizen of Europe', one needs to have a set of competences and a predisposition towards European integration. Knowledge of English and a particular demographic profile are considered a bonus.

It is also not easy to introduce truly participatory modes of policy making. As discussed above, the first steps towards e-government were described as managerial in their ethos. Thus far, the new 'participatory' processes employed by the European Commission can be defined as consultative in type; the flow of information is mainly unilinear (from the Commission to the citizens), and the interactive modes are either formal consultations, mainly focusing on stake-holder organizations (Magnette 2003), or venting forums with no direct link to any regulatory processes (e.g. comments on blogs or discussion forums; cf. the discussion of Wallström's blog above). Although the commission is using social media tools such as blogs and video sharing sites, the use is not 'social' in the full sense of the word; the aspects of collaboration, crowd-sourcing and sharing are rarely present. Obstacles to truly participatory processes, peer-to-peer interaction and universal access indicate that the Commission still has a long way to go before its governance model could be described as participatory in practice, and not merely on the discoursal level (for managerial, consultative and participatory modes of e-government, see Chadwick and May 2003:277).

Finally, for researchers interested in institutional communication, the digitization and multimodalization of the field poses new challenges. In addition to the challenge of simply keeping up with new communication strategies, basic research steps such as data collection and analysis need to be reconsidered and new methods employed. One thing is certain: institutional text production will provide fascinating material for researchers for many years to come.

References

Atickan, Ece Ozlem (2006) 'Citizenship or Denizenship: The Treatment of Third Country Nationals in the European Union', *SEI Working Paper No 85, Sussex European Institute.*

Beaton, Morven (2007) 'Interpreted Ideologies in Institutional Discourse. The Case of the European Parliament', *The Translator* 13(2): 271-96.

Bell, Allan (1984) 'Language Style as Audience Design', *Language in Society* 13(2): 145-204.

------ (2001) 'Back in Style: Reworking Audience Design', in Penelope Eckert and John R. Rickford (eds) *Style and Sociolinguistic Variation*, Cambridge: Cambridge University Press, 139-68.

Bora, Alfons and Heiko Hausendorf (2006) 'Communicating Citizenship and Social Positioning. Theoretical Concepts', in Heiko Hausendorf and Alfons Bora (eds) *Analysing Citizenship Talk. Social Positioning in Political and Legal Decision-making Processes*, Amsterdam & Philadelphia: John Benjamins, 23-49.

Chadwick, Andrew and Christopher May (2003) 'Interaction between States and Citizens in the Age of the Internet: E-Government in the United States, Britain, and the European Union', *Governance: An International Journal of Policy, Administration, and Institutions* 16(2): 271-300.

Cronin, Michael (2003) *Translation and Globalization*, London & New York: Routledge.

-------- (2008) 'Downsizing the World. Translation and the Politics of Proximity', in Anthony Pym, Miriam Schlesinger and Daniel Simeoni (eds) *Beyond Descriptive Translation Studies. Investigations in Homage to Gideon Toury*, Amsterdam & Philadelphia: John Benjamins, 265-75.

Eurobarometer (2006) *Europeans and their Languages* 243. Available at http://ec.europa.eu/education/languages/pdf/doc631_en.pdf (accessed 25 March 2009).

Goodin, Robert E. (1980) *Manipulatory Politics*, New Haven & London: Yale University Press.

Häyhtiö, Tapio and Jarmo Rinne (2008) 'Introduction: Seeking the Citizenry on the Internet – Emerging Virtual Creativity', in Tapio Häyhtiö and Jarmo Rinne (eds) *Net Working/Networking: Citizen Initiated Politics,* Tampere: Tampere University Press, 11-34.

Jones, R.J. Barry (2001) 'The Political Economy of European Citizenship', in Richard Bellamy and Alex Warleih (eds) *Citizenship and Governance in the European Union*, London & New York: Continuum, 143-62.

Kantola, Anu (2003) 'Loyalties in Flux. The Changing Politics of Citizenship', *European Journal of Cultural Studies* 6(2): 203-17.

Koskinen, Kaisa (2008a) *Translating Institutions. An Ethnographic Study of EU Translation*, Manchester: St. Jerome Publishing.

-------- (2008b) 'Kansalaiset keskustelevat – kuuleeko EU?' [Citizens are Debating – Does the EU hear them?], in Heli Katajamäki, Merja Koskela and Suvi

Isohella (eds) *Lukija- ja käyttäjälähtöinen viestintä/ Reader- and User-Oriented Commmunication*, Vaasa: University of Vaasa, 138-44.

-------- (2009) 'Going Localized – Getting Recognized. The Interplay of the Institutional and the Experienced Status of Translators in the European Commission', *Hermes* 42: 93-110.

Lönnroth, Karl-Johan (2005) 'How to Ensure the Total Quality in a Changing Translation Market – A European Approach', in Leena Salmi and Kaisa Koskinen (eds) *Proceedings of the XVII World Congress*, Tampere: International Federation of Translators, 30-34.

Magnette, Paul (2003) 'European Governance and Civic Participation: Beyond Elitist Citizenship?', *Political Studies* 51(1): 144-60.

Mason, Ian (2000) 'Audience Design in Translating', *The Translator* 6(1): 1-22.

Molinari, Francesco (2008) '(E-)participation: A Complement to Good Legislation?', in Tapio Häyhtiö and Jarmo Rinne (eds) *Net Working/Networking: Citizen Initiated Politics*, Tampere: Tampere University Press, 127-62.

OECD (2001) *Citizens as Partners. Information, Consultation and Public Participation in Policy-making*, Paris: OECD.

OECD (2003) *The E-Government Imperative*, Paris: OECD.

Key EU documents (accessible through http://eur-lex.europa.eu)

European Commission (2001) *White Paper on European Governance, COM(2001)428*.

European Commission (2004) *Report on European Governance (2003-2004), SEC(2004)1153*.

European Commission (2005a) *Action Plan to Improve Communicating Europe by the Commission, SEC(2005)985*.

European Commission (2005b) *The Commission's Contribution to the Period of Reflection and Beyond: Plan-D for Democracy, Dialogue and Debate, COM(2005)494 final*.

European Commission (2006) *The Period of Reflection and Plan D, Communication from the Commission to the European Council, COM(2006)212*.

European Commission (2007) *Communicating Europe in Partnership. Communication from the Commission to the European Parliament, the Council, the European Economic and Social Committee and the Committee of the Regions, COM(2007)568*.

European Commission (2008) *Communicating Europe through audiovisual media, SEC(2008)506/2*.

European Parliament (2009) *Council of the European Union and European Commission Declaration: Communicating Europe in Partnership, 2009/C 13/02*.

European Union (1992) *Treaty on European Union, 92/C 191/01*.

Positioning and Fact Construction in Translation

JI-HAE KANG
Ajou University, Republic of Korea

Abstract. *This paper investigates the interplay between fact construction and positioning of a translated news magazine article by tracing an intertextual chain in the reporting of a political interview. By investigating how a political interview (speech event) of a South Korean president is recontextualized, first into a Newsweek article and then into a Newsweek Hankukpan – Korean edition – article, the present study argues that the Newsweek Hankukpan (NWH) article's portrayal of itself as a factual information provider is achieved via explicitly distancing itself from its corresponding article in Newsweek (NW). At one level, the level of the magazine as a whole, an overt and formal intertextual relationship based on resemblance and alikeness is evident in terms of a comparable design, layout and colour scheme. However, at the level of the individual text, the NWH article claims that it is an authentic and factual report of the interview and alludes to the possibility that its corresponding NW article may be flawed and misleading in certain parts. By raising questions about the possible lack of journalistic integrity on the part of NW, NWH asserts its commitment to the truth and constructs itself as a reliable and independent source of information. The findings of this study suggest that the relationship between texts in a translational chain is far from stable or consistent and that the positioning of a text, and by extension the positioning of a news institution, is highly flexible, adapting to the distinctive identities and interests of the target readership.*

I n his discussion of translation as rewriting, André Lefevere (1992:9) argues that "translation is the most obviously recognizable type of rewriting and... is potentially the most influential because it is able to project the image of an author and/or (a series of) work(s) in another culture, lifting that author and/or those works beyond the boundaries of their culture of origin". While this view of translation as a form of rewriting is accepted and embraced by many translation scholars (cf. Tymoczko 2007), the issue of whether translation is in fact a 'recognizable' type of rewriting is debatable. For example, Munday (2007:197) argues that deviations in meaning in translation are often "misrecognized" as they "so often [tend] to pass unnoticed, absorbed into reports feeding on a variety of sources or in the co-existence of multiple versions of the same text on websites of all sorts of commercial, governmental and non-governmental organizations". Similar arguments are found in discussions of translations that focus on how changes in meaning may be concealed or obscured as translating agents or institutions decontextualize and metadiscursively recontextualize texts so that they become new texts embedded in a new context of use for a new audience (Mason 1994/2009, Hatim and Mason 1997, Baker 2006a, 2006b).

In the context of the translation of political texts in news media settings, the issue of 'recognizability' of changes or omissions in translation becomes complex due to several key factors that characterize the production and reproduction of news texts. News translation involves working with discourse that is already heavily mediated and recontextualized. The "dynamic transfer-and-transformation of something from one discourse/text-in-context (the context being in reality a matrix of field or contexts) to another" (Linell 1998:144-45) may result in different degrees of extraction of some aspect of prior discourse and of fitting this aspect into another context. Nevertheless, news discourse, whether translated or non-translated, purports to be referential, factual, accountable and reliable, making it particularly challenging for readers to 'recognize' appropriations and deviations in meaning. Translation strategies and methods, including choice of wording, are critically influenced by institutional criteria regarding what constitutes 'factual' and 'credible' discourse.

Despite the accelerated flow of information resulting from spatio-temporal contraction and the intensification of interconnectedness that together characterize globalization (Cronin 2005), the limited number of major news institutions, coupled with the development of state-of-the-art communication technology, have served to centralize the role of these news organizations in the global generation of news content (Boyd-Barrett 1997). The crucial position filled by a limited number of major news organizations has raised serious concern regarding imbalances in the global flow of news content and the worldwide diffusion of reporting about the same events (Marchetti 2002, Morley and Robins 1995), one of the consequences of which is the homogenization of news, i.e., the global spread and imposition of the news-values, frames and categories espoused by these few major players (Giddens 1990). Nonetheless, the trend towards the homogenization of global news is counterbalanced by local pressures (cf. Appadurai 1990); these pressures favour a domesticating strategy which aims at putting news content into frameworks that render these events comprehensible, relevant and acceptable in the local context, as pointed out by Bielsa (2005).[1] Local and national news organizations play an important role in making international news acceptable

---

[1] The emergence and growth of national and regional news media institutions are also challenging the penetration of Western-based news institutions' influence in various regions of the world (Banerjee 2002).

and familiar by particularizing and recasting international information in accordance with the particular frameworks of interpretation shared by local audiences (Clausen 2003, 2004). As Gurevitch *et al.* (1991:206) have argued, news "simultaneously maintains both global and culturally specific orientations" by "constructing the meanings of these events in ways that are compatible with the culture and the 'dominant ideology' of the societies they serve".

To approach the issue from the perspective of a translation of an item of global news by a local news organization is to interrogate the interaction between the practice of news translation and the needs of the global economy, which requires information transfer in the form of news. Tension between the requirements of information transfer and the context of target audience reception poses an ongoing challenge in that there is a constant need to embed and contextualize the source text within the narrative framework of the local context. This point has been argued from diverse perspectives: Barnard (2000) uses the term 'self-censorship' to describe news translation at *Newsweek Japan*; Fujii (1988) describes news translation in terms of 'gatekeeping'; and Orengo (2005) views news translation as a process of 'localization'. These studies point to the cultural and political differences between the relevant cultures and institutions, to differences in journalistic culture, and to the norms and processes that lead to the domestication of news content to accommodate distinctive local perspectives.

In what follows, I intend to explore the ways in which an interview article in a translated news magazine is reframed for a new context by analyzing how news institutions endorse or contest different states of affairs as participants occupy different positions of speaking. I argue that the interview article published in *Newsweek Hankukpan* – Korean edition (NWH) – recontextualizes its relationship with *Newsweek* (NW) by suggesting that the reporting by NW (NWH's putative source) of the particular event under discussion is not accurate. What is suggested is that the positioning of the article in NWH is intricately related to the way in which the local news organization articulates the global organization's projection of the local, and the way in which NWH explicitly and intentionally displays a commitment – which it implies is in contrast to the source text (NW) – to what NWH purports to be the pursuit of journalistic integrity. Because there is no definitive version of truth which can be described unequivocally or in relation to which news articles can be said to 'misinform', what is examined below is how different news institutions may occupy different positions of speaking, and how the positions of speaking may be neither stable nor consistent, especially where translation is involved.

1.   News translation and fact construction

If we accept that most translations involve a translating agent taking a text out of its original spatio-temporal setting and resituating it in a new site for a new audience, the process of translation may be understood as a form of recontextualization (Slembrouck 1999). News translation, in particular, stands out as a uniquely interesting instance of recontextualization in that the two activities involved in news translation, i.e., 'news reporting' and 'translation', respectively involve processes of recontextualization. Given that it generally consists of "embedded talk" (Bell 1991:60) with a metadiscursive context added to the text, news discourse frequently adds to, deletes, compresses or departs from the prior discourse to different degrees during the process of recontextualization (Fairclough 1992). Bell thus suggests that the term *news article* is a misnomer in that the process of making news usable for general consumption entails transforming it into a 'story' with a recognizable "structure, direction, point, viewpoint" (1991:147). What is interesting is that the recontextualized text functions as an 'original'; insofar as readers are not in a position to verify the 'truth' of an event directly or to access anterior discourse, what is reported by journalists often becomes *the* reality.

This 'constructing' function of news is persuasively discussed in Paterson's description of the Bosnian civil war, where he claims that "the war news agencies manufactured for the world was the very war they covered" (Paterson 1997:150). The shaping of perceptions and realities discussed by Paterson is evident in diverse cases of news translation. For example, in her discussion of different English translations of a speech by Osama Bin Laden in 2004, Baker (2006a:333-35) shows how different narratives and disparate realities can be constructed by different translations.[2] Baker's analysis of translated texts, including possible reasons or motivations behind specific choices, reveals that translation is a product of sociocultural processes that involve crucial questions of power and, at the same time, local sites where specific social agendas may be elaborated and pursued.

The discussion above is indicative of the nature of news translation as a socially situated practice (Inghilleri 2003, 2005, Blommaert 2005). Similar to other modes of translation in which the transfer and transformation of information is carried out in a specific institutional setting, news translation is characterized by the centrality of the institutionally embedded processes

---

[2] Translation into English of a passage containing a potentially ambiguous Arabic word, *wilaya*, meaning either "state in the sense of nation/country" or "state in the modern sense of electoral region", resulted in the elaboration of different narratives. *Al-Jazeera* translated the problematic passage as "Your security is in your own hands. And *every state* that doesn't play with our security has automatically guaranteed its own security". In contrast, *MEMRI*, a pro-Israel, US-based monitoring organization, translated the passage as "Your security is in your own hands, and *any [U.S.] state [wilaya]* that does not toy with our security automatically guarantees its own security" (Baker 2006a:333-34; emphasis added). Compared to *Al-Jazeera*'s translation, MEMRI's translation, which was circulated by numerous news agencies and websites – including WorldNetDaily (*"any U.S. state* that does not toy with our security automatically guarantees its own security"*) – presents a different version of events and constructs an altogether different reality for its audience.

involved (Kang 2009). These processes dictate not only how information is transferred but also how voices are managed and orchestrated (Bielsa and Bassnett 2009). Created according to different, sometimes competing, institutional criteria which reflect the attitudes and positions of those involved in the production of (translated) news texts, translations are adapted to the new context of use and made to conform to the norms and practices of the news institution.

2. Textual interaction in news translation

All texts are woven out of threads of other discourses and texts and thus combine or blend multiple voices (Bakhtin 1986). They draw not only on other specific discourses and texts but also on "anonymous discursive practices, codes whose origins are lost" (Culler 1981:103), thus making the task of tracing the origins of specific stretches of a given text immensely difficult, if not impossible in some instances. However, texts also relate to one another in a more visible and chronological sequence which shapes the channels of textual interaction. Fairclough (1992:130) uses the term **intertextual chain** to refer to the textual connection among "series of types of texts which are transformationally related to each other in the sense that each member of the series is transformed into another member in regular and predictable ways".[3] In the case of translation, the intertextual chain formed between the source and target text is 'regular' and 'predictable', in that the interlingual, chronological and formal features that characterize a translation are fairly conventionalized. A target text is sequentially linked to a source text because the process of language transfer normally occurs after the publication of the source text. Formal connection is also crucial in that a target text marks its relationship to the source text in overt ways that can include the display of the title or the source text writer's name, often in the source language.

In the case of news translation, intertextual chains created as a result of recontextualization are characterized not only by their sequential and interlingual nature but also by the way in which their inter-institutional conditions of production influence the transformation of the text. Since news translation is undertaken at various points in the overall process of news gathering and dissemination, intertextual chains are created in different phases of actual speech events and of the generation of texts, with each phase being mediated by individuals working in different institutional contexts.

---

[3] As Solin (2004) points out, most discussions of intertextual relations focus on a distinction between two types of relationships: one based on a view of texts as related to specific prior discourses/texts and the other based on a view of texts as associated with abstract sets of conventions, as evident in the use of such terms as *manifest* and *constitutive intertextuality* (Fairclough 1992), *intertextuality* and *architextuality* (Genette 1997), and *referential* and *generic intertextuality* (Devitt 1991).

In news translation, moreover, the embedded nature of news discourse leads to the formation of an intertextual chain which is characterized by a level of complexity and opacity that may exceed those found in other types of translation. The connection between the source and target text may simultaneously be characterized as 'one-to-many' and 'many-to-one', in the sense that one text may generate multiple versions and, at the same time, multiple texts may produce one text. The 'one-to-many' relationship implies the existence of multiple, sometimes divergent, versions of translations, as exemplified by Baker's account of multiple translations of Bin Laden's speech, discussed above. On the other hand, a 'many-to-one' relationship exists when a variety of source texts are woven into one target text, as Bielsa and Bassnett (2009:16) explain:

> What the study of news translation adds to the debate is in endeavoring to define quite what an original text might be. An original may be thousands of words of text that have to be cut down to a minimum, or it may be a string of loosely connected interviews and versions that have been derived from different sources, and those sources may well have originated in entirely different linguistic and cultural contexts. There is no clear sense of what an original is when we are looking at news translation, and in such circumstances the old idea of translation being an act that takes place across a binary line between source and target can no longer be upheld.

Although Bielsa and Bassnett's comments are made in reference to translation in news agencies, plurality of source texts and intricacy and opacity in the assigning of a translational relationship between texts are both often found in various other modes and contexts of news translation (Palmer 2009).

The many-to-one relationship established between source and target texts, in particular, directly impacts on a news translator's understanding of what constitutes legitimate translation. According to García-Suárez (2005:175-76, cited in Bielsa and Bassnett 2009:65-66), "what is characteristic is that faithfulness to the original text is subordinated to faithfulness to the narrated facts, which, on some occasions and whenever there exists a clear justification allows for the introduction of alterations of meaning". The result is that translators often combine the translating task with other tasks, including that of the journalistic editor (Hess 1996, Palmer and Fontan 2007, Tumber and Webster 2006). According to Palmer (2008:187), news translation is carried out by people "for whom translation is only part of the job description, and may not even be its most important part". Similarly, Stetting (1989:371) uses the term *transediting* to denote "the grey area between editing and translating". Transediting often entails changes in the title and lead, elimination of unnecessary information, addition of important background information, changes in the order of paragraphs and summarizing information.

The intertextual relationship established between the source and target texts in news translation is central to the news translators' intricate act of re-narrating the source text in order to construct and elucidate the reported event for target readers. Furthermore, because news translation is subject to the same requirements of genre and style that dictate journalistic production in general within the target culture, translated news articles manifest different degrees of variation in form, style, content and meaning when compared to the source text.

3. Data and analysis

The data for this study consist of an article published in *Newsweek U.S. Domestic Edition* on 3 March 2003 and its corresponding Korean article, published two days later in *Newsweek Hankukpan*. The articles are based on an interview of the then newly elected South Korean President Roh Moo Hyun, which was conducted on 19 February, shortly before Roh's inauguration on 25 February. The NW article was written by NW journalists George Wehrfritz and Byung Jong Lee, both of whom participated in conducting the interview with Roh; their names appear in the byline of both articles. The NW article is one page long and has the typical format of a news magazine interview article, including the headline and subhead as well as a byline. Introductory paragraphs that outline some background information and the interviewers' impressions of the interviewee are followed by a sequence of questions and answers. As such, the article is different from a typical news article whose structure includes a headline, a subhead, attribution information and a main story consisting of episodes (Bell 1991). The questions in the interview mostly focus on the relationship among South Korea, North Korea and the US. The article is followed by a three-page, in-depth item about Roh and his politics.[4] The NWH article has a similar format, with a headline, a byline and introductory paragraphs followed by questions and answers. However, the interview section is longer (three pages, including a page showing a picture of Roh) and the questions deal with a wider range of issues, both domestic and international. Similar to its corresponding NW article, the NWH article is also followed by the same three-page, in-depth item on Roh.

NWH is a South Korean news magazine published by Joongang Ilbo, one of the largest news companies in South Korea. Under a licensing arrangement

---

[4] As far as the actual interview is concerned, it is not known who did the interpreting or how many people were involved in the interpreting process. As high ranking officials' interviews with foreign press typically involve interpreting processes, it is likely that this interview was mediated by an interpreter. An interpreter for Roh may have mediated the entire communication process alone or may have interpreted only Roh's utterances. The latter scenario is more likely if an interpreter for NW journalists was present or if one of the journalists carried out the interpreting task.

established in 1991 with *Newsweek*, a US-based news magazine published since 1933 and distributed throughout the United States and internationally, Joongang Ilbo publishes a Korean version of this weekly news magazine, retaining similar values and a similar look as well as the *Newsweek* brand name and editorial formula (Joongang Ilbo 1997). The 'licensing arrangement' is an important feature of the South Korean magazine industry, which ranks tenth in the world in terms of volume (Korea Press Foundation 2001). Although the total number of magazines that are published under a licensing arrangement is not large – only 48 magazines in 2001 – many of these, termed 'licensed magazines', have proved successful in the South Korean market (Chun 1997), due in no small part to the prestige of their source magazines. *Newsweek Hankukpan*, for example, is considered a success story, with more than 150,000 copies sold annually since 1994. The Korea Press Foundation (2001:53) attributes this success first and foremost to the "brand power of *Newsweek*".

Each issue of NWH, usually published two days after the publication of NW, consists of both translated articles and articles originally written in Korean by NWH journalists. Due to a 15% ceiling that went into effect at the time NWH was established in 1991, only 15% of the articles included in an issue could be written by NWH journalists (Korea Press Foundation 2001). However, this ceiling was eliminated in 2001 when an agreement was reached concerning the need to include a larger number of news articles tailored specifically to Korean readers. NWH attempts to ensure that up to 30% of an issue consists of stories written by NWH journalists.

The larger sociopolitical and historical context surrounding the interview should also be noted. Of particular relevance here is the status of the relationship between South Korea and the US at the time of the interview, as well as Roh Moo Hyun's positioning vis-à-vis this relationship. Support for the newly elected Roh Moo Hyun largely came from South Koreans who wanted to change the status quo and supported policies that were sympathetic towards North Korea. North Korea still occupies an important place in many South Koreans' vision of nationhood, despite the division of the nation into the capitalist South and the communist North following the end of World War II, the experience of a fratricidal war in the 1950s, and the ensuring antagonism that has lasted for more than 50 years. Furthermore, the South Korean government's policy of engagement with North Korea, implemented since the end of the 1990s, contributed to raising serious questions about US policies towards North Korea; these policies have been based on what some South Koreans consider to be an unfair portrayal of North Korea as threatening and inherently evil. Meanwhile, the US government and media have continued to condemn North Korea due to issues that included its development of a nuclear programme and human rights violations. The tension was most clearly evident in President George Bush's labelling of the North as part of an 'Axis of Evil' in 2002. The data in this study is analyzed against this background.

3.1 Assumed status of source and target text and the image of sameness

A key feature characterizing the intertextual chain connecting NWH and NW is the assumed status of the source and target text. The general assumption is that the starting point of any translation is the source text and that the end point is the target text, although the trajectory between the two points may be marked by complex and recursive processes of translation as well as revision and editing. This conventional translation process characterizes NWH's translation, in that an intertextual chain between NW and NWH is triggered by the selection of an article for translation and because NW and NWH exist in a chronological relationship to each other.[5] The assumed status of NW as the source text and NWH as the target text is verified by such signals as NWH's use of the title *Newsweek*, the formal similarity between the two magazines and the appearance of the original headline and byline in English in small print next to the Korean headline and byline in NWH.

NW   NWH

Figure 1. Front Covers of English and Korean Magazine Issues[6]

Formal similarity between the two magazines brings us to the second key feature of the intertextual chain: the image of sameness. As an explicit and powerful feature of the chain, visual and graphic resemblance is displayed not only in the matching layout and colour but also in photographs, illustrations and graphics, all of which are reproduced and convey an impression of sameness (Figure 1). It is this image of identity that may function as the crucial device

---

[5] See Kang (2007) for a discussion of the process of translation at *Newsweek Hankukpan*.
[6] Every effort has been made to secure permission for reproducing the *Newsweek* covers discussed here.

in reassigning the 'brand power' of NW to NWH. The visual and graphic image of sameness, however, weakens somewhat when the wording of the title is considered. On the cover of NWH, the title declares: 'The Roh Moo Hyun Era, Hope and Unease', followed in smaller print by 'The Participatory Government Raises the Anchor and Sets Sail amid Trouble at Home and Abroad' and 'An Exclusive Interview with President Roh Moo Hyun' (my translation). In the case of NW, the title reads: 'In the Hot Seat' and 'Can Roh Moo Hyun Defuse the Crisis on the Korean Peninsula?'. While both headlines emphasize the challenges that lie ahead for Roh, the article in NW is mainly framed in terms of tension, conflict and a high-pressure situation, as illustrated by the use of such expressions as *hot seat* and *defuse the crisis*. This contrasts with the title of NWH, which juxtaposes *Hope* and *Unease* to frame the article on Roh in more ambivalent terms.[7]

Having briefly outlined formal signals that create an image of sameness between NH and NHW, the rest of the analysis offered below will focus on aspects of the intertextual chain established through choices within the articles themselves. All examples from NWH are back-translated from Korean (see Appendix for full text of Korean article).

3.2 Reframing

As meta-texts, the headline and subhead frame the article and encourage the reader to interpret it from a particular vantage point (Bell 1991, van Dijk 1998, Smith 1999, Geer and Kahn 1993, Price *et al.* 1997). The use of a headline and/or a subhead is a crucial feature of news reporting in that these devices work as strategic cues to direct or manipulate the way people read and make sense of news, as is evident in Extract 1 below.

---

[7] The intertextual chain between the two magazines becomes more complex when both the magazine covers and the articles are compared with their sources texts. The English article examined in this study comes from *Newsweek U.S. Domestic Edition*. However, the intertextual chain established at the level of the magazine cover is formed between NWH and *Newsweek International Edition* rather than *Newsweek U.S. Domestic Edition*. Figure 1 shows the covers of the 5 March issue of NWH and the 3 March issue of *Newsweek International Edition*. The covers display the same picture of Roh Moo Hyun and use a similar layout and similar colours, signalling similarity between NWH and *Newsweek International Edition*. Nevertheless, in terms of news content, the NWH article is connected to one featuring in the *Newsweek U.S. Domestic Edition*. The 3 March issue of *Newsweek U.S. Edition* has a completely different cover, and the 3 March issue of *Newsweek International Edition* does not feature the interview article. NWH is free to choose a news article or part of the editorial material from any of the latest editions of *Newsweek*, including the *U.S. Domestic Edition* and the *International Edition*, which may be further broken down into the *Atlantic Edition*, the *Pacific Edition*, and the *Latin American Edition* (Joongang Ilbo 1991). This policy further complicates the relationship between the source and target text and has consequences for the intertextual chain analyzed in this study.

Extract 1

NW	NWH
A Life-or-Death Issue Some in Washington worry that Roh Moo Hyun is naive about the dangers posed by North Korea. Roh worries that America could ignite a devastating war. By George Wehrfritz and B. J. Lee	**"If North Korea is given what it wants, it will give up nuclear [program/ambition]"** An exclusive interview / Declaring a continuation of the Sunshine Policy, Roh [said] "Rather than punish an immoral government, it would be better to persuade and support [it]" Interview [by]: George Wehrfritz, Tokyo Bureau Chief Byong Jong Lee, Correspondent in Seoul [Article] Presented [by]: Newsweek Hankukpan

The NW headline 'A Life-or-Death Issue', which is part of a quote from Roh, creates a sense of urgency and suggests that the issue discussed in the interview has crucial consequences for those concerned. The nature of this issue is clarified in the subhead, which also foregrounds tension by polarizing Roh and the US government in terms of their views on North Korea. By contrast, the NWH headline and subhead reiterate Roh's views on the solution to the North Korean problem and explicitly state that the article is based on an exclusive interview. The schism between Roh and the US and Roh's concern about a destructive war, both evident in the NW headline and subhead, are replaced with a plain and matter-of-fact description of the new government's North Korean policy and quotes from Roh. The byline in NWH is also different compared to that in NW: more specific information about the interviewers' identities is provided and NWH is clearly presented as the agent responsible for the reporting of the interview.

Other areas of divergence in the way the articles are framed via headlines and subheads are evident here: NW frames Roh as a political leader with intractable differences vis-à-vis the US on matters related to North Korea, while NWH is more descriptive, quoting Roh's assessment of the North Korean problem and its solution. The conflict frame, one of the most dominant frames in news reporting in the US (Neuman *et al.* 1992, Fallows 1996, Zillmann *et al.* 2004), is much more in evidence in NW. While a clear contrast in positions is used as a rhetorical device in NW to evoke the conflict frame, this contrast is backgrounded in NWH, where the difference in opinions is expressed more generally (the act of *punish[ing] an immoral government* is not attributed to any party) and the headline and subhead merely report Roh's plans to continue his predecessor's policy of engagement with North Korea. The articles diverge from each other at the level of lexical choice as well. In NW, the use of modifiers such as *life-or-death* and *devastating* and the phrase *ignite a war* create an atmosphere charged with extreme anxiety and tension. However, the few evaluative lexical items and phrases used in NWH (e.g. *immoral, it would be better to*) lack the sense of urgency communicated in NW.

Differences in the bylines are also significant. NWH not only contains more detailed information in terms of the journalists' titles and the bureaus with which they are affiliated, creating an impression of thorough research and accurate reporting, but also invokes an independent institutional presence (*Presented by Newsweek Hankukpan*) – something not commonly found in other NWH articles.[8] This is especially important when viewed in the context of NWH explicitly making an attempt to distinguish its voice from that of NW. The nature and significance of such choices is examined in detail in the following analysis of the introductory paragraph(s).

3.3   Explicit distancing and strategic use of voicing

While the articles in NWH, published after their corresponding articles in NW, have the status of translated texts, the interview article analyzed in this paper denies its status as a derived version, as evident in the introductory paragraphs that precede the interview with President Roh (see Extract 2).

The introductory paragraphs in Extract 2, which precede the interview with President Roh, provide background information and set the scene for the reader's subsequent understanding of the interview. In the introductory paragraph to the NW article, presented as an *excerpt* of the interview, the tension between Roh and the US is specific and overt. The expressions *loves a good fight, pugnacity, overbearing influence of the U.S.* and *never "kowtow" to America* cumulatively foreground a particular aspect of Roh's character and his evaluation of the US government. The use of *kowtow* within quotation marks is particularly significant in that it resonates with North Korean propaganda.[9] Without any overt signal of the status of the quotation marks, *kowtow* is likely to be interpreted as a verbatim report of what Roh said, thus aligning him with pro-North Koreans and anti-Americans. The diametrically opposed attitude of Roh toward North Korea and the US, as constructed here, is also signalled in the way 'to keep economic and diplomatic channels open to Pyongyang' is juxtaposed with 'he would never "kowtow" to America, but would demand to be treated as an equal'.

---

[8] Most bylines of articles published in NWH in 2003 state only the name of the journalist who wrote the original article. Specific information about the identity of a journalist, such as the name of the bureau, is not provided. However, translated articles that deal with Korea sometimes contain more specific information about the identity of the reporter.

[9] *Kowtow* is one of the many evaluative lexical items often used in English translations of North Korean news provided by the Korean Central News Agency (KCNA), the official news agency of the North Korean government. The word is typically used in a negative and derogatory way to condemn South Korea's close ties with the US (e.g. 'kowtow to such foreign forces of aggression', 'kowtowing to its imperialist master').

Extract 2

NW	NWH
More than just about anything else, Roh Moo Hyun loves a good fight. It was his pugnacity that helped the 56-year-old former human-rights lawyer to win South Korea's presidential election in December, against all expectations. By standing for a clean break from the status quo – as exemplified by the sometimes overbearing influence of the United States – Roh drew unprecedented support from the country's chronically disaffected youth. He promised to keep economic and diplomatic channels open to Pyongyang. And he vowed he would never "kowtow" to America, but would demand to be treated as an equal. Days before his Inauguration – and ahead of a key meeting this week with Secretary of State Colin Powell – Roh talked to NEWSWEEK's George Wehrfritz and B. J. Lee. Excerpts:	President Roh Moo Hyun's interview with *Newsweek* is creating controversy at home and abroad. In the introduction to the interview article (one page long) published in the latest issue (3 March) of *Newsweek US edition*, *Newsweek* [reported] "Roh Moo Hyun likes a fair fight. It was his 'contentious character (pugnacity)' that helped the 56-year-old former human-rights lawyer to win South Korea's presidential election in December, against all expectations. President Roh vowed he would never 'kowtow (kowtow)' to America, but would demand to be treated as an equal."
	However, these expressions do not feature in President Roh's interview. Thus, the two problematic words appear to be *Newsweek* Tokyo Bureau Chief George Wehrfritz's own expressions based on his 'understanding' of President Roh up to that point. When the content of the introduction to the interview with Chief Wehrfritz created a controversy, President Roh's aides protested, stating that "such expressions were never used". Chief Wehrfritz's interview article was published only in the US edition. In the Asian edition/s, an article dealing with President Roh's life was published based on the interview. *Newsweek* is published in several overseas editions including the US edition.
	Newsweek's interview of President Roh took place at his presidential transition office on 19 February, before the inauguration ceremony. He was interviewed by Tokyo Bureau Chief George Wehrfritz and Seoul correspondent Byong Jong Lee.
	Newsweek Hankukpan obtained the entire content of the problematic interview with *Newsweek* and is publishing it [here]. President Roh's remarks at the interview are presented without any additions or omissions.

What is interesting is that the conflict frame, so obvious in NW, is transformed into something very different in NWH. By clearly stating that NWH is an accurate replication of what Roh originally said, 'without any additions or omissions', NWH brings to the fore the issue of fact construction rather than tension and conflict surrounding the complex tripartite relationship and Roh's positioning in relation to it.

The first part of NWH's introductory paragraph ('President Roh Moo Hyun's interview ..... would demand to be treated as an equal') is exceptional in that it makes a deliberate and blatant reference to the prior text, especially in terms of singling out the name *Newsweek*. Not only is *Newsweek* directly referred to but the occurrence of a controversy surrounding the prior text's reporting of the interview is also mentioned. NW's problematic passage is quoted in its entirety, and *pugnacity* and *kowtow* are provided in parentheses in English to help readers gain a better understanding of the nature of the issue.

We see here a distinctive NWH voice which is not only autonomous and separate from NW but also given full textual visibility. By explicitly signalling that NW and NWH are not a unified entity, NWH unequivocally asserts its independent status, contrary to what is conveyed by its overt similarity to NW in terms of the design, layout and use of colours at the level of the magazine as a whole. The NWH voice, which distances itself from the controversy in terms of locally recontextualizing its relationship with NW, seems to be making it clear that the readership, which might include Roh, should not be misled into thinking that NW and NWH are the same entity. This is further reinforced in the next stretch of text ('However, these expressions .... in several overseas editions'). In this stretch, NWH explains the controversy by making an overt distinction between reporting based on facts and reporting based on someone's 'understanding'. Reporting based on facts is attributed to NWH, which is portrayed as having access to specific information (as asserted in the next paragraph) and as reporting from a privileged epistemic position. By contrast, NW is presented as reporting on the basis of one individual's 'understanding'. NWH thus explicitly attributes blame, albeit indirectly, to NW – or to be more specific, a specific NW journalist – for using the problematic words in the article.

What is of particular relevance here is how different actors and their voices are interwoven into the narrative in order to construct NWH's version of events. In particular, the statements of Roh's aides, produced within direct quotes and thus presented as "incontrovertible facts" (Bell 1991:207), assume evidential status by functioning as the main evidence used in holding NW journalists responsible for the act of problematic reporting. This stretch of text thus positions NWH not only as a factual information provider but also as an ethical news outlet that is competent and comfortable in coping with contradictory views and conflicting versions of facts, presented respectively by NW and NWH. This is achieved by drawing a professional, institutional and ethical boundary between NW and NWH, thereby securing NWH's institutional credibility.

NWH also assumes a role in exercising damage control by mentioning that the edition containing the interview article is only one of many editions and thus has limited circulation at the global level. This amounts to NWH acknowledging, albeit implicitly and indirectly, that its institutional identity and credibility remain in certain ways tied to those of NW. Nevertheless, significant sections of the introductory paragraphs are clearly dedicated to distancing NWH and recontextualizing its ties to NW. This is particularly evident in the last two paragraphs of this introductory section (*'Newsweek'*'s interview of President Roh ... without any additions or omissions'); NWH claims legitimacy and accuracy regarding its reporting, as evidenced by its assertion that it has 'obtained the entire content of the problematic interview with Newsweek' and that 'President Roh's remarks at the interview are presented without any additions or omissions'.

3.4 Narrative transformation

Interview questions fulfil an important function in a news story since the design of the question can influence and transform the message of the interviewee to a significant extent. In his study of broadcast interviews, Nylund (2003) argues that the final news output is more similar to the assumptions expressed in interviewers' questions than it is to the replies of the interviewees. The preliminary idea of what the news story should look like determines how the interview is conducted and how it is edited into the final story. This observation is echoed by other scholars, who suggest that the story that reaches the audience is no longer the interviewee's but instead the journalist's (Helland and Sand 1998, Clayman 1995). Altheid goes as far as saying that journalists "seek evidence which support the storyline" (1974:76) and that a news story is already fairly set before the journalists set out for the interview.

The questions asked by the interviewers constitute an important dimension along which the interview articles published in NW and NWH diverge. The articles differ primarily in terms of the total number of questions asked: eight questions in NW and eighteen in NWH. The eighteen questions that appear in NWH include the eight NW questions; the key issue here concerns the nature of the questions selected for publication in NW. Extract 3 (overleaf) details a list of specific questions included in NW, followed by another list of questions that were not included but that appear in NWH.

The questions in NWH seem designed to allow readers to gain an understanding of Roh's thinking on social, political, economic and foreign affairs issues and to obtain insight into his past experiences. In contrast, the questions that appear in NW focus on anti-Korean sentiment within the US government, Roh's assessment of US policy, and the North Korean nuclear issue. What is

Extract 3

NW Questions (eight questions)	Questions not included in NW (but included in NWH)
(a) You have demanded an equal partnership with the United States, which worries many Americans. Do you fear an anti- Korean backlash? (b) You praise American values. But do you also think, as do many Asian and European leaders, that Washington is trying to impose its value system on the rest of the world? (c) Can you elaborate? (d) This week Pyongyang threatened to abandon the 1953 armistice agreement that ended the Korean War. How should Seoul and Washington respond? (e) This week the U.S. ambassador in Seoul, Thomas Hubbard, suggested reducing the number of American combat troops in Korea. Might such a move serve to reduce mistrust? (f) You fear abandonment? (g) British Prime Minister Tony Blair has made a very strong moral case for regime change in Iraq. He argues that Saddam has maintained power by causing the deaths of more than a million of his people. Should the same case be made against North Korea's Kim Jong Il? (h) When you meet President Bush, what priorities will you stress regarding North Korea?	(a) A tragic accident has taken place just before your inauguration ceremony. What are your thoughts regarding the Taegu subway fire? (b) One of your aides has told us of your struggle during the 1980s, when you used your car to move and distribute anti-government leaflets in the Pusan area. How has your thinking on political matters changed since then? (c) What is the reason behind your writing a book about President Lincoln? (d) The Bush administration is considering imposing sanctions on North Korea. Do you think that this is an appropriate measure? (e) Won't allegations made against former president Kim Dae Jung regarding his remittances to North Korea hurt your policy of engaging North Korea? (f) Then, will the details [regarding remittances to North Korea] be made public? (g) How is your policy of engaging North Korea different from that of former President Kim? (h) There is concern in Korea that inequality between the rich and the poor is deepening. What priority will policies to enhance equality receive? (i) Attracting foreign investment is necessary for the East Asian economic bloc, but foreign investors are concerned about labour problems in South Korea. As an old friend of labourers, how do you feel about Korean labourers' situation at present? (j) You surprised many people by going to a public bath house even after you were elected president. This kind of open and young behaviour, is this the face of the new government?)

not included in NW are questions dealing with South Korea's social issues (three questions), Roh's personal history (three questions), different aspects of South Korea's North Korean policy (three questions), and the relationship between the US and North Korea (one question). The questions that do appear in NW relate to issues that not only have relevance for US foreign policy and American interests but also support the conflict frame and highlight controversial aspects of Roh's thinking, already evoked in the introductory paragraphs (Extract 2 above). Thus, the interview questions selected for publication by NW function to draw out answers that provide support for creating an image of Roh that is critical of and uncooperative towards the US government.

The articles in NW and NWH also differ in terms of Roh's response to the interviewers' questions. The part of the reply selected for inclusion in a final news output is typically determined by numerous factors, including narrative relevance, conspicuousness and extractability (Clayman 1995). Narrative relevance, in particular, is important in that the quotes that fit into the developing narrative frameworks are the ones most likely to be extracted for use in the final text, as can be seen in Extract 4 (stretches not included in the NW article are shown in italics).

A number of differences can be seen between NW and NWH in Extract 4. Compared to NWH, the question in NW is more direct and straightforward: the demand for an equal partnership is attributed to Roh and the second person pronoun *you* ('You have demanded...', 'You fear ...') is used to single out Roh directly as the actor and the experiencer of an emotion. The NWH question, by contrast, is indirectly formulated. The appeal for an equal partnership is not specifically attributed to one person – perhaps to Koreans in general ('Americans are concerned about the move in Korea towards wanting ...'; 'Won't this situation give rise to anti-Korean sentiment ...').[10] The difference in transitivity ('Do you fear' vs. 'Won't this situation give rise to') and the level of intensity attributed to anti-Korean responses (e.g., 'anti-Korean backlash' vs. 'anti-Korean sentiment') have the combined effect of making the question in NWH more moderate and mitigating the potential for a face-threatening situation.

In response to the question 'Do you fear an anti-Korean backlash?', Roh, in NWH, begins by confirming the interviewers' assumption ('South Koreans are concerned about the threat of an inter-Korean war resulting from a possible US military strike on North Korea') but ends on a positive note, expressing hope for more dialogue with the US and a continuation of cooperative ties. In NW, by contrast, Roh's answer is presented as providing evidence of and support for the view that there is a conflict ('South Koreans feel threatened

---

10 Note also that in contrast to some *Americans* in NW, NWH simply uses 'Americans' – 'Americans are concerned about ...'. This type of generalization makes the claim broader and hence more generally applicable.

Extract 4

NW	NWH
Newsweek: You have demanded an equal partnership with the United States, which worries many Americans. Do you fear an anti-Korean backlash? **Roh:** Most Koreans like the United States and also like Americans. When we think we have been unfairly treated, we may complain or object, but this is different from anti-American sentiment. [Now] major U.S. media and government officials are mentioning the possibility of attacking North Korea. It is a life-or-death issue. A president is responsible for his people's safety. That is why I am asking the United States to refrain from taking too much risk. Some people in the United States are not happy because they interpret this as South Korea siding with the North. They are calling us disloyal, or are saying that we have forgotten what we owe to the United States.	**Newsweek:** Americans are concerned about the move in Korea towards wanting an equal relationship with the US. Won't this situation give rise to anti-Korean sentiment in the US? **Roh:** Most Koreans like the United States and also like Americans. *But sometimes problems occur and* when we think we have been unfairly treated, we may complain or object. However, this is different from anti-American sentiment. *Korean youths stand up to their father and protest when they consider their father to be wrong. (We) are well aware of the historical fact that Korea received a great deal of help from the US and that even now (we) are maintaining stability and achieving economic prosperity through cooperation with the US.* Normal Korea-US relations are not about anti-Americanism or pro-Americanism but about consistently maintaining a friendly and cooperative relationship and resolving conflicts through rational dialogue. Although there are occasionally people in Korea and the US who use extreme expressions and make extreme demands, they are not the majority. Korea up to now has always followed and never opposed the opinion of the US. Korea participated in the Vietnam War and the Gulf War. Korea has sided with the US even when the US went against world opinion. This is natural because of the special nature of the US relationship and even now (we) are trying to do that. *But I have a problem.* Major US media and government officials are mentioning the possibility of attacking North Korea. *Because this could immediately lead to war, Koreans cannot easily agree. In the past, this kind of problem did not exist. Complying with the opinion of the US had never put us in danger of a war. However,* this is a matter of life or death. A president is responsible for the people's safety.

That is why I am asking the United States to refrain from taking too much risk. Some people in the United States are not happy because they interpret this as South Korea siding with the North. They are calling us disloyal, or are saying that we have forgotten what we owe to the United States. *Koreans are worried about this kind of a situation.*

I expect a common position to be reached by consistently engaging in a dialogue with many American policymakers. Korea-US relations will become more cooperative and consolidated when [we] make an effort to find common ground amid different opinions. This will also enable the US to protect its security and economic interest in Northeast Asia.

and the US government feels that South Korea is being disloyal in siding with North Koreans'). In particular, NW ends on a negative note, with Roh stating that the US government has failed to understand the current situation in South Korea.

The difference between NW and NWH becomes clearer when we examine the parts that are left out in NW. The omitted parts include a description of the history of the close relationship between South Korea and the US, Roh's vision of the South Korea-US relationship, the cause for South Koreans' concerns about America's policy towards North Korea, and Roh's eagerness to engage in dialogue and cooperation with the US. In NWH, these same parts (omitted in NW) play an important role in elaborating Roh's narrative – specifically his attempt to reject what is presented as given in the question (that Roh and/or South Koreans are harbouring anti-American sentiment) and to address the issue of possible 'anti-Korean backlash' in a positive way. In NW, however, the interviewers' assumption is weakly denied in that no evidence is provided – note how 'but this is different from anti-American sentiment' is stated without any evidence or elaboration – and Roh's answer is formulated as simply confirming the interviewers' question about the fear of a backlash.

Extract 5 provides another instance of a shift in the narrative, albeit from a different perspective. The interviewers evoke a voice that is critical of the US government (the voice of 'many Asian and European leaders' in NW, the voice of those 'outside the US' in NWH) to ask Roh what he thinks of the US. Compared to NW, NWH is more overt in terms of displaying Roh's resistance to the line of questioning pursued by the interviewers. In particular, when asked to elaborate on what he means by 'unilateralist' aspects, Roh makes a direct reference to the interviewer and the design of the question, and refuses to elaborate on the grounds that it would not be 'polite' to the US

Extract 5

NW	NWH
Newsweek: You praise American values. But do you also think, as do many Asian and European leaders, that Washington is trying to impose its value system on the rest of the world?	**Newsweek:** There is a view outside the US that sees the US as imposing that kind of value system on other countries. Don't you think that the US is going too far with this?
Roh: The new order the U.S. is demanding is, in the main, just. But it also has unilateralist characteristics.	**Roh:** The world order the US is demanding is, in the main, just. But it also has unilateralist aspects.
Newsweek: Can you elaborate?	**Newsweek:** Can you elaborate on 'unilateralist' aspects?
Roh: Aha. [18-second pause] Let's not go too deep into this. I love my wife very much even though I have some dissatisfaction with her.	**Roh:** Ah. [Silence for a moment.] I don't think it would be good to go too deep into this. *[I] think the interviewer will be imagining a couple of things about this. I don't think specifically confirming those thoughts is polite to the US.* I love my wife very much even though I have some dissatisfaction with her.

to do so. Although NW and NWH both convey Roh's reluctance to elaborate, NW's failure to relay Roh's reasons for his refusal to do so (as this would be potentially 'impolite' to the US) appears to have the effect of constructing an image of Roh as odd (his remarks on marriage could be interpreted as peculiar) and inconsistent (because he refuses to talk about an issue – the 'unilateralist aspects' of US actions – despite the fact that he has brought it up himself).

4.   Concluding discussion

The above analysis suggests that the NWH article not only reframes the NW article and constructs a different narrative of events but also evokes a distinct and independent NWH voice which explicitly comments on and questions the NW article. In particular, NWH hints at possible misreporting on the part of NW, thereby constructing itself as a trustworthy and ethical news institution while potentially discrediting NW's reporting practice. The use of distancing strategies and the management of multiple voices combine strategically to underline NWH's adoption of a reflexive and metacommunicative stance with regard to its reporting practice. The NWH article is presented as self-indexical, constructed to show NWH at work as part of doing its own job of news reporting, at the same time as raising the possibility of NW's failure to do the same.

This paper has also shown that the image of sameness and the assumed status of the source and target text that characterize the intertextual chain between NWH and NW do not necessarily extend to the level of the articles that are linked together in a translational relationship. The image of sameness, which plays a key role in strengthening NWH's reputation and identity as a credible news magazine, is strategically downplayed when NWH wishes to distance itself and suggest that its corresponding NW article may be flawed and misleading. The NWH article backgrounds, and even nullifies in certain parts, its direct ties to the NW article and foregrounds its ties to the speech event (interview), thus invoking divergent intertextual relationships and blurring the boundaries between the source and target texts. This may be explained in terms of NWH adapting the problematic news article for a new audience, one which would likely include Roh and members of his government, an audience who would expect the NW article to be re-narrated and made commensurable with the discursive, cultural and political reality of the target readership. While the NW article constructs an image of Roh as uncooperative and critical with respect to the US and as siding with anti-Americans, the NWH article shifts the focus to issues of fact construction and its own commitment to convey Roh's opinion in an accurate and balanced way in relation to a range of social, economic, political, diplomatic and personal issues.

The recontextualization of a text across linguistic, discursive and institutional boundaries and the multiplicity of relationships a text may form with related texts in an intertextual chain are intricately linked to the ways in which discursive resources available to text producers at particular historical moments in particular social communities are utilized and certain narratives are (re)shaped in order to achieve a desirable outcome. This has consequences for our understanding of what constitutes a source and target text: complex intertextual chains in translation problematize the very concept of a source and target text and require clarification in such a problematic context. In other words, source and target texts are no longer 'given' here but become fluid, multi-layered, inconsistent and contradictory concepts.[11] This highlights the need to situate discussions of source and target texts in a wider context of analysis. The status of a source text or a target text may become a *resource* to be utilized and exploited so that a narrative congruent with the identity and value system of the translating agent or the target readers is foregrounded and given a special status in the process of producing a translation. The attribution of the status of a source text or the rejection of the status of a target text may thus serve the translating agent or institution in terms of declaring the place of enunciation, constructing the state-of-affairs, and legitimating the translation. Lending credibility to and ensuring the acceptability of the target text by embedding and contextualizing the original text within the narrative

---

[11] The concepts of 'source' and 'target' text are among the most widely discussed and controversial topics in translation studies (cf. Toury 1995, Schäffner 1999), but the difficulty of identifying source and target texts has been exacerbated in recent years by the proliferation of new and more complex modes of translation.

framework of a translating institution may not only involve aspects of giving, silencing, distorting and blending voice but also evoking intertextual relationships that may deviate from the typical source-target relationship. It may be precisely those variant and atypical uses of source and target text concepts that can offer us a fresh perspective on the 'misrecognized' appropriations in meaning, power relationships and the not necessarily innocent nature of institutional translation.

References

Altheid, David (1974) *Creating Reality: How TV News Distorts Events*, Beverly Hills, CA: Sage.
Appadurai, Arjun (1990) 'Disjuncture and Difference in the Global Culture Economy', *Theory, Culture, and Society* 7(2): 295-310.
Baker, Mona (2006a) 'Contextualization in Translator- and Interpreter-Mediated Events', *Journal of Pragmatics* 38(3): 321-37.
----- (2006b) *Translation and Conflict: A Narrative Account*, London & New York: Routledge.
Bakhtin, Mikhail (1986/1952) 'The Problem of Speech Genres', in Caryl Emerson and Michael Holquist (eds) *Speech Genres and Other Late Essays*, Austin: University of Texas Press, 60-102.
Banerjee, Indrajit (2002) 'The Locals Strike Back?: Media Globalization and Localization in the New Asian Television Landscape', *International Communication Gazette* 64: 517.
Barnard, Christopher (2000) 'The Tokaimura Nuclear Accident in Japanese *Newsweek*: Translation or Censorship?', *Japanese Studies* 20(3): 281-94.
Bell, Allan (1991) *The Language of News Media*, Oxford: Blackwell.
Bielsa, Esperança (2005) 'Globalisation and Translation: A Theoretical Approach', *Language and Intercultural Communication* 5(2): 131-44.
------ and Susan Bassnett (2009) *Translation in Global News*, London & New York: Routledge.
Blommaert, Jan (2005) 'Bourdieu the Ethnographer: The Ethnographic Grounding of Habitus and Voice', *The Translator* 11(2): 219-36.
Boyd-Barrett, Oliver (1997) 'Global News Wholesalers as Agents of Globalization', in Annabelle Sreberny-Mohammadi, Dwayne Winseck, Jim McKenna and Oliver Boyd-Barrett (eds) *Media in Global Context: A Reader*, London: Arnold, 131-44.
Cen Yeng-Phyo (1997) *Chwulphanmwunhwawa Capci Cenellicum* [Book Publishing and Magazine Journalism], Seoul: Taykwangmwunhwasa.
Clausen, Lisbeth (2003) *Global News Production*, Copenhagen: Copenhagen Business School.
------ (2004) 'Localizing the Global: "Domestication" Processes in International News Production', *Media, Culture and Society* 26(1): 25–44.
Clayman, Steven (1995) 'Defining Moments, Presidential Debates and the Dynamics of Quotability', *Journal of Communication* 45(3): 118-46.

Cronin, Michael (2005) 'Bringing the House Down: Translation in a Global Setting', *Language and Intercultural Communication* 5(2): 108-19.

Culler, Jonathan (1981) *The Pursuit of Signs: Semiotics, Literature, Deconstruction*, Ithaca, NY: Cornell University Press.

Devitt, Amy (1991) 'Intertextuality in Tax Accounting: Generic, Referential, and Functional', in Charles Bazerman and James Paradis (eds) *Textual Dynamics of the Professions: Historical and Contemporary Studies of Writing in Professional Communities*, Madison: University of Wisconsin Press, 336–57.

Fairclough, Norman (1992) *Discourse and Social Change*, Cambridge: Polity Press.

Fallows, James (1996) *Breaking the News: How the Media Undermine American Democracy*, New York: Pantheon.

Fujii, Akio (1988) 'News Translation in Japan', *Meta* 33(1): 32-37.

García-Suárez, Pablo (2005) 'Noticias de agencia: características, problemas y retos de su traducción', in María del Carmen Cortés Zaborras and María José Hernández Guerrero (eds) *La traducción periodística*, Castilla-La Mancha: Ediciones de la Universidad de Castilla-La Mancha, 175-98.

Geer, John G. and Kim F. Kahn (1993) 'Grabbing Attention: An Experimental Investigation of Headlines during Campaigns', *Political Communication* 10(2): 175-91.

Genette, Gérard (1997) *Palimpsests: Literature in the Second Degree*, Lincoln, NE: University of Nebraska Press.

Giddens, Anthony (1990) *The Consequences of Modernity*, Stanford: Stanford University Press.

Gurevitch, Michael, Mark Levy and Itzhak Roeh (1991) 'The Global Newsroom: Convergences and Diversities in the Globalization of Television News', in Peter Dahlgren and Colin Sparks (eds) *Communication and Citizenship*, London: Routledge, 195–216.

Hatim, Basil and Ian Mason (1997) *The Translator as Communicator*, London: Routledge.

Hess, Stephen (1996) *International News and Foreign Correspondents*, Washington DC: Brookings Institute.

Inghilleri, Moira (2003) 'Habitus, Field and Discourse: Interpreting as a Socially Situated Activity', *Target* 15(2): 243-68.

------ (2005) 'The Sociology of Bourdieu and the Construction of the 'Object' in Translation and Interpreting Studies', *The Translator* 11(2): 125-45.

Joongang Ilbo (1997) *Newsweek Hankwukphan Suthailpuk* [*Newsweek Hankukpan Stylebook*], Seoul: Joongang Ilbo.

Jucker, Andreas (1986) *News Interviews: A Pragmalinguistic Analysis*, Amsterdam & Philadelphia: John Benjamins.

Kang, Ji-Hae (2007) 'Recontextualization of News Discourse: A Case Study of Translation of News Discourse on North Korea', *The Translator* 13(2): 219-42.

------ (2009) 'Institutional Translation', in Mona Baker and Gabriela Saldanha (eds) *Routledge Encyclopedia of Translation Studies*, 2nd edition, London & New York: Routledge, 141-45.

Korea Press Foundation (2001) *Hayoymaycheyuy Kwuknay Swuyong Hyenhwang* [International Media and Their Reception in Korea], Seoul: Hankwuk Enlon Caytan [Korea Press Foundation].

Lefevere, André (1992) *Translation, Rewriting, and the Manipulation of Literary Fame*, London & New York: Routledge.

Linell, Per (1998) 'Discourse across Boundaries: On Recontextualizations and the Blending of Voices in Professional Discourse', *Text* 18(2): 143-57.

Marchetti, Dominique (2002) 'L'internationale des images', *Actes de la recherche en sciences sociales* 145: 71-83.

Mason, Ian (1994/2009) 'Discourse, Ideology and Translation', in Robert de Beaugrande, Abdullah Shunnaq and Mohamed Heliel (eds) *Language, Discourse and Translation in the West and Middle East*, Amsterdam & Philadelphia: John Benjamins, 23-34; reprinted, with a postscript, in Mona Baker (ed.) *Critical Concepts: Translation Studies*, Volume III, London & New York: 141-56.

Morley, David and Kevin Robins (1995) *Spaces of Identity: Global Media, Electronic Landscapes and Cultural Boundaries*, London: Routledge.

Munday, Jeremy (2007) 'Translation and Ideology: A Textual Approach', *The Translator* 13(2): 195-218

Neuman, Russell, Marion R. Just and Ann N. Crigler (1992) *Common Knowledge: News and the Construction of Political Meaning*, Chicago: University of Chicago Press.

Nylund, Mats (2003) 'Asking Questions, Making Sound-Bites: Research Reports, Interviews and Television News Stories', *Discourse Studies* 5(4): 517–33.

Orengo, Alberto (2005) 'Localising News: Translation and the Global-National Dichotomy', *Language and Intercultural Communication* 5(2): 168-87.

Palmer, Jerry (2009) 'News Gathering and Dissemination', in Mona Baker and Gabriela Saldanha (eds) *Routledge Encyclopedia of Translation Studies*, 2nd edition, London & New York: Routledge, 186-189.

------ and Victoria Fontan (2007) 'Our Ears and Our Eyes: Journalists and Fixers in Iraq', *Journalism* 8(1): 5-24.

Paterson, Chris (1997) 'Global Television News Service', in Annabelle Sreberny-Mohammadi, Dwayne Winseck, Jim McKenna and Oliver Boyd-Barrett (eds) *Media in Global Context: A Reader*, London: Arnold, 145-60.

Price, Vincent, David Tewksbury and Elisabeth Powers (1997) 'Switching Trains of Thought: The Impact of News Frames on Readers' Cognitive Responses', *Communication Research* 24: 481-506.

Schäffner, Christina (1999) *Translation and Norms*, Clevedon: Multilingual Matters.

Slembrouck, Stef (1999) 'Translation, Direct Quotation and Decontextualization', *Perspectives: Studies in Translatology* 7(1): 81-108.

Smith, Edward (1999) 'Leadlines May Be Better than Traditional Headlines', *Newspaper Research Journal* 20(1): 55-64.

Solin, Anna (2004) 'Intertextuality as Mediation: On the Analysis of Intertextual Relations in Public Discourse', *Text* 24(2): 267-96.

Stetting, Karen (1989) 'Transediting – a New Term for Coping with a Grey Area between Editing and Translating', in Graham Caie, Kirsten Haastrup, Arnt Lykke Jakobsen, Jorgen Erik Nielsen, Jorgen Sevaldsen, Henrik Specht and Arne Zettersten (eds) *Proceedings from the Fourth Nordic Conference for English Studies*, Copenhagen: University of Copenhagen, 371-82.

Toury, Gideon (1995) *Descriptive Translation Studies*, Amsterdam & Philadelphia: John Benjamins.

Tumber, Howard and Frank Webster (2006) *Journalists under Fire: Information War and Journalistic Practices*, London: Sage.

Tymoczko, Maria (2007) *Enlarging Translation, Empowering Translators*, Manchester & Kinderhook: St. Jerome Publishing.

van Dijk, Teun (1998) 'Opinions and Ideologies in the Press', in Allan Bell and Peter Garrett (eds) *Approaches to Media Discourse*, Oxford: Blackwell, 21-63.

Zillmann, Dolf, Lei Chen, Silvia Knobloch and Coy Callison (2004) 'Effects of Lead Framing on Selective Exposure to Internet News Reports', *Communication Research* 31(1): 58-81.

APPENDIX

"북한 원하는 것 들어주면 핵 포기할 것"

단독 인터뷰/ 햇볕정책 유지 선언한 노대통령, "부도덕한 정권 응징하기보다 설득·지원해야"

대담: George Wehrfritz 도쿄 지국장
     이 병 종 서울 특파원
정리: 뉴스위크 한국판

노무현 대통령의 뉴스위크 인터뷰가 국내외에 논란을 불러일으키고 있다. 뉴스위크는 미국판 최신호(3월 3일자) 노대통령 인터뷰 기사(1쪽 분량) 전문에서 "노무현은 정당한 싸움을 좋아한다. 이 56세의 전직 인권변호사가 지난해 12월 한국 대선에서 모든 예측과는 달리 승리하도록 도운 것은 바로 그의 '투쟁적인 성격'(pugnacity)이었다. 노대통령은 결코 미국에 '아첨'(kowtow)하지 않고 대등한 관계로 대우받기를 요구할 것이라고 맹세했다"는 내용을 실었다.

하지만 이같은 표현은 노대통령의 인터뷰 내용 속에는 등장하지 않는다. 이로 보면 문제가 된 두 단어는 담당기자인 조지 워프리츠 도쿄 지국장이 그간 노대통령에 대한 '인식'을 바탕으로 나름대로 표현한 부분인 것으로 보인다. 노대통령측에서는 워프리츠 지국장의 인터뷰 전문 내용이 문제가 되자 "그런 표현을 쓴 적이 없다"며 반발하고 있다. 워프리츠 지국장의 인터뷰 기사는 미국판 뉴스위크에만 게재됐고, 아시아판에는 이번 인터뷰를 토대로 노대통령의 삶을 전반적으로 다루는 기사가 실렸다. 뉴스위크는 미국판과 몇종의 해외판으로 나뉘어 발행되고 있다.

노대통령과 뉴스위크의 인터뷰는 취임식 전인 2월 19일 인수위 사무실에서 이뤄졌으며 대담은 조지 워프리츠 도쿄 지국장과 이병종 서울 특파원이 함께 진행했다. 뉴스위크 한국판은 문제가 되고 있는 뉴스위크와 노대통령의 인터뷰 전문을 입수해 게재한다. 이날 진행된 인터뷰에서 나온 노대통령의 발언을 가감없이 정리한 것이다.

취임식도 하기 전에 비극적인 일이 일어났습니다. 대구 지하철 방화 사건을 보면서 어떤 생각을 하셨나요.

아주 불행한 일입니다. 이같은 사회에 대한 공격 행위가 왜 생기는가 생각해 보았습니다. 그런 행위를 완벽하게 방어할 방법은 무엇인가 하고 깊이 생각해 봤지만 한마디로 말할 수 있는 대책은 생각나지 않더군요. 다만 절망과 분노, 증오가 우리 사회에 대단히 위험한 현상으로 나타나고 있고, 사람들로부터 희망을 빼앗지 않으면서 서로 사랑할 수 있는 사회를 만드는 게 중요하다는 생각이 들었습니다. 이번 사고를 보면서 우리가 가진 물적 설비나 시스템의 문제가 없었는지 재평가해야 한다는 생각이 들더군요. 피해자와 그 유족들에게 심심한 위로를 보냅니다. 차기 대통령으로서 피해를 회복하고 마음을 위안할 수 있도록 필요한 조치를 다할 겁니다.

미국인들은 미국과 동등한 관계를 원하는 한국의 움직임을 우려하고 있습니다. 이런 상황이 미국 내 반한 감정을 일으키지는 않을까요.

대부분의 한국 사람들은 미국과 미국인을 좋아합니다. 그러나 때때로 문제가 발생하기도 하고, 우리가 부당한 대우를 받았다고 생각하면 불평하고 항의합니다. 하지만 그건 반미감정과는 별개입니다. 한국의 젊은이들은 아버지에게도 잘못된 것이 있다면 당당하게 항의합니다. 한국이 미국으로부터 많은 도움을 받았다는 역사적 사실과 지금도 미국과의 협력을 통해 안정을 유지하고 경제적으로 번영하고 있다는 사실을 잘 알고 있습니다. 정상적인 한·미 관계는 반미냐 친미냐가 아니라 합리적 대화를 통해 꾸준히 우호적이고 협력하는 관계를 유지하고 갈등을 풀어가는 것입니다. 가끔 한국과 미국에서 지나친 표현이나 극단적 요구를 하는 사람들도 있지만, 그런 사람들이 주류인 것은 아닙니다. 그동안 한국은 미국의 의견을 항상 따라 왔고 반대한 적이 없습니다. 베트남전에 이어 걸프전에도 참전했죠. 세계 여론과 미국의 입장이 부딪칠 때도 한국은 미국의 입장을 따라왔습니다. 한·미 관계는 특수한 관계이기 때문에 당연히 그렇게 해온 것이고 지금도 마찬가지로 그렇게 하려고 노력하고 있습니다.

하지만 고민이 있습니다. 미국의 주요 언론과 정부의 책임 있는 사람들이 북한에 대한 무력 공격 가능성을 자주 얘기하고 있습니다. 그것은 곧바로 전쟁으로 이어질 수 있기 때문에 한국인들은 쉽게 동의하기 어렵죠. 예전에는 이같은 어려운 문제가 없었습니다. 미국의 의견을 따랐다고 해서 우리가 전쟁의 위험에 처한 적이 없었던 거죠. 하지만 이 문제는 우리가 죽느냐 사느냐 하는 문제입니다. 대통령은 국민의 안전을 보호할 책임이 있습니다. 그래서 미국에 대해 너무 위험한 일은 피하자고 말하는 겁니다. 미국인들은 우리가 미국 편을 들지 않고, 북한 편을 든다고 생각하고 섭섭해 하고 있습니다. 의리도 없고 배은망덕하다는 얘기도 나오는데, 한국인들은 그같은 상황을 걱정하고 있습니다. 나는 미국의 여러 정책 당국자와 꾸준히 대화하면서 의견을 합치시켜 나갈 수 있을 것으로 기대하고 있습니다. 다른 의견이라도 대화를 통해 서로 합치시켜 나가는 노력을 기울일 때 한·미 관계는 좀더 돈독한 협력관계로 발전할 수 있습니다. 그렇게 해서 미국도 동북아에서 안보적·경제적 이익을 관리해 나갈 수 있을 것입니다.

노대통령 측근 중 한명은 지난 80년대에 당선자의 승용차로 부산지역에서 반정부 유인물을 돌리며 투쟁하던 얘기를 전해주었습니다. 그후에 노대통령의 정치적인 견해는 어떻게 변했습니까.

내 의견이 바뀌는 않았지만 좀더 풍부해졌습니다. 그때와는 상황도 많이 달라졌죠. 나는 미국의 역사를 존중하고 부러워합니다. 역사적으로 보자면, 미국은 부당한 압제에 저항해 싸웠고 이겼습니다. 그 바탕 위에 합리주의 문화를 건설했습니다. 바로 그런 점을 부러워하고 있습니다. 나도 그렇게 해보고 싶습니다.

링컨 대통령에 관한 책을 쓴 이유는 무엇입니까.

한국에도 훌륭한 인물들은 많습니다. 하지만 지난날 한국의 역사에서 정의의 편에 섰던 사람들은 대체로 성공하지 못했습니다. 그러한 실패의 역사를 극복하고 싶습니다. 우리도 정의의 깃발을 든 사람들이 성공하고 승리하는 역사를 만들고 싶은 겁니다. 링컨 대통령이 바로 그 사례라고 봤던 겁니다. 또 하나는 링컨 대통령이 국가의 통합을 위해 부득이 전쟁을 했지만, 국민 사이에 분노와 증오를 부추기는 일을 매우 자제했다는 겁니다.

미국 밖에서는 미국이 그러한 가치 체계를 타국에 강요한다는 인식이 있습니다. 미국이 이 점에서 너무 심하다고 생각하지 않으십니까.

미국이 요구하는 세계 질서는 주로 정당합니다. 그러나 일방적 강요라는 측면도 함께 있습니다.

'일방적' 측면을 좀더 설명해주시겠습니까.

아... (잠시 침묵) 너무 깊이 들어가지 않는 것이 좋다고 봅니다. 질문자도 그런 면에 관해 몇가지 상상하는 게 있을 거라 생각합니다. 내가 그 점을 구체적으로 확인해주는 것은 미국에 대한 예의가 아니라고 봅니다. 나는 아내를 사랑하지만 몇가지 불만도 있습니다.

최근 북한은 정전협정을 파기하고 국제원자력기구(IAEA) 사찰단을 추방하는 등 자극적인 행동을 하고 있습니다. 한국과 우방은 어떻게 대처해야 한다고 보십니까.

나는 북한이 핵무기에 대한 집착을 버리기를 바랍니다. 국제 사회의 제반 규칙들을 존중하고 준수하는 합리적인 행동을 하기 바랍니다. 문제는 북한이 특별한 나라라는 겁니다. 북한이 처해 있는 상황도 특수하고, 생각하고 행동하는 방법도 특별합니다. 우리로서는 어떻게 하면 북한을 합리적인 대화의 상대로 만드는가 하는 것이 중요하고 또 어려운 문제이기도 합니다.

부시 행정부는 북한에 대한 제재를 고려하고 있습니다. 이런 방법이 북한에 대한 적절한 대책이라고 생각하십니까.

북한과 한국, 북한과 미국 사이에 문제가 안 풀리는 가장 큰 이유는 신뢰가 없기 때문입니다. 불신을 해소해 나가는 방법이 가장 효과적입니다. 협상은 일종의 게임의 성격이 있기 때문에 여러 가지 수단이 필요하겠죠. 하지만 궁극적으로 전쟁이 발생할 수도 있는 대결적 수단은 굉장히 조심스럽게 사용해야 합니다.

최근 주한 미군의 재조정 논의가 있고 허바드 주한 미국 대사도 조정 및 감축에 대한 언급을 했습니다. 이러한 방법이 북한과의 불신을 제거할 수 있다고 생각하십니까.

나와 대부분의 한국 국민도 주한 미군이 지금 같은 상태로 한반도에 주둔하기 바랍니다.

그러나 또한 많은 사람들이 주한 미군문제에 관한 한 한국민의 요구가 그대로 받아들여지지 않는다는 것을 이해하고 있습니다. 한국 사람이 가지 말라고 아무리 부탁해도 미국이 마음만 먹으면 갈 수 있다는 것을 한국민은 잘 알고 있습니다.

(주한 미군이) 한국 사람들을 두고 떠나는 것에 대한 우려가 있습니까.

많은 국민들이 거기에 대해 불안감을 갖고 있습니다.

블레어 영국 총리는 사담 후세인을 제거하는 데 도덕적 측면을 강조하고 있습니다. 살인적이고 전체주의적인 후세인 정권을 제거해야 한다고 주장하고 있죠. 북한의 김정일 정권에 대해서도 같은 측면이 있다고 보십니까.

나는 모든 정권이 민주적이고 도덕적이기 바랍니다. 그러나 어떤 한 국가가 민주성이나 도덕성, 인권이라는 기준으로 한 국가나 정부의 존립을 좌우할 수는 없습니다. 그러한 국제질서는 아직까지는 성립되지 않았습니다. 이 기준은 그 국가가 힘이 약하면 적용할 수 있지만 힘이 강한 국가에는 적용할 수 없습니다. 그같은 기준으로 세계 평화를 유지하는 것은 아직 어렵습니다. 그리고 부도덕한 정권을 응징을 통해 무너뜨릴 수도 있지만 설득과 지원을 통해 그 국가가 좀 더 개방적이고 민주적이며 도덕적인 국가가 될 수 있도록 유도할 수도 있습니다. 동구권이나 중국·베트남도 개방적이고 국제질서를 존중하는 자유로운 국가로 변화하고 있습니다. 그런 국가들의 변화는 외부의 공격에 의한 것이 아닙니다.

김대중 전 대통령의 대북 송금 의혹이 귀하의 대북 포용정책을 손상시키지는 않겠습니까.

대외적으로는 국가적 위신, 대내적으로는 국민으로부터의 신뢰를 상실한 것이 사실입니다. 외교와 안보에 관한 한 여러 나라 역사에서 많은 비밀 거래들이 있었고 시간이 지난 후에 그것이 정당한 일로 승인받은 적이 많습니다. 그런 문제들이 그 당시에 밝혀졌다면 시끄러웠을 겁니다. 그래서 우리는 사실을 밝힐 것은 밝히고 책임질 것은 져야 한다고 봅니다. 다만 이 과정에서 외교관계가 심각하게 손상되지 않기 바랍니다. 이 문제는 국내적 문제와 대외적 문제가 함께 얽혀 있습니다. 은행을 통한 자금 대출 과정 등은 국내 실정법상 금융질서나 경제원칙을 어기는 범죄가 될 수도 있습니다. 또 대외적으로 돈이 북한에 어떤 경로로 누구에게 어떻게 갔는가 하는 문제가 있습니다. 북한과의 거래에 관한 문제는 민감한 외교적 문제가 포함되어 있습니다. 국내에서 자금 조달 과정의 문제에 대해 (사실을)밝히기를 거부하는 것은 어렵다고 봅니다.

그럼 모든 사항이 공개되어야 합니까.

양면성이 있기 때문에 국민들에게 공개해야 할 범위와 절차에 관해 국회에서 일차 조사하고 이 범위와 절차에 따라 그 다음 단계로 검찰이나 특검에 맡기는 것도 한 방법입니다.

김대중 전 대통령의 햇볕정책과 노대통령의 대북 포용정책은 어떻게 다릅니까.

　김대통령이 남북대화와 교류를 적극적으로 하지 않았다면 한반도에는 긴장과 불안이 계속됐을 겁니다. 그랬다면 한국 경제의 회복도 어려웠을 것입니다. 이것은 한국 경제에 대한 또 하나의 희망입니다. 김대통령이 남북대화를 적극적으로 하지 않았다면 우리는 지금 이런 희망을 말하기 어려웠을 겁니다. 지금 남북간에 철도와 도로가 연결되고 있습니다. 북핵 문제만 잘 해결되면 동북아시아가 새로운 도약의 시대로 가게 될 것입니다. 대북정책면에서는 김대통령과 크게 다를 것이 없을 겁니다. 다만 동북아시아라는 큰 비전을 가지고 적극적으로 국제적 사업과 자본을 조직하고, 남북관계를 풀어나갈 생각입니다. 대북 정책은 공개적으로 추진하면서 여야간 협의를 거치는 등의 국민적 합의를 모아갈 것입니다.

한국사회에는 가진 자와 못 가진 자 사이의 불평등이 심화되고 있다는 우려가 있습니다. 평등을 제고하기 위한 정책에 어느 정도 우선순위를 둘 생각이십니까.

　우리가 시장경제와 경쟁체제를 유지하는 한 빈부간 소득 차이는 어쩔 수 없이 수용해야 한다고 봅니다. 그러나 빈부차는 적대감과 갈등의 원인이 되기 때문에 적절하게 조절해야 합니다. 보다 더 많은 사람들이 일자리를 가지고 열심히 일할 수 있게 하고 노동의 결과에 대한 소득이 공정하도록 여러 제도를 개선하는 노력을 할 것입니다. 또 하나 중요한 것은 규칙과 절차의 공정성에 대한 사람들의 믿음입니다. 그 동안 한국에서는 시장의 공정한 규칙을 준수하며 경쟁하지 않았습니다. 지금의 빈부차가 공정한 경쟁의 결과가 아니라는 생각을 하고 있습니다. 같은 차이라도 과정이 공정했느냐에 따라 그 차이를 받아들이는 느낌이 달라집니다. 나는 이 문제를 해소하기 위해 공정한 게임의 룰을 만들고 운영할 겁니다. 나 역시 그렇게 해서 성공했습니다. 그래서 내가 하는 말이 사람들에게 설득력을 갖는다고 생각합니다. 이 계획이 성공한다면 한국이 국제 시장에서 새로운 경쟁력을 갖추게 될 것입니다. 빈부격차나 분배에 대한 관심은 결코 성장이나 경쟁력과 서로 배치되는 것이 아닙니다.

동북아시아 경제권을 위해서는 외국 자본의 유치가 필요하지만 외국인 투자자들은 한국의 노사 문제에 대해 우려하고 있습니다. 노동자의 오랜 친구로서 한국 노동자들이 처한 현재 상황에 대해 어떻게 생각하십니까.

　한국의 노동자나 직장인의 숙련도·기술적 수준·일에 대한 열정은 우수합니다. 나는 여기에다 사람의 능력을 향상시킬 수 있는 프로그램을 집중적으로 진행할 겁니다. 그동안 일부 공공 부문의 집단 해고를 둘러싸고 강경 투쟁이 있었지만 지금은 마무리 단계에 있습니다. 외국 기업이 한국에 진출하는 데 노사문제로 인해 갈등을 겪지는 않을 겁니다.

　현장에서 사업에 지장을 줄 만한 노사 갈등은 거의 없습니다. 미국이나 유럽에 투자해 사업하는 한국인들의 말을 들어보면, 개별 노동자의 요구사항은 한국의 노동자가 (외국의 노동자들에 비해) 훨씬 더 온건하며 요구 수준도 낮고 부지런하다고 합니다.

부시 미국 대통령과 만났을 때 북한 문제에 대해 어떤 점을 언급할 생각이십니까

부시 대통령에게 말하고 싶은 것은 북한이 개방을 원하며 변화하고 있다는 점입니다. 평화체제, 안전보장, 국제사회에서의 정상적 대우, 경제적 지원 같은 북한이 간절히 원하는 사항을 들어주면 핵도 포기할 것이라는 점을 말하고 싶습니다. 그들을 범죄인이 아니라 협상의 상대로 대하면 문제는 풀린다는 확신이 있습니다. 만일 대화로 문제를 풀지 않고 핵포기를 위해 여러 수단을 강구하다 결국 전쟁을 선택하게 된다면 그것은 우리에게 너무나 치명적인 결과를 가져옵니다. 전쟁의 위험은 피해야 한다고 강조할 겁니다.

대통령 당선 후에도 공중목욕탕을 방문해 주위를 놀라게 했는데 이렇게 자유롭고 젊은 행보가 바로 새로운 정부의 모습입니까.

한국은 보다 더 자유롭고 수평적이며, 개방적인 사회로 가야 하고 또 그렇게 가고 있습니다. 이런 변화 속에서 인권이 존중되고, 경제가 효율화되며, 민주적이고 창조적인 사회가 이뤄질 수 있다고 믿습니다. 내가 당선된 것은 사회가 그렇게 변화하고 있다는 증거입니다. 나는 보다 더 역동적인 사회, 미래를 합리적으로 예측할 수 있는 사회를 만들 겁니다. 원칙·신뢰·공정·투명·분권·자율·대화·타협이라는 8개의 키워드가 향후 5년간 정착시키려는 질서입니다.

On Trust

Relationships of Trust in Interpreter-mediated Social Work Encounters

REBECCA TIPTON
University of Salford, UK

Abstract. *The provision of high quality and culturally sensitive services in interpreter-mediated social work encounters involves complex interaction and negotiation between the service provider and interpreter, the success of which is considered to depend to a large extent on the level of mutual trust invested in the communicative approaches adopted by both agents. This paper explores the socio-cultural norms that underpin the relationships of trust between service providers and interpreters in the social work field which often remain implicit during interaction and which, it is argued, could usefully be negotiated at the 'edges' of the role boundaries of both agents in order to improve the quality of communication. The discussion involves a re-interpretation of the 'server-served' relationship in interpreter-mediated social work encounters and is informed by findings of focus-group work designed to allow social work practitioners to articulate and evaluate their experiences of practice in light of what might be termed a new reality of social work practice. The aim of this research is to promote cross-fertilization between the interpreting and social work professions and research disciplines, and develop theoretical insights that may have applications at the level of both interpreting and social work practice.[1]*

T he health and social services are often grouped together under the banner of the 'caring professions' and in Britain this translates into policy through the placing of social service provision under the auspices of the

---

[1] I would like to pay tribute to the very significant contribution Ian Mason has made to establishing public service interpreting as a serious research field within the academy through his extensive publications in the field and in the timely bringing together of scholars, notably through two edited volumes (Mason 1999, 2001) to establish the state of the art and examine new directions in research. The text-linguistic approach to interpreting developed with Basil Hatim (Hatim and Mason 1997) and, in particular, the problems of textuality identified in relation to the liaison interpreting mode draw attention to the fragility of interaction in the interpreter-mediated encounter as a result of the fragmentation of information to be processed by the interpreter; such fragility informs the discussion on trust that follows. These insights, together with the foregrounding of context in the liaison interpreting mode have served as an important springboard for my research interests with respect to the way they inform the examination of socio-cultural aspects of interpreter-mediated encounters at both the micro and macro levels. Interpreting studies, and in particular the sub-field of public service interpreting, owes a great debt to his scholarship and doubtless his work will continue to inspire generations of researchers to come.

Department of Health. Yet, despite areas of overlap at an occupational level, conflating the two services is unhelpful in public service interpreting research because the division between clinical and social aspects of practice in these fields has implications for understanding the nature of the interpreter's role, and, more specifically, the relationship between interpreter, service provider and service user. To date, research into the use of interpreters in the health-care professions has dominated interpreting studies under the umbrella of the 'caring professions'; however, drives to improve the take-up of social service provision for service users of limited or no proficiency in English and increased efforts to improve and monitor the effectiveness and quality of service delivery to minority groups[2] in all public service domains means that there is consider-able justification for examining interpreting practice in the social service field as a discrete object of study. It also constitutes one of the 'emergent themes' identified in qualitative research in the health and social care professions (e.g. Popay and Williams 1998), namely, the analysis of taken-for-granted practices in social work and organizational culture and management, since the use of interpreters in the delivery of services has become a reality for increasing numbers of social work practitioners in Britain. The concept of trust, which forms the focus of this paper, has long proved difficult to define and measure (Misztal 1996). In the discussion that follows I adopt a descriptive approach to the concept based on a re-examination of the service provider-interpreter relationship in social work encounters and an emphasis on the socio-cultural norms that underpin the communicative relationship between the two. The discussion does not assume that the so-called problematics of trust constitute a more complex phenomenon in the social work field compared to other fields of interpreting in the public services, but the socio-cultural norms identified here are considered to impact on the interpreter-mediated interaction and levels of trust created therein. As a result, if service provision is to be improved, these socio-cultural norms merit particular attention by the academy. The discussion also considers the extent to which these socio-cultural norms are shaped by social work policy and practice as well as by the 'server-served' relationship between the social worker and interpreter in the wider context of the triadic exchange; the latter is explored by recasting the server-served relationship as one that is fluid rather than fixed, as is often assumed. Stakeholders who are external to the communicative process and the potential impact they exert on the interaction are also examined in the context of this relationship.

In examining the importance and impact of socio-cultural norms on the professional relationship between social worker and interpreter in this field,

---

[2] Improvements to the quality of social care delivery in the past decade have been driven by the White Paper on *Modernising Social Services* (Department of Health 1998) and, more recently, by the creation of the Care Quality Commission in 2009, a regulator for health and adult social care.

the paper considers the extent to which the concept of trust can be considered as a potential norm of interaction. In this regard, Carole Smith (2001:303) suggests that "although trust and discretion cannot be said to *characterize* social work, trust can be practised in the negotiable spaces or interstices at the edge of role performance as Seligman (1997) suggests" (original emphasis). Although Smith's observations suggest that perhaps trust should not be viewed as a norm of social work practice, the emphasis she places on trust-as-*practice* draws attention to the importance of the 'doing' or 'praxis' of trust, which is echoed in Edwards *et al.*'s (2006) conceptualization of trust-as-*process* (my emphasis), and which is central to the discussion here. Despite concluding that trust does not characterize social work practice, Smith believes it is *necessary* for social work practice; that is, service users need to "experience trust in order to feel able to give truthful/authentic accounts of themselves" (Smith 2001:294; original emphasis). The service user's *experience* of trust is seen as contingent on the service provider and interpreter's *doing* of trust and therefore cannot simply be assumed.

It is important to stress at the outset that the discussion here does not suggest that where there is an absence of trust, distrust automatically follows. On a general level, Anthony Pym (2000:187) in his article 'On Cooperation' suggests that participants from different cultures might have greater grounds for mutual distrust in communicative encounters, since they have little knowledge about how the other is going to act. This assertion finds ample support in studies in the asylum field, for example, where generally low level of so-called 'basic trust' (following Giddens 1990, 1991) on the part of minority speakers is well documented (Blommaert 2001, Maryns 2006). By contrast, it seems reasonable to assume that participants from different *professional* cultures generally have fewer grounds for distrust, if it is considered, for example, that the very co-presence of two professionals serves as an *a priori* condition for trust to be invested in the other from the outset of the interaction (i.e. trust that the 'other' will execute his or her role as required). However, research in the health and social service fields in Britain highlights the generally low levels of (inter-professional) trust in interpreting service provision (see, for example, Chamba *et al.* 1999, O'Neale 2000, Brophy *et al.* 2003, Chand 2005) and the general levels of dissatisfaction on the part of service providers in terms of the quality of the communication experienced. For Pym (2000:187), the quality of communication obtained in an intercultural encounter can be affected by "the relative weakness of the cultural norms shared by the participants". Although Pym's comments chiefly relate to participants from different cultures, they also apply to the communication between the social worker and interpreter, since, in spite of the fact that these two agents are likely to share an understanding of the cultural norms of the country in which the interaction is taking place (and may have a greater understanding of these than the service user), many of the socio-cultural norms specific to the field are seen to remain implicit between the two in the course of interaction, which can impact on the quality of communication. In other words, the interpreter-mediated social work encounter is often characterized by a lack of negotiation and explicitation of the socio-cultural norms, that is, the 'professional socio-cultural norms', especially at the 'interstices' mentioned by Smith above. If service provision is to be improved in the field, there is a need to examine the reasons behind the lack of trust between these two agents as well as the connection between trust and the negotiation of the socio-cultural norms in question.

In reviewing qualitative approaches to data collection in the social work and interpreting fields, Edwards *et al.*'s (2005) study emerged as a particular point of reference with its focus on users' experiences of interpreters in public service fields. The study concluded (among other things) that trust involves belief about the way that other people, and even institutions, are likely to behave. This observation has served, in part, to inform the choice of methodology for data collection in the present paper, since the use of focus groups is designed to foreground the intersubjective nature of trust in social relationships through the elicitation of practitioners' perceptions *about* practice and the beliefs that shape their professional relationships with interpreters. This approach draws on Möllering's (2001) reflexive approach to trust and his contention that trust research should concern the subjective reality as interpreted by the person who trusts; this contrasts, for example, with a behaviourist approach to cause-effect relationships of trust which assumes that trust is a stable, observable, variable. Trust, therefore, is considered (following McEvily *et al.* 2003) as more of a heuristic than as a given of the interaction in this context. As Luhmann (1979:33) highlights, it should not be assumed "that empirical research will yield strong law-like relationships between bases for trust, treated as causes, and demonstrations of trust, treated as effects", although he does contend that statistical correlations may emerge "since one may assume that on average trust is more likely to be conferred when certain preconditions are met" (*ibid.*). The present discussion is concerned primarily with the foundational aspects of the preconditions to which Luhmann refers.

The discussion that follows draws on findings from focus-group work conducted in the Greater Manchester region between September and November 2008, which involved 30 participants in three sessions lasting between 45 and 90 minutes. Participants in the study were recruited (following authorization by Manchester City Council research ethics committee) from several social services in the region: adult and child social care, asylum support, equipment and adaptations, tenancy compliance and family information service, among others. Permission was granted by participants for two of the sessions to be recorded and for field notes to serve as the basis of data collection in the case of the third session. The sessions were conducted by the same facilitator and were semi-structured. The purpose of semi-structuring was to allow scope for participants to formulate and comment on ideas generated within the group but for some degree of comparison to be achieved. This meant that the nature of the topics covered varied between the groups. As I wished to gain as great an insight as possible into the range of practitioner experiences, trust was not foregrounded as the main feature of the sessions but it did inform most of the discussion points.

1.   Trust and goal achievement in the social work encounter

According to Mason (2000:217), trust is an integral part of the negotiation process in interpreter-mediated encounters, a process which he suggests is inherent in progressing towards a mutual goal. For Mason, such negotiation primarily involves non-cognitive features such as socio-cultural norms, over and above translatorial equivalence. If it is assumed that the interpreter is acting as "a medium through which the speaker reaches the target" (Mason 2001:54, with reference to Kang 1998), the role of negotiation in goal achievement is viewed as potentially problematic, since it raises questions of when, where and how precisely such negotiation is carried out and coordinated. Furthermore, the notion of the mutual goal is open to question in the relationship between service provider and interpreter in the field under review; in other words, while the service provider and interpreter can often be *assumed* to pursue a mutual goal during interaction, the reality of practice in the social work field suggests that goal determination and goal achievement are complex and highly differentiated activities. This is because social work practitioners often simultaneously orient practice to the achievement of short, medium and longer term goals of which the interpreter may or may not be aware. Pincus and Minahan (1973) provide an illustration of multiple goal setting through the case of a mother who visits a mental health centre for help because of the excessive acting-out behaviour of her 6 year-old child. The authors refer to a meeting with the mother that involves a data collection task that has two aims: to collect important data on the child's behaviour and to actively involve the mother in the treatment process.

In practice, goal differentiation is articulated by the social worker, for example, through particular approaches to 'audience design'[3] and encounter management, which can appear to skew goal achievement in the encounter from the interpreter's perspective. This is supported by the following quote from a participant in the second of the three focus groups in relation to the social worker's use of 'codification' as an audience design and goal differentiation strategy (i.e. the use of particular terms and questioning strategies that

---

[3] 'Audience design' is understood as the way in which a producer of discourse adapts the discourse or 'text' to the 'perceived receiver group' – following Hatim and Mason (1997:62), who draw on Bell (1984). When applied to the social work field, adaptation assumes that the social work practitioner also takes the goals of the encounter into account in the process of audience design.

are designed to assess a particular aspect of the service user's behaviour or response) and its impact on the interpreter's task:

> Just interpreting words is not as simple as it seems because you [the social worker] are codifying words … and so, as a result, things can get very interesting.

The use of codification strategies by social workers is informed by 'expert' knowledge; the implicitness of such knowledge and the difficulties this poses in the sense-making process of the interpreter were acknowledged by the same respondent quoted above:

> And even when you use an interpreter, you are not 100% sure that they've [interpreters] understood what you are saying… because they haven't got the professional knowledge that underpins what you are saying.

In short, there is a risk that, if the goals of interaction remain implicit and the processes through which they are achieved remain obscure (e.g. through the use of 'codification'), the level of trust that the social worker places in the interpreter's ability to make sense of clues and cues to meaning in the service provider's discourse, gaze, gesture, etc. is likely to be considerably overestimated and, as a result, the likelihood is diminished that conditions will be created that foster quality communication and successful goal achievement (as defined by the social work practitioner). This was acknowledged by a participant in the third focus group who was keen to stress that the expert role of the service provider and the subtleties of the communicative situation that needed to be 'controlled' by the provider in effect override the need to make the information explicit to the interpreter, the implication being that it was not worth the risk to disclose the specific goal(s) of the encounter to the interpreter in case she or he somehow compromises their achievement. This was felt to apply even if this meant more work on the service provider's part to compensate for the potential difficulties encountered by the interpreter. Compensation strategies cited by all focus groups ranged from systematically double-checking responses given to questions and paying attention to the body language of the service user, to applying strategies for assessing whether the interpreter (not just the service user) had understood the questions being posed.

The notion of the interpreter as a medium through which the speaker reaches his or her goal is therefore perhaps more complex than it first appears. Furthermore, it is suggested that goal achievement in the social work encounter needs to be viewed as contingent on factors that typically extend beyond the interaction at a particular point in time, which necessarily limits the extent to which a goal (and the understanding of the goal) is shared by the service provider and interpreter. This is also felt to limit the extent to which a goal can be negotiated at the edge of the role boundaries mentioned earlier (i.e. in one of the "sub-dialogues" (Mason 2001:ii) that may be initiated between these two agents in a dyadic exchange), especially if the factors that are 'external' to the interaction (e.g. long term goals and social work policy approaches) are not explicitly mentioned in the course of interaction.

The focus group findings appear to suggest an inherent contradiction at the level of social work practice; that is, practitioners appear to assert that the sharing of expert knowledge about the nature and purpose of goals in the interaction with the interpreter is a risk because it could compromise his or her control over the interaction, and yet, by providing explicit cues and clues to meaning for the benefit of the interpreter, goals could perhaps be achieved in a more straightforward manner than through reliance on the compensation strategies suggested above. This suggests an unwillingness to negotiate these aspects at the boundaries of the respective roles (especially on the part of the service provider), possibly as a result of general distrust in interpreting provision; however, this assertion would need to be examined using a much larger sample size if these findings are to be generalized.

1.1   Goal achievement and the server-served relationship

The problem of goal achievement in the interpreter-mediated triadic exchange and associated problems of trust can be further examined through the lens of the server-served relationship. In this regard, the framework proposed by Goffman (1961) in his work on mental health institutions is of note, chiefly because it presents a 'traditional' picture of the server-served relationship, which serves as a useful point of contrast with recent developments in the social work field. In Goffman's account, the "server's" work can include work that is "mechanical in nature" but also "verbal exchanges" which, for Goffman, break down into three parts: a technical part, a contractual part and a sociable part (*ibid.*:287); this underscores the server as gatekeeper and controller of the interaction. Although Goffman's comments relate to the specific context of the asylum, the three elements of the server's practice cited above are considered true of many other professional contexts that involve interaction between a service provider and client or service user, including relationships in the social work field. Goffman (*ibid.*:288) also asserts that

> [i]t is important to see that everything that goes on between server and client can be assimilated to these components of activity, and that any divergences can be understood in terms of these normative expectations. The full assimilation of the interaction between server and client to this framework is often for the server one of the tests of a 'good' service relation.

In spite of the fact that such a framework of institutional interaction is still frequently considered today by the layperson and professional alike as the 'normal order' of things, it is subject to challenge at two levels in the contemporary social work field. At the level of policy, the service user is increasingly seen as 'empowered' and involved in the 'negotiation' of the future direction/nature of the goals of social intervention that concern him or her (Butler and Drakeford 2005), as opposed to a more passive and 'served' agent. At the level of the interpreter-mediated encounter, the service provider is effectively cast in the role of both 'server' and 'served' (as the recipient of the interpreting service), which leads to a temporary (and potentially not inconsequential) relinquishing of control over goal achievement, in the sense that the 'coding' strategy used by the social worker may be diluted or compromised by the linguistic limits imposed on the interpretation.

In short, when applied to the contemporary social work field, Goffman's triad is subject to considerable challenge, largely as a result of ideological changes which place emphasis on the ability of the service user to move from 'served' to 'server' (as in 'self server') and to take responsibility for choices and for achieving goals as soon as possible. The nature of the contract, but also the assumption of the service provider as an 'expert' (i.e. the 'technical part' in Goffman's triad) has been called into question as a result of these emerging trends in practice and policy. It is this shifting nature of the service provider's role as 'server' and the resulting change to the way in which goals are determined and achieved that is seen as potentially significant for the relationships of trust between provider and interpreter, not least because of the implications it has for the power relations between the participants in the exchange and the service provider's expectations regarding the interpreter's involvement in the process of negotiation.

1.2   Trust 'in' and trust 'between'

The traditional server-served relationship outlined in the section above is also shaped by wider societal forces. For example, the visibility of other, external 'stakeholders' in the processes and outcomes in the social work field has arguably increased in recent times, which calls for a re-examination of the server-served relationship from a broader (macro) perspective. Placing the general public in the role of the 'served' opens up the possibility of examining the relationship in terms of the contribution made by the social work profession to the welfare of the wider nation. Public perception of this contribution undeniably has significance for the performance levels of the front line social workers, at the level of morale, for example. Similarly, public service interpreting can also be articulated in the same relationship with the general public who, in this case, are seen as (indirect) recipients (i.e. 'served') of the wider social benefits (or losses, depending on the individual's perspective) that interpreting provides. Any examination of the socio-cultural norms and the conceptualization of trust in the social work encounter must therefore take due account of this additional layer of relationships in the server-served framework, since the layers are intertwined and potentially impact on the level of inter-professional solidarity between service provider and interpreter at the level of interaction. In other words, at any given time in the interaction one agent will always play the role of layperson to the other's role of professional (except in cases where a trained bilingual interpreter might also be working as a trained social work professional), which is likely to colour beliefs and expectations about how the other might (re)act. Equally, lay perceptions of professional roles (developed through media representations, word-of-mouth, and so forth) can also generate 'myths' of practice which become embedded in professional roles (e.g. in the form of generalized distrust) and which are perpetuated through practices over time.

Such 'myths' of practice have developed partly as a result of the problems of identity which are experienced by both the social work and interpreting professions and which impact on the level of trust invested in the services by wider society. The status of both as 'full' professions, for example, has often been called into question (in relation to social work, see, for example, Wilding 1982). What is more, given the general decline of trust in the professions in contemporary society, there is a perception that the foundations of 'system trust' (following Giddens 1990) have been considerably weakened by these myths, even though this might not necessarily translate into actual changes in behaviour. This point is well illustrated by Onora O'Neill (2002) through her assertion that people still often call out the police in an emergency although they might have declared, for example in an opinion poll or survey, that their faith in the police has diminished. O'Neill challenges the idea that a crisis of trust has developed in the professions, and instead suggests that a 'culture of suspicion' has developed among the population largely as a response to increased emphasis on audit and accountability in all institution-related areas of society. However, every now and then events occur that perhaps tip the balance towards a perception of 'crisis' on the part of the public, which, in turn, can develop in some cases beyond a culture of suspicion into a culture of blame, and can impact negatively on the level of professional solidarity alluded to above. For example, the cases of the tragic deaths of Victoria Climbié (a case in which language and a lack of professional interpreting input were considered major factors in the tragedy) and Baby P which occurred, eight years apart, in the London borough of Haringey, have both served to thrust issues of trust in social services into the spotlight in recent times.[4] While these events may have served to diminish general public trust in the social work profession, they more particularly draw attention to the complexity of

---

[4] The deaths, as a result of abuse and neglect, of eight-year old Victoria Climbié in 2000 and seventeen-month old Peter Connelly in 2007 (the child referred to as Baby P until reporting restrictions were lifted in August 2009) received wide press coverage at the time and led to reviews of the child protection system in England .

the inter- and intra-professional relationships in the field: the lines of communication, decision-making, accountability, and so forth, which are further
complicated by the involvement of an interpreter. The fallout from the latest
high profile case of Baby P and others may be seen by some as the result of a
culmination of changes in social work practice which are documented briefly
in the following section and which underpin the socio-cultural norms of social
work practice today.

By contrast, public trust in interpreting service provision is not often called
into question in terms of its overall fitness for purpose, largely because of the
general lack of awareness about the profession in public life; however, distrust
in the profession has grown significantly in recent years (as evidenced by
growing media attention) with regard to its *need* in contemporary Britain, as
a result of well-publicized audits of police, court, NHS and council budgetary
expenditure on interpreting services (Tipton, forthcoming).

In sum, therefore, it can be argued that trust *in* the professions of social work
and interpreting is not peripheral to the discussion of trust *between* the two. As
Hale (2007:145) notes, "[a]t the macro level, the attitudes towards interpreters from the other participants and their understanding and expectations of
their work and their role impinge on the performance of the interpreter". This
statement could equally apply to the performance and attitude of the service
provider in the encounter, given the extension of 'other participants' to include
external stakeholders such as the general public as mentioned above. Public
attitudes are considered to have an impact on professional roles during situated
action (for example on staff morale as mentioned earlier) and, furthermore,
can shape the perception of justice (and value for taxpayer's money) being
delivered where it matters most. This helps to ascertain the roots of some of
the inter- and intra-professional trust-related issues at the level of interaction,
which, it is suggested, lie principally in individual experience or myth (or a
combination of the two).

2.   Changes in the social work profession and implications for intra-/inter-professional trust

It is not within the scope of this paper to discuss the nature of the recent
changes in the social work profession in depth; however, in order to identify
and understand the range of socio-cultural norms present in interpreter-mediated
encounters in this field, some of the changes that have affected social work
practice in recent years are charted briefly here.

Many researchers in social work refer to the rise of 'managerialism',
'evidence-based practice' and the 'commodification of services' in the social
work profession, an increase in detailed procedural methods of practice (e.g.
assessment for eligibility), and a concomitant decline in the autonomy and
discretion of the social work practitioner (Howe 1996, Martin 2000, Lymbery

2000, 2001, Butler and Drakeford 2005). Smith (2001) charts this change, for example, through reference to several White Papers on Modernizing Social Services (in particular the Department of Health 1998), which place emphasis on performance indicators and measurable outcomes, monitored by the Commission for Social Care Inspection created in 2004 (replaced by the Care Quality Commission in 2009). Parton (2008) interprets such changes as marking a paradigmatic shift which has seen the 'informational' supersede the 'social' in social work practice. Further, he asserts that, by the early to mid-1990s, the emphasis on the relationship in social work practice had been "stripped of its social, cultural and professional significance" (*ibid.:*260). Parton's article emphasizes the growing importance of 'auditable' information collection, which, while it might make decisions more transparent and professionals more accountable, inevitably leads to some information loss. For Parton, this has "particular implications for the way in which identities are constructed and the type of human experience that can be represented" (*ibid.*:262); there is a risk that the situation is exacerbated in multilingual encounters. Parton refers to the work of Scott Lash (2002), who concludes that the emphasis in such a culture shifts from 'meaning' to 'operationality', summed up by Smith (2001) as the pre-eminence of the quantitative and objective over the qualitative and the subjective. According to Smith, this shift has impacted on the nature of trust relationships in the social work encounter in the sense that the need to 'trust' in services has been supplanted by Government rhetoric which privileges the service user's *right* to services (Smith 2001:288, original emphasis). Arguably, service users requiring interpreting services are unlikely to have an understanding of such a shift, which is why trust remains an important aspect of interpreter-mediated interaction, as Edwards *et al.*'s (2005, 2006) work highlights.

The future direction of social work practice is still the subject of much debate; however, several authors, among them Lymbery (2001), suggest that future developments in the field need to place greater emphasis on collective action and negotiation. Butler and Drakeford (2005:650) support this by asserting that "users rely upon a recognition of reciprocal relationships and shared decision making as the basis upon which improvements can best take place", and furthermore that "trust is the key that allows us to understand both users and providers as jointly engaged in a common pursuit" (*ibid.*), which again draws attention to the need to review the traditional server-served relationship between service users and providers in the modern context. The problem facing practitioners is that, while shared decision making and negotiated outcomes appear to be gaining primacy in the rhetoric of Government, the nature of the 'exchange' between provider and user is likened by some, such as Smith (2001:287), as akin to any other impersonal contractual relationship "rather than as the kind of engagement that thrives on trusting relationships". There therefore appears something of a paradox emerging in the profession, a paradox that is further complicated by the involvement of the interpreter in the exchange.

It might legitimately be argued that changes in the nature of social work practice are of little or no consequence for the interpreter, whose role is to interpret the interventions of participants regardless of the ideological shifts that lie behind the social worker's practice. This view is consistent with treating the interpreter as medium or conduit (Reddy 1979), which privileges the transfer of the basic propositional meaning of an utterance and can be said to form the 'basic contract' between interpreter, service provider and service user. However such a view neglects the broader social and linguistic issues at play in the social work encounter that can directly or indirectly affect the interpreter's performance, including the pragmatic and semiotic aspects discussed at length in Hatim and Mason (1997). It also leaves little scope for considering the extent to which differentiation occurs in the interpreter's role, a role which could also be viewed in terms of Goffman's triad mentioned earlier, since in many respects the interpreter, like the service provider, plays a technical, contractual and social role in the encounter. What is more, the conduit view does not allow full account to be taken of the shifts in the server-served relationship between the service provider and interpreter, nor between the service provider and service user.

Wadensjö's (1998) conceptualization of the interpreter as the 'coordinator' of others' talk offers an alternative perspective to the conduit role and draws attention to the potential of the interpreter to be viewed as a 'server' in his or her own right (such is the level of power afforded the 'coordinator of others' talk). This has implications for the level of the interpreter's involvement in the negotiation of goals in the encounter, since the role of coordinator is often subject to considerable challenge by the service provider. For example, the interpreter-as-coordinator can easily become engaged in a power struggle for control of the floor if the service provider 'over-rides' the turn-taking sequence (sometimes completely but often partially) by not allowing the interpreter to complete his or her turn before taking the floor again (Englund Dimitrova 1997, Tipton 2008). The interpreter can construe this as unfair practice on the service provider's part, with the result that she or he is faced with the decision of whether to assert his or her presence as coordinator and 'promote justice' for the service user by making sure that the complete turn is interpreted. However, if, from the social worker's perspective, the dominant socio-cultural norm in the encounter has shifted away from meaning and narrative (i.e. *why* users behave as they do) to *what* they do – following Parton (2008:259; original emphasis), and echoed by Howe (1996) – it becomes easier to understand both the approach(es) of the social worker to discourse in the encounter and the possible tendency to curtail the narrative being conveyed by the interpreter, since this is no longer often the main focus and does not necessarily assist the social worker in "judging the nature and level of risk" and "allocating resources" (Parton 2008:260). The resulting lack of trust that might develop on the interpreter's part as a result of being denied the opportunity to complete a turn may lead to a sense of antagonism that could be avoided if this socio-cultural norm were made more explicit by the service provider as part of the process of negotiation "around institutionalized roles" (Smith 2001:291).

I began this paper by suggesting that the 'traditional' server-served re-lationship is contested in the new context of social work policy as well as within the interpreter-mediated encounter, in particular because of the (often implicit) differentiation in goal achievement. If indeed the relationship between service provider and service user is to be developed on the basis of shared engagement/negotiated outcomes, to allow service users to engage with social workers as fellow travellers on the road to discovery, as Smith (*ibid.*) asserts, the implications this has for the involvement of an interpreter on such a jour-ney merit particular attention by the academy. This is why a re-examination of the relationship between server and served is deemed necessary. So far the discussion has not focused on the specific nature and purpose of trust in the interpreter-mediated social work exchange, aside from a brief indication that my approach to trust is variable and process-driven and the suggestion that it can be negotiated (possibly more explicitly than often seems the case) in the spaces 'around the institutionalized roles' of the service provider and interpreter. In the final section of this paper I address the nature and meaning of trust in the interpreter-mediated encounter by examining some of the (very extensive) literature on trust and by contrasting aspects of this scholarship with the findings presented so far; the aim is to tease out a working conceptualization of trust in the interpreter-mediated social work encounter that can be subject to further investigation in the field.

3.   Nature and meaning of trust in the interpreter-mediated social work encounter

Attempts to define the concept of trust have proved extremely difficult, as is well documented (Shapiro 1987, Misztal 1996, Möllering 2001). For example, early conceptualizations of trust as a 'psychological event' were effectively supplanted by approaches placing more emphasis on social context, as illus-trated by Lewis and Weigert (1985:969), who assert that "individuals would have no occasion or need to trust apart from social relationships". An emphasis on the social nature of trust lends support to the idea that a degree of basic trust exists between two professionals in interaction. It is further suggested that such basic (professional) trust is rooted to a large extent in the habits or routinized practices of the workplace (in the sense that very little would be undertaken if this trust were completely absent). However, it is interesting to note that the so-called routinized practices of the interpreter-mediated social work encounter do not appear to generate a particularly strong level of basic trust; on the contrary, some practitioners in the focus groups indicated that their experience over time was felt to have eroded basic levels of trust in their working relationship with interpreters.

Edwards *et al.*'s (2006) assertion that trust has the possibility of being started afresh in each new interaction is perhaps one reason that it is seen as unstable and process-oriented; this is why I refer in this paper to relationships of trust in the plural, as this opens the possibility that trust serves different purposes at different times in interaction, that it is potentially weak or strong. It also allows a distinction to be drawn between the relationships of trust that are generated variously between the interpreter and service provider and the interpreter and the service user.

Edwards *et al.*'s (2006) study on user views of working with interpreters is an example of an empirical approach that is theorized using the process approach mentioned above. Despite the fact that their initial research project was not designed specifically to analyze issues of trust, in the course of their investigations – semi-structured interviews with 50 users – it emerged as one of the most salient aspects of the users' experiences. The theoretical framework that these authors developed to analyze their findings is based on the distinction between 'personal' and 'abstract' trust (following Giddens 1990, 1991) according to which personal trust relates to trust in kin, friends and so forth, in contrast to trust in impersonal and often 'faceless' systems. The service user's position of vulnerability in the institutional encounter, which stems from his or her assumed level of cultural/linguistic limitations in the context, requires a considerable leap of faith to trust in the systems represented variously by the service provider (i.e. the institution of social work) and the interpreter,[5] who are both seen as the 'faceworkers' of systems, following Giddens and as mentioned by Smith (*ibid.*:298). The leap of faith the service user has to take means that it is not surprising that 'abstract trust' was found to have primacy over 'personal trust' in the study.

By contrast, it is more difficult to account for the nature of the interpreter's relationships of trust with the service provider under this framework. It could be argued, for example, that the interpreter as the 'coordinator of talk' and 'facilitator' of the speakers' goal achievements does not need to be concerned with either personal or abstract trust in order to perform the role in the manner required of the basic contract mentioned earlier. However, in practice, this is perhaps more true of abstract trust than personal trust. This is because, in the dyadic exchanges between interpreter and service provider, a degree of personal trust serves to mitigate the problems posed by the basic contract, since the contract assumes that interlingual and intercultural information

---

[5] Here interpreting is viewed as a system in its own right, one that is sanctioned by society and that is governed by rules (such as impartiality) with which the user is unlikely to be familiar, hence the need for the service user to take a 'leap of faith' to trust in the interpreting service provided.

transfer is inherently unproblematic in interpreter-mediated exchanges. The interpreter, however, needs to place personal trust in the service provider to ensure that the negotiation of any problems that occur in the communicative process is made possible.

Even though the interpreter and service provider are, in effect, both 'servers' of abstract systems, neither has to take the leap of faith on the scale of the service user in terms of trusting these abstract systems in the field during practice. They do, however, have to develop a degree of mutual trust in the other's approach to the communicative process. The primacy of personal trust between provider and interpreter is therefore seen first and foremost as a feature of the shifting nature of the server-served relationship between these two agents, although it is understood in a 'looser' sense than the personal trust that exists between family and friends.

3.1   Trust as a mechanism for reducing complexity

Luhmann's conceptualization of trust as a way of reducing complexity (1979, 1988) supports the approach to trust as a heuristic mentioned at the start of this paper and is considered a more appropriate conceptualization than the personal/abstract trust framework for examining the relationship between the service provider and interpreter. For Luhmann, trust acts as a mechanism for reducing the complexity of situations and takes "special forms on account of its subjective nature"; these forms are described as "changes in the level at which uncertainty is absorbed or made tolerable" (1979:26-27). Although his remarks chiefly concern the level of basic trust between humans (without which, he claims, society would be likely to collapse), they also apply to the discrete instances where trust is generated/deployed on the basis of need or risk, as mentioned by Smith (2001), suggesting that various forms and strengths of trust are always present in any one interaction.

The need to reduce complexity in the liaison interpreting encounter is apparent through the understanding of texture in this mode (following Hatim and Mason 1997) and the 'incompleteness' and fragmentation occasioned as a result. In other words, the interpreter working in the liaison mode is forced to draw on contextual clues (e.g. pragmatic and semiotic) to construct meaningful output and compensate for the restricted quantity of information and idea development that the mode imposes. The relationship between trust and incompleteness in general interaction is taken up by Misztal (1996:18), who argues that "[t]rust always involves an element of risk resulting from our inability to monitor others' behaviour, from our inability to have a complete knowledge about other people's motivation and, generally, from the contingency of social reality". Similarly, Luhmann (1979:37) asserts:

> It is not possible to acquire information on the future behaviour of others except in an incomplete and unreliable fashion. But one can shift

this problem into a realm where it can be mastered more effectively. One can inform oneself instead about certain structural properties of the system which one shares with others, acquire thereby the supports necessary for building trust, and so overcome the need for information which is lacking. As in many other functional contexts, structure reduces the need for information.

Luhmann's observations are particularly pertinent to the present discussion because of the earlier points made with regard to the information that is sometimes left implicit between the service provider and interpreter and that can impact on the effectiveness of communication; this information is considered of a 'structural' nature first and foremost (i.e. not about meaning but about intention behind the meaning). The reason for such implicitness is considered to be directly related to the socio-cultural norms of the field, i.e. the role of the social worker's expert knowledge which, as the focus group findings suggest, take primacy over the interpreter's 'need to know'. Fukuyama's (1995) work is also of note in this regard as he asserts that trust can only become active between individuals who base their interactions on commonly shared norms. While service providers and interpreters might share some norms in common about professional practice (ranging from the need to not get involved with clients on a personal level to basic norms about conversation turn taking, among many others), it has been observed that socio-cultural norms of the social work field, particularly those relating to goal differentiation, often preclude the sharing of certain norms of social work practice with the interpreter, which limits the level of negotiation around the institutionalized roles of these agents and the concomitant levels of trust generated between the two.

Luhmann's work on trust finds echo in work on norms in the field of translation studies. Hermans' work is apposite in this regard since he characterizes a norm as a psychological and social 'mechanism' that mediates between the individual and the collective (1999:80). Crucially, Hermans (*ibid.*) asserts that "[n]orms contribute to the stability of interpersonal relations by reducing uncertainty", which is precisely the function Luhmann ascribes to trust. Further, for Hermans, norms "make behaviour more predictable by generalizing from past experience and making projections concerning similar types of situation in the future. They have a socially regulatory function" (*ibid.*). Hermans' observations again foreground the importance of building up structural knowledge of the interaction, as this is seen as the basis on which trust is generated between the two agents concerned. In this regard, the possibility that trust can be considered a norm of interaction is raised.

3.2   Trust and normalcy

In seeking to reduce complexity and create the 'illusion of normality' (i.e. the belief that the interaction will take place as though it were being conducted in the social worker's mother tongue, following Wadensjö 1998), it could be argued that the social worker involved in an interpreter-mediated encounter needs to conserve cognitive resources for the technical aspects of his or her work, and that investing basic trust in the interpreter is a way to achieve this. This not only helps the service provider to reduce uncertainty but also, and perhaps more importantly, it allows scope for the service provider to promote two aspects of institutional-based trust for the service user's benefit, that McEvily *et al.* (2003:478, drawing on the work of Garfinkel 1963) describe as 'situational normality' (i.e. the belief that success is likely because the situation is normal) and 'structural assurances' (i.e. the belief that success is likely because such contextual conditions as promises, contracts, regulations and guarantees are in place). It is the contention of this paper that the latter of the two can only be provided through negotiation at the interstices of the boundary roles between service provider and interpreter, since such structural assurances pose cultural issues to be overcome in the interpreting process. Success in the social work interpreter-mediated encounter therefore needs to be understood in terms of the creation of the best possible communicative conditions during the encounter and not in terms of the outcome of the encounter (i.e. that it will necessarily achieve the service user's aims).

Finally, it is important to mention the importance of time to relationships of trust and normalcy. This is especially relevant in relation to the problem of basic trust, which many scholars assume begins low and ends high, as information and knowledge about the other accumulates (McKnight *et al.* 1998). In the interpreter-mediated encounter, relationships of trust can develop on a fairly solid, predictable basis during the encounter over time, if the service provider and interpreter work together on a regular basis. Pöchhacker (2000) found, through a survey of the interpreter's role and tasks in the health and social care settings in Austria, that this familiarity could lead to interpreters being granted greater autonomy to 'lead' questions as the service provider's trust in the interpreter's ability to do this grew on the basis of exposure to similar situations. While there was no evidence of such control being relinquished to the interpreter in the focus group work I conducted, the 'structural' information that was exchanged between provider and interpreter prior to an encounter involving the same interpreter did appear to help to improve the quality of the communication, as this quotation from the second focus group illustrates:

> You can then build up a history with them [interpreters] and say things like 'do you remember when we were with that other woman? Well, this is I think a similar situation'... And it is a short cut to them understanding what you are talking about.

However, for many practitioners, initial encounters with new interpreters were characterized by generally low levels of initial trust, and exposure to practice over time did not necessarily diminish this problem. The level of erosion in basic trust and strategies adopted to compensate for it are illustrated in the following quote from the same participant, in which the marked use of the word *now* highlights the extent to which practice has developed, over time and through exposure to working with interpreters, suggesting that compensation strategies are a means of generating the desired level of 'normalcy' in the encounter for the service provider:

> I'm much more rigorous now in saying [to the interpreter] 'I want you to say this *exactly* as I'm saying it'…you know, my colleagues get very, very disconcerted when they say something like 'when did this incident happen?' and there'll be a huge discussion, and it'll take for ages, and you are sat there thinking 'I only asked a simple question'. And you say to the interpreter 'what's been said?', 'what's been happening?' and they'll say 'oh I'm just explaining… I'm just making sure I understand it' and you [the social worker] wonder what's really happening.

4.   Conclusion

This paper has highlighted the extent to which changes in social work practice and policy, and increased public scrutiny at both a general level (public perception) and a formal level (audit), have impacted on the practitioner's role in recent times and have served to question the traditional server-served relationship between the service provider and service user. These changes are not inconsequential to the interpreter-mediated encounter, especially if the interpreter-as-coordinator role is foregrounded.

The social function ascribed to trust draws attention to its potential variability in interaction and its inherently process-driven nature. In terms of its purpose, trust is first and foremost viewed in the social work interpreter-mediated encounter as a heuristic, that is, a mechanism that can be deployed to reduce complexity where appropriate, although the discussion here is premised on the fact that it is not perhaps sufficiently deployed in interaction as it needs to be to facilitate optimum quality in communication. No level of trust (or rather propensity to trust) is therefore simply assumed on the part of either party to the exchange.

Although it is argued that there is likely to be a general degree of basic trust between professionals, the focus group findings suggest that this has often been eroded and has led to particular compensation strategies being deployed in the encounter to overcome the problems this poses and to establish a degree of 'normalcy' as a backdrop against which the social work practitioner carries out his or her technical work. The reasons behind such erosion appear to stem from negative individual experience in the field and in the myths generated about practice that impact on the communicative relationship with the interpreter. The lack of negotiation over the more structural aspects of social work practice (i.e. the socio-cultural norms of the social work field) between the social worker and interpreter at the boundaries of their respective roles is considered one of the main reasons behind the lack of mutual trust between the two agents in relation to the quality of the communication obtained. Although it may be concluded that the two agents discussed here do not need necessarily to negotiate the goals of the encounter (since this falls within the technical remit of the social work practitioner as 'expert'), they do perhaps need to devote greater consideration to the need to negotiate *expectations* at the boundaries of their respective roles. This is because if the future direction of social work practice is to be based on collective negotiation and action, the interpreter's role as a coordinator of others' talk implies a potentially greater need for structural awareness in the encounter (i.e. the intentions and goals behind the discourse) in order for culturally sensitive and appropriate services to be delivered.

References

Bell, Allan (1984) 'Language Style as Audience Design', *Language in Society* 13(2): 145-204.

Blommaert, Jan (2001) 'Investigating Narrative Inequality: Analyzing African Asylum Seekers' Stories in Belgium', *Discourse and Society* 12(4): 413-49.

Brophy, Julia, Jagbir Jhutti-Johal and Charlie Owen (2003) *Significant Harm: Child Protection Litigation in a Multi-Cultural Setting*, London: Lord Chancellor's Department.

Butler, Ian and Mark Drakeford (2005) 'Trusting in Social Work', *British Journal of Social Work* 35(5): 639-53.

Chamba, Rampaul, Waqar Ahmad, Michael Hirst, Dot Lawton and Bryony Beresford (1999) *On the Edge: Minority Ethnic Families Caring for a Disabled Child*, Bristol: The Policy Press.

Chand, Ashok (2005) 'Do you Speak English? Language Barriers in Child Protection Social Work with Minority Ethnic Families', *British Journal of Social Work* 35(6): 807-21.

Department of Health (1998) *Modernising Social Services*, London: The Stationery Office.

Edwards, Rosalind, Claire Alexander and Bogusia Temple (2006) 'Interpreting Trust: Abstract and Personal Trust for People Who Need Interpreters to Access Services', *Sociological Research Online*, 11(1). Available online: http://www.socresonline.org.uk/11/1/edwards.html (accessed 1 March 2009).

Edwards, Rosalind, Bogusia Temple and Claire Alexander (2005) Users' Experiences of Interpreters: The Critical Role of Trust', *International Journal of Research and Practice in Interpreting* 7(1): 77-95.

Englund Dimitrova, Birgitta (1997) 'Degree of Interpreter Responsibility in the Interaction Process in Community Interpreting', in Silvana E. Carr, Roda P. Roberts, Aideen Dufour and Dini Steyn (eds) *The Critical Link: Interpreters in the Community*, Amsterdam & Philadelphia: John Benjamins, 147-64.

Fukuyama, Francis (1995) *The Social Virtues and the Creation of Prosperity*, London: Free Press.

Giddens, Anthony (1990) *The Consequences of Modernity*, Oxford: Polity Press.

------ (1991) *Modernity and Self Identity*, Oxford: Polity Press.

Goffman, Erving (1961/1968) *Asylums: Essays on the Social Situation of Mental Patients and other Inmates*, Harmondsworth: Penguin.

Hale, Sandra Beatrice (2007) *Community Interpreting*, Basingstoke, Hampshire & New York: Palgrave Macmillan.

Hatim, Basil and Ian Mason (1997) *The Translator as Communicator*, London & New York: Routledge.

Hermans, Theo (1999) *Translation in Systems: Descriptive and System-Oriented Approaches Explained*, Manchester: St Jerome Publishing.

Howe, David (1996) 'Surface and Depth in Social Work Practice', in Nigel Parton (ed.) *Social Work Theory, Social Change and Social Work*, London: Routledge, 77-97.

Lash, Scott (2002) *Critique as Information*, London: Sage.

Lewis, David, J. and Andrew Weigert (1985) 'Trust as Social Reality', *Social Forces* 63(4): 967-85.

Luhmann, Niklas (1979) *Trust and Power: Two Works by Niklas Luhmann, intr. G. Poggi*, Chichester: John Wiley & Sons; first published 1968.

------ (1988) 'Familiarity, Confidence, Trust: Problems and Alternatives', in Diego Gambetta (ed.) *Making and Breaking Co-operative Relations*, London: Basil Blackwell, 94-108.

Lymbery, Mark (2000) 'The Retreat from Professionalism: From Social Worker to Care Manager', in Nigel Martin (ed.) *Professionalism, Boundaries and the Workplace*, London & New York: Routledge, 123-38.

------ (2001) 'Social Work at the Crossroads', *British Journal of Social Work* 31(3): 369-84.

Martin, Nigel (ed.) (2000) *Professionalism, Boundaries and the Workplace*, London & New York: Routledge.

Maryns. Katrijn (2006) *The Asylum Speaker: Language in the Belgian Asylum Procedure*, Manchester: St. Jerome Publishing.

Mason, Ian (ed.) (1999) *Dialogue Interpreting*, special issue of *The Translator* 5(2).

------ (2000) 'Models and Methods in Dialogue Interpreting Research', in Maeve Olohan (ed.) *Intercultural Faultlines: Research Models in Translation Studies I*, Manchester: St Jerome Publishing, 215-32.

------ (ed.) (2001) *Triadic Exchanges: Studies in Dialogue Interpreting*, Manchester: St Jerome Publishing.

McEvily, Bill, Vincenzo Perrone and Akbar Zaheer (2003) 'Trust as an Organizing Principle', *Organization Science* 14(1): 91-103.

McKnight, D.Harrison, Larry L. Cummings and Norman L. Chervany (1998) 'Initial Trust Formation in New Organizational Relationships', *The Academy of Management Review* 23(3): 473-90.

Misztal, Barbara (1996) *Trust in Modern Societies: The Search for the Bases of Moral Order*, Cambridge: Polity Press.

Möllering, Guido (2001) 'The Nature of Trust: From Georg Simmel to a Theory of Expectation, Interpretation, and Suspension', *Sociology* 35(2): 403-20.

O'Neale, Vivienne (2000) *Excellence Not Excuses: Inspection of Services for Ethnic Minority Children and Families*, London: Department of Health Publications.

O'Neill, Onora (2002) *A Question of Trust: The BBC Reith Lectures 2002*, Cambridge: Cambridge University Press.

Parton, Nigel (2008) 'Changes in the Form of Knowledge in Social Work: From the 'Social' to the 'Informational'?' *British Journal of Social Work* 38(2): 253-69.

Pincus, Allen and Anne Minahan (1973) *Social Work Practice: Model and Method*, Itasca, Illinois: F.E. Peacock Publishers.

Pöchhacker, Franz (2000) 'The Community Interpreter's Task: Self Perception and Provider Views', in Roda P. Roberts, Silvana E.Carr, Diana Abraham and Aideen Dufour (eds) *The Critical Link 2: Interpreters in the Community*, Amsterdam & Philadelphia: John Benjamins, 49-66.

Popay, Jennie and Gareth Williams (1998) 'Qualitative Research and Evidence Based Health Care'. *Journal of Royal Society of Medicine* 91 (Suppl. 35): 32-37.

Pym, Anthony (2000) 'On Cooperation', in Maeve Olohan (ed.) *Intercultural Faultlines: Research Models in Translation Studies I*, Manchester: St Jerome Publishing, 181-92.

Reddy, Michael (1979) 'The Conduit Metaphor: A Case of Frame Conflict in our Language about Language', in Andrew Ortony (ed.) *Metaphor and Thought*, Cambridge: Cambridge University Press, 284-324.

Seligman, Adam, B. (1997) *The Problem of Trust*, Princeton, N.J.: Princeton University Press.

Shapiro, Susan P. (1987) 'The Social Control of Impersonal Trust', *The American Journal of Sociology* 93(3): 623-58.

Smith, Carole (2001) 'Trust and Confidence: Possibilities for Social Work in 'High Modernity'', *British Journal of Social Work* 31(2): 287-306.

Tipton, Rebecca (2008) 'Reflexivity and the Social Construction of Identity in Interpreter-Mediated Asylum Encounters', *The Translator* 14(1): 1-19.

------ (forthcoming) 'Public Service Interpreting and the Politics of Entitlement for New Entrants to the United Kingdom', *Journal of Language and Politics*.

Wadensjö, Cecilia (1998) *Interpreting as Interaction*, London: Routledge.

Wilding, Paul (1982) *Professional Power and Social Welfare*, London, Boston & Henley: Routledge & Kegan Paul.

Institutional Identities of Interpreters in the Asylum Application Context

A Critical Discourse Analysis of Interpreting Policies in the Voluntary Sector

MATTHEW MALTBY
University of Manchester, UK

Abstract. *Interpreter impartiality and notions of interpreter neutrality have long been enshrined in interpreter codes of conduct, but there are nonetheless clear distinctions evident between models of interpreting prescribed in codes of conduct and the way that these notions are articulated in institutional interpreting policies. Drawing on Critical Discourse Analysis, this article considers the interpreting policies of two voluntary sector advocacy organizations in the UK asylum application context (Asylum Aid and Refugee Action) to argue that institutional interpreting policy might act as an interface between codes of conduct and institutionally specific conceptualizations of interpreters and their roles. The author reconstructs two interpreter identities on the basis of interpreting policy articulations which diverge from professional codes of conduct and argues that these conceptualizations are, in part, ideologically shaped by institutional operational objectives.*

For many, interpreter neutrality and impartiality in public service settings such as courts of law, immigration hearings and healthcare contexts have long been a point of contention. Conceptualizations of 'impartiality' and 'neutrality' vary considerably. Morris (1995:30) argues that in some institutions, assumptions are made that "one language can be switched into another with no loss of substance or form and, furthermore, that a standard of absolute accuracy will be achieved". This positivist view of language as a transparent code underpins a conceptualization of the interpreter as a language conduit; interpreting is thus a matter of switching code while leaving the messages expressed intact and unaltered. Since the interpreter is viewed as a mere presence with no active engagement with what he or she is interpreting, interpreter impartiality and neutrality are taken for granted and are assumed to remain unchanged throughout the duration of the interpreted interaction. Other conceptualizations assume that "only clearly expressed personal attitudes or opinions can endanger impartiality and neutrality" (Leinonen 2007:231).

The ways in which interpreter impartiality and neutrality are articulated in codes of conduct appear to be intricately linked to conceptualizations of the role and function of the interpreter and notions of interpreter professionalism. In many national contexts, public service interpreters are bound by professional codes of conduct which enshrine particular notions of interpreter impartiality and neutrality and oblige interpreters, at the risk of serious professional (and potentially personal) consequences, to observe often vaguely formulated articulations of how they should interact within the institution/client relationship as they engage in their professional duties. And yet, several studies conducted in a range of different settings which consider actual interpreter-mediated interactions against the backdrop of a code of conduct suggest that "the interpreter is not a neutral and uninvolved machine but rather an active participant in the talk exchanges, fulfilling a crucial role in coordinating others' talk" (Mason 1999:150). Evidently, there is a gap between the codes of conduct which interpreters in public service contexts are often obliged to uphold and the observable dynamics which unfold in mediated interactions. Wadensjö (2008:187) views this gap as "communicative wiggle room" which can partly account for the "variability of interlocutors' local 'readings' of one another in social interaction". Tipton (2008a:190) argues that the institutional context of the exchange frequently leads to a breakdown in interpreters' ability to maintain impartiality; she suggests that it is not the site of practice *per se* which affects (interpreter) neutrality, but rather the commitment of the interlocutors to establishing that site as one of neutral practice and maintaining a 'baseline neutrality' of interaction.

It seems clear that interpreters often approach interactions with a notion of impartiality informed by a code of conduct, but other interlocutors' perceptions of the interpreter's role and function subsequently lead to a situation in which impartiality becomes increasingly difficult, even undesirable, to maintain. Inghilleri (2003) argues that perceptions of the interpreter's role and activity – hence notions of impartiality and neutrality – are largely conditioned by habitualized routines of institutional structures, ranging from "training institutes, to participation in a particular discourse community, to a particular institutional body, and/or a wider set of social beliefs and practices concerning cross-cultural/linguistic communication and notions of exclusion/inclusion" (*ibid.*:255). Wadensjö argues that public service interpreters should properly be viewed as "actors within the *service system of society* and at the same time within the *public system of control*" (1997:36; emphases in original). Since "institutions live partly by their routines" (Wadensjö 1998:45), it seems that, in these contexts, interpreter behaviour is as much shaped by the habitual institutional routines in which the interpreted exchanges take place as by codes of conduct. Leinonen (2007) suggests that notions of impartiality and neutrality enshrined within codes of conduct are forms of professional ideologies which orient interpreters towards particular definitions of their role and function. She also argues that these professional ideologies do not pay enough attention to the contextual complexities and institutional requirements of interpreting (*ibid.*:239).

This article investigates the ways in which two voluntary sector organizations in the UK asylum context articulate notions of interpreter impartiality in their policies, in an attempt to illustrate how institutional requirements might inform interpreting at a more immediate level. Using a Critical Discourse Analysis approach (Fairclough 1992, 2003), I reconstruct institutional notions of interpreter impartiality and neutrality by considering the institutions' policies as a 'moment of discourse' (Fairclough 1992). The impact of the relevant policy articulations on the role of the interpreter, specifically with regard to notions of impartiality and neutrality, may elucidate the extent to which interpreting policies could determine interpreter orientations within institutional contexts.

1.   Policy as a 'moment of discourse'

Discourse is a difficult concept to define; Fairclough and Wodak (1997:258) regard discourse – language use in speech and writing – as a form of social practice which "implies a dialectical relationship between a particular discursive event and the situation(s), institution(s) and social structure(s) which frame it". Moreover, they view discourse as "socially constitutive as well as being socially constituted" (*ibid.*). I consider elsewhere how interpreting policy in the asylum application context might be viewed as being constituted by particular discourses in this setting, such as discourses on immigration and multiculturalist discourses (Maltby 2008). I confine my discussion in this article to the idea that policy articulations reflect the ways in which institutions conceptualize interpreting and, more specifically, interpreter impartiality. I highlight the *Code of Professional Conduct* of the National Register of Public Service Interpreters (NRPSI 2007)[1] and the *Diploma in Public Service Interpreting* handbook (DPSI 2007)[2] as examples of a specific discourse on normative, prescriptive modes of action within interpreter-mediated exchanges. The articulations of the two institutional interpreting policies under consideration in this article, namely those of Asylum Aid and Refugee Action, are presented to illustrate the dialectical relation between their own conceptualizations of impartiality and neutrality and those enshrined in the NRPSI and DPSI codes of conduct.

---

[1] The NRPSI accreditation is administered by the Chartered Institute of Linguists (IoL). Full membership status of the register requires an interpreter to be over the age of 18 and eligible to work in the UK, in addition to holding accreditation with DPSI, the Metropolitan Police Test or an honours level degree in interpreting, plus more than 400 hours of proven public service interpreting experience.

[2] DPSI accreditation is also administered by the IoL.

In defining policy, Crowley argues that, in general terms, "policy is a *self-conscious framework for authoritative action*" (emphases in original) and that its effectiveness within any given context "depends on its compatibility with the nature of the social reality it is designed to modify" (1996:228-29). Freeman also suggests that "policy is essentially problem-defining rather than problem-solving" (1994:228), a perspective which Gentile suggests is regularly witnessed in discourses on interpreting in public service contexts, as institutional policies identify "problem clients in problem contexts" (1997:118). Ager makes reference to the notion of 'overt' and 'covert' policies. He argues that overt policies are declared as such and are enshrined in texts or documents. Covert policies, on the other hand, "are represented simply by what people do or the attitudes they adopt" (2001:195). He goes on to stress that, for example, "a policy of rejection or discrimination is nonetheless real for not being openly stated" (*ibid.*). This is particularly pertinent with respect to CDA's approach to discourse analysis, developed by Fairclough (1992) and Fairclough and Wodak (1997), which sees itself as a "critical and engaged" form of intervention, laying bare to scrutiny the more opaque, hidden elements of discourse which do "ideological work" (Fairclough and Wodak 1997:259).

The dialectic nature of discourse, according to Fairclough, implies that "on the one hand discourse is shaped and constrained by social structure in the widest sense ... on the other hand, discourse is socially constitutive" (Fairclough 1992:64). In essence, a discourse represents the world as perceived by an institution, and the constitutive nature of a discourse is sanctioned within a network of power relations. The constitutive force of discourse is central to Fairclough's notion of CDA; he argues that it comprises three elements. First, discourse contributes to the construction of social identities and subject positions, operating very specifically at the local level. Second, as these identities are constructed and reiterated, they are positioned in relation to each other, and social relationships are thus established. And third, discourse contributes "to the construction of systems of knowledge and belief" (*ibid.*). For Fairclough, discourse thus constitutes social interaction at three distinct but intertwined levels, moving from the specific and local through to the wider, macro levels. As I have already indicated, this article focuses solely on the first constitutive aspect of discourse, i.e. the ways in which the discourses of institutional policies construct a specific interpreter identity.

2.   Data collation and methodology

Under the terms of the *1951 United Nations Convention Relating to the Status of Refugees*, which the UK has agreed to observe, an individual who has a "well-founded fear of being persecuted for reasons of race, religion, nationality, membership of a particular social group or political opinion" (UNHCR

2001) may apply for asylum.

In order to apply for asylum in the UK, an individual must make themselves and their intention to apply for asylum known to the Borders and Immigration Agency (BIA)[3] at the Home Office. Once an application has been presented, an initial screening interview takes place. It is at this point that the applicant is given details of legal representation, law firms specializing in asylum cases or, alternatively, voluntary sector support groups such as Asylum Aid or Refugee Action, both discussed below. A further 'substantive' interview takes place at the BIA, during which the applicant presents their case for asylum, often making use of a Home Office appointed interpreter. The applicant's legal representative is entitled to attend this interview and to bring their own interpreter. The BIA may make a decision on the case at any point during the process. If the decision means that asylum is refused and the applicant must leave the UK, an appeal may be made through the mechanisms of the Asylum and Immigration Tribunal (AIT). The appeal hearing consists of a lengthy interview presided over by an immigration judge or judges at one of the AIT hearing centres. In addition to the asylum applicant and his or her legal representation, a representative from the BIA is also present to defend the initial decision of refusal made by the Home Office. As required, the AIT also employs interpreters in order for non-English speaking appellants to communicate with the court and to understand the general proceedings of the court. If the appeal fails, the decision is final and the appellant must leave the UK.

Founded in 1990 in London, Asylum Aid (AA) is an organization with charitable status. It describes itself on its website as "an independent, national charity assisting refugees in the UK" and explains that its chief remit is to provide specialist, legal advice and representation to asylum-seekers and refugees in the UK if their initial application for asylum is rejected. AA is also engaged in campaigns which seek to influence national immigration policy within the framework of the law. Its activities are two-pronged; one strand actively engages in refugee casework, with a particular specialization in 'Article 3 protection claims'[4] and medical cases, and the other strand is more campaign-led. Therefore, there is a specifically legal focus to AA's work.

Like Asylum Aid, Refugee Action (RA) is an organization with charitable status but it operates more widely than AA, across 10 regions of the UK. Each regional office has a core remit to provide refugees and asylum-seekers with expert advice, advocacy and support at any point during their application for protection in the UK. Unlike AA, which mostly takes on casework as part of

---

[3] The BIA was the new identity for the Immigration and Nationality Directorate (IND) from May 2007 until April 2008. By May 2008 the BIA had been replaced by a restructured body, the UK Borders Agency (UKBA).

[4] This refers to Article 3 of the European Convention on Human Rights, which prohibits the use of torture or other inhuman and degrading forms of punishment.

an appeal, RA could be involved with a case for its full duration.

The RA offices also develop and implement projects specific to the needs of refugee and immigrant communities in each region. Founded in 1981, RA's initial function as indicated on its website was to "provide a radical new approach towards the successful resettlement in the UK of refugees and asylum-seekers". The underlying approach remains focused on supporting refugee communities in partnerships, with the principal activity being the provision of "high quality practical advice and assistance for newly arrived refugees and asylum-seekers" with "a long-term commitment to their settlement in the UK". Additionally, local projects aim to engage with refugee communities to establish partnerships with refugee community groups, refugee-led support networks and other voluntary organizations. In contrast to the legal frame-work within which the representation services and campaigns of Asylum Aid operate, Refugee Action's advice and support work are less specialized and are oriented more towards the long-term social needs of asylum-seekers and refugees as they arrive and then settle in a new society.

On the basis that both organizations may be involved in providing legal representation, advice, support and advocacy at any stage through the asylum application process, the interpreting policies of Asylum Aid (AA) and Refugee Action (RA) were selected as data for this study. The interpreting policy documents provided by each organization are assumed to represent official institutional positions with respect to interpreting in that organization. Whether a text defines itself as an interpreter code of conduct or an interpreting procedure is not seen as devaluing its worth as a reflection of a particular institutionalized practice; the texts are assumed to be the official, on-record positions of each organization with respect to interpreting policy, even if – as in the case of AA – the texts are viewed as examples of covert policy rather than self-conscious and explicit policy articulations.

The following documents were provided by AA:[5] *Interpreting and Translation Procedure*; *Interpreters Quality Criteria* (Appendix 1 to *Interpreting and Translation Procedure*); *Code of Practice for Interpreters* (Appendix 2 to the same document). The analysis of these written interpreting policy documents is supplemented with interview data. In addition to allowing for clarification of aspects of the policies, this also serves the purpose of avoiding one of the limitations of CDA identified by Blommaert (2005), i.e. that a CDA analyst may have a tendency to impose a particular reading onto a text, projecting interpretations onto data with their own "stentorian voice" (*ibid.*:33). The Casework Manager at Asylum Aid agreed to participate in a semi-structured interview, which was recorded and transcribed. Any extracts incorporated into the analysis were approved by AA and therefore, along with the policy documents, the data represents an official, on-the-record position taken by AA

---

[5] Each source is referenced in the discussion using its full title.

with respect to its interpreting policy[6] and allows AA to articulate its discourse in its own terms.

RA provided a copy of the *Refugee Action Interpreting Policy and Guidelines*, clearly an example of an overt policy in that it defines itself as such. No one was available to be interviewed and, thus, the analysis of RA's interpreting policy is based solely on the articulations of the policy text.

2.1 Methodology

Fairclough argues that the way people choose to express themselves through their texts amounts "to choices about how to signify (and construct) social identities, social relationships and knowledge and belief" (1992:76). At a micro level of textual analysis, "the meanings of words and the wording of meanings are matters which are socially variable and socially contested, and [are] facets of wider social and cultural processes" (*ibid.*:185); the vocabulary of a text reflects certain in-built social principles, which manifest themselves in the identities of social agents. He argues that "the meaning potential of a form is generally heterogeneous, a complex of diverse, overlapping and sometimes contradictory meanings" (*ibid.*:75), and that interpreters of texts draw on different aspects to construct meaning. Although the meaning of a particular concept can be quite open to different interpretations, texts reduce this openness to a specific set of possible meanings. It is these sets of potential meanings that are of key importance to understanding how the policy texts under consideration conceptualize the interpreter's identity. Since interpreter impartiality and neutrality are assumed to be key concepts in the policy texts, the analyses offered here consider how meaning is attached to these concepts, based on the ways in which they are worded and how interpretation of 'impartiality' and 'neutrality' is reduced to a specified set of meanings. This is achieved by addressing the following conceptualizations of interpreting evident in the policies:

- – how the policies define the role and function of interpreting within the institutional setting;
- – how the policies conceptualize interpreting as an activity;
- – how the policies define notions of interpreter professionalism.

Addressing these aspects of the policies enables a particular identity of the interpreter in a given institutional context to be (re)constructed; this potential identity is rooted in institutional notions of interpreter impartiality and neutrality.

---

[6] Extracts from the interview incorporated into the analysis are referenced as *Interview with Asylum Aid.*

3.   Data analysis

Before presenting the analyses of the two interpreting policies of Asylum Aid and Refugee Action, it is useful to illustrate briefly how the NRPSI and the DPSI codes of conduct articulate notions of interpreter impartiality and neutrality. These codes may be expected to function as a central point of reference for interpreting policies and may inform and shape the articulation of the interpreting service provision within institutions such as those discussed here. As a result, these codes of conduct might be considered particularly powerful institutional discourses since they make their presences known in the discourses of others.

As Tipton (2008a) indicates, the NRPSI *Code of Professional Conduct* fails to adequately qualify or quantify how 'impartiality' or 'neutrality' should to be understood by interpreters and other interlocutors during interpreter-mediated exchanges, even though it features the term 'impartial' prominently. Paragraph 3.12 states that "[p]ractitioners shall at all times act impartially and shall not act in any way that might result in prejudice or preference on grounds of religion or belief, race, politics or gender, otherwise than as obliged to in order faithfully to translate, interpret or otherwise transfer meaning" (NRPSI 2007:4). This explicates the notion of interpreter impartiality to a certain extent, but, as Tipton (2008a) argues, assumptions as to how interpreters (and those working with interpreters) should understand 'impartial' are built into this articulation: that impartial interpreting is contingent on a faithful (and accurate) transfer of meaning; that non-impartial interpreting would lead to bias in the direction of either interlocutor, and that impartial interpreting is achievable and warranted in the context of public service interpreting. In a similar vein, the *Diploma in Public Service Interpreting (DPSI)* handbook states that "in order to work reliably and effectively, the [DPSI accredited] Public Service Interpreter must have … complete impartiality of attitude, speech and script" (DPSI 2007:3).

Prominent in both sources are the requirements that the accredited interpreter will "always act with integrity and in accordance with the high standards appropriate to practitioners within the profession" (NRPSI 2007:2), that he or she "shall be of good character and shall not bring the status of Chartered Linguists, the bodies named in 2.1 [i.e. the Chartered Institute of Linguists] or the profession generally into disrepute by conducting themselves in a manner at variance with the high standards expected of a professional person" (*ibid.*), and that he or she will respect confidentiality at all times unless required by law to do otherwise. It is notable that, while implicit, there are no explicit mentions of 'neutrality' in either source. As the institutional policies are analyzed, it becomes clear that notions of impartiality, neutrality, the role of interpreting and the interpreter as a professional are defined in institutionally very specific and relative terms, and are anchored only to a limited degree in what Tipton argues is "an unfathomable norm of which the boundaries are ill-defined" (2008a:184).

3.1   Asylum Aid

As noted above, casework forms AA's core activity, with around 150 active cases at any one time; the vast majority of these require interpreting services (*Interview with Asylum Aid*). Many of AA's cases require interaction between AA caseworkers and clients on a face-to-face basis, by telephone and, to a lesser extent, through written correspondence. AA views the provision of interpreter services as part of "its commitment to client care" and specifies that interpreters must be used at times when "there are language difficulties in communicating" (*Interpreting and Translation Procedure* 2001/2004:2). Even when a client may have some demonstrable level of English competence, interpreters may be called on to assist. The rationale underpinning AA's interpreting service provision is illustrated in Extract 1, from *Interview with Asylum Aid*.[7]

Extract 1

R   Narrowing this down then to interpreter services, what are the underlying objectives that the organization has for providing interpreter services?

AA   I think that it's to facilitate people's experiences of the asylum process. I guess it's quite daunting really to go through the asylum process and the anxieties and managing the anxieties of the clients and reducing their anxieties is a major concern. And for us, maintaining a professional stance of independence of the interpreting and translation services. It's also a fundamental part to offer female interpreters to female clients. Those I think are the main concerns.

Interpreter services are used by AA on the basis of a commitment to facilitate a client's progression through the asylum process and to enable communication to take place. The extract is also interesting in that it introduces a further element to the service provision; interpreters are specified as professionally 'independent'.

AA's policy refers to a list of approved interpreters who meet preferred accreditation requirements of London Open College Network (LOCN) Community Interpreting, Community Translating at Level 3 or the DPSI

---

[7] In extracts from the Interview, the researcher's words are attributed as **R**, and those of the Asylum Aid Casework Manager as **AA**. The interview data has been transcribed with written-language punctuation for ease of reading; specific features of the utterances themselves were not the focus of attention.

qualification. But such policy articulations seem to be largely irrelevant in practice and to have been abandoned, as is evident in Extract 2, from the same interview.

Extract 2

R   So tell me about the relationship that Asylum Aid has with its interpreters. How do interpreters, and translators I suppose to a certain extent, fit within the overall service provision?

AA   The majority of our clients don't speak English, so it's a communication element primarily. And in terms of the procurement…when I came we had a whole load of people, lists and lists, but basically now, we've reduced it down to a couple of agencies. I think it's more the professional stance the control of the quality of the interpreting which we. I think the reason that drove that. Because inevitably, the agencies will have some sort of liability insurance, if there are mistakes and you'll have a bigger pool, access to a bigger pool of interpreters when you use an agency rather than one. We have used individual interpreters, which I don't have a problem with but our preference is to use agency interpreters.

In this regard, the quality control mechanisms, accreditation provisions, interpreter recruitment and selection of interpreters set out in AA's policy text become redundant as AA procures its interpreters directly from agencies and these issues are passed directly to the agency.

The interpreter's role is defined in Extract 3 below, quoted from AA's *Code of Practice for Interpreters* (2001/2004:1); the means by which that role should be fulfilled are also outlined.

Extract 3

The Code of Practice
A General Principles
- You will facilitate in-depth communication between Asylum Aid (or their agent) and the client.
- You will interpret accurately to the best of your ability between the parties without anything being added or omitted, and without distorting the information provided by either the client or the adviser. You should ensure that you will be and will be seen to be in a position of neutrality and not appear to be siding with the client or the adviser.
- You must not accept an assignment involving relatives or anyone who you know closely through work, at home or in any situation where your partiality might be challenged: if you know the person for whom you have been asked to interpret, you should inform the adviser/Asylum Aid immediately.

- You will treat information that may come to you in the course of your work with Asylum Aid as strictly confidential.

AA directly addresses its interpreters in this Code and defines their professional obligations as integral elements of the AA interpreting service provision. Directly addressing interpreters in the second person *you* indicates that these tasks are specific to interpreters; other agents within AA might not necessarily be required to work in this particular manner. The interpreter's primary function is to "facilitate in-depth communication" between interlocutors in such a way as to ensure that he or she is "seen to be in a position of neutrality" and that the interpreting is "accurate … without anything being added, or omitted and without distorting the information provided". The responsibility for interpreting in the required manner is placed firmly with the interpreters, who are expected to exercise their own controls and checks to maintain the required service, particularly underlining impartiality and confidentiality.

This is a familiar approach to the role of the interpreter, echoing articulations in the NRPSI *Code of Professional Conduct* and the DPSI handbook. However, AA extends the role of the interpreter in an interesting and somewhat divergent way; it does not confine its concept of facilitating communication solely to the rendering of statements into another language, as Extract 4 from *Interpreting and Translating Procedure* (2001/2004:2) shows:

Extract 4

1. Choosing to use an interpreter
Staff members must use interpreters where there are language difficulties in communicating with clients. They should bear in mind that clients may not be the best judges of their own linguistic abilities, and should exercise their own judgment as to when it is appropriate to use an interpreter. Telephone interpretation may be used when, in the judgment of the member of staff, there are significant linguistic difficulties in communicating the required advice/information to the caller.

Where clients speak and understand English, but imperfectly, it may be appropriate to allow the client to speak in English with an interpreter on hand to assist in case of difficulty.

It is the adviser's responsibility to ensure that the client has the choice of language and dialect in which they wish to communicate. In the case of on-going clients, the front sheet on each client's file is marked with this information.

Interpreters must act in the additional capacity of a language adviser, ready to intervene in an interaction conducted in English should effective communication prove to be problematic, as the second paragraph indicates. Suggesting that an interpreter can 'assist' in ensuring that communication takes place between client and institution in the case of difficulties is consistent with the overriding advocacy principles of AA as an institution, but it positions the interpreter in a slightly different way from what the General Principles in Extract 3 might suggest. In such cases, the interpreter facilitates communication between client and Asylum Aid; but such an approach also appears to allow decisions to be made on the client's behalf by the AA caseworker *and* the interpreter. This potentially undermines the principle of interpreter neutrality expressed in the second point of Extract 3. Moreover the interpreter has access to both languages and is therefore in a position to exercise and act on his or her judgement on behalf of either interlocutor.

A further role for the AA interpreter is outlined in Extract 5, from *Interpreting and Translating Procedure* (2001/2004:5), which describes how interpreters might be used as a quality control mechanism during AIT appeal hearings.

Extract 5

> Advisers may also consider it necessary to bring an independent interpreter to an official interview or appeal hearing to check on the performance of the official interpreter and facilitate communication with the client. Where concerns arise over the official interpreter (see below) these must be raised privately by the Asylum Aid interpreter with the adviser, and, if appropriate, by the adviser with the interviewer or adjudicator (and not directly by the interpreter with the interviewer or adjudicator, or with the official interpreter her/himself).
>
> As a general rule, advisers must immediately make the interviewing officer or adjudicator aware of any problems with an official interpreter (naturally, with the greatest possible tact and courtesy to all concerned). This is notwithstanding any request that may have been made by an interviewing officer not to interrupt an interview (advisers are reminded that their duty to a client takes precedence over restrictions imposed by officials). In the case of minor or exceptional instances that have not seriously affected understanding, advisers should exercise their judgment as to whether it may be better to allow the interview or hearing to proceed uninterrupted. Advisers should, without exception, ask for the interview or appeal to be terminated in the event of persistent or serious misunderstandings, mistakes or misconduct by an official interpreter.

Here, AA interpreters are assigned the additional role of a language expert, as evident also in Extract 6 below (from *Interview with Asylum Aid*); the role of the interpreter now becomes increasingly complex, bearing in mind the

explicit requirement for interpreting to be conducted in a way which renders
it 'neutral'.

Extract 6

R   When you use interpreters for instance in a court, to check on the
      quality of the court interpreter, do you feel that changes the role of the
      interpreters at all because in that sense they're being used as a sort of
      quality control mechanism – do you think that changes the role of the
      interpreter at all?

AA   The asylum process, once it's past the decision stage, is adversarial so
      clearly your interpreter is going to explain to you, what he thinks, he or
      she thinks what's happening. I had a particular case which is very stark.
      Because my client came from western Armenia, spoke western Arme-
      nian rather than eastern Armenian. Had a negative reaction to the court
      interpreter and I couldn't understand why. And we had our interpreter
      in court and my client was getting agitated and he couldn't express it
      and we said 'Why?' and he said 'This was the same guy who was in my
      Home Office interview'. And I said to him 'what's the problem?' And
      our interpreter said 'Well, this guy actually speaks a different Armenian'.
      For me, as a person who practises, it's quite difficult to tell, so yes, you
      know, it does have a different impact. Because what we were saying
      was that this interpreter, he was previously involved before, obviously
      it came to light and there are discrepancies which may have arisen out
      of that and our interpreter's telling us, 'actually this cannot happen' be-
      cause it's not the same language. So yes, they do play a very important
      part of quality assurance.

R   This is quite interesting you see, so in that sense, could you say that
      the interpreter was fulfilling a role over and above interpreting? In that
      Asylum Aid are using interpreters to exercise their own quality controls
      rather than necessarily using the interpreters simply for interpreting
      processes?

AA   No, what we do is to facilitate our clients' experience of the asylum
      process so in that sense it's no different if we take our own interpret-
      ers to a Home Office interview or to a court proceedings because what
      we're doing is saying 'Can we know what is going on? Can we be sure
      about what's going on?' and I think that's no different for the role of the
      interpreter interpreting for us, in that sense.

In this case, the interpreter not only drew AA's attention to the fact that the
Home Office interpreter had been previously involved in the client's case, but
also that he or she was interpreting into a different form of Armenian, which
the client had difficulty in understanding. While the interpreter maintained
a position of neutrality in the interaction in that he or she did not directly

intervene, it is understood from this scenario that AA explicitly expects the interpreter to assume a double role. The interpreter acts as a quality control mechanism (a language expert to check that the interpreting offered meets the required standard), and also interprets "for us", AA as an institution, in order to facilitate the *institution's* understanding of proceedings conducted in a language to which the institution has no other access. The interpreter thus becomes AA's own – an extension of the institutional structure and processes. It is unclear whether the interpreter's role is consciously extended by AA or if it is understood more as an inevitable aspect of interlingual communication. Either way, the AA interviewee sees no conflict of interests in drawing interpreters into relationships with AA that could compromise their neutrality. The complexity of the AA interpreter role is thrown into sharper relief when we now consider AA's conceptualization of interpreting as activity and interpreters as professional individuals.

AA's policies construct the activity of interpreting as being a means to facilitate communication; the interpreter must not intervene in the interaction in order to ensure that his/her position of neutrality and impartiality remains intact. Extract 7, from *Interpreting and Translating Procedure* (2001/2004:6), suggests that interpreters might be required to change their relation to other interlocutors as certain factors beyond their own professional control come to bear on the interpreting activity.

Extract 7

3. Telephone interpreting

AA has 24 hour access to telephone interpreters through its contract with National Interpreting Service. Detailed guidance on use of the NIS service is outlined in the 'Quick Reference Guide', available in Public/Interpreters/Telephone interpreting quick reference guide on the computer network.

Calls made through NIS cost £2 per minute, and the Deputy Coordinator monitors the use of this service monthly. To facilitate this, all staff are required to log each use of the NIS service immediately after each call, detailing the date and length of call and language used, in a central record. This is stored in Public/Interpreters/ Using telephone interpreters.

It may also be appropriate to use private telephone interpreters from time to time, in particular where the client has established trust with a particular interpreter, without which communication could not take place.

It is clear from the last sentence that specific interpreters will be used by AA in preference to others, on the basis of a past relationship of trust between a client and interpreter. AA stresses that this approach may be appropriate under certain circumstances only. This seems to indicate that AA is aware that client perceptions of interpreter impartiality within a relationship based on 'trust' may be radically different from the interpreter's understanding of that impartiality. The selection of interpreters may lead clients to misconstrue the relationship as one of a more subjective nature. AA's policy underlines the need for caseworkers to exercise caution when selecting a particular interpreter; the selection of one interpreter rather than another could potentially undermine all efforts to maintain interpreter impartiality.

Extract 8 below, from the same document (2001/2004:6) indicates that the AA interpreter may need to negotiate other forms of client subjectivity in interpreting:

Extract 8

4. Choice of interpreter/translator

Advisers must bear in mind the need for sensitivity in choosing an interpreter or translator, in particular the fact that the client and the interpreter may share a common language but may have very different cultural, political or religious beliefs.

Advisers should also bear in mind the need for an interpreter of the same sex as the client, particularly bearing in mind any reasons why the client might find it difficult to speak through a person of the opposite sex.

Factors such as ethnicity, cultural background, gender and religious beliefs are explicitly acknowledged as potentially adding an involuntary and fundamental subjectivity to the interpreted interactions, and are set alongside the definition of the interpreter as a professional individual occupying a neutral space in the interpreting interaction in Extract 9 (*Code of Practice for Interpreters* 2001/2004:2).

Extract 9

You should intervene in the session in any of the following circumstances:
- you have not fully understood the concept you are asked to interpret and you need to seek clarification;
- you need to point out that a client has not fully understood the message, although the interpreting was correct;
- you need to alert the client to a possible missed inference – i.e. an inference which has not been stated by the advice worker because knowledge of it was assumed.

  - You will inform both parties for the reasons for your intervention.
  - If you feel at any time during the session that your impartiality is jeopardised, you should immediately notify the advice worker.

There are echoes here of the NRPSI *Code of Professional Conduct* and the DPSI handbook, which require interpreters to avoid intervention in interpreted interactions in order to maintain a professional distance from the proceedings and thus any subjective alignment with either party. The interpreters are directly addressed, indicating that the principles outlined in Extract 9 are obligatory aspects of interpreters' professional behaviour within the AA interpreter-mediated interviews. These obligations are entirely consistent with those of Extract 3, that interpreters "will be and will be seen to be in a position of neutrality and not appear to be siding with the client or the adviser". As in the NRPSI *Code of Conduct*, AA's policy underlines notions of neutrality and impartiality on several occasions.

However, for all that, and taking into account the articulations of Extracts 6, 7 and 8, interpreting is considered as a socially motivated action: AA's account adds complexity by offering a distinction between two (acceptable) aspects to subjectivity. Active subjectivity and intervention by the interpreter are aspects of interpreting which are sanctioned when "inferences" have been missed by either AA adviser or the client, when the interpreter requires further clarification or when it is clear that the interpreter's "impartiality is jeopardised". There is also an acknowledgement of an *involuntary* subjectivity, as the interpreter enters into interaction with clients and elements of their professional 'impartial' selves become inextricably implicated in subjective social interactions. The interpreter's own gender, evident "cultural, political or religious beliefs" and a perceived relationship of trust may elicit particular responses from a client and draw the interpreter into an interaction which is more subjectively oriented and less characterized by impartiality and neutrality.

Drawing together these layers of AA's articulations of interpreter identity shows a clear difference between notions of the objectivity of interpreters as professional individuals set against an involuntary, inalterable subjectivity of interpreting as an activity in a specific space and time. In AA's *Code of Practice for Interpreters*, the interpreter is *required* to side neither with the client nor the AA adviser, and is obliged to be seen to occupy a position of professional neutrality. It is also clear that AA recognizes that interpreters often enter into interactions which could be construed as being less impartial, particularly by the client. It seems that AA recognizes an inherent subjectivity in any and all interpreting activity, based on the gender, cultural history and religious affiliation of the interpreter and as a consequence of the social nature of interpreting. This is a complex and multilayered perspective which defines interpreting as a socially oriented activity with an intrinsic subjectivity of action, rather than an objective mechanistic process.

3.2   Refugee Action

Turning to the second of the two organizations under study, the analysis addresses a broadly similar theme: how Refugee Action (RA) conceptualizes and articulates its notion of interpreter neutrality and impartiality. In 2006, the organization gave "independent advice" to more than 29,000 individual asylum-seekers/refugees (*Refugee Action Interpreting Policy and Guidelines* 2002/2006:6). During 2005/2006 over 150 volunteer staff, many of whom were themselves asylum-seekers or refugees who have since settled in the UK, donated their time and expertise to RA in a range of roles, including interpreting (*ibid.*). Indeed, many of RA's interpreters are former asylum-seekers themselves, and this appears to be instrumental in shaping the way RA conceptualizes interpreter impartiality in a number of ways. I return to this issue later in the discussion.

Extract 10 below, from the RA website, sets out the organization's vision, values and aims:

Extract 10

Our vision
We want a society in which refugees are welcome, respected and safe, and in which they can achieve their full potential.

Our values
All our work must be guided by the aspirations and needs of refugees, and their empowerment.
- Strong and organised refugee communities are essential to settlement.
- We must facilitate partnerships with refugee and with wider groups in carrying out our work, and we will do this in a creative and non-competitive way.
- We must seek to advance refugee rights through innovation and leadership, and through delivering high quality service and evaluation.
- Our role must be to provide additional services which refugee communities, or other voluntary or statutory services, cannot provide.
- We must enjoy the diversity of our staff and stakeholders, and promote a culture in which everyone can express their potential.

Our aims
- To provide the highest quality reception, advice and information to refugees and asylum-seekers, and other displaced people.
- To promote the development of refugee communities as distinctive parts of wider British communities.
- To improve access to employment and mainstream services, and enhance opportunities for refugees and asylum-seekers.
- To raise awareness of refugee issues, influence policy, and campaign for refugee rights.
- To establish high quality organisational policies and practices, as befits a refugee agency.

It is clear from this extract that a large proportion of RA's work is undertaken in an advisory capacity, dispensing advice, support and advocacy to asylum-seekers and refugees newly arrived in the UK. Much of this involves RA advice workers conducting face-to-face meetings with asylum-seekers and refugees. Eligibility for RA support is not determined solely by immigration status. In order to ensure that communication between RA and its clients progresses meaningfully, RA makes extensive use of interpreters. Interpreting is provided by RA at no financial cost to the client, to ensure that "clients who don't communicate in English ... are offered advice, information and assistance through a skilled and impartial interpreter, in a language and manner that ensures respect, clarity and confidentiality" (*Refugee Action Interpreting Policy and Guidelines* 2002/2006:2). Interpreters are recruited to the Refugee Action Interpreter Register either as part of a proactive campaign which aims to fill gaps identified in service provision in terms of language, gender or geographical location, or as a response to specific individual enquiries. Potential candidates are interviewed and their interpreting skills assessed. Accreditation through programmes such as the DPSI or membership of the NRPSI may exempt a candidate from a full assessment, but such accreditation is not required by the RA. A short interview is also conducted with accredited candidates to ensure that the prospective interpreter demonstrates personal "commitment to the needs and hopes of refugees and asylum-seekers" (*ibid.*:12). The underlying principle of the RA interpreting service is that interpreters facilitate communication between parties, clients and RA advice workers who do not share a common language. Extract 11 below (from *Refugee Action Interpreting Policy and Guidelines* 2002/2006:7), provides a point of departure for consideration of RA's interpreting policy; the heading of the extract indicates that this is offered as a definition of the role of the interpreter:

Extract 11

The interpreter's role
The interpreter's role when working with the Refugee Action is to be a channel of communication between the caseworker and the client. Their interpretation should be an accurate translation of what is being said, neither adding, omitting, or changing anything, unless it is necessary to ensure that the meaning of what is being said is effectively communicated.

RA conceptualizes the interpreter's role as a 'channel of communication'. Although the nature of the communicative channel is not explicitly defined, its link to the next sentence suggests that fulfilment of this role requires an interpreter to produce an "accurate translation of what is being said, neither adding, omitting, nor changing anything". This is similar to the NRPSI articulations outlined above. The implicit drawing together of conceptualizations is significant because, throughout RA's policy, 'interpreting' as an activity and 'the role of the interpreter' are assumed to be the same thing, with no distinction between the two.

According to the RA policy, "the practices and principles described ... draw upon widely established and accepted models of 'good practice' as currently operated in a range of advice work and interpreting projects" (*ibid.*:7). While the recommended practices and principles are legitimated because they are representative models of "good practice", it remains unclear which models are being drawn on, why they should be construed as good practice and what implications these models might have for the RA interpreter. Nonetheless, the guidelines are defined as neither 'complete' nor 'definitive' (*ibid.*:7), and the RA policy is thus not closed to further development. As I observe above, the interpreter, as he or she fulfils their role successfully, is presented as a 'channel of communication' between client and RA caseworker. Extract 12 (*ibid.*:2) offers further insight into how RA constructs the identity of its interpreters:

Extract 12

> **Introduction**
> Clients who speak little or no English ... depend upon the professional co-operation of skilled interpreters and advice workers to enable them to effectively access our services. The aim of this document is to describe Refugee Action's operational principles, practice, commitments and expectations regarding the delivery of services in partnership between advice workers and interpreters. Our aim is to ensure that clients who don't communicate in English ... are offered advice, information and assistance through a skilled and impartial interpreter, in a language and manner that ensures respect, clarity and confidentiality.

Interpreters are described here in a range of ways. They are "skilled", "professional" and "impartial". They offer a service which non-English speaking clients can "depend upon" to allow effective access to RA services, including its "advice, information and assistance". The language and manner in which this service is delivered must ensure "respect, clarity and confidentiality", all of which assumes that RA interpreters are trained and competent to carry out their duties in the required manner. The services of "advice, information and assistance" are offered "through" an interpreter and delivered by RA advice workers and interpreters in "partnership". This is particularly significant; it suggests that interpreters in the RA are actively involved in general service provision as well as the provision of interpreting (language) services. The aim of the RA policy is not expressed as 'RA's aim', or 'the aim of the advice workers'; the phrase "partnership between advice workers and interpreters" is prominent and the use of "our" in the following sentence implicates *both* groups of agents (interpreters *and* RA advice workers) in the institutional aims of the service provision. There is a clear suggestion here of collaborative cooperation in advocacy which I return to later. While RA's interpreters are identified as highly-trained and competent professionals, what constitutes interpreting as an activity is less clearly defined.

RA's policy presents a complex account of the interpreter's role and how it affects the activity of interpreting. Extract 10 above defines the interpreter's role. As a "channel of communication" between the RA advice worker and the client, the interpreter's activity is limited to transferring the meaning of what is said throughout the interaction as "an accurate translation". The interpreter is to remain "impartial" to the interaction and intervention in the form of omissions or additions to what is said is ruled out, even if what is said is "threatening, offensive, obscene or [constitutes] expressions of anger" (*ibid.*:9). A key aspect of RA's conceptualization is that the interpreter *facilitates* communication *between* the other interlocutors. As I have indicated, this draws on the model of community interpreting set out in the NRPSI's (2007) *Code of Professional Conduct*. In this regard, the *Code of Professional Conduct* appears to underpin much of RA's policy on interpreting, and the NRPSI's key articulations of impartiality with the implicit assumption of neutrality are also evident in the RA policy text.

However, the RA policy diverges from the NRPSI's (2007) *Code of Professional Conduct* in two very distinct and marked ways. The first is with respect to intervention. As evident in Extract 13 below (*Refugee Action Interpreting Policy and Guidelines*:7), RA permits interpreter intervention during the interaction, albeit under very specific conditions and for specific reasons:

Extract 13

> **Giving advice / making suggestions**
> Provision of advice, guidance and information to the clients is the responsibility of the advice worker, not the interpreter. Interpreters may and often do have varying degrees of knowledge relating to advice work with refugees and asylum-seekers, gained through a variety of experiences or work roles. However, to ensure clarity of roles and accountability, it is important that all advice and information is offered to the client exclusively through the advice worker, through the medium of the interpreter.
>
> If an interpreter feels it is necessary to offer ideas, dispute information or offer suggestions relating to the options available to the client, this should be done before or after the interview, or during a break – not during the process.

It is clear from the first sentence that the RA advice worker, not the interpreter, is responsible for the "provision of advice, guidance and information to the clients". It is also explicitly recognized that interpreters themselves "may and often do have varying degrees of knowledge relating to advice work with refugees and asylum-seekers" due to previous personal experience or the nature of their professional roles; interpreters might have a breadth of knowledge and experience useful to providing advice and information to RA's clients. The policy makes provision for interpreters to engage with the advice session and intervene in a way that conflicts with the provisions set out in the NRPSI's *Code of Professional Conduct*; an interpreter is permitted to "offer ideas, dispute information or offer suggestions relating to the options available to the client" and to have an active, advocacy role as an additional adviser in client consultations. To maintain clarity in role definition and responsibility, however, the interpreter is not permitted to intervene during the advice session; off-the-record interpreter intervention alone is permitted so that information given to the client is always *seen* to be that of the RA advice worker. The interpreter may nevertheless have specific and distinct input into the advice session. This is an interesting approach because it introduces a double-faced conceptualization of the interpreter. On one hand, the RA policy text constructs a client-facing interpreter who is neutral, impartial and whose remit, as far as the client is concerned, is to establish the "channel of communication". On the other hand, there is a more institutionally oriented face of the interpreter, whose intervention in advice sessions is permitted and whose role ranges from language interpreting activities to working alongside and speaking through the RA adviser to give advice to clients. This is a double role, one which is consciously hidden from the client to maintain client perceptions of role clarity during interpreted interactions.

A further aspect of RA's policy adds an additional complexity; it is apparent that RA, as an institution, requires a very specific type of personal and political engagement on the part of its interpreters, as evident in Extract 14 (*Refugee Action Interpreting Policy and Guidelines* 2002/2006:12).

Extract 14

Essential experience and abilities:
– An understanding of the role of an interpreter in an independent advice service.
– Fluency in English and specialist language.
– An awareness and understanding of the refugee situation in the UK and a commitment to the needs and hopes of refugees and asylum-seekers.
– An ability to interpret in an impartial manner.
– An ability to work with clients in distress.
– An understanding of and a commitment to equal opportunities and confidentiality.
– Reliability and punctuality.
– Effective communication and listening skills

Desirable experience and abilities:
- An ability to write your specialist language to a good standard
- Experience of interpreting in a similar setting (either paid or voluntary)
- A recognized interpreting qualification

Extract 14 distinguishes between what RA considers to be "essential experience and abilities" of interpreters and those which are "desirable". The essential criteria include a "commitment to the needs and hopes of refugees and asylum-seekers" and an "awareness and understanding of the refugee situation in the UK", criteria which are listed after "an understanding" of the role of the interpreter in an advisory setting and "fluency" in English and another language. Experience of interpreting in a voluntary sector setting and interpreting qualifications, by contrast, are listed as "desirable" and are positioned below the ability to write the specialist language to a "good standard". What is of central concern to RA is that its interpreters are personally and ideologically committed to the ongoing welfare of its clients. This, in addition to the space allowed to interpreters to intervene in interpreted interactions, creates a complex and highly politically motivated account of an activist, advocate interpreter.

4.   Concluding discussion

Both policies analyzed here position interpreters as impartial and neutral agents to greater or lesser extents. However, there are some crucial distinctions in the ways in which impartial and neutral interpreters are conceptualized.

The AA interpreter is oriented towards the kind of impartiality that Tipton (2008a) proposes in her notion of "baseline neutrality". However, the AA account of the interpreter is one in which impartiality of interpreting can shift in response to certain factors. The AA interpreter must, on occasion, interpret for the benefit of AA as an institution, as well as for the client, and act as a quality control mechanism at official hearings when AA represents a client. The interpreted interaction may also draw the interpreter into a less distanced or objective relationship with the client because of factors beyond their control, such as gender and ethnicity. The AA interpreter is anchored in notions of objectivity and impartiality but, as a range of factors come to bear on the interpreter, he or she responds accordingly, in a way which may sacrifice "baseline neutrality".

In contrast, active intervention for the RA interpreter is explicitly endorsed. RA interpreters are presented as often being former asylum-seekers or refugees themselves and, as such, are a source of knowledge and expertise. Provision is made to allow interpreters to engage with RA advice sessions in a collaborative partnership with RA advice workers. It is true that such intervention must be conducted in a way that preserves the client's perception of interpreter impartiality – any interpreter intervention should be conducted off-record and communicated to the client *through* the advice worker. Importantly, however, RA interpreters are required to demonstrate a personal commitment to the welfare of refugees and asylum-seekers, and an awareness of the asylum process in the UK. Thus, the RA interpreter is far less an impartial, disinterested conduit, and much more an active advocate, motivated by an explicit political activism and a vested interest in the outcome of each interpreted interaction.

Both interpreting policies (and many others) demonstrably echo the 'best practices' of interpreting evident in the DPSI and NRPSI codes of conduct, but there are divergent meanings attached to these conceptualizations, suggesting that these notions are highly flexible and open to subjective, institutionalized readings. What is significant is that both interpreting policies orient the service provision in such a way that "impartial and neutral" interpreting can also offer advocacy and advice to clients negotiating the "daunting process" (*Interview with Asylum Aid*) of applying for asylum in the UK. They are ideologically motivated policies underpinned by particular institutional notions of impartiality but which depart from these normative models to allow client interests to remain of central concern.

Inghilleri (2003, 2007) and Maltby (2008) argue that interpreting in the asylum context has political and social implications. I suggest that, since interpreter impartiality and neutrality is quite clearly a relative concept, research needs to focus less on how to maintain interpreter impartiality and neutrality (Tipton 2008b) and give further consideration to the wider social and political implications of institutionalized notions of interpreter impartiality. In addition, interpreters themselves may need to consider why it is that particular modes of interpreter behaviour are enshrined in policy, over and above others, and to engage explicitly with the ramifications of what they do professionally in the institutional contexts in which they do it. It seems to be of utmost importance that, in accepting interpreting assignments for specific organizations, interpreters in this sector fully reflect upon the institutional interpreting policies with which they become complicit. Interpreters need to make a living, so this is not to suggest that they should turn down assignments on the basis of the policy commitments of a particular institution, but it does seem to be important, in the interests of interpreter ethics, that they take a measure of responsibility for what they do to make that living. I would argue that interpreters could be encouraged to view themselves more actively as intrinsic elements of an ideologically motivated institutional power structure; while an interpreter may operate under a code of conduct that explicitly calls for an impartiality or neutrality of approach to interpreting, there are tangible implications to what they do as part of the wider commitments of the institution that employs them.

References

Primary Sources

Documents Issued by Asylum Aid

Interpreting and Translation Procedure (2001, updated 2004)
Interpreters Quality Criteria (Appendix 1 to the *Interpreting and Translation
    Procedure*)
Code of Practice for Interpreters (Appendix 2 to the *Interpreting and Translation
    Procedure*)

Interview with Asylum Aid

Interview with Asylum Aid Casework Manager, Kahiye Alim, at Asylum Aid
    offices in London on 7 March 2008.

Document Issued by Refugee Action

Refugee Action Interpreting Policy and Guidelines (2002, revised 2006)

Websites

Asylum Aid: www.asylumaid.org.uk (accessed 5 March 2009).
Refugee Action: http://www.refugee-action.org.uk/ (accessed 5 March 2009).

Secondary Sources

Ager, Dennis (2001) *Motivation in Language Planning and Language Policy*,
    Clevedon: Multilingual Matters.
Blommaert, Jan (2005) *Discourse: A Critical Introduction*, Cambridge: Cambridge
    University Press.
Crowley, John (1996) 'The Theory and Practice of Immigration and Race-Relations:
    Some Thoughts on British and French Experience', in Naomi Carmon (ed.)
    Immigration and Integration in Post Industrial Societies, Basingstoke &
    London: Macmillan, 227-47.
DPSI (2007) *Diploma in Public Service Interpreting*. Available online: http://
    www.iol.org.uk/qualifications/DPSI/DPSIHandbook.pdf (accessed 5 March
    2009).
Fairclough, Norman (1992) *Discourse and Social Change*, Cambridge & Oxford:
    Polity Press.
------ (2003) *Analysing Discourse: Textual Analysis for Social Research*, London
    & New York: Routledge.
------ and Ruth Wodak (1997) 'Critical Discourse Analysis', in Teun van Dijk (ed.)
    Discourse as Social Interaction, London: Sage, 258-84.

Freeman, Gary (1994) 'Britain, The Deviant Case', in Wayne Cornellius, Philip Martin and James Hollifield (eds) *Controlling Immigration*, Stanford: Stanford University Press, 297-302.

Gentile, Adolfo (1997) 'Community Interpreting or Not? Practices, Standards and Accreditation', in Silvana Carr, Roda Roberts, Aideen Dufour and Dini Steyn (eds) *The Critical Link: Interpreters in the Community*, Philadelphia & Amsterdam: John Benjamins, 109-18.

Inghilleri, Moira (2003) 'Habitus, Field and Discourse: Interpreting as a Socially Situated Activity', *Target* 15(2): 243-68.

------ (2007) 'National Sovereignty versus Universal Rights: Interpreting Justice in a Global Context', *Social Semiotics* 17(2): 195-212.

Leinonen, Satu (2007) 'Professional Stocks of Interactional Knowledge in the Interpreter's Profession', in Cecilia Wadensjö, Birgitta Englund Dimitrova and Anna-Lena Nilsson (eds) *Critical Link 4: Professionalisation of Interpreting in the Community*, Amsterdam & Philadelphia: John Benjamins, 227-40.

Maltby, Matthew (2008) *Interpreting Policy in UK Asylum Applications*, unpublished PhD thesis, Manchester: Centre for Translation & Intercultural Studies, University of Manchester.

Mason, Ian (1999) 'Introduction', in Ian Mason (ed.) *Dialogue Interpreting*, special issue of *The Translator* 5(2): 147-60.

Morris, Ruth (1995) 'The Moral Dilemmas of Court Interpreting', *The Translator* 1(1): 25-46.

NRPSI (2007) *Code of Professional Conduct*. Available online: http://www.iol. org.uk/nav.asp?r=MRK50R16495 (accessed 5 March 2009).

Refugee Action (2006) *Annual Report 2006*, London: Refugee Action.

Tipton, Rebecca (2008a) 'Interpreter Neutrality and the Structure/Agency Distinction', in Carmen Valero Garcés, Carmen Pena Díaz, Raquel Lázaro Gutiérrez (eds) *Research & Practice in Public Service Interpreting and Translation: Challenges and Alliances*, Alcalá: University of Alcalá, 183-97.

------ (2008b) 'Reflexivity and the Social Construction of Identity in Interpreter-Mediated Asylum Interviews', *The Translator* (14)1: 1-19.

UNHCR (2001) *Global Consultations on International Protection/Third Track: Access to Procedures*. Available online: www.unhcr.org/refworld/docid/ 3b39a152d.html (accessed 5 March 2009).

Wadensjö, Cecilia (1997) 'Recycled Information as a Questionning Strategy: Pitfalls in Interpreter-Mediated Talk", in Silvana Carr, Roda Roberts, Aideen Dufour and Dini Steyn (eds) *The Critical Link: Interpreters in the Community*, Philadelphia & Amsterdam: John Benjamins, 35-52.

------ (1998) *Interpreting as Interaction*, London: Longman.

------ (2008) 'In and Off the Show: Co-constructing 'Invisibility' in an Interpreter-Mediated Talk Show Interview', *Meta* 53(1): 184-203.

IV. The Impact of Translation & Interpreting in a Changing World

Rethinking Activism

The Power and Dynamics of Translation in China during the Late Qing Period (1840-1911)[1]

MARTHA P.Y. CHEUNG
Hong Kong Baptist University

Abstract. *One significant development in translation studies in the last two decades has been the emergence of both empirical research and theoretical discourse on the relationship between translation and power. This paper explores one facet of the power and dynamics of translation by examining the use and usefulness of translation in serving activist ends and effecting concrete change – total or partial change, change in the individual or in some supra-individual system, or both. Drawing on a model for classifying social movements borrowed from the anthropologist David Aberle, and focusing on a particular period in the past – the late Qing era (1840-1911) in China – this paper analyzes the aims and aspirations of political activists of different orientations, and the complex relationship between translation and activism during that period. The analysis is followed by a more reflective section on the relevance of research on this topic to the present generation of translator-activists.*

With the shift of critical attention from decontextualized texts to the whole context of interaction in translation studies over the past couple of decades, a number of case studies have been conducted that problematized the notion of translation as an innocent, bridge-building activity devoted to narrowing the linguistic and/or cultural gaps between peoples, to promoting communication and to transferring information with minimal distortion (Alvarez and Vidal 1996, Bassnett and Trivedi 1999, Mason 1994/2009, Venuti 1995, 1998a). Research has repeatedly shown that translation is a means of effecting social change and/or bringing about cultural transformation. It can undermine, contest and subvert structures of power in society. It can play a crucial role in situations of conflict – through manipulation, fabrication and even falsification, as attested in a number of essays in Salama-Carr (2007); Baker (2006a) also contains a wealth of material on the topic. Translation can further function as a tool of resistance – against

---

[1] I am grateful to the Research Grants Council of Hong Kong for providing me with a General Research Fund (GRF 240907) to conduct research on translation during the late Qing.

the policies of repressive regimes, or the encroachment of ideologies deemed unacceptable or threatening (see the essays in Tymoczko 2006). But it can also be an act of complicity – serving to assert military and/or political power, for example – and deceit. Where colonization is concerned, translation can be used in the service of dispossessing the indigenous population (Cheyfitz 1991, Venuti 1998b, Tymoczko and Gentzler 2002, Mutu 2003, Fenton and Moon 2003).

In addition to empirical and historical studies, a number of scholars have attempted to elaborate theoretical frameworks to account for the power of translation in effecting change,[2] drawing, for example, on postcolonial theory (Tymoczko 1999), poststructuralist theory (Venuti 1998c), and narrative theory (Baker 2006b). These theoretical accounts focus on why translation can, and should, participate in political and/or ideological struggles, aim to form and reform mindsets, and even to shape and/or reshape the world. They form a fast-growing area of scholarship – characterized perhaps a little too readily by Tymoczko and Gentzler (2002: xvi) as the new 'power turn' in translation studies – in which the present discussion is to be located. The current study focuses on the way in which translation, in a particular period of Chinese history, was used to serve activist ends and effect change – partial and/or total, in the individual and/or in the established order. The focus, however, is not just on the actual (documented) changes that took place and how they served the purpose(s) of the translators and/or activists involved. Works of translation, as skopos theory has taught us, are oriented towards aims and intended outcomes. They can produce their intended outcomes, or fail to produce them. What skopos theory has not discussed, but is crucially important to any study of the relationship between translation and activism, is the fact that works of translation can also produce unanticipated outcomes, and in unpredictable ways, because of a variety of factors which interact with and impinge upon the translator's work; this is what I refer to as the 'dynamics of translation'. By paying attention to such 'dynamics of translation' in the analysis, it is hoped that this article can add one further dimension to current theoretical discussions of the power of translation, specifically of its power to effect change, in all spheres of its operation.

'Activism' is a potentially confusing term in the current context, and it is worth explaining how I intend to use it before proceeding with the analysis. I do not propose to study the relationship between translation and contemporary activist movements in this article; instead, I will focus on one particular period (1840-1911) in imperial China. Usually called the late Qing period, it

---

[2] For a succinct review of literature on translation and power, see the 'Introduction' to Tymoczko and Gentzler (2002), which also provides an account of the intellectual and political climate that has given rise to interest in questions of power in discussions of translation history and strategies of translation. Tymoczko has dealt with many of these issues in an earlier monograph (1999).

encompasses the last decades of the Qing Dynasty and is one that witnessed a major translation movement in China. Baker (2009) argues that scholars of translation have traditionally focused on historical studies, perhaps as a way of taking shelter in the past, or – in her words – of avoiding any "spillage of risk" or "political controversy" that might "contaminate the orderly world of scholarly research" (*ibid*.:222). She may have a point, and this paper is open to such criticism. It must be pointed out, however, that in the context of China, and especially in view of the strong reaction from the PRC government and sections of the Chinese populace towards the Tibet separatist movement, the very use of the term 'activism' is anathema to some and spells danger to others, even in the world of scholarly research, which has witnessed a gradual loosening of state control and a greater degree of academic freedom in the last decade. Irrespective of whether the material to which the term 'activism' is applied is drawn from the present or the past, the very use of such a concept and the attempt to flesh it out theoretically and analytically is in itself a challenge to the status quo, or would be perceived as such, and hence as ideologically subversive. And indeed, one of the purposes of this paper is to test the possibility of employing perspectives that might be construed as ideologically sensitive in translation studies *in China*. I am of course aware that this paper cannot serve as the litmus test, since I am writing it in English – a relatively safe language in the context of politics in China – and in the relative security provided by Hong Kong, where freedom of speech and other freedoms are by and large guaranteed to its citizens. Looking further afield at the state of translation studies outside China, where the relationship between translation and activism is only just beginning to receive scholarly attention,[3] studying the past not only enhances our understanding of the past but also facilitates reflections on present realities, both the reality of 'doing activism' (in the sense of fighting for a special cause) and of 'being an activist' (in the sense of explicitly identifying oneself as part of a community that is focused on effecting change in society).[4]

---

[3] The fact that the relationship between translation and contemporary activist movements is only just beginning to draw the attention of researchers in translation studies can be seen in the date of the 'First International Forum of Translation/Interpreting and Social Activism', which was held at the University of Granada from 28 to 30 April 2007. The proceedings of the forum are to be made available online in the near future. In this sense, the work of Tymoczko (2000), Baker (2006b), Boéri (2008) and Baker (2009) constitutes a pioneering contribution to the discipline.

[4] This distinction is drawn by Chris Bobel, who conducted a study, based on interviews with thirty-three individuals involved in the Menstrual Activism movement in the US, of why the identity 'activist' is resisted among some of those engaged in front-line activist work. Bobel offers an interesting discussion of why many individuals would 'do' activism but refuse to be called, or refuse to call themselves, activists (Bobel 2007).

1.   Translation and activism

The word 'activism', as a designation for "the doctrine or practice of vigorous action or involvement as a means of achieving political or other goals, sometimes by demonstrations, protests, etc." (Flexner 1993:20), has a twentieth-century ring and is normally associated with contemporary social and political movements. The *Oxford English Dictionary*, quoting from the *Glasgow Herald*, gives 12 August 1920 as the date that saw the first usage of the term 'activism' in a political context. Despite a relatively short history of usage of the word in this sense, the meaning and set of activities and behaviours signalled by the term, i.e., action taken to challenge the status quo (in, for example, the prevailing social norms, embedded practices, policies, and power relationships) and to effect change, have been documented throughout history. The difference lies in the vocabulary used. Rather than characterizing such action as 'activism', other terms and expressions such as 'reform movement' (which carries positive connotations) or 'political conspiracy', 'plots engineered by secret societies' and 'rebellion', all of which are negative in connotation in official Chinese historical documents, would often have been used instead.

To replace these terms and expressions with the term 'activism' is therefore to announce a different discursive position, one which introduces a different grouping of individuals in history and which calls for the spotlight to be cast differently, so that a particular dimension of the power and dynamics of translation could be revealed. From this position, I will be asking a set of research questions which include the following. What was the relationship between translation and activism during the late Qing period? Who were the players, the 'activists' in modern terms? What cause(s) did they fight for or against? What made them commit themselves to those causes? Was translation used as a tool of activism (in a non-colonial setting), in more or less the same way as it has been used as a weapon of, or against imperialism? How well did translation fulfill its function(s)? What impact did it have? What relevance does the story of the success or failure of translation and/or translators to advance specific activist agendas in that context have for our generation?

To structure my discussion of the relevant historical material, I propose to draw in the first instance on a set of categories from a theoretical model outlined by the anthropologist David F. Aberle (1966), who devised them to classify social movements (Table 1).

		Locus of Change	
		Supra-individual	Individual
Amount of Change	Total	Transformative	Redemptive
	Partial	Reformative	Alterative

Table 1. Aberle's Model for Classification of Social Movements

Aberle's model identifies four types of social movement – transformative, reformative, redemptive and alterative – and classifies them along two dimensions (1966:316). One is the dimension of the locus of the change sought (i.e. in the individual or in some supra-individual system such as the economic order, the political order, a total society or culture, the world, or indeed the cosmos). The other is the extent of change (i.e. partial or total) at which the movement is aimed. *Transformative movements*, for example revolutionary movements, aim at a total change in supra-individual systems (*ibid.*:317). *Reformative movements* aim at a partial change in supra-individual systems. Some of the examples of reformative movements Aberle offers include the women's suffrage movement, movements in favour of compulsory vaccination, and rebellions (*ibid.*).[5] *Redemptive movements* aim at a total change in individuals rather than supra-individual systems. They can be secular or religious in orientation. Sectarian movements aiming at a state of grace (such as the peyote religion among the Navaho) are cited by Aberle as examples. *Alterative*[6] *movements* aim at a partial change in individuals. According to Aberle, various birth control movements exemplify alterative movements, insofar as they do not involve attempts to change anti-birth control legislation, in which case they would be classified as reformative in orientation (*ibid.*).

Aberle's model is arguably too rigid and static. It is hard to imagine how it can reflect adequately the complexity and interdependence of activist strategies in real life. Will a social movement fall so neatly into any of these four classes? Will it not exhibit the characteristics of more than one class? Will it not evolve over time? Aberle himself is aware of these problems of classification. "Some movements are probably close to pure types of one or another of these four classes", he says, while others can ordinarily be classified as "predominantly of one or another major type, with less emphasis on a different type" (*ibid.*). In still other cases, "a movement is better described by reference to its particular blend of transformative, reformative, redemptive, and alterative elements, without being forced into one or another major category" (*ibid.*). Aberle also admits that any given movement may change in type over time: "Any concrete historical instance may change radically, so that the appropriate classification at one time may be quite inappropriate later" (*ibid.*). In addition, he cautions that "not everything that starts as a social movement finishes as one", for "a movement may succeed and turn into the Establishment" (*ibid.*).

---

[5] 'Rebellion' has different connotations, depending on the user's discursive position. For some, 'rebellion' is a positive word indicating a collective challenge to the status quo. For the authorities, however, labelling a mass movement as a rebellion is an official act of indictment.

[6] The term 'alterative' has been more or less replaced by the term 'alternative' in subsequent literature on activism. See for example, Zoller (2005).

These problems are real. Any attempt at classification runs the risk of slippage, of overlap. The researcher must be alert to signs of historical phenomena playing havoc with the category that seeks to contain them. Nonetheless, these categories, like all heuristic categories, are useful as long as they are not taken as 'pure types', to use Aberle's term, but as categories with fuzzy boundaries. I find them particularly useful for an analysis such as the present one, which examines not single issues but the theme of change at all different levels of society and within individuals. For that is what late Qing China was – a period of social unrest, political upheavals, ideological power struggle, military conflicts, and rude awakening for both the intellectuals and the populace. I will thus use Aberle's categories in this study to provide a notional classification of the aims and purposes for which translation was undertaken, by a few prominent individuals committed to the pursuit of change. The aims and purposes of these translator-activists in late Qing China, however, were almost always mixed, and hence more than one category will be deployed where the immediate purpose(s) differed from the long term goal(s), or where different strands of activism were intertwined.

2.   Activist translation in the late Qing period

An activist agenda relies on activists for its realization. To analyze the relationship between translation and activism during the late Qing period, I will focus on the translators as well as the translation patrons (i.e. those who initiated/financed the activity of translation or who adopted works of translation for activist purposes). These human agents came from both the elite and the grassroots. I use 'the elite' here to refer to those who were educated (unlike the majority of the populace) but who worked outside or on the margins of the imperial government. The grassroots are the ordinary people, with no connections to authority. My decision to treat the elite working on the periphery of the Establishment as actual or potential activists is perhaps the major difference between the current analysis and other analyses of contemporary activist groups. The latter tend to focus, sometimes exclusively, on non-government organizations and individuals working together as a community outside the Establishment. In the days of feudal China, however, the structure of power and the rate of literacy were such that any meaningful study of the relationship between translation and activism must include the educated (i.e. the elite) seeking to effect change, either within or outside the political and social institutions of the day.

2.1   Translation and activism – predominantly reformative, with some alterative elements

In the initial stage, reformative activism (aiming at partial change of supra-individual systems) was the major driving force behind some of the translation activities of the time, specifically those aimed at changing the dominant ideology of the imperial court. The dominant ideology was that of a Middle Kingdom, which saw its legitimacy as mandated by heaven and its superiority as founded on the resilience of over two thousand years of civilization. The view of the world upheld by such an ideology was that of 'Us and the Rest', the Rest being tributary states of the Celestial Empire. That ideology was challenged by Western nations pursuing a policy of economic expansionism, and particularly by the United Kingdom, which at the time was trying to force China to import British opium, to the detriment of the health of the Chinese people. The result of this confrontation was the Opium War (1838-1842). But that Middle-Kingdom ideology was also challenged by the Chinese themselves, though only a handful of intellectuals were involved. These intellectuals were no less arrogant in their view of the world than the ruling conservatives, but they were critical of the Establishment for having allowed the country to fall into a state of decline, and called for immediate action to redress the problem. Wei Yuan 魏源 (1794-1857) was a key figure in this movement.

Wei Yuan was a Confucian scholar who advocated a range of reforms in handling state affairs (also called statecraft). However, he was merely an advisor to the provincial officials rather than an official himself. When news of China's defeat in the Opium War reached him, Wei became convinced that reforms in statecraft must begin with a change in the ruling conservatives' attitude towards the Celestial Empire's relations with other countries. His sentiments, therefore, were predominantly reformative, but his reformative activism was blended with alterative elements, for he sought to bring changes to the system through changing the attitudes of the individuals running the system.

At the instigation of Lin Zexu 林則徐 (1785-1850), the Imperial Commissioner to Guangzhou who had been sent to exile by the imperial court for his inept handling of the war, Wei undertook the compilation of the *Haiguo tuzhi* 海國圖志 ('Illustrated Gazetteer of the Maritime Countries', hereafter the *Gazetteer*). The work was encyclopedic in content. There were Western-style and Chinese-style maps, tables and diagrams, traditional Chinese geographical writings, Wei's own writings, portions of official memorials on China's defence needs written by high government officials such as Lin, and, most importantly, translations. The translations were of various types. There were translations of Western sources, including articles (or excerpts of articles) from English-language newspapers published in the Far East. These were mostly done by Chinese working in the translation bureau set up by Lin when he was Imperial Commissioner in Guangzhou.[7] The translations were intended to expose Western designs on China, and to show how much the Westerners knew

---

[7] Four Chinese were employed by Lin in the translation bureau. See Wong (2007) for a description of these translators and a preliminary assessment of their competence.

about China, in contrast to the ignorance of the Chinese about the world. In addition, there were geography books and history books, mostly by Protestant missionaries, who drew their material from sources such as Elijah Bridgman's *Geographical History of the United States* and translated and rewrote them for the Chinese readership. There was also the *Sizhou zhi* 四洲志 ('Gazetteer of the Four Continents'), a geographical work based on translations from Hugh Murray's *Cyclopaedia of Geography* (Leonard 1984:91, Hsü 1990:275). According to Wei, it was upon this work that the whole *Gazetteer* was based (Wei 1998:1). These materials provided up-to-date information about Western history and geography. They also served to reinforce the point about Chinese ignorance of the outside world.[8]

Not only did the *Gazetteer* provide information on maritime Asia and countries in the West, but it was also the first to explore the significance of such information from a broad geopolitical perspective. As such, it was a powerful critique of the mindset of the ruling conservatives. Behind the new maritime policy it advocated, there was in fact a new paradigm of thinking, one that looked afresh at China's relation to the world.

In the preface to the *Gazetteer*, Wei asks: "What is the purpose of this work? It is to argue for the need to use the foreigners against the foreigners, to befriend the foreigners in order to manage them, and to learn the superior techniques of the foreigners in order to control them" (Wei 1998:1; my translation, in Cheung forthcoming). The sense of superiority typical of the Establishment was still there. But the admission that there was a need to learn from the 'foreigners' was new – radically so, dangerously so. It was dangerous because learning from the foreigners would make a person vulnerable to charges of traitorous conduct. As Wei remarks, "if Chinese are involved in translating foreign books, imitating the foreigners' skills, and briefing themselves on the foreign situation in the same way as the foreigners spy on all aspects of our situation, these people will be punished for committing crimes, causing trouble and communicating with foreigners" (*ibid.*:449; my translation).

From these two passages, we can see how translation was meant to serve the political agenda of an intellectual committed to reformative activism – not reformative activism of the pure type but one interwoven with alterative strands. More specifically, translation was undertaken here with the purpose of introducing a new attitude towards foreigners, for intelligence gathering and for the strategic formulation of a new maritime policy. We can see, too, the risks involved. As a matter of fact, Lin Zexu, the first translation patron in modern Chinese history,[9] was denigrated by his successor, Qi Shan 琦善 (1790-1854), precisely for "spying on the foreigners" (Wei 1976:178), thus

---

[8] For detailed information on the sources used by Wei Yuan, see Xiong (1994:258-66) and Barnett (1970).

[9] See Wong (2001, 2005:112-113) for a portrayal of Lin Zexu as the first translation patron in modern Chinese history.

bringing disgrace to the Empire. Wei had thus committed himself to compiling the *Gazetteer* with a full awareness of the risks involved.

Was Wei successful in achieving his aims? Not really. The *Gazetteer* failed to bring about any change in mindset, or in policy, or in the operation of the system. The inertia, the political myopia and the sense of cultural superiority were too strong to be shaken. Wei's mode of activism was both too advanced for his time and too much of an isolated effort.

2.2   Translation and activism – at once transformative and redemptive

While Wei Yuan was working on his *Gazetteer*, another form of activism – at once transformative and redemptive – was being undertaken in China. The movement was led by a strong leader with support from the grassroots, and it promised to be more effective in bringing cataclysmic social and political change. Translation once again played a significant role in the process.

The Taiping Revolution broke out in 1850. It lasted for fourteen years and was the largest anti-government movement in nineteenth-century China. Its leader was Hong Xiuquan 洪秀全 (1814-1864), a scholar who suffered attacks of delirium and was driven to the verge of mental breakdown by his repeated failure to pass the imperial examinations, which was a necessary prerequisite to a career in the Chinese civil service at the time. In his frustration, he turned his back on such a career and pursued a programme of fundamental social change. He drew his inspiration for this programme not only from the Confucian classics such as the *Liyun* 禮運 ('The Evolution of Li') and the *Datong* 大同 ('The Grand Union'), but also from what he claimed to be visionary encounters with the Heavenly Father, from some religious tracts he had read, and from a work of translation – the missionary Gützlaff's 1840 Bible.[10] These two sources of influence became most visible when the religious society set up by Hong (called Bai Shangdi Hui 拜上帝會, or the Association of God Worshippers) grew powerful, clashed with government troops, and Hong declared the establishment of a new regime with the title 'Taiping Tianguo', or 'Heavenly Kingdom of Great Peace'. The term 'Taiping' 太平 (Great Peace) appeared in the Chinese classics and had been the title used by several emperors in earlier periods (Hsü 1990:229). And 'Tianguo' 天國 (Heavenly Kingdom) was derived from the phrase 'the Kingdom of Heaven', taken from the Gospel of Matthew (Boardman 1952:86).

Hong endorsed Gützlaff's 1840 Bible as the 'Taiping Bible' which, along with other sources from which he haphazardly selected and freely interpreted, formed the basis of the beliefs of the God Worshippers. Hong had obtained a copy of Gützlaff's Bible in 1847 in Guangzhou, either from Gützlaff's native

---

[10] For a more detailed description of Gützlaff's translation of the Bible and an in-depth analysis of the role played by Gützlaff in the Taiping Revolution, see Cheung (1998a:264-66).

helpers or from Gützlaff's assistant, Issachar Jacox Roberts.[11] Based on these, Hong set down the Ten Commandments for the God Worshippers: (1) Thou shalt worship God; (2) Thou shalt not worship evil spirits; (3) Thou shalt not mention God's name superfluously; (4) Thou shalt worship God and praise him on the seventh day of the week; (5) Thou shalt have filial piety; (6) Thou shalt not kill or harm people; (7) Thou shalt not commit adultery and treachery; (8) Thou shalt not steal and rob; (9) Thou shalt not lie; (10) Thou shalt not covet (Luo and Wang 2004:5-6, Hsü 1990:228-229). The Bible was also relied upon for preaching and for the inculcation of Hong's brand of Christian ideas among the people.

But the Taipings were not engaged in a narrowly evangelical movement. Their movement was politically motivated, aimed at overthrowing the Manchu rule, and it was visionary in the social changes which it sought to achieve. Hong the 'Heavenly King' and his five senior associates put into action an elaborate programme of social engineering. It included not only the prohibition of ancestor-worship and the destruction of idols and temples, but also plans to stem out social evils such as opium-smoking, gambling, prostitution, sale of slaves and polygamy. There were social welfare plans to support the disabled, the sick, the widowed and the orphaned. The programme upheld the egalitarian idea that all men were brothers and all women sisters, and men and women were equal, both enjoying the right to serve in the civil and military administration. It abolished private ownership of land by introducing a new land system based on communal use. It even held civil service examinations in the vernacular, that is, the plain language of the masses rather than the classical style of writing required in the imperial examinations of the Qing government.[12] This was Hong creating a parallel universe, a utopia, in which the power dynamics were turned upside down and things were run the way he felt they should be.

In short, the Taipings had laid down the infrastructure of a new government, with an ideology founded on Confucian doctrines and ideas, and on Gützlaff's 1840 Bible, a work of translation, however 'impure' or 'compromised' Hong's interpretation of this work was deemed to be in the eyes of the missionaries in China.[13]

---

[11] I. J. Roberts (1802-1871) was an American Baptist who came to China in response to the appeal for missionary workers launched by Gützlaff. He was Gützlaff's assistant in Hong Kong until 1844, when he was assigned to work in Guangdong. In the spring of 1847, Roberts met Hong Xiuquan and his cousin Hong Rengan and gave them Christian instruction for two months (Boardman 1952:43).

[12] For details of the Taiping institutions, see Hsü (1990:232-36).

[13] The missionaries working in China, "either through a closer scrutiny of Taiping beliefs or through detection of lamentable change in the religious beliefs of the rebellion's leader", came to the conclusion that Hong did not understand "Christianity in the real sense of the term" (Shih 1972:402).

In the end, however, because of internal dissension, blunders in strategy, crises in leadership and a host of outside factors, the Taiping Revolution was crushed. The radical social and political changes and the transformation of the individual envisaged by the Taipings' brand of activism came to various degrees of realization in the course of the fourteen years of the history of the 'Heavenly Kingdom of Great Peace', but they could not be sustained.

Nonetheless, the Taiping Revolution had far-reaching and profound reper-cussions.[14] One that pertains to our topic of translation and activism was that the movement drew the attention of Christian missionaries stationed in China to the enormous potential power that a work of translation (Gützlaff's 1840 Bible) can exercise. This generated a strong momentum for the use of translations (of the Bible and other religious tracts) as a tool for the spread of Christianity, or, in the parlance of this paper, for the realization of redemptive activism and/or alterative activism. In the context of China in the mid 19th century, when Christian teachings were considered a force that alienated the Chinese from their cultural tradition, the spread of Christianity did partake of the nature of an activist movement, aimed either at reform through the individual or at the pursuit of alternative life styles and alternative cultural values by individuals. But since this involves a critical study of the foreign missionaries in China, and since the focus of the present paper is on the Chinese themselves, I shall not venture into a discussion of this repercussion at this point.[15]

For about thirty years after the Taiping Revolution (1865-1895), the Qing government took the initiative to introduce a range of social reforms, and translation was pressed into the service of reinforcing the feudal order. In fact, during what came to be known as the Ziqiang Yundong 自強運動 (the Self-strengthening Movement), translation featured as an integral part of the government-led modernization programme, modernization being equated with the acquisition of Western technical know-how – in firearms, ships, machines, railroads, mining, light industries and applied science generally. It was only

---

[14] One result was the shift of military power to the Han Chinese, for it was the new army led by Zeng Guofan曾國藩 (1811-1872) and Li Hongzhang 李鴻章(1823-1901) that defeated the Taipings. Another was that revolutionaries of a later time found inspiration from the Taiping Revolution. It was well-known that Dr Sun Yet-sen (1866-1925), father of the Chinese Republic, wanted to emulate Hong and that his revolutionary philosophy was influenced by the Taiping ideology. Karl Marx, disappointed by the failure of the 1848 revolution in Europe, was greatly encouraged by the Taiping movement and gained from it a new perspective on the possibility of peasant revolution (Hsü 1990:251-53).

[15] The foreign missionaries in China have been studied by scholars from different perspec-tives. See Gu Changsheng (1991) for a standard account from a revised Marxist point of view, and Luo Guanzong (2003) for a collection of essays representing the views of patriotic Chinese and of the China Christian Council towards the relationship between Christianity and imperialism in China. For an opposite view and a classic study in English, written by a former missionary who also had a long career as a Yale University historian, see Kenneth Scott Latourette (1929). Two other important critical introductions to the topic are Cohen (1963) and Fairbank (1974).

after China's disastrous defeat in the First Sino-Japanese War (1894 to 1895), and especially after the Boxer Uprising (1899 to 1901), when China was faced with the threat of partition by aggressive foreign powers, that activists once again took the lead in pressing for change. This time, the power of translation was released by a number of scholars. Their works changed the course of development of the modernization of China, in a way never intended or anticipated by the reformers within the government.

2.3 *Translation and activism – redemptive in immediate goals, transformative in ultimate aspirations*

Liang Qichao 梁啟超 (1873-1929) was one of the scholars involved in this new movement. He was a student of Kang Youwei 康有為 (1858-1927), a charismatic scholar-activist who advocated vociferously for reforms. After the defeat of China by Japan in 1895, Liang helped Kang prepare a 10,000-word 'memorial' – or petition in today's terms – and gather the signatures of 603 provincial graduates to protest the peace treaty, an incident considered by some historians as the first 'mass political movement' in modern China.[16] The memorial did not reach the emperor. But that only strengthened the resolve of Kang and Liang to work harder towards their goals. After many more memorials, Kang and a number of his associates, including Liang, inaugurated a programme for radical institutional reform. But their effort was crushed by a *coup d'état* staged by the Empress Dowager Cixi 慈禧太后, the ultra conservative who was the main target of most of the efforts to overthrow the Qing. The 'Hundred-Day' Reform thus came to an end, and Liang fled to Japan. There he devoted his time to political writing and argued for setting up a constitutional monarchy in preference to a complete overthrow of the Manchu dynasty and setting up a republic.[17]

At the same time, Liang added a new item to his agenda – education of the masses through the translation of fiction – and gave it top priority. His argument, based on the view expressed by his mentor Kang Youwei, was that not everyone would read the Chinese classics, but anyone who could read would read fiction, especially fiction in the vernacular (see Kang 1897:13). In particular, Liang advocated the translation of political novels.[18] In his portrayal, the political novel embodied the loftiest political sentiments and

---

[16] The incident was known as the Gongche Shangshu 公車上書, or 'Public Vehicles Presenting a Memorial', 'public vehicles' being the nickname for the provincial graduates who came to Beijing by public transportation for the metropolitan examinations (Hsü 1990:367).

[17] See Song (1990) for a survey of Liang's political views.

[18] The term 'political novel' (*zhengzhi xiaoshuo*) was first used in Liang's essay (2001) published in the first issue of the magazine *Qingyi bao* (The China Discussion). An English translation of this preface, in which Liang elaborated the merits of this genre, appears in Cheung (forthcoming).

the most enlightening political ideas, and hence would provide the most direct access to the political consciousness of the people and effect change in that sphere. Not only did he espouse these views in writing, he also translated the Japanese writer Shiba Shirō's political novel *Kajin no kigu* into Chinese. This translation, entitled *Jiaren qiyu* 佳人奇遇 (Romantic Encounters with two Fair Ladies), was serialized in *Qingyi Bao* 清議報 (The China Discussion), an influential journal published by Liang in Japan and read not only by the Chinese overseas but also by those at home. The novel called for the independence of Japan from oppressive Western powers; Liang intended his translation to rouse similar feelings in his countrymen.[19] Liang also started to write his own political novel – *Xin Zhongguo weilai ji* 新中國未來記 (The Future of New China) – but the project was never completed.[20]

Liang's privileging of the political novel showed that the failure of the 'Hundred-Day' Reform had taught him a valuable lesson. While total transformation in the political order remained his long-term aspiration, he was shrewd enough to see that this aspiration would not be realized through political measures alone. He had to take the more circuitous route of reaching the individual first, and, through transformation of the individual, prepare the nation for political change. Translation and political writing were the means he relied upon for reaching his first destination.

As an influential political and cultural figure, Liang was successful in stimulating enthusiasm for using the novel as a tool of social criticism, for debating controversial issues of the day, and for bringing political enlightenment to the masses (Yi 1997:15-16), but he failed to produce a critical mass of translated political novels of impact. No more translations of political novels appeared in *Qingyi bao* after the serialization of *Jingguo meitan* 經國美談, a translation by an anonymous translator of another Japanese political novel, Yano Ryuukei's *Keikoku bidan* (A Beautiful Story of Statesmanship).[21] This was significant, since *Qingyi bao* was published by Liang and served as the mouthpiece of his political views.

2.4 The power and dynamics of translation: an unexpected trajectory

The power of translation to effect change, as seen in the stories of Wei Yuan, Hong Xiuquan and Liang Qichao, was manifested in results which either fell

---

[19] See Wong (1998) for an analysis of textual evidence of manipulation. Liang reworked sections of the source text in his translation so that the differences in political situations between China and Japan would not invalidate his attempt to stir up political sentiments among his readers.

[20] For a succinct summary of the possible reasons why Liang did not finish writing this novel, see Wong (1998).

[21] *Jiaren qiyu* (Romantic Encounters with two Fair Ladies) was serialized in *Qingyi bao* from December 1898 to February 1900. *Jingguo meitan* (A Beautiful Story of Statesmanship) was serialized from February to December 1900. After that, the column which published these translations was cancelled.

short of, or within, the range of expectations envisaged by these individuals. With the threat of partition by aggressive foreign powers becoming increasingly real, however, the psychology of reading began to change. Translation, in the hands of two extraordinarily accomplished writers – Yan Fu 嚴復 (1854-1921) and Lin Shu 林紓 (1852-1924) – and a host of others, became a catalyst which, once activated, operated with a dynamic of its own, setting off results that surprised even the translators themselves.

Yan Fu produced what is often considered to be the single most important translation in early modern China. His partial translation of Thomas H. Huxley's *Evolution and Ethics* (1891), entitled *Tianyan lun* 天演論 (Theory on Natural Evolution, 1898), was both profound and far-reaching in impact. But Yan was not a banner-waving activist. He received his education at the Fuzhou Dockyard (a naval academy of the new style), spent two years in Britain (1877-1879), and was superintendent of the North Sea Naval Academy in Tianjin when the war with Japan broke out. He translated Huxley's work because he was driven by an impulse to do something, anything, to change the deplorable state of his country. In this he was behaving in a manner all too familiar to many activists today, who are also often initiated into activism through impulse rather than careful planning. Yan selected *Evolution and Ethics* for translation because it enabled him to introduce Social Darwinism into China. He saw a real danger of 'racial extinction' if the Chinese people did not rise to repel Western imperialism, and he wanted to declare this message loud and clear. That was why his translation was characterized by an abundant use of paratextual devices such as annotations and commentary. Through these devices, Yan expressed his views on the political situation in China and provided background explanations of the intellectual content and key concepts of Huxley and his age. The work was, in fact, translation-cum-political writing. At a deeper level, perhaps one of which Yan himself was not fully conscious, but which becomes more visible from the perspective of activism, the work was a manifesto – of redemptive activism interwoven with reformative strands. Like Wei Yuan before him, Yan realized that social and political change could not be achieved without attitudinal change. But unlike Wei Yuan, who aimed only to change the attitude of those in power towards foreigners and foreign nations, Yan aimed at a complete change in mindset, though the classical style he used for his translation showed that his intended readers were not the common people but the literati and court officials who could initiate change in the political system.

The dynamics of translation, however, were such that *Tianyan lun* (Theory on Natural Evolution) set off trains of reaction totally unexpected by Yan. Because 'racial extinction' touched the very nerve-centre of the nation at that point in history, the work reached a wide readership. It was read not only by the literati but also by students. The notions of 'natural selection' and 'survival of the fittest' came to the forefront of people's attention, with intellectuals debating them in newspapers (Xiong 1994:683). Terms such as 'evolution', 'struggle', 'elimination' and 'natural selection' became slogans on the lips of the patriotic youths. Even school children were asked to write essays on these topics.[22]

Yan subsequently translated other seminal works in the social sciences. They included Adam Smith's *An Inquiry into the Nature and Causes of the Wealth of Nations* (1776), Herbert Spencer's *A Study of Sociology* (1873), John S. Mill's *On Liberty* (1859) and *A System of Logic* (1843), C. L. S. Montesquieu's *De l'esprit des lois* (1743), Edward Jenk's *A History of Politics* (1900) and William S. Jevon's *Primer of Logic* (1876). Through these translations, which provided Yan with the opportunity to comment on the urgent problems in society, Yan showed that Western learning had a lot more to offer than just science and technology. The reforms introduced by the Qing government had merely scratched the surface of modernization. Below the surface were ideas, values, cognitive processes and epistemological frames – all waiting to be explored. Change at a deeper level was needed. Yan was using his translations to serve precisely that purpose. The irony was that the classical style of writing Yan employed in his translations was a hindrance to popular reception, the notable exception being *Tianyan lun*. So while his vision became more transformative in scope, his presentation of such a vision militated against its realization, for it largely restricted comprehension to the intelligentsia.

The power of translation to effect change was tapped by other translators, many of whom were as desperate as Yan Fu had been to 'do something' for their country. Few, however, produced translations with the kind of catalytic force released by *Tianyan lun* (Theory on Natural Evolution). The exception was Lin Shu.

Lin Shu was by far the most influential translator of fiction in late nineteenth- and early twentieth-century China. It was extraordinary that Lin, a Confucian scholar with no foreign languages, would take up translation.[23] He was at home recovering from the death of his wife when, to divert Lin from his grief, a friend told him the story of *La Dame aux camellias* and Lin wrote it down in elegant classical Chinese. Entitled *Bali chahua nü yishi* 巴黎茶花女遺事(Anecdotes of the Lady of the Camellias in Paris, 1899), the 'translation' became enormously popular. When Lin saw what he could achieve with the translation of fiction, he devoted himself wholeheartedly to collaborative translation.

---

[22] This is recollected by Hu Shi, a prominent literary and cultural figure in the early 20th century (Hu 1959:49-50).

[23] Lin is a legendary figure in the history of translation in China. Even today it is well known that he could turn his collaborators' oral rendition into a style evocative of the classical style at the amazing speed of "6000 Chinese characters in mere four hours per day"; see Lin (1914), an English translation of which can be found in Cheung (forthcoming).

A total of 163 works, by 98 writers from 11 countries, were produced by
this collaborative method (Yu 1983:403). Of these, the most influential was
Heinu yutian lu 黑奴籲天錄 (A Chronicle of the Black Slaves' Appeals to
Heaven, 1901) – a translation, by Lin Shu and Wei Yi, of the well-known
anti-slavery and religious novel *Uncle Tom's Cabin, or Life among the Lowly*
by Harriet Beecher Stowe. Published immediately after the Boxer Uprising
(1899-1901) and the humiliating presence of the Allied Expeditionary Forces in
Beijing in 1900, the translation, which carried an emotionally charged preface
urging people to rally round their country or become slaves, stirred up strong
patriotic feelings and hardened people's anti-imperialistic stance.[24] Its impact
was enormous – as seen, for example, in letters published in newspapers and
poems registering the reaction of the common reader, and in the fact that the
translated text was adapted in 1907 into a play for performance in Japan, where
it elicited a strong patriotic response.[25] Lin became convinced that the translation of novels was the most effective means for liberating the minds of the
people. Through the translated novels, he hoped to introduce his countrymen
to all aspects of Western society – Western customs, social problems, ethical
concepts, familial relations and so on. And he made full use of his prefaces to
educate the masses. He even spoke of translation as an enterprise for saving
the country (Zhang 1992:96-97).

In short, Lin initially used translation to serve the purpose of redemptive
activism, but he was quick to appreciate its transformative potential. He soon
saw the power of translation to break down the insularity in which the Chinese
people had been trapped for centuries, to bring radical change in consciousness
and even in the intellectual climate and social fabric of the time. He was, like
Yan Fu, a stubborn defender of the classical style, and his translated novels
were popular with the literati and government officials, but he was able to reach
a large readership because the type of works he translated, novels in particular,
as Liang Qichao had already noted, had a strong appeal among the public.

3. The contemporary implications of translation and activism in the late Qing period

From the examples discussed above, it can be seen that the relationship between translation and activism was complex during the late Qing period and
changed quite dramatically over time. In the initial stage, translation was

---

[24] See Cheung (1998b) for a detailed analysis of how the translation shows signs of subtle
attempts by Lin Shu to shape his readers' reaction.

[25] Ouyang Yuqian (1962: 1) contains quotations excerpted from letters sent to newspapers
by readers and poems on how deeply moved people were by Lin Shu's translation of *Uncle
Tom's Cabin*. See also Chen Yugang (1989:68) for the reaction of Lu Xun, the writer who
exerted what many would consider to be the greatest influence on the literary and translation scenes in twentieth-century China.

almost always used as a tool by translators and/or translation patrons to attain the goals of various activist projects. Following the unexpected impact produced by Yan Fu's translation of *Evolution and Ethics* and Lin Shu's translation of *Uncle Tom's Cabin*, the readership for activist translation grew, and the relationship between translation and activism became more intricate, more unpredictable. The activity of translation might have been undertaken with a purely utilitarian purpose, but the success of a particular work of translation, as noted above, at times released a catalytic effect – on both the translator and the community. This then strengthened the patriotic sentiment in society and among individuals. Heightened activist fervour would, in turn, generate further momentum for the activity of translation, thus changing the pattern of growth and development of translation, especially of certain types of translation. The following sets of figures are significant in this respect.

Between 1840 and 1920, a total of 2,504 titles (of fiction) were translated, 1,488 of which were produced between 1911 and 1920. For the years 1902-1907, the number of translated titles (of fiction) exceeded that of works of fiction written in Chinese (Tarumoto 1998:39). These figures reveal a burst of energy in the translation of fiction. It would perhaps be rash to attribute the reason for such a boom in fiction translation to the success of Liang Qichao's translation of *Kajin no kigu* (Romantic Encounters with Two Fair Ladies), published in 1898, or Yan Fu's translation of *Evolution and Ethics*, also published in 1898, and/or Lin Shu's translation of *Uncle Tom's Cabin*, published in 1901. But it would be equally rash to dismiss such a possibility. In any case, given the Chinese pride in their literature and culture, and bearing in mind that the Self-strengthening Movement was only interested in learning science and technology from the West, these figures must be taken seriously, so long as the political events of the time are factored into our understanding of the dynamics of translation. At the very least, the numbers show that the relationship between translation and activism had evolved from one that is akin to a one-sided affair to a relationship characterized by interaction, reciprocity and mutual reinforcement. Rather than just a tool of activism or a catalyst for change, translation became something more – and more complex – at the turn of the 20th century in China. It focused people's minds and emotions, providing a point of anchor for their hopes for their country and their dreams of a strong nation. At the same time, it became a site where change actually took place – as evidenced in the passionate intensity with which intellectuals and writers threw themselves into the task of translating, and the equally passionate intensity with which their translations were read by the populace. Such passion is akin to the kind of energy that activists aim to release today, expressed clearly in the motto of the World Social Forum: "Another world is possible". It is this belief that "Another world is possible" that worked, and will continue to work, in a fundamental way on people's psyche and, when combined with the forces of circumstances, drove and will continue to drive people to seek change, whether in China or other parts of the world, and whether people see themselves as activists or reject the label but just 'do' activism. Certainly, the fact that translation could function not just as a tool but also a site where change actually took place should provide an illuminating lesson for the activists of today. They do well to explore the way the internet technology might be used more productively – so that the translation websites devoted to the release of information aimed at contesting or offering alternative perspectives to the information released by pro-government or dominant media can also serve as a site for recruitment, a site where goodwill and the simple desire to offer one's service for the promotion of a good cause can be harnessed, a site where translators can be transformed into translator-activists.

There are other ways in which the late Qing story of the power and dynamics of translation can have relevance to the present generation. From the story, the conclusion can be drawn that when the intended readership of a translator-activist is relatively small (if it is confined to the Confucian scholars or court officials, for example), it is easier to predict the outcomes, but as the readership grows and the scope of dissemination of activist values and ideas introduced through translation also grows, there is an increased likelihood that people might run off with newly translated or borrowed ideas and use them to their own ends, that is, interpret them in ways that were never intended. Some twentieth-century examples that come readily to mind include the rise of Maoism, which was based on translated Marx and Lenin plus Chinese characteristics, or the Peruvian movement 'The Shining Path', which took Maoist ideas from the Little Red Book of Mao Zedong and transplanted them to Peruvian activism. These examples all go to show that in the great exchange and cross-fertilization of ideas across language and nations, there is always an element of unpredictability. The advance in information technology, which has resulted in faster and easier worldwide dissemination of ideas than during the late Qing period, makes the unpredictability of interpretation, and of results, that much more inevitable.

This does not mean, however, that everything should be left to chance, or that the unpredictability principle rules over everything. Precisely because it is hard to predict the impact of translation on activist movements, it is even more necessary to study the dynamics of translation by conducting strategic thinking on the variety of factors – domestic and international, contextual and circumstantial – that might interact with and impinge upon a translator's work. Understanding the dynamics of translation does not guarantee attainment of change, but the awareness that unpredictability is an integral part of the processes of change can help a translator-activist develop resilience and manage frustration in the face of setbacks. This is why historical research is important. All too often, it is thought that activism is a distinctly twentieth-century phenomenon. All too often, it is thought that studies of activism should focus on the present, on the urgent and compelling problems of the day. But if our sight is so firmly trained on the present, we deny ourselves the opportunity to forge with people of the past a sense of community based on shared values and aspirations across time and space, and we run the risk of idealizing activism as a unique, unprecedented pursuit. It would be much more productive to seek a fuller understanding of how translation works in the complex and intricate power struggles of history and to draw lessons from this for the future, or the present. It is for this reason that I have sought to rethink activism in this article by conducting a case study of the power and dynamics of translation in a particular period in Chinese history – the late Qing period (1840-1911).

References

Aberle, David (1966) *The Peyote Religion Among the Navaho*, Chicago: Aldine.

Alvarez, Román and M. Carmen-Africa Vidal (eds) (1996) *Translation, Power, Subversion*, Clevedon; Philadelphia: Multilingual Matters.

Baker, Mona (2006a) *Translation and Conflict: A Narrative Account*, London & New York: Routledge.

----- (2006b) 'Translation and Activism: Emerging Patterns of Narrative Community', *Massachusetts Review* 47(3): 462-84.

----- (2009) 'Resisting State Terror: Theorising Communities of Activist Translators and Interpreters', in Esperança Bielsa Mialet and Chris Hughes (eds) *Globalisation, Political Violence and Translation*, Basingstoke & New York: Palgrave Macmillan, 222-42.

Barnett, Suzanne Wilson (1970) 'Wei Yuan and Westerners: Notes on the Sources of the *Hai-kuo t'u-chih*', *Ch'ing-shih wen-t'i* 2(4): 1-20.

Bassnett, Susan and Harish Trivedi (1999) *Post-colonial Translation: Theory and Practice*, London; New York: Routledge.

Boardman, Eugene Powers (1952) *Christian Influence Upon the Ideology of the Taiping Rebellion, 1851-1864*, Madison: University of Wisconsin Press.

Bobel, Chris (2007) '"I'm not an activist, though I've done a lot of it": Doing Activism, Being Activist and the "Perfect Standard" in a Contemporary Movement', *Social Movement Studies* 6(2): 147-59.

Boéri, Julie (2008) 'A Narrative account of the Babels vs. Naumann Controversy: Competing Perspectives on Activism in Conference Interpreting', *The Translator* 14(1): 21-50.

Chen, Yugang (ed.) (1989) *Zhongguo fanyi wenxue shigao* [A Draft History of Chinese Translated Literature], Beijing: Zhongguo duiwai fanyi chuban gongsi.

Cheung, Martha P. Y. (1998a) 'Translation and Power: A Hong Kong Case Study', *Perspectives: Studies in Translatology* 6(2): 259-74.

----- (1998b) 'The Discourse of Occidentalism? Wei Yi and Lin Shu's Treatment of Religious Material in Their Translation of *Uncle Tom's Cabin*', in David Pollard (ed.) *Translation and Creation: Readings of Western Literature in Early Modern China, 1840-1918*, Amsterdam & Philadelphia: John Benjamins, 127-49.

----- (ed.) (forthcoming) *An Anthology of Chinese Discourse on Translation.
Volume 2: From the 13th Century to the Beginning of the 20th Century*, Manchester: St. Jerome Publishing.

Cheyfitz, Eric (1991) *The Poetics of Imperialism: Translation and Colonization
from The Tempest to Tarzan*, New York: Oxford University Press.

Cohen, Paul A. (1963) *China and Christiantiy: The Missionary Movement & the
Growth of Chinese Antiforeignism, 1860-1870*, Cambridge, MA: Harvard
University Press

Fairbank, John King (ed.) (1974) *The Missionary Enterprise in China and America*,
Cambridge, MA: Harvard University Press.

Fenton, Sabine and Paul Moon (2003) 'Survival by Translation: The Case of Te
Tiriti o Waitangi', in Sabine Fenton (ed.) *For Better or For Worse: Translation
as a Tool for Change in the South Pacific*, Manchester: St. Jerome Publishing,
37-61.

Flexner, Stuart Berg (ed.) (1993) *Random House Unabridged Dictionary*, New
York: Random House.

Gu, Changsheng (1991) *Chuanjiaoshi yu jindai zhongguo* [Missionaries and
Modern China], Shanghai: Shanghai renmin chubanshe.

Hsü, Immanuel C. Y. (1990) *The Rise of Modern China*, New York: Oxford
University Press.

Hu, Shi (1959) *Sishi zishu* [A Self-account at the Age of 40], Taipei: Yuandong
tushu gongsi.

Kang, Youwei (1897/1989) 'Riben shumu zhi shiyu' [On "A Bibliography of Japanese Books"], in Chen Pingyuan and Xia Xiaohong (eds) *Ershi shiji Zhongguo
xiaoshuo lilun shiliao* [Theoretical Materials on Chinese Fiction in the Twentieth
Century], Volume 1. Beijing: Beijing daxue chubanshe, 13-14.

Leonard, Jane Kate (1984) *Wei Yuan and China's Rediscovery of the Maritime
World*, Cambridge, MA: Council on East Asian Studies, Harvard University.

Liang, Qichao (2001) 'Yiyin zhengzhi xiaoshuo xu' [A Preface to the Translation
and Publication of Political Novels], in *Yinbingshi wenji dianjiao* [A Punctuated Edition of the *Essays from the Ice-drinking Chamber*], Kunming: Yunnan
jiaoyu chubanshe, Volume 2, 758-60.

Lin, Shu (1914) 'Xu' [Preface] to *Kaonü naier zhuan* [A Biography of the Filial
Daughter Naier], Chinese translation of Charles Dickens' *The Old Curiosity
Shop*, Shanghai: Shangwu yinshu guan, 1-4.

Luo, Ergang and Wang Qingcheng (eds) (2004) *Taiping tianguo* [The Taiping
Heavenly Kingdom], vol. 1, Guilin: Guangxi shifan daxue chubanshe.

Luo, Guanzong (ed.) (2003) *Qianshi buwang, houshi zhishi: diguo zhuyi liyong
jidujiao qinlue zhongguo shishi shuping* [Past Experience as a Guide for the
Future: A Critical Account of How the Imperialists used Christianity as a Tool
to Invade China], Beijing: Zongjiao wenhua chubanshe.

Mason, Ian (1994/2010) 'Discourse, Ideology and Translation', in Robert de Beaugrande, Abdulla Shunnaq and Mohamed H. Heliel (eds) *Language, Discourse
and Translation in the West and Middle East*, Amsterdam: John Benjamins,
23-34. Reprinted, with new postscript, in Mona Baker (ed.) *Critical Readings*

in: Translation Studies, London & New York: Routledge, 83-95.

Mutu, Margaret (2003) 'The Humpty Dumpty Principle at Work: The Role of Mistranslation in the British Settlement of Aotearoa. The Declaration of Independence and He Whakaputanga o te Rangatiratanga o nga hapü o Nu Tïreni', in Sabine Fenton (ed.) *For Better or For Worse: Translation as a Tool for Change in the South Pacific*, Manchester: St. Jerome Publishing, 12-35.

Ouyang, Yuqian (1962) *Heinu hen* [Persecution of the Black Slaves], Beijing: Zhongguo xiju chubanshe.

Salama-Carr, Myriam (ed.) (2007) *Translating and Interpreting Conflict*, Amsterdam & New York: Rodopi.

Shih, Vincent Y. C. (1972) *The Taiping Ideology: Its Sources, Interpretations, and Influences*, Seattle & London: University of Washington Press.

Song, Ren (ed.) (1990) *Liang Qichao zhengzhi falü sixiang yanjiu* [A Study of the Political and Legal Thoughts of Liang Qichao], Beijing: Xueyuan chubanshe.

Tarumoto, Teruo (1998) 'A Statistical Survey of Translated Fiction 1840-1920', in David Pollard (ed.) *Translation and Creation: Readings of Western Literature in Early Modern China, 1840-1918*, Amsterdam & Philadelphia: John Benjamins, 37-42.

Tymoczko, Maria (1999) *Translation in a Postcolonial Context: Early Irish Literature in English Translation*, Manchester: St. Jerome Publishing.

----- (2000) 'Translation and Political Engagement: Activism, Social Change and the Role of Translation in Geopolitical Shifts', *The Translator* 6(1): 23-47.

----- (ed.) (2006) *Translation as Resistance*, special section of *Massachusetts Review* 47(III).

----- (2007) *Enlarging Translation, Empowering Translators*, Manchester: St. Jerome Publishing.

----- and Edwin Gentzler (eds) (2002) *Translation and Power*, Amherst: University of Massachusetts Press.

Venuti, Lawrence (1995) *The Translator's Invisibility: a History of Translation*, London & New York: Routledge.

----- (1998a) *The Scandals of Translation: Towards an Ethics of Difference*, London & New York: Routledge.

----- (1998b) 'American Tradition', in Mona Baker (ed.) *Routledge Encyclopedia of Translation Studies*, London & New York, 305-16.

----- (1998c) 'Introduction', in Lawrence Venuti (ed.) *Translation and Minority*, special issue of *The Translator* 4(2): 135-44.

Wei, Yuan (1976) *Wei Yuan Ji* [Works of Wei Yuan], vol. 1, Beijing: Zhonghua shuju.

----- (1998) *Haiguo tuzhi* [Illustrated Gazetteer of the Maritime Countries], vol. 1, Changsha: Yuelu shushe.

Wong, Lawrence Wang-Chi (1998) '"The Sole Purpose is to Express My Political Views": Liang Qichao and the Translation and Writing of Political Novels in the Late Qing', in David Pollard (ed.) *Translation and Creation: Readings of Western Literature in Early Modern China, 1840-1918*, Amsterdam & Philadelphia: John Benjamins, 105-26.

----- (2001) 'Quanli yu fanyi: wanqing fanyi huodong zanzhuren de kaocha' [Power and Translation: An Investigation of the Translation Patrons of the late Qing Dynasty], *Zhongwai wenxue* 30(7): 94-127.

----- (2005) 'From "Controlling the Barbarians" to "Wholesale Westernization": Translation and Politics in Late Imperial and Early Republican China, 1840-1919', in Eva Hung and Judy Wakabayashi (eds) *Asian Translation Traditions*, Manchester: St. Jerome Publishing, 109-34.

----- (2007) 'Translators and Interpreters During the Opium War Between Britain and China', in Myriam Salama-Carr (ed.) *Translating and Interpreting Conflict*, Amsterdam & New York: Rodopi, 41-57.

Xiong, Yuezhi (1994). *Xixue dongjian yu wanqing shehui* [The Eastward Spread of the Western Learning and the Late-Qing Society], Shanghai: Shanghai renmin chubanshe.

Yi, Xinding (ed.) (1997) *Ershi shiji zhongguo xiaoshuo fazhanshi* [History of Chinese Novel in the 20th Century], Beijing: Shoudu shifan daxue chubanshe.

Yu, Jiuhong (1983) 'Lin Shu fanyi zuopin kaosuo' [An Investigation of Lin Shu's Translations], in Xue Suizhi and Zhang Juncai (eds) *Lin Shu yanjiu ziliao* [Material for the Study of Lin Shu], Fuzhou: Fujian renmin chubanshe, 403-27.

Zhang, Juncai (1992) *Lin Shu ping zhuan* [Lin Shu: A Critical Biography], Tianjin: Nankai daxue chubanshe.

Zoller, Heather M. (2005) 'Health Activism: Communication Theory and Action for Social Change', *Communication Theory* 15(4): 341-64.

'Ad-hocracies' of Translation Activism in the Blogosphere
A Genealogical Case Study

LUIS PÉREZ GONZÁLEZ
University of Manchester, UK

Abstract. *This paper sets out to explore how translation is increasingly being appropriated by politically engaged individuals without formal training to respond effectively to the socio-economic structures that sustain global capitalism. Drawing on a generative conceptualization of translation activism and insights from globalization studies and media sociology, the paper traces the genealogy of an activist community subtitling a televised interview with Spain's former Prime Minister, José María Aznar López, originally broadcast by BBC News 24 against the background of the ongoing military conflict between Lebanon and Israel. The analysis suggests that these communities of 'non-translators' emerge through dynamic processes of contextualization, involving complex negotiations of narrative affinity among their members. It is argued that, in contrast to more traditional groupings of activist translators, these fluid networks of engaged mediators constitute 'ad-hocracies' that capitalize on the potential of networked communication to exploit their collective intelligence. The paper concludes by exploring the implications of the growing importance of such ad-hocracies for the future of activist translation and its theorization.*

This paper sets out to explore the part that networks of politically engaged individuals without formal training in translation ('non-translators') are playing within the wider process of cultural resistance against global capitalist structures and institutions through interventionist forms of mediation, including translation. Ultimately, it aims to ensure that the idiosyncrasies of such collectivities are not overlooked by current scholarly initiatives to elaborate research programmes on and theorize the emergence and functioning of groupings of politically committed translators. Drawing on a generative conceptualization of activism pursued through translation, I argue that these communities of 'non-translators' emerge through dynamic processes of contextualization, involving complex negotiations of narrative affinity among their members. Their structural instability, their reliance on 'collective intelligence' (Levy 2000) to oppose capitalist institutions and their preference for engaging in the mediation of audiovisual contents, vis-à-vis written texts, are found to be some of the reasons why these 'ad-hocracies' (Jenkins *et al.* 2006) differ from typical activist networks.

The study of such *ad hoc* activist mediators requires a robust conceptual framework that draws on translation studies, globalization theory and media sociology – as outlined and critiqued in sections 1, 2 and 3, respectively. Section 4 focuses on the genealogy of a specific community of engaged individuals, some of whose members assume an *ad hoc* interventionist role during a single episode of mediation – in what constitutes a clear manifestation of the generative power of fluid activist identities. Presented with an audiovisual text which resonates strongly with their own 'narrative location' (Baker 2006), Spanish readers of a progressive blog appropriate, subtitle and circulate an audiovisual programme in an attempt to tamper with the dynamics of the global media marketplace and to promote their shared set of narratives vis-à-vis the 'public narratives' (*ibid.*) that circulate in their environment.

1. Structuralist and generative conceptualizations of activism through translation

Activist communities of translators and interpreters are becoming a recurrent object of scholarly enquiry in our discipline, as evidenced by the proliferation of recent international conferences and publications seeking to theorize the emergence and scope of this social phenomenon as well as to identify and scrutinize the different agendas that prompt the critical engagement of activist networks with mainstream public discourse in the communities in which they are embedded. The body of disciplinary discourse in circulation during the inception stages of this strand of scholarship attests, unsurprisingly, to the malleability of the very notion of **activism**. My own survey of conferences and publications purporting to serve as a platform for academic debate on activism in translation and interpreting reveals how these disparate understandings of activism by different scholarly groupings appear to have resulted in important foundational differences. The study of activist translation and interpretation would appear to gravitate around two poles that, for the purposes of systematic discussion, I propose to label as **structuralist** and **generative** conceptualizations of activism.

In Simon's (2005) introduction to a collection of papers entitled *Traduction engagée/Translation and Social Activism*, the term 'activism' designates a range of interventionist approaches to interlingual and intercultural mediation whereby translators and interpreters seek to promote the agendas and redress the grievances of minorities and/or oppressed social groups, largely bound together by their affinity in terms of social class, gender, sexual orientation, religious beliefs or colonial status. These resistant, often entrenched constituencies which Simon presents as the would-be beneficiaries of activist translation are well-established categories in translation and interpreting scholarship, having importantly informed the "cultural politics of translation in the 20th century" (*ibid.*:10) in their explorations of power struggles, both from a contemporary and a historical perspective. Against this background, the role of activist translation is one of 'valorizing', 'reinforcing' or 'reanimating' these social groupings, depending on whether the translator is dealing with 'marginalized', 'dominated' or 'neglected' communities, respectively. Simon's conceptualization of activism relies heavily on a set of crystallized collective identities forged by power differentials and inflected by one or more of the affinities above. The central role of these stable and static categories in activist scholarship is underscored by Simon's claim that "translation has become an ally in representing, reinscribing or reinforcing these identities" (*ibid.*) – which in turn shape the translators' textual interventions. This set of discrete cultural categories reflects the prominence that Simon gives to social structures over individual agency, and it is on this basis that her stance on activism can be regarded as structuralist.[1]

In contrast to Simon's conceptualization of socio-cultural resistant communities as discrete, static groupings of individuals clustered on the basis of mutual affinity and shared affiliations, Baker (2006a, 2006b, 2009) explores the generative potential of activism. For the purposes of this overview, I will argue that the starting point in the development of the generative strand of activism lies in its opposition to a number of widely held disciplinary narratives, including the portrayal of translators as inhabitants of interstitial spaces between discrete cultural communities and as mediators entrusted with bridging resulting intercultural gaps (Pym 1998). Baker (2009), whose critical appraisal of the interculturality narrative builds on previous critiques of the metaphor of interstitial mediation by Tymoczko (2003) and Krebs (2007), challenges the idealization of translators as agents who conduct their mediation work without regard to their own positioning in the socio-political order and the ideological, ethical or religious alignments that the latter brings about; the assumption that translators are located within spaces in-between cultural groupings, Baker argues, allows proponents of the interculturality narrative "to downplay commitment to real people caught up in real contemporary conflicts, and to avoid the responsibility of using language and translation as a tool for political change" (2009:223).

It may be argued that Baker's acknowledgement of the inevitability, even desirability, of the translator's political engagement with the power imbalances

---

[1] The role of static categories in Simon's understanding of activism is in line with her conceptualization of other constructs, such as national cultures (Simon 1996). As Tymoczko (2003:200) notes, Simon's "monolithic, homogeneous" characterization of national cultures "contrast[s] markedly with contemporary ideas about culture that stress the heterogeneity of culture and that assert that any culture is composed of varied and diverse – even contradictory and inconsistent – competing viewpoints, discourses, and textures".

and ideological conflicts inherent to most episodes of social interaction is not, essentially, very dissimilar to Simon's call for the translator's intervention in "situations of discourse where there are discrepancies of power, knowledge or status" (2005:16). A major difference between these two approaches to activism can be found, however, in their conflicting theorization of the collective identities that determine the forms of intervention chosen by translators. While Simon draws on static groupings delimited on the basis of stable socio-cultural and political affiliations, Baker (2009:223) argues that "translators, like other human beings ... negotiate their identities, beliefs and loyalties as we do on the basis of various aspects of the context and their own developing judgement of the issues involved in any given interaction". Drawing on the social strand of narrative theory, Baker describes social life as the product of a constant interaction between individual narratives and publicly constructed attempts to make sense of reality. Identities, forged at the interface between the shifting ways in which individuals narrate themselves and the changing collective narratives circulating around them, are thus best described as transient narrative locations. According to this stance, activists could be defined as highly critical individuals whose personal narratives fail to align, totally or partially, with public narratives at a given point in time and space and who, consequently, set out to bring one or more aspects of their personal narrative to bear on the collective ones. Activism networks would thus consist of individuals sharing one or more aspects of their identity – and hence aiming to renegotiate their position in relation to public narratives in similar ways – that may cut across traditional constituencies. In that collective affiliations are increasingly subject to inflection and redefinition, as are the agendas of activist translator networks (Baker 2006b:463), collective identities are to be understood as temporary and hence dynamic constructs.[2]

As Baker (2009) notes, this conceptualization of identity informed by narrative theory makes it possible to account for the emergence and consolidation

---

[2] Baker's account of social identities as dynamic and ongoingly negotiated narrative locations should be assessed against the gradual shift from 'context' to 'contextualization' that has become increasingly prominent in our disciplinary discourses. Recent studies have shown, for example, how translators and interpreters mediating in institutional settings, traditionally described in terms of the asymmetrical distribution of power between professional and lay interactants, are able to engage in and bring about processes of 'recontextualization' and renegotiation of the initial powerful/powerless identities (Pérez-González 2006a). Even in institutional settings, "effects of power and dominance are always inscribed within processes of (re)contextualization and [hence] ... closer engagement with these processes can provide us with better insight into the shifting agendas of participants and the dynamic goals of interaction than any static listing of contextual variables, however extensive" (Baker 2006c:318). The shift from a static context towards a dynamic process of contextualization problematizes "the notion of a source text as an entity with a stable, definable meaning", highlighting instead the role that the actual mediation process plays in the process of negotiation of meaning among participants (Mason 2006:359).

of communities of activists on the basis of narrative affinity, even when the affinity among the members of the network is partial, i.e. when activists subscribe to a broad narrative which gives cohesion to the group but disagree on other intersecting narratives. Baker's approach to activism is thus able to account for the formation of collective affiliations, and their potential shifts over time, "and still accommodate endless variation at the individual level" (*ibid.*).[3] It is on the basis of the emphasis on agency over social structure and the individuals' constant need to negotiate their identity around traditional socio-cultural categories that I propose to label Baker's account of activism as generative.

The generative conceptualization of activism goes a long way towards recognizing and harnessing the complexity of this interventionist form of mediation at a time when the clustering of narrative affinities is increasingly reliant on fluid identities. As discussed in section 2 below, the dynamics of globalization and the proliferation of new and more sophisticated platforms for social interaction have enhanced the permeability of hard-core and hitherto stable social groupings. Irrespective of their positioning in the political and socio-cultural order, individuals are increasingly engaging in activism on the basis of partial affinity with other network members. The 'mobilization' of only some aspects of one's identity (Baker 2009) – a process which unfolds dynamically on the basis of an individual's political engagement in social inter-action – has thus become the linchpin of contemporary activist networking.

The blog-based site of activism constructed by those individuals involved in the subtitling of the political interview under scrutiny in section 4, for instance, revolves mainly around their opposition to American, Israeli and European foreign policies in relation to the Arab World. But while it may be possible to account for this instance of blog-centred clustering in terms of collective opposition to the 'War on Terror' narrative (and the commitment of its mem-bers to a progressive political discourse), this community of *ad hoc* activist translators is best defined in terms of its gravitational core, rather than discrete external boundaries. As we move away from the core, entropy increases, with community members mobilizing other aspects of their identity and subscribing to intersecting narratives that may differ from those favoured by their fellow network members. Narrative entropy inflects members' identities and affilia-tions, thus detracting from the cohesion of any given community.

---

[3] In her study of activist networks as narrative communities, Baker proposes to "refrain from using categories which pre-exist the research or analysis and instead allow ... (temporary) categories to emerge from the analysis itself" (2009:224). Her study of activism prioritizes agency to the detriment of structure, thus acknowledging the potential for individual vari-ation. Gambier (2007) takes a diametrically opposed perspective on this matter: the starting point for his study on networks of 'traducteurs/interprètes bénévoles' (voluntary translators/interpreters) is, precisely, a close analysis of the structural underpinning of this phenomenon in 'sociotecnique' (sociotechnical), 'processuel' (processual) and 'militant' terms.

This paper acknowledges the strengths of the generative approach and its theoretical apparatus but sets out to explore issues which have so far received relatively little scholarly attention at this foundational stage of research on activism. The aim of this piece of work is not to advance the study of activism, as mapped so far, from a narrative theoretic standpoint; instead, it seeks to chart new ground and draw attention to sites and manifestations of activism that feature less visibly in the research programme of this scholarly strand – as illustrated by a set of research questions proposed by Baker (2009) in the second half of her paper.

Despite expressing her intention to gain a deeper insight into the formation of activist collective identities, Baker has so far concentrated on the outcome, rather than on the unfolding of the actual formation process. In this sense, only one of the set of research questions listed by Baker as part of her research programme pertains to the reasons why individuals are attracted to activist groups. The remaining research questions cover different aspects of the activities and practices of *already formed* groups of activists, including the way in which they choose to narrate themselves and their use of the Internet as a symbolic space "to elaborate and practise a moral order in tune with their own narratives of the world" (2006b:481). This paper looks at the dynamic construction of a narrative community, placing particular emphasis on the role played by the Internet in that spontaneous process of network formation and, hence, paying less attention to the use of the Internet as a medium for the circulation of activist-mediated messages. Ultimately, this essay investigates an extreme manifestation of dynamic identity generation, where individuals take on an activist role during a single episode of mediation.

Secondly, although generative activism envisages the engagement of both "professional and non-professional" (Baker 2006b:463) translators in activist networks, the formulation of Baker's research questions gives particular prominence to the role of professionals in activist communities. In her occasional references to non-professionals, Baker tacitly assumes that this group will consist of translation/interpreting students and academics. This paper looks at an instance of mediation undertaken by individuals who do not hold any qualifications in translation, a category which would seem to have been largely overlooked in Baker's research programme.[4] This essay intends to examine the reasons why non-translators engage in activist translation on an '*ad hoc*' basis, in relation to the subtitling of the political interview under

---

[4] Even if one or more individuals happened to be formally trained translators, this information may not necessarily be available to other community members. Networks of *ad hoc* activist translators thus differ from most of the narrative communities studied by Baker, in that the former (*i*) are not initially bound together by their members' shared skills or professional/academic interests; (*ii*) do not regard translation as the only or main form of social intervention; (*iii*) may be more likely to disband after the completion of an individual translation project.

scrutiny. Attempts will also be made to gauge the relative stability of these communities vis-à-vis other activist groupings formed by professional and/or trainee translators/interpreters and academics; and to establish whether the emergence of communities of *ad hoc* activists translators is circumscribed to specific textual genres or formats.

Finally, as has been the case throughout the history of translation studies, the body of scholarship on activist translation[5] available to date has focused exclusively on the mediation of written texts. This paper deals with an instance of mediation ultimately resulting in the subtitling of the chosen audiovisual text, thus aiming to make this form of engaged translation more central to the agenda of generative activism.

2.   Translation in the era of global 'simulacra'

The audiovisual text mediated by the *ad hoc* activist community under scrutiny in section 4 is a televised interview conducted in English and broadcast by *BBC News 24* – a channel which is available digitally as well as on cable and satellite networks around the world and, therefore, forms part of the trans-national media establishment that has so decisively contributed to widening the geopolitical reach of capitalist economic structures in recent decades. According to Venuti (2008:19),

> The global capitalist economy is maintained by what Jean Baudrillard has called the "precession of simulacra", an effect of mass print and electronic media which do not so much reflect as construct reality through encoded forms and images that are determined by various ideologies and elicit, in Baudrillard's words, "a fascination for the medium" over "the critical exigencies of the message".

In turn, the global distribution of simulacra has been facilitated, to a large extent, by the 'time-space compression' which Harvey (1989) regards as a distinctive feature of postmodernity (Venuti 2008). Technological develop-ments and, in particular, the digitization of audiovisual content, have allowed media to overcome spatial barriers and speed up the circulation of information and knowledge. This 'de-materialization of space', in Cronin's (2003) terms, is responsible for the creation of supraterritorial and interconnected audiences and accounts for the centrality of 'transworld simultaneity' and 'instantaneity' (Scholte 2005) in the contemporary media landscape.

As noted by Bielsa and Bassnett (2009), there has been a tendency for theorists of cultural globalization to put a positive spin on the instantaneity

---

[5] In making this point, the term 'translation' is used to refer exclusively to the mediation of written texts; interpreting is therefore not to be subsumed into what is often used as a generic term encompassing both forms of mediation.

of global flows within the media industry, on the grounds that it facilitates "the rapid and extensive juxtaposition of, and comparison between, different cultures and spaces" (Lash and Urry 1994:243). Indeed, this view seems to enjoy wide acceptance, not least because it underpins the monolingual strategy adopted by the powerful Anglophone media corporations, whereby they assume that viewers of global broadcasts are equipped with a tool kit of cultural and linguistic resources – notably their familiarity with English as the *lingua franca* of global communication – to be smoothly deployed when juxtaposing and drawing comparisons between the abovementioned cultures and spaces. Some globalization theorists, like Castells (2000), have gone so far as to suggest that viewers inhabiting the deterritorialized space of global flows speak a 'universal digital language' which spans and underpins both the encoding and decoding of global audiovisual broadcasts. In this digitally 'monolingual' sphere of the global flows, whose instantaneity sets it apart from the linguistically diverse, physical spaces of everyday life, translation plays a secondary role. From a translation studies perspective, Bielsa and Bassnett (2009:18) argue that the prioritization of instantaneity by globalization theorists "has obscured the complexities involved in overcoming cultural and linguistic barriers, and made the role of translation in global communications invisible". In downplaying the role of translation in the context of global information flows, globalization theorists would appear to be raising the expectation that translation must "approximate more and more to the ideal of instantaneous transparency" (*ibid.*:29). According to Venuti (2008:18-19), this perception of translation is largely informed by the 'simulacral quality' of postmodern culture, understood as the capacity to perfectly replicate reality on a screen by subordinating the message to the medium and generating the illusion of total identity between the original and its virtual reproduction.[6]

In the deterritorialized (digitally monolingual) sphere of the global media marketplace, the simulacral quality of the audiovisual content in circulation is particularly consequential. The technical feasibility of instant distribution and perfect replication of audiovisual programmes on a global scale contributes to the perception of production and consumption as two seamlessly joined processes and, by extension, to the "illusory effect of transparency whereby the translation" may be, under some circumstances, "taken as the foreign text regardless of the translating language" (Venuti 2008:20). The impact that the combination of instantaneity and serial reproduction has on the degree of political engagement of individuals embedded in capitalist social structures has been articulated in conflicting terms by different scholars. For Baudrillard, as critiqued by Venuti (*ibid.*), the mechanical replication of simulacra erodes

---

[6] Venuti's critique of the simulacral quality of postmodernity is not restricted to audiovisual messages and the media industry; in fact, his paper explores that key concept in relation to the translation of a number of written texts.

ideological idiosyncrasies and fosters standardization, which often results in the minoritization of critical social groups. Other theorists, such as Lash and Urry (1994), contend that our society's constant exposure to simulacra fosters the emergence of aesthetic variation across individuals which, in turn, serves as a basis for the diversification of the social agents' subjectivity and their perceptions of social events. For Lash and Urry, the fragmentation of subjectivity is highly conducive to the proliferation of critical reflexivity in the form of resistant communities, as it reinforces "individuation in the sense of the atomization of normalized, 'niche-marketed' consumers" (1994:113; quoted in Venuti 2008:21).

Unsurprisingly, Venuti's alignment with Lash and Urry's stance regarding the place of social critique and political engagement in the era of postmodern simulacra has implications for his conceptualization of translation as a "cultural means of resistance that challenges multinational capitalism and the political institutions to which the economy is allied" (2008:18). In his attempt to articulate the interventionist quality of translation, Venuti challenges previous approaches to this issue (e.g. Tymoczko 2000), that are often based on the assumption that politically engaged translation can only be effective when it (*i*) addresses large constituencies clustered around static socio-cultural categories, which makes it easier to control the reception and consumption of the simulacra; and (*ii*) serves to promote or undermine "metanarratives that build totalizing explanations of social forces" but, in Venuti's view, "have lost their epistemological power" in the postmodern context (2008:22). In line with Lash and Urry's contention that the quick circulation of postmodern simulacra ultimately engenders reflexivity through the fragmentation of traditional audiences and constituencies, Venuti claims in no uncertain terms that the use of translation for the purposes of political intervention is only conceivable through the discursive practices of 'small-scale' resistant communities. According to Venuti (2008:21),

> [t]ranslation, then, might intervene into the postmodern situation by tampering with the simulacra that drive the global economy. A translator might use the images on which capital relies to short-circuit or jam its circulation by translating so as to question those images and the practices of consumption that they solicit. This sort of intervention is distinctly postmodern because it contends with the globalized flow of simulacra that is a hallmark of multinational capitalism and that permeates cultural and social institutions.

Although Venuti does not use the terms 'activist' or 'activism' in his paper, the tampering with simulacra that he places at the heart of resistant translation clearly has similarities with activist practices, as examined in section 1. In particular, I submit that the importance that Venuti accords to the subversive role of small-scale resistant communities – arising from the redefinition and atomization of traditional socio-cultural groupings – is tantamount to prioritizing individual agency (temporary narrative locations) over social structures and, by extension, acknowledging the generative potential of socio-political engagement through translation, irrespective of whether the latter is labelled as 'activism' or 'resistance'. Similarities can also be found between the formulation of the narrative theoretic framework in terms of the interaction between personal and public narratives and Venuti's definition of postmodernity as a site of interplay between socio-economic and cultural practices. Just as personal narratives may be in line with or in opposition to public ones, Venuti envisages a "disjunctive or contradictory relation" between the socio-economic and cultural practices underpinning global capitalism, such that "capital can be variously reproduced or frustrated by the cultural products to which it gives rise" (2008:22), depending on how translators choose to engage with the simulacra in circulation, whether by reinforcing or tampering with them.

In the concluding paragraphs of section 1, it was argued that the narrative theoretic framework which informs generative approaches to the study of activism through translation contributes to the present study with its dynamic conceptualization of social identities as temporary narrative locations. As noted then, this is particularly relevant to the data discussed in section 4, where individuals interact within a temporary network to carry out a single episode of mediation. This section has argued that Venuti's account of resistant translation as the product of the engagement of small communities in disjunctive cultural practices to challenge socio-economic structures shares with the narrative theoretic model a dynamic understanding of identity which foregrounds the generative power of agency.

3.   Activist intervention in non-linear communication structures

Ad hoc activist translators mediating audiovisual political programmes engage critically with the monolingual strategy favoured by global media corporations and challenge their assumption that global broadcasts fall into two categories: contents which are readily intelligible to digitally savvy viewers all over the world and programmes requiring translation, conceived as a "transparent medium of fluid exchange" (Cronin 2000:111). This section aims to explore how *ad hoc* activist translators go about tampering with the simulacra circulated by global media corporations, thus enhancing the disjunctive potential of their mediated texts, understood as instances of resistant cultural practices, vis-à-vis their respective socio-political context.

In comparison to other types of text, audiovisual simulacra have been, until very recently, difficult for individuals outside media organizations to tamper with. With the advent of the Internet and, more specifically, the widespread digitization of audiovisual footage, the technological tools required to manipulate audiovisual texts have become ubiquitous and affordable. Indeed, the key for activist communities to articulate their disjunctive approach to audiovisual mediation has been the feasibility of appropriating audiovisual simulacra whose circulation had so far been restricted to the supraterritorial monolingual sphere of global flows. In the era of digitization, the copies of those audiovisual programmes that activist communities choose to mediate have become virtually indistinguishable from the originals which were first distributed by the broadcaster. The appropriation of audiovisual footage is the first of a series of steps, which include the subtitling of the spoken dialogue or any written text featured in the programme and culminate in the superimposition of subtitles on the visuals. Once the mediation is completed, programmes are released by activist networks into the spatio-temporally and linguistically constrained space(s) that their target audience inhabits. Unsurprisingly, the appropriation of audiovisual content is highly 'selective'.[7] Out of the limitless pool of simulacra that are constantly circulating in the space of global flows, *ad hoc* activists choose their objects or sites of intervention strategically. As is also the case with activist networks mediating written political texts (Baker 2006b, 2009), *ad hoc* activists mediating audiovisual texts show a preference for messages that either reinforce their temporary narrative location or, alternatively, contribute to undermining one or more of the collective narratives that their communities oppose.[8]

The interventionist engagement of activist communities with the circuitry of the global audiovisual marketplace represents a challenge to the control that media corporations have traditionally exerted over the distribution and consumption of their products. This challenge manifests itself in two ways. The first manifestation pertains to the role of self-appointed translation commissioners that activist communities assume when selectively appropriating the simulacra they intend to tamper with. The very selection of audiovisual simulacra represents an act of resistance against the dynamics of global audiovisual flows, in that the chosen messages would not have otherwise reached the activists' target constituencies.[9] The second manifestation is inextricably linked to the first. As a result of the politically motivated transfer of audiovisual simulacra from the deterritorialized global sphere to linguistically diverse geographies, the global capitalist structures responsible for the production of the original message lose control of the receiving situation. In this respect, audiovisual programmes often take on new resonances, in terms of narrative

---

[7] For an extended discussion and illustration of the notion of selective appropriation, see Baker (2006a:71-76).

[8] Activist mediators of political television programmes are not alone in favouring an 'appropriation-based' approach to intervention in the media landscape. A case in point is that of fan communities intervening in the global circulation of their favourite products and genres (Pérez-González 2006b).

[9] Venuti notes that "[t]he selection of foreign texts for translation and the development of discursive strategies to translate them inevitably involve taking sides to a certain extent, aligning with some constituencies and institutions more than others" (2008:32).

reinforcement or clash, when displaced from the dematerialized global circuits they were originally intended for and brought to intersect with the here and now of the audience's space. But this loss of control not only affects the spatial dimension of the receiving situation, but also its temporal counterpart. Along with the ease of retrieval and storage of mediated simulacra, digitization has created the conditions for the asynchronous and 'iterative consumption' (Crewe *et al.* 2005) of audiovisual messages.

These two challenges mounted by activist communities can be explored further in relation to two major socio-cultural developments which are increasingly receiving attention from media sociologists, i.e. the shift from a 'linear' to a 'non-linear model of communication' and the consolidation of 'participatory cultures' in the media industry; each of these developments is considered in turn in the remainder of this section.

The now superseded linear model of communication (McNair 2006) – that is, the organization of the media industry in the form of top-down, elite-controlled structures – was offer-driven; editors and chief executives, as the embodiment of traditional power structures, were able to mobilize public opinion and exercise a certain degree of political and ideological control over their readership and audiences. The dynamics of activist mediation in audiovisual contexts, however, are to be interpreted as non-linear. The emerging non-linear model of communication is demand-driven, as the new generation of media consumers demands that ever more content be delivered when, how and as they want it. According to McNair (2006), this scenario of unprecedented diversity and unpredictability, both in terms of the variety of content available to audiences and the increasingly atomized receiving communities, is best understood as

> a movement from a *control* to a *chaos* paradigm; a departure from the sociologist's traditional stress on the media's functionality for an unjust and unequal social order, towards greater recognition of their capacity for the disruption and interruption, even subversion of established authority structures. ... The chaos paradigm acknowledges the *desire* for control on the part of elites, while suggesting that the performance, or exercise of control, is increasingly interrupted and disrupted by unpredictable eruptions and bifurcations arising from the impact of economic, political, ideological and technological factors on communication processes. (*ibid.*:3)

The generative potential of individual agency is central to McNair's account of the political disruptions that have upset the foundations of traditional linear models. Against this background of growing structural volatility in the media marketplace, it is easier to theorize the role of translator activists as agents of chaos – in the sense that this term is used in media sociology. Activists' interventions represent 'unpredictable eruptions' of resistance, in McNair's terms, against the increasingly deterritorialized media and their 'habitualized discursive practices' (Mason 1994/2010). In their struggle to oppose narratives circulated by the media elites and the socio-political structures they represent (i.e. 'control culture'), activist communities (i.e. 'agents of chaos') clustered around fluid social identities resort to disjunctive practices of cultural mediation which have disruptive ramifications for the circulation of simulacra outside the erstwhile uncontested global broadcasting highways.

The consolidation of the non-linear model of communication as a platform for the expression of participatory cultures – in the form of grassroots movements of civic engagement and political empowerment – relies heavily on the ubiquity of media technologies. Recent studies on the role of participatory culture in contemporary media (e.g. Jenkins *et al.* 2006) highlight the crucial role of information technologies in the articulation of 'affinity spaces', defined as "highly generative environments, from which new aesthetic experiments and innovations emerge" (*ibid.*:9), as the building blocks of participatory cultures. As a form of highly generative environment, audiovisual activism perfectly illustrates the contribution of technologies to the dynamics of participatory cultures, i.e. empowering their members to "archive, annotate, appropriate, and recirculate media content" (*ibid.*:8) along the lines suggested earlier in this section.

Interestingly, the opportunities to subvert established authority structures through the use of technologies are so embedded in the non-linear model of communication that it is possible to envisage a short-term scenario in which resistant mediation practices might lose their radical edge to other non-politically motivated forms of engagement with audiovisual simulacra. This perception is shared by recent studies on participatory culture in the media, in their appraisal of 'grassroots creativity' as an important engine of cultural transformation:

> The media landscape will be reshaped by the bottom-up energy of media created by amateurs and hobbyists as a matter of course. This bottom-up energy will generate enormous creativity, but it will also tear apart some of the categories that organize the lives and work of media makers ... A new generation of media makers and viewers are emerging which could lead to a sea change in how media is made and consumed. (Blau 2005:3-5)

The place that activism occupies within the broader movement of grassroots participatory culture, in terms of the ease with which individuals take on and step out of a politically interventionist role while interacting online, will be explored in more depth in the following section. It is envisaged that the discussion of the selected data will provide the basis from which a more probing statement can be made as to whether, and if so to what extent, the concept of activism needs to be reconsidered.

4.   The genealogy of sites of activism in the blogosphere

The conceptual framework outlined in preceding sections enables the study of activist mediation in postmodern non-linear communication structures. Against this background, the second part of this paper focuses on fortuitously generated affinity sites, some of whose members assume an activist identity during a single episode of mediation, in what constitutes a clear manifestation of the generative power of fluid activist identities. In this section, the discussion focuses on the genealogy of a specific grouping of *ad hoc* activist mediators, rather than on the actual mediation practices deployed by those engaged individuals. Following an account of the context leading to the emergence of the narrative community under analysis, I will then examine the negotiation of narrative affinity between members of the community and the role that intersecting narratives play in relation to the sustainability of the network.

4.1   Setting the context: The HARDtalk interview

On Monday 24 July 2006, *BBC News 24* broadcast an exclusive *HARDtalk* interview with Spain's former Prime Minister, José María Aznar López,[10] against the background of the ongoing military conflict between Lebanon and Israel. The interview includes a discussion of Spanish internal politics but it is Aznar's opinions on international affairs that receive particular attention. Given his firm support of the Bush administration's foreign policy, his hard-line stance on the 'War on Terror' and his public alignment with Israel's security policies,[11] both during and after his period in office, it is hardly surprising that the BBC website chose to contextualize this interview for prospective viewers in the following terms:

> **Excerpt 1** (*Hardtalk* Website, BBC News 24)
>
> Iraq, Afghanistan and now Lebanon. All of them are on the frontlines in the global war on terror according to the Bush administration.
> This view causes unease in some parts of Europe but not for former Spanish Prime Minister Jose María Aznar. He is still a close ally of George W Bush.
> Is he out of step with his own continent?
> In an exclusive interview for HARDtalk he talks to Stephen Sackur.

During the interview, Stephen Sackur refers to Aznar's lobbying campaign to redefine the objectives of NATO and make it more effective at combating

---

[10] At the time of writing, the interview can be accessed via the *BBC News Website* at: http://news.bbc.co.uk/1/hi/programmes/hardtalk/5209566.stm (last accessed 15 May 2009).
[11] For an English overview of Aznar's views on Israel's role in the Middle East, published shortly before the invasion of Lebanon, see Aznar (2006).

what the former Prime Minister regards as the new global threat: Islamist terrorism. In his response, Aznar outlines his vision on this matter and advocates that future enlargements of NATO should prioritize those countries which can help to fight terror:

Excerpt 2 (Transcript of the *HARDtalk* interview; abridged)[12]

SS: Which countries?

JMA: Israel.

SS: Israel?

JMA: Israel.

SS: You believe Israel should be in NATO?

JMA: Yeah, absolutely.

SS: Well, let's stop there for a moment. Israel currently is bombarding Lebanon.

JMA: Yeah.

SS: It says that its actions in Lebanon are a part of a war against terrorism. Do you believe that?

JMA: Yes. Hezbollah ... Hezbollah is a terrorist group ... it's considered a terrorist group ... Hamas is a terrorist group ... it's considered a terrorist group ... both are supported by Iranian regime, maybe by Syrian regime, but Hezbollah is a terrorist group, and Hezbollah entered in the Israel territory ... catch two soldiers ... kidnap the soldiers ... killing another people... and this is an attack, terrorist attack.

SS: So let's be clear. You are saying you believe Israel should be in NATO.

JMA: Yeah.

SS: NATO, as you know, runs upon the idea of collective security and mutual self-defence, so you are now saying that NATO should be bombing Lebanon?

JMA: If it's necessary, yes. Because I consider that Israel is a part essential of the Western World.

During his two final years in office, Aznar faced an unprecedented level of public anger for being one of the few European leaders who actively supported the Bush administration's invasion of Iraq in 2003 on the basis of what would turn out to be faulty intelligence on Iraq's alleged arsenal of weapons of mass destruction. His popularity suffered a devastating blow with the Madrid train bombings on 11 March 2004 (only three days before the General Election)

---

[12] The transcription reflects Aznar's command of and fluency in English at the time of the interview. The full transcription is available at http://piezas.bandaancha.st/aznar.html#trans_eng#trans_eng (last accessed 15 May 2009).

by Islamist terrorists, which much of the Spanish public regarded as "a direct result of Spain's decision to send troops to the Middle Eastern country" (Govan 2009).[13] Against this background, some of the views Aznar expressed in the interview – mainly those pertaining to his alleged 'demonstrated capacity' to defeat terrorism and his openly proclaimed lack of regrets on his handling of Iraq's intelligence fiasco and the investigations of the Madrid bombings – had the potential to elicit more visceral reactions from large collectivities of the Spanish public. It will therefore come as no surprise that the Spanish leading (and left-leaning) newspaper *El País* published, on the very same day as the interview was being broadcast by the BBC, a news story entitled 'Aznar, partidario de que la OTAN bombardee Líbano "si fuera necesario"' (Aznar in favour of NATO's bombardment of Lebanon "if necessary"), complete with an audio link to the relevant soundbite (*El País* 2006). The liberal daily *El Mundo* presented it in the following terms: 'Aznar cree que la OTAN podría bombardear el Líbano si Israel fuera miembro de la Alianza' (Aznar believes that NATO could bomb Lebanon if Israel was a member of the Alliance) (*El Mundo* 2006). Aznar's views – which many interpreted as yet another refusal to accept responsibility for his alleged lapses in political judgement during his final years in power – received ample coverage by the Spanish media over the following days, attracting criticisms from a wide range of individuals and organizations positioned to the left of the political spectrum, including senior members of the governing Socialist Party (PSOE). On Tuesday 25, one day after the interview was broadcast, the Spanish newspaper *El Mundo* reported attempts from Aznar's own party to frame his words from a slightly different perspective:

Excerpt 3 (Remírez de Ganuza (2006), writing for *El Mundo*)

[f]uentes próximas a Aznar aseguraron … que el PSOE «tergiversa» la entrevista. Precisaron que Aznar presentó en Londres el informe de FAES que aboga por la ampliación de la OTAN a Australia, Japón e Israel. A la pregunta de si, en ese futurible, la OTAN podría «intervenir» (no «bombardear») en el Líbano, Aznar dijo que sí, «si fuera necesario» y si así lo decidieran los estados miembros.

[sources close to Aznar claimed … that PSOE is 'purposefully misinterpreting' the interview. They added that Aznar had travelled to London to present a report by FAES [a conservative think-tank directed by Aznar] advocating the enlargement of NATO to incorporate Australia, Japan and Israel. When asked whether, in a hypothetical future,

---

[13] At the time of writing, "Spain's Supreme Court is to rule whether the former prime minister, Jose María Aznar, can be prosecuted for the country's involvement in the US-led invasion of Iraq" (Govan 2009).

NATO might 'intervene' in (not 'bomb') Lebanon, Aznar replied yes, 'if it was necessary' and member states decided so.[14]]

Despite the controversy surrounding Aznar's words, the BBC interview was not broadcast by any public or private Spanish television channel. Short clips of the interview were shown in a number of news programmes by way of simulacra, i.e. visual back-up to the Spanish correspondents' reports, with their voices superimposed on the original soundtrack. The lack of extended audiovisual coverage of the interview had implications which are worth spelling out in the context of this paper. English-speaking viewers situated within the space of global flows were presented with unmediated access to a televised event in which Aznar threw his weight behind the 'War on Terror' narrative and showcased his own achievements on the fight against terrorism, including on the domestic front. Moreover, members of the deterritorialized audience of *HARDtalk* also had an opportunity to see how Aznar repeatedly expressed his unreserved commitment to the neo-conservative doctrines circulating during the Bush years, despite being offered by the interviewer multiple (and not always subtle) prompts to qualify, tone down or reflect on the implications of his statements, as illustrated in Excerpt 2 above. Aznar's decision not to distance himself from what, at the time, was already regarded as a widely contested narrative is so unambiguous that the BBC ended up 'framing' this televised event, noting that Aznar's view "causes unease in some parts of Europe" and inviting viewers to consider whether he is "out of step with his own continent".[15]

As Excerpt 3 above demonstrates, even the former Prime Minister's party (PP) found Aznar's candour problematic.[16] His views on both domestic and international matters could provide progressive collectivities in Spain with useful ammunition to continue fuelling the wider public narrative regarding the reasons which led to PP's electoral defeat in March 2004. For Aznar's detractors, however, the patchy journalistic coverage which the interview received in the Spanish printed media was insufficient to capitalize on this opportunity to lambast the former Primer Minister and, in so doing, reinforce their own narratives. The following subsection examines precisely how Aznar's

---

[14] Unless otherwise stated, the translations provided in these excerpts are my own.

[15] The text presented in Excerpt 1 is both displayed on the page providing access to the streaming broadcast of the interview and also delivered by Stephen Sackur in the opening seconds of the programme (with the exception of the last sentence of the excerpt). Sackur is filmed in an unidentified outdoor location, with his gaze directed at the viewer; it is impossible to establish whether that segment was incorporated into the programme before or after the interview was conducted.

[16] A number of former Cabinet members during Aznar's presidency argued, for instance, that Aznar's words had been 'manipulated' by the government. See, for instance, *20 Minutos* (2006).

interview was imported from the sphere of the global flow into the domain of geographical materiality by engaged individuals with a clear interventionist agenda. Given the unrivalled capacity of audiovisual media to resonate with public perceptions, this intervention sets out to disrupt the dynamics of global media circulation by turning the viewers' attention away from the untranslated fragments of an audiovisual simulacrum onto a full translated message allowing for the audience's critical engagement with its content.

4.2 Negotiating narrative affinity within spontaneous networks of engaged mediators

On 25 July 2006, amid the emerging political and media furore over Aznar's interview, Spanish progressive journalist Ignacio Escolar posted an entry in his political blog *escolar.net* entitled 'La Tercera Guerra Mundial de Aznar' (*Aznar's Third World War*).[17] In this short entry, Escolar comments briefly on the *HARDtalk* interview broadcast the previous day, placing Aznar's views on the future role of NATO in the broader context of his unequivocal alignment with Bush (as showcased by the picture chosen to illustrate the text). Between 25 July and 7 August 2006, a total of 182 comments would be posted by blog readers under this entry.

In the first 26 comments,[18] posted in a period of approximately 6 hours after the publication of Escolar's entry, Aznar is subjected to fierce criticism on a number of counts; some pertain to his record in office (including his unwavering support for Bush's foreign policy), while others relate to his personal 'flaws' (e.g. megalomania, smugness and poor command of English). Overall, these posts are used by blog readers to (*i*) negotiate their narrative location relative to that of other members of this temporary online community;[19] (*ii*) mutually reinforce their shared political affiliation against occasional challenges from Aznar's supporters (e.g. comments #19, 25 and 26); and (*iii*) jointly construct the gravitational core of their emerging affinity space. In line with the principle of 'mutual accountability' that underpins interaction-based communicative encounters (Taylor and Cameron 1987), each contribution is simultaneously

---

[17] This entry is available at: http://www.escolar.net/MT/archives/2006/07/la_iii_guerra_m.html (last accessed 15 May 2009). Escolar is one of Spain's most prominent and established bloggers, both in the fields of politics and independent music. Subjectivity and interactivity, as measured by the degree of user-generated content, are some of the key features that distinguish his (and most) blogs "from traditional media outlets" and provide the space "for driven, determined individuals [like Escolar] to establish a media presence of their own" (McNair 2006:122).

[18] In referring to the readers' comments, the discussion will use the numbering of entries as it appears online.

[19] Although their transient narrative location is negotiated there and then, readers can also challenge or reinforce the narratives of future blog visitors, as comments remain accessible and searchable through the blog archives.

context-shaped and context-renewing; interventions react to previous comments while determining the unfolding of the next ones.

In the initial stages of interaction under this blog entry, readers comment on the interview only on a 'hear-say' basis, that is as an item of information that they have only read about or heard in part (see, for instance, comment #12, where *Nena* shares the URL of the audio link to a soundbite of Aznar's interview), and they focus almost exclusively on Aznar's NATO-related responses. By the end of this initial stage, it is clear that an effective 'architecture of intersubjectivity'[20] is in place within this blog-centred constituency; readers feel reassured that their collectively negotiated political affiliation is (almost) unanimously critical of Aznar and their contributions are designed accordingly. Comment #27, posted 7 hours after the publication of Escolar's entry, is the first contribution by a blog reader showing evidence of actually having watched the interview – indeed, he even provides time cues for specific climatic moments. In contrast to most of the preceding posts, *Valensiano* (#27) chooses to draw the community's attention to Aznar's opinions on Spanish internal politics and opts to frame his account of the event in accordance with the prevalent narrative. Emphasis is thus placed on the interviewer's 'shocking disbelief' at Aznar's views and the former Primer Minister's disingenuousness showing through his 'body language'. *Valensiano*'s mocking summary, which resonates deeply with other readers, is swiftly followed by a request for information on how to access the interview (#28) and the circulation of the relevant URL (#29). More importantly, it succeeds in turning the domestic implications of Aznar's responses into the object of discussion throughout the remainder of this communicative encounter.

Only 45 minutes after expressing an initial interest in the programme (#28), *Gong Duruo* appears to have watched the interview. His first comment (#31) draws on the same framing strategies as *Valensiano*'s earlier one. It delivers an overtly subjective assessment ('the interview is hard to believe'), disambiguates the interviewer's perception of Aznar's words ('the interviewer cannot believe his ears') and articulates his constituency's likely reaction ('I would also find it difficult to believe it if this fellow had not been my Prime Minister for 8 years'). However, *Gong Duruo* is called to play a focal role in displacing the simulacrum out of the space of global flows into the 'here and now' of this politically engaged Spanish-speaking community. Five hours after posting his first comment, *Gong Duruo* is back online and ready to engage in a more detailed mediation of the interview. His first comment (#40), which concentrates on the first adjacency pair (question and answer) of the interview, is reproduced in Excerpt 4 as it offers a good illustration of his approach to mediation:

---

[20] Taylor and Cameron (1987:103) define this term as "the means by which individuals participating in the same interaction can reach a shared interpretation of its constituent activities and of the rules to which they are designed to conform".

Excerpt 4 (Gong Duruo's comment #40)[21]

#40. Publicado por *gong duruo* - Julio 25, 2006 10:13 PM.

la entrevista ésta es para enmarcarla y regalarla en bodas:
Primera pregunta:
PERIODISTA: "Jose María Aznar, welcome to Hard Talk. I would like
to quote to you your own words from a big speach [*sic*] you made in
march of this year, you said 'we are at war, terrorists must be defeated,
no other policy exists' ... those words could have been spoken by
George Bush, couldn't they?

ÁNSAR: [traduzco tan literal como puedo]: "Ha Ha ... Well, George
Bush is a very good friend for me, no? But I think that terrorists can
be defeat, and that terrorists should be defeat, and during my life me
fighting terrorists, at home, abroad, and errr I think err I have demonstraid that terrorism can be defeat ... i don't support the idea of contain?,
apaseament, and eerrr surrender terrorism".

Es decir, que el periodista abre la entrevista con una pulla no demasiado
sutil ('hablas como Bush, macho'), y el Ánsar no lo pilla y además el
muy lelo presume de ser muy buen amigo del Emperador ... después
de algo así, ¿a quién puede sorprenderle que asegure que él 'ha dem-
ostrado que el terrorismo puede ser derrotado'?
¿dónde? ¿cuándo? ¿cómo?

#40. Published by *gong duruo* - July 25, 2006 10:13 PM.

this interview should be framed and handed out at weddings:

First question:
JOURNALIST: "Jose María Aznar, welcome to Hard Talk. I would
like to quote to you your own words from a big speach [*sic*] you made
in march of this year, you said 'we are at war, terrorists must be defeated, no other policy exists' ... those words could have been spoken
by George Bush, couldn't they?

ÁNSAR: [I am translating as literally as I can]: "Ha Ha ... Well,
George Bush is a very good friend for me, no? But I think that terrorists can be defeat, and that terrorists should be defeat, and during my
life me fighting terrorists, at home, abroad, and errr I think err I have

---

[21] Available at: http://www.escolar.net/MT/archives/2006/07/la_iii_guerra_m.html (last
accessed 15 May 2009). This is a literal reproduction of the text available online, complete
with spelling mistakes and other editing infelicities.

demonstraid that terrorism can be defeat ... i don't support the idea of contain?, apaseament, and eerrr surrender terrorism".

In sum, the journalist begins with a not very subtle jibe ('you speak like Bush, mate'), and Ánsar does not get it; he is so thick that he boasts being a very good friend of the Emperor ... after this, who can be surprised to hear him [Aznar] claim that 'he has demonstrated that terrorism can be defeated'?
where? when? how?

In this first mediating move, *Gong Duruo* opts to leave the question and answer untranslated. His understanding of what 'translation' involves becomes apparent in the transcription of Aznar's reply ('I am translating as literally as I can'): ensuring that Aznar's lack of fluency in English becomes evident, mainly through conspicuously wrong spellings, even to readers with a basic knowledge of English. Framing devices are present throughout, whether in the form of subtle winks to *anti-aznaristas*[22] or a suggested interpretation of what, in *Gong Duruo*'s mind, was the illocutionary force behind Sackur's question.

From this point onwards, *Gong Duruo*'s mediation becomes more selective, focusing only on key (and increasingly shorter) contributions, by combining either (*i*) personal narration and translation of individual sentences (e.g. #40); or (*ii*) personal narration and transcription of English sentences (e.g. #46). Other instances of mediation on *Gong Duruo*'s part include comments #47, 54, 56, 59, 61 and 63. However, it is comments #48-49 that convey the climatic moment of the interview. Perhaps assuming that his mediation of this exchange will be subjected to close scrutiny, *Gong Duruo* opts for a more 'transparent' approach involving the juxtaposition of English transcriptions and Spanish translations as well as the use of square brackets to identify other elements of intervention on his part (e.g. the description of Aznar's facial expression as angry and body language as nervous or fidgety):

Excerpt 5 (Gong Duruo's comment #49)

ÁNSAR: [cara de cabreo, moviéndose en la silla]:

"No. This isn't true. The circumstances of march 11th attack in Madrid, that's created special circumstances in my country, and the opposition,

---

[22] Take, for instance, the spelling of the former Spanish Prime Minister's surname as 'Ánsar', a parody on Bush's pronunciation when referring to Aznar during their joint press-conferences over the years. Opting for 'Ánsar' is thus an affiliation-enhancing strategy; it indirectly lends support to attempts by Aznar's detractors to present the relationship between both leaders in terms of dominance-submission rather than equality.

the current government, take advantage in this moment to declare guilty of this attack the government, not the terrorists. It's the first time in history that it 'occurs'??"

[No, eso no es verdad. Las circunstancias del 11M en Madrid, han creado circunstancias especiales en mi país, y la oposición, el actual gobierno, se ha aprovechado para declarar culpable del ataque al gobierno, no a los terroristas. Es la primera vez en la historia que pasa esto (?)]

As suggested earlier, *Gong Duruo* recognizes the need to articulate some of what is being communicated by Aznar and Sackur through non-verbal meaning-making modes – notably paralinguistic features and body language. As illustrated above, he often takes advantage of these opportunities for intersemiotic mediation to boost narrative affinity among members of the blog-based community by accentuating the domestic resonance of the message circulating in the sphere of global flows (e.g. #46: 'Ánsar le contesta en un tono ridículamente condescendiente, con esa falsa risita suya que tan bien conocemos por aquí' – Ánsar replies in a stupidly patronizing tone, with that forced laugh of his that we know so well over here). Weaving the different strands of meaning into his posts proves difficult, however, and *Gong Duruo* becomes increasingly aware that his text-restricted mediation detracts from the potential impact that the audiovisual text may have on progressive collectivities in Spain – a point which is also made by other readers in #77 and 81. Regretting not having the technical expertise required to appropriate the audiovisual simulacrum and make it available to the target collectivities in the early stages of his mediation (#43), *Gong Duruo* concludes his intervention by calling for a subtitled version to be circulated via one of the 'broadcast yourself' platforms.[23] This call is taken up by *Piezas*, in two of the very last comments posted that night (#130 and 132).

Much of the interactional activity on the morning of 26 July takes place between *Gong Duruo* and *Piezas*.[24] Comment #137 marks the beginning of a long exchange of messages in which both readers discuss the technical feasibility of the appropriation stage. As their conversation unfolds, decisions are made on how to share the video files to undertake the subtitling work, as well as on the most suitable format and platform for the distribution of the subtitled version. On 27 July, *Piezas* draws *Gong Duruo*'s attention to a well-known subtitling freeware application (#155) and announces the availability of the

---

[23] It is worth noting that, while carrying out the translation/narration of the interview, *Gong Duruo* refuses to confront the two blog readers who occasionally publish posts in support of Aznar. It is not until his mediation is completed that he acknowledges these occasional challenges and responds to them a number of times before signing off (11.15 pm, #90).

[24] Although this is not explicitly signalled in the blog posts, their messages suggest that they have interacted in the past.

'raw' files on a popular video website (#156). On 7 August, *Piezas* announces the availability of the Spanish subtitled version of the *HARDtalk* interview online (#176), together with the list of 3 participants in the project and the nature of their contribution.[25] In their follow-up posts, *Andaqueno* (credited as the translator) confesses his lack of translation experience (#177), while *Gong Duruo* expresses his interest in undertaking further subtitling projects, preferably based on other 'Ánsar shows'.

On the same day of *Piezas'* announcement, Escolar published a new entry on his blog entitled 'Bombas de la OTAN contra Hizbolá' (NATO bombs against Hezbollah).[26] Escolar's entry showcases the subtitled version of the interview produced by his blog readers, whose work is duly acknowledged, complete with an embedded, ready-to-play screenshot of the version available online. Cross-links to previous entries of his blog on this same topic as well as to the website of one of the mediator-readers[27] illustrate the interconnectivity which characterizes blog-based online journalism (McNair 2006:119-25).

In the long list of comments published under this entry, there is extensive praise for the translators, as well as multiple requests for access to alternative formats of the subtitled programme. The community soon moves on to discuss the growing problems experienced by individual members in accessing the subtitled interview, as this is successively deleted from a number of video-broadcasting platforms due to copyright claims by the BBC.[28] At the time of writing, this subtitled version of the *HARDtalk* interview can only be accessed through a lesser-known video hosting service website.[29]

4.3   Intersecting narratives and the redefinition of collective identities

The process leading to the subtitling of the *HARDtalk* interview reflects the dynamics of the decentralized global 'infosphere' brought about by the shift

---

[25] The organization of the workflow in this project adheres to standard practices among networks of audiovisual mediators. For a detailed account of the footage appropriation and role distribution processes operating within stable networks of anime fansubbers, see Pérez-González (2006b).

[26] Available online at: http://www.escolar.net/MT/archives/2006/08/bombas_de_la_ot.html (last accessed 15 May 2009).

[27] Within *Piezas'* website, a dedicated page provided access to the English transcript, the Spanish translation, subtitles file, embedded screenshots of the subtitled interview and a portable version of the original video file. See http://piezas.bandaancha.st/aznar.html (last accessed 15 May 2009).

[28] Gambier (2006) and Pérez-González (2006b) have drawn attention to the increasingly complex relationship between copyright holders and distributors in the era of digitization in the contexts of professional audiovisual translation and amateur audiovisual translation, respectively.

[29] Available online at: http://www.dailymotion.com/video/x1ozzd_entrevista-a-aznar-subtitulada-13 (last accessed 15 May 2009).

from linear models of communication (control paradigm) to non-linear ones (chaos paradigm). As McNair (2006:xviii) notes,

> [i]n the context of globalised news culture, to talk about chaos is to argue that the journalistic environment, far from being an instrument or apparatus of social control by a dominant elite, has become more and more like the weather and the oceans in the age of global warning – turbulent, unpredictable, extreme. Like storm fronts, journalistic information flows around the world in globally connected streams of real-life data, forming stories which become news and then descend through the networked nodes of the world wide web to impact on national public spheres.

In the case of Aznar's interview, the descent from the global to the national is the result of the interventionist agenda of a collectivity of progressive individuals who, instead of letting this message blow itself out in the sphere of the global flows, turn it into news for a specific target audience. The starting point in this process consists in the mobilization of certain aspects of their individual identities, whereby they join the community of readers of a progressive political blog. The publication of a news item that resonates strongly with their own personal narratives leads them to engage in interaction with fellow blog readers and, in doing so, establish the scope and depth of the collectivity as an affinity space. By ongoingly mobilizing additional aspects of their identity, not least their linguistic and technological mediation skills, a network of activists is spontaneously created. Working under a clearly interventionist agenda, this grouping appropriates an audiovisual simulacrum and circulates the mediated product in an attempt to promote their shared set of narratives vis-à-vis the public narratives that circulate in their environment.

To a large extent the gravitational core of this site of engaged mediation is defined by the interface between a global and a local narrative ('War on Terror' and 'Aznar as a leader of international stature', respectively), both of which have been highly contested in Spanish progressive circles over a number of years. The relative weighting of each of the constituencies interacting within this site of engagement is, however, difficult to establish. In contrast to organized networks of activist mediators, some of which have explicitly articulated their agenda and vision (Baker 2009), spontaneously generated networks of activist translators operate on the basis of ongoingly negotiated appraisals of mutual affinity spaces. As part of these constant negotiations to gauge the strength of collective affinity on other discursive practices and perceptions, it becomes possible for spontaneous networks of activists to differentiate between nuclear and intersecting narratives. In the case study at hand, the nuclear narratives gravitate near the narrative interface which defines the core of the site of mediation, in that they are subscribed to by a significant majority of members whose engagement with the socio-political order relies on the mobilization of similar aspects of their identity. Intersecting narratives, on the other hand, are subscribed to by specific individuals or subgroups within the broader community whose social affiliations involve the mobilization of an additional set of aspects to their identities. Given the fluid nature of social identities, intersecting narratives enable individuals to step out of their current site of activism in search of other sites where they are positioned closer to the gravitational core.

A survey of the reactions to the subtitled version of the *HARDtalk* interview, as illustrated by readers' comments on the second entry of Escolar's blog, reveals signs of narrative entropy inflecting the readers' identities and affiliations. Some members (e.g. #20) appear to be drawn to the community by purely instrumental considerations, i.e. the possibility of accessing and understanding an interview that would otherwise have been beyond their reach. For others (e.g. #30, 60, 64, 85) – convinced that "the Spanish still have reason to cower, as they did in the years of Franco, in the face of the superior civilisations of the north" (Carlin 2004) – when it comes to standards in political life and journalism, the subtitled interview offers the opportunity to appreciate the adversarial interviewing style that characterizes British and American media. Finally, other members opt to introduce ramifications of the core narrative interface into tangential issues like the need to marginalize Israel (e.g. #76) or the need to redefine the place of progressive political parties after the fall of communism. But while the arborization of core narratives through identity inflection can detract from the cohesion of any given community, it also contributes to the propagation of nuclear narratives to other areas of the blogosphere gravitating around similar narrative locations. *Migeru*, for instance, 'exports' the mediated interview onto a blog created to foster debate 'on politics and public life from a left-of-centre and pro-European-integration perspective', as a follow-up to a post he had sent earlier on the changing role of NATO.[30]

5.   Concluding remarks

This paper has attempted to illustrate how translation is increasingly being appropriated by politically engaged individuals to respond effectively to the socio-economic structures that sustain global capitalism by intervening in the reception of its cultural manifestations. Unlike the networks of activist translators which are starting to come under scrutiny within translation studies, the members of the mediating collectivity studied in this article have no formal training in translation, lack a formal organizational structure or manifesto and rely heavily on information technologies for the purposes of constructing

---

[30] Available at: http://www.eurotrib.com/comments/2006/8/7/161752/7603/5 (last accessed on 15 May 2009).

themselves as a narrative community. While strengthening the case for the investigation of collectivities of activist translators, the existence of fluid networks of mediation such as the one responsible for the subtitled version of the *HARDtalk* interview problematizes the very notion of activist translation. To what extent can such fluid groupings be characterized in structural terms? How can the term 'translator' be applied to designate individuals without training in translation, regardless of their status as professionals or amateurs at any given time?

Specialists on participatory culture propose the label 'ad-hocracies' for these configurations of individuals "brought together because their diverse skills and knowledge are needed to confront a specific challenge and then dispersed onto different clusters ... when new needs arise" (Jenkins *et al.* 2006:41), and this appears to be a useful way to address the taxonomic issues at hand. Fluid networks of engaged mediators like the ones studied in this paper would thus constitute ad-hocracies of activist translators, i.e. groups of like-minded individuals gathering online and capitalizing on the potential of networked communication to exploit their 'collective intelligence' (Levy 2000) regardless of their professional affiliation. The notion of collective intelligence is particularly important in the study of ad-hocracies of activist translators, in view of the differences between the collectivities involved in the translation of written texts (Baker 2009) and those responsible for the mediation of audiovisual content. Whereas the former typically consist of members producing new language versions of written texts, the latter also comprise individuals who specialize in the appropriation and distribution stages of the mediation process.

Although I argued above that only a generative conceptualization of translation activism can help to theorize the genealogy of *ad hoc* activist networks, it should also be noted that the mediation of audiovisual texts – a recurrent object of mediation for such ad-hocracies – has not so far featured prominently in the agenda of this scholarly strand. If, as predicted by Tymoczko, the proliferation of audiovisual texts is bound to bring about "yet another expansion of the concept of translation, necessitating the retheorization of various aspects of the entire field of translation studies" (2005:1090), it is important to ensure that any potentially idiosyncratic feature of activist subtitling is adequately theorized at this incipient stage in the development of translation activism and of this new scholarly strand.

References

20 Minutos (2006) 'El PP afirma que las palabras de Aznar sobre el Líbano se han manipulado' (PP [Popular Party] claims that Aznar's views on Lebanon have been manipulated), 25 July. Available online: http://www.20minutos. es/noticia/144509/0/aznar/libano/bomardeos (accessed 15 May 2009).

Aznar, José M. (2006) 'Europe's Response to the Threat of Global Terror', *Jerusalem Issue Brief* 5(23). Available online: http://www.jcpa.org/brief/brief005-23.htm (accessed 15 May 2009).

Baker, Mona (2006a) *Translation and Conflict: A Narrative Account*, London & New York: Routledge.

------ (2006b) 'Translation and Activism: Emerging Patterns of Narrative Community', *The Massachusetts Review* 47(III): 462-84.

------ (2006c) 'Translation and Context', *Journal of Pragmatics* 38(3): 317-20.

------ (2009) 'Resisting State Terror: Theorising Communities of Activist Translators and Interpreters', in Esperança Bielsa Mialet and Chris Hughes (eds) *Globalisation, Political Violence and Translation*, Basingstoke & New York: Palgrave Macmillan, 222-42.

Barsky, Robert F. (2005) 'Activist Translation in an Era of Fictional Law', *TTR: traduction, terminologie, rédaction* 18(2): 17-48.

Bielsa, Esperança and Susan Bassnett (2009) *Translation in Global News*, London & New York: Routledge.

Blau, Andrew (2005) 'The Future of Independent Media', *Deeper News* 10(1). Available online: http://www.integratedmedia.org/files/Media/030207_051_0090401.pdf (accessed 15 May 2009).

Carlin, John (2004) 'A Really Bad Case of Penis Envy', *New Statesman*, 12 January. Available online: http://www.newstatesman.com/200401120014 (accessed 15 May 2009).

Castells, Manuel (2000) *The Information Age*, *Volume 1: The Rise of the Network Society*, Second Edition, Oxford: Blackwell.

Crewe, Louise, Andrew Leyshon, Nigel Thrift and Pete Webb (2005) 'Otaku Fever? The Construction of Enthusiasm and the Coproduction of Markets'. Paper presented to the Royal Geographical Society Conference, London, 1st September 2005. Available online: http://www.nottingham.ac.uk/geography/contacts/staffPages/louisecrewe/documents/ibgfans.final.pdf (accessed 15 May 2009).

Cronin, Michael (2000) *Across the Lines: Travel, Language, Translation*, Cork: Cork University Press.

Cronin, Michael (2003) *Translation and Globalization*, London & New York: Routledge.

El Mundo (2006) 'Aznar cree que la OTAN podría bombardear el Líbano si Israel fuera miembro de la Alianza' (Aznar believes that NATO could bomb Lebannon if Israel was a member of the Alliance), 24 July. Available online: http://www.elmundo.es/elmundo/2006/07/24/espana/1153762521.html (accessed 15 May 2009).

El País (2006) 'Aznar, partidario de que la OTAN bombardee Líbano "si fuera necesario"' (Aznar in favour of NATO's bombardment of Lebanon "if necessary"), 24 July . Available online: http://www.elpais.com/articulo/espana/Aznar/partidario/OTAN/bombardee/Libano/fuera/necesario/elpepuesp/20060724elpepunac_9/Tes (accessed 15 May 2009).

Gambier, Yves (2006) 'Orientations de la recherche en traduction audiovisuelle', *Target* 18(2): 261-93.

------ (2007) 'Réseaux de traducteurs/interprètes bénévoles', *Meta* 52(4): 658-72.

Govan, Fiona (2009) 'Lawsuit filed against Spain's ex-PM over Iraq', *The Daily Telegraph*, 3 April. Available online: http://www.telegraph.co.uk/news/worldnews/europe/spain/5100640/Lawsuit-filed-against-Spains-ex-PM-over-Iraq.html (accessed 15 May 2009).

HARDtalk Website, BBC News 24. Available online: http://news.bbc.co.uk/1/hi/programmes/hardtalk/5209566.stm (accessed 15 May 2009).

Harvey, David (1989) *The Condition of Postmodernity: An Enquiry into the Origins of Social Change*, Oxford: Blackwell.

Jenkins, Henry, Katie Clinton, Ravi Purushotma, Alice J. Robison and Margaret Weigel (2006) 'Confronting the Challenges of Participatory Culture: Media Education for the 21st Century', Chicago: The MacArthur Foundation. Available online: http://www.digitallearning.macfound.org/atf/cf/%7B7E45C7E0-A3E0-4B89-AC9C-E807E1B0AE4E%7D/JENKINS_WHITE_PAPER.PDF (accessed 15 May 2009).

Krebs, Katja (2007) *Cultural Dissemination and Translational Communities: German Drama in English Translation 1900-1914*, Manchester: St. Jerome Publishing.

Lash, Scott and John Urry (1994) *Economies of Signs and Space*, London: Sage.

Levy, Pierre (2000) *Collective Intelligence: Man's Emerging World in Cyberspace*, New York: Perseus.

Macintyre, Donald and Eric Silver (2006) 'UK Calls Israeli Attacks 'Disproportionate'', *The Independent*, 24 July. Available online: http://www.independent.co.uk/news/world/middle-east/uk-calls-israeli-attacks-disproportionate-409087.html (accessed 15 May 2009).

Mason, Ian (1994/2010) 'Discourse, Ideology and Translation', in Robert de Beaugrande, Abdulla Shunnaq and Mohamed H. Heliel (eds) *Language, Discourse and Translation in the West and Middle East*, Amsterdam & Philadelphia: John Benjamins, 23-34. Reprinted, with new postscript, in Mona Baker (ed.) *Critical Readings in: Translation Studies*, London & New York: Routledge, 83-95.

------ (2006) 'On Mutual Accessibility of Contextual Assumptions in Dialogue Interpreting', *Journal of Pragmatics* 38(3): 359-73.

McNair, Brian (2006) *Cultural Chaos: Journalism, News and Power in a Globalised World*, London & New York: Routledge.

Pérez-González, Luis (2006a) 'Interpreting Strategic Recontextualization Cues in the Courtroom', *Journal of Pragmatics* 38(3): 390-417.

------ (2006b) 'Fansubbing Anime: Insights into the Butterfly Effect of Globalisation on Audiovisual Translation', *Perspectives: Studies in Translatology* 14(4): 260-77.

Pym, Anthony (1998) *Method in Translation History*, Manchester: St. Jerome Publishing.

Remírez de Ganuza, Carmen (2006) 'Aznar defiende que Israel esté en la OTAN', *El Mundo*, 25 July. Available online: http://www.elmundo.es/papel/2006/07/25/espana/2003339.html (accessed 15 May 2009).

Scholte, Jan Aart (2005) *Globalization: A Critical Introduction*, Second Edition, Basingstoke: Palgrave Macmillan.

Simon, Sherry (1996) *Gender in Translation: Cultural Identity and the Politics of Transmission*, London & New York: Routledge.

------ (2005) 'Presentation', *TTR: traduction, terminologie, rédaction* 18(2): 9-16.

Taylor, Talbot J. and Deborah Cameron (1987) *Analysing Conversation: Rules and Units in the Structure of Talk*, Oxford: Pergamon Press.

Tymoczko, Maria (2000) 'Translation and Political Engagement: Activism, Social Change and the Role of Translation in Geopolitical Shifts', *The Translator* 6(1): 23-48.

------ (2003) 'Ideology and the Position of the Translator: In What Sense is a Translator 'In Between'?', in María Calzada Pérez (ed.) *Apropos of Ideology – Translation Studies on Ideology – Ideologies in Translation Studies*, Manchester: St. Jerome Publishing, 181-201.

------ (2005) 'Trajectories of Research in Translation Studies', *Meta* 50(4): 1082-97.

Venuti, Lawrence (2008) 'Translation, Simulacra, Resistance', *Translation Studies* 1(1): 18-33.

Accessing Contextual Assumptions in Dialogue Interpreting

The Case of Illegal Immigrants in the United States

ROBERT BARSKY
Vanderbilt University, USA

Abstract. *This article considers the importance of Ian Mason's work, on accessing contextual assumptions in dialogue interpreting, by evaluating its implications as regards the kinds of translation and interpretation issues that arise when authority figures encounter 'illegal' immigrants in the Southern US. Based on findings from a large-scale research project completed in 2009, the author argues for a higher level of engagement on the part of the interpreter, such that he or she truly will assume the role of 'interpreter' as opposed to 'translator', active participant instead of a (disingenuously) 'objective' intermediary. On the basis of this work, the author suggests methods of alleviating some of the horrific consequences of the xenophobic lust for 'security' through border enforcement, and the misguided efforts to create immigration law out of a series of haphazardly assembled proposals and guidelines that hapless police officers are forced to enforce.*

Ian Mason's work provides theoretical sophistication to analyses of crucial real-life cases of translation and interpretation, illustrations of which can be found in his own corpus of writings and in applications of his insights to important interpreting settings. An interesting implication of his work is that it helps us think about how interpreters come to be involved in the production of the output of a dialogue in settings where it could be politically valuable. I have suggested elsewhere (Barsky 2007)[1] that activist translation presumes that translators ought to be involved and engaged in the process of communicating information, over and above the act of substituting one lexical item for another, and I will recall sections of this work in order to argue that this could be a positive contribution to the translator's work, in particular if the activism is directed to lofty causes (such as properly representing the views of persons regularly maligned or misrepresented, like asylum seekers, homeless persons

---

[1] Arguments and sections from this work are taken up in the current discussion, since Mason offers grounds for their re-elaboration, and for clarification of their importance.

or 'illegal immigrants'). I will also argue that when the 'translator' decides to become an 'interpreter', a move for which I have argued in the past (Barsky 1996), the subjectivity of the latter will trump the so-called 'objectivity' of the former, but it will also offer the possibility that the interpreter will more adequately represent the victim of intercultural or inter-class misunderstandings which are bound to arise in certain translation settings. I will work under the assumption that the situations in which the interpreter could be most valuable are those in which at least one party to the hearing is a 'foreigner', either in terms of class, race, religion or nationality. I am willing to take the risk that advocating activism over machine-like fidelity in these interpreting settings is salubrious, because the abuses in certain realms of law are so egregious, and the stories so horrendous, that most translators who are given the right to speak out will take the road towards humanity, in my opinion, and my own work in these realms has borne out this suspicion (Barsky 1994, 2001).

One point that is not fully articulated in this position is that any determination of how the interpretation process is unfolding is contingent upon our accessing the 'contextual assumptions' at work during the process of interpreting, and Ian Mason's 2006 article entitled 'On Mutual Accessibility of Contextual Assumptions in Dialogue Interpreting' provides tools for doing so. This work is of particular importance in realms such as legal settings in which individuals from cultures deemed foreign are accused of some misstep because this area almost always involves the 'dialogue interpreting' that Mason describes. I would argue that simultaneous interpreting (with which he deals variously in his writings) and face-to-face dialogue are indeed prevalent examples of what he calls 'on-line' interactions, and that these interactions are especially prevalent in translation settings in which lives of vulnerable persons are at stake. Non-native speakers who are (say) seeking refugee status, or describing life-threatening ailments or injuries, or attempting to free themselves from legal prosecution, generally deal in the crucial first instances with individuals (not texts) whose role in the process is more administrative than functional. By the time they land up in a courtroom, or in recovery from surgery, or – in the example that Mason discusses – in the immigration office providing relevant details of their cases, they have already had several dialogue-interpreting encounters, which in many ways structure or even determine the proceedings and the outcome of the case at hand. For the purposes of this article, the example of this dialogue interpreting to which I will refer occurs when an immigrant or a visitor to the United States is suspected of having illegitimate immigration status in the country by an officer of homeland security, a prison guard or, most frequently, a police officer responding to an alleged traffic violation. And it is here that the contextual assumptions really matter, and that Mason's efforts to understand them can be applied.

1.   Background

The examples I am recalling here emanate from a project on immigrant incarceration in the Southern USA (Barsky 2009),[2] and I will therefore take positive activism in this case to mean efforts that help people who are arrested for immigration violations in the United States (or anywhere else) to obtain justice. But what I will consider to be a positive outcome for a case like this – the liberation of the 'illegal' immigrant from the grips of a manifestly punitive and unfair judicial system – is not likely to occur, not only because translators are not supposed to be activists, and indeed are explicitly discouraged from being anything other than 'impartial', but because the realm of law that deals with immigration violations is so unevenly applied, so internally inconsistent across local, regional, state, federal and national lines, and so variously construed depending upon the person doing the construing, that it does not really deserve the nomenclature of 'law'. The latter point is the subject of a prolonged discussion elsewhere (Barsky 2006), but Mason helps us understand why such injustice occurs in a legal setting when he looks with precision at very specific utterances to determine how such elements as the modal *would* can affect the way a crucial question might come to be interpreted for the benefit of (say) an immigrant seeking status, in an utterance such as: "That immigration officer would ask you some questions" (Mason 2006:360). The import of such a statement can be clarified by the interpreter because she shares a "mutual cognitive environment" with the immigration officer and thus, says Mason, "accounts of the contextual environment of instances of interpreter-mediated communication need to include mapping from utterance meanings and linguistic meanings to actually received meanings, crucially dependent upon mutual accessibility of contextual assumptions" (*ibid.*:361). What is valuable here is that Mason adds to the idea of interpreter activism some very clear descriptions of what needs to be done by the interpreter, notably, "the need for communicators to make assumptions about (others') assumptions" (*ibid.*). In this case, the communicator, or the interpreter, needs to understand the contextual elements that motivate the questions posed by (say) the police officer who has stopped a Latin American for some infringement of the highway code, as well as the contextual elements that motivate the driver of the vehicle to respond to the officer in particular ways. Or, because the burden ought to be placed upon the officer in this case, and because it is unlikely that an interpreter would be present in the squad car during a routine traffic stop, we can expand our idea of interpreter activism by suggesting that not only should the officer understand Spanish if he or she lives in the Southern USA, but should also be trained to understand the situation of migrants so that he or

---

[2] Citations of interviews are all taken from transcriptions recorded in the course of that research and, as per Institutional Review Board guidelines, no other data about interviewees can be provided.

she will be able to understand the specific utterances that might be produced in their presence.

The role I am assigning to the activist translator, or the burden that I am placing upon the official from the host country who is charged with understanding the utterances of (say) an immigrant at a traffic stop, is one of the insider who actively chooses – or is obliged to choose, through regulations governing the workplace – to understand the outsider by putting himself in the outsider's shoes, in this case those of an undocumented immigrant in a country that is overtly uncertain about how to deal with 'illegals'. To do so, we need to expand Mason's idea about 'context' to include the mindset of the officer before the encounter even begins, a step that would be in accord with Stanley Fish's (1990) approach to literary texts, in which he considers the 'interpretative community' as an integral part of the subsequent interpretation. In this case, the interpretative community is one that has already criminalized the immigrants the moment they enter upon our soil, and this after having overtly enticed them here with seemingly un-enforced, and practically unenforceable, laws. Then we expect the police officer, who through his enforcement of the traffic code is on the front lines of dealings with immigrants and therefore immigration law, to properly assess and act upon information that he himself does not understand. As one lawyer interviewed in Tennessee indicated to me, the system seems rigged from the get-go, towards ulterior motives:

> It seems like the public as a whole is more interested in getting rid of people who aren't here legally. I said things were bad in 1994, when the tide started to turn, and it has just gotten worse and worse and worse. I think that to the public, this is the most unsympathetic kind of client. There's a knee-jerk reaction: 'You're here illegally anyway, you're lucky.' I had this conversation with somebody in NY, and I happened to be there the weekend of the Republican Convention. I was talking to someone about the situation and he said, 'What? This person even has rights? How is this person protected by our constitution?' I just turned the conversation around and said, 'Yes, and that is how great this country is, you patriot, that is how awesome our constitution is'!

This is a telling observation, and an interesting example: when someone threatens to limit the sale of firearms in the United States, the immediate response is that the right to bear arms is guaranteed by 'the' constitution; but as this anecdote suggests, when that same constitution is applied to ensure equal rights to all persons living on our soil, then 'the' constitution is treated as 'our' constitution, i.e. that which applies only to 'us' Americans. This perhaps explains how it is that, while our *Wall Street Journal* lauds undocumented immigrants for their entrepreneurial spirit and our corporations hire them for their work ethic and low hourly wage, everyone is outraged when they find out that these useful immigrants actually have rights. The message is clear: illegal immigrants are great to have around when we need them, to undertake the tasks we do not want to take on, and when we don't need them anymore, when they have finished building our stadiums, painting our homes, weeding our gardens, picking our crops, or when they turn out to be human, in particular young human males trying to earn a living but also having some fun, and then they make the mistakes that the rest of us make when we slip behind the wheel of our automobile en route to an inebriated ride upon the suddenly blurry interstates that provide us convenient pathways to our malls and our suburban retreats, then we can unceremoniously make them disappear through incarceration and deportation, as opposed to rehabilitating them through courses, or advocating avoiding such disasters through the building of public transportation.

2. Guilty by virtue of being here

So what we land up with is cheap and available labour that is always in the wrong, human beings who only have the rights we choose to accord, and only as long as we wish to accord them. Being 'illegal', these individuals are criminals; and if they are not technically wrong, they are often made out to be wrong because they cannot communicate their rightness, which means that if we cannot get rid of them for legitimate reasons, we can always claim that they could not make themselves understood in our 'language' – and here I mean both national language and also the kind of professional language described in so much of Pierre Bourdieu's (1990) work on language and symbolic power. In this language exist the rights accorded to all persons on a territory, including the right to refuse (say) an illegal search, without fear of repercussion. As one lawyer in my data states,

> There have been linguists and sociologists who will tell you that people
> in circumstances will consent to anything. It is common for all people
> not empowered to feel that way when asked by an authority figure to
> do something. And if you refuse, it's true as a practical matter that it'll
> bring more pressure down on you.

The guarantee of such protections as those offered by the constitution should outweigh the excuse often made by officials, including judges, that on the basis of a 'hunch', officers have found narcotics, weapons or other signs of illegal activity. These are the exceptions, and Miranda[3] and search requirements have been put into place in the United States to ensure that these searches do not become routine, to the detriment of everyone in society.

---

[3] Miranda rights provide Americans in a custodial situation or in police custody with a warning and a explanation of their rights. An elicited incriminating statement from someone who has not been read these rights, and has not waived them in a voluntary, knowing and intelligent manner, is not admissible as evidence.

3.   The objectives of activist translation

It is in cases like this, when people are made out to be wrong just because they are exercising their rights, where activist interpreters can play a role because they can help both sides in this setting understand what are the "set of premises used in interpreting an utterance" and the "subset of hearer's assumptions about the world" (Sperber and Wilson 1986/1995:15). Mason is helpful here because he insists, in very careful readings, upon our considering the 'participants' communicative intentions', and in offering a way for the interpreter to intervene on the basis of this knowledge. On both sides of an event, such as the arrest of an 'illegal' immigrant for immigration violations, are a set of these 'intentions' which can be, to name but a few mentioned by Mason, "emotive, personal, practical and so on" (2006:363). The most obvious for immigrants would of course be the practical concerns, which would lead them to say whatever seems to be the most efficacious to simply make the situation go away as quickly as possible, whatever the consequences. Many lawyers and interpreters make reference to this tendency through descriptions of police officers requesting the right to search a car for drugs during a routine traffic stop, which inevitably brings up issues of how officers communicate crucial information to the person begin pulled over. For example, Miranda rights must be read to people in a language that they can understand, to ensure that there are no miscarriages of justice which would result either in inappropriate convictions, or in cases being overturned after long and complex review. One interpreter in my data noted the problems that arise when the formal act of reading the rights is fulfilled, but the obligation to ensure that what has been read is being understood is not:

> The big issue that comes up in all of the court proceedings and it does directly affect us has to do with the Miranda rights, and there are some officers out there who think that they speak Spanish. Or they have taken, and we hear this a lot, they had a one week Spanish survival course. These people have this little card, and some of them carry the card with them, containing the text of the Miranda rights. Some of them have learned a few phrases like: "May I have permission to search your car?" Others just think they speak Spanish when they really don't, so they do not even bother to carry around those little cards, and we are having more and more challenges on that because they, the officers, will claim to have asked, in Spanish, "May I search your car". We had this in a case recently, and the guy on the stand was from Mississippi. They asked him to say how he would have said in Spanish "may I search your car." I was doing the interpreting and I had to stop; I did not know what language he was speaking when he said that. It happened so quickly, and as an interpreter, you are always a few steps behind what is going on, you are listening and you are speaking what

> was just spoken so by the time they got back to English, I was sitting
> there thinking: "What was that?" Oh, that was supposed to be Spanish.
> I mean I had a total blank in my interpretation. I had no idea what he
> said. And, you know this guy, on the basis of the fact that he thought
> he was asking for the right to search the car, and that in response the
> Mexican sort of smiled, he thought he was fulfilling his responsibility.
> The driver of the car was nervous, and he smiled; so the officer said
> okay, that means yes. So he searched the car and got the evidence. We
> are just seeing more and more of that. The basic rights that Americans
> have guaranteed … are not being afforded to some of these immigrants.
> They offer these one week courses and the officers think that is all they
> need to get permission to search the car.

If the translator decides to act upon his or her experience in order to provide useful information, in this case (following the lawyer's suggestion) declaring during the hearing that the translation is incomprehensible, then this could be a powerful activist intervention. This is particularly true because translators could be considered 'disinterested' parties, that is, they have no particular claim on the victory of one side or the other in a case against an illegal immigrant.

The second role for activist translators is in the day-to-day dealings with authorities. Undocumented migrants in the so-called First World are criminalized to such a degree as to render virtually any case unarguable, or un-winnable, particularly if there is discretion-sanctioned abuse in the early stages leading to the arrest. In many cases, this abuse is purely linguistic, relating to the simple fact that the immigrants, particularly immigrants without legal papers, are not given the opportunity to 'be heard', or even to speak, because of the shortage of competent linguistic and cultural interpreters who could intervene at crucial moments of interaction with authority. That translators could make a crucial difference flows from the fact that so much of the problem of migrant incarceration happens on the ground, as they say in NGO circles, that is, on the freeways, in the farming communities, and in places where immigrants are called to appear, such as traffic court. This is where the worst abuses of translation meet the potentially nefarious system of vague laws and ordinances which can ensnare foreigners, and what allows the movement from the traffic violation to the federal indictment often has a linguistic element to it. A lawyer who represents farmworkers, who in the South are mostly illegal immigrants, notes the following:

> Language skills on both ends of this equation exacerbate the problem
> tremendously, and in fact lead to an actual shift in the legal categories
> into which people are likely to fall. If an immigrant speaks good Eng-
> lish, or if there is a translator present to ensure that this isn't just racial
> profiling, then the chances of escaping from such random identification
> fishing trips is of course much stronger.

Activist translators therefore need to work in both directions, informing the general public, through whichever intermediary is appropriate, and informing immigrants of their rights; and translators are often the best intermediaries in this sense (Barsky 1994). A public defender[4] I interviewed provides a description of why this is so:

> After interviews, I often ask the translators what they think. We'll accept cases sometimes provisionally, and if there's nothing there there's no sense in wasting our time, so since we have to represent their case, we need to figure it out. So comprehension with a translator was often such that I would have to talk to the translator afterwards. I have read critiques of asylum officers saying 'Why didn't you say that before, why didn't you mention that fact?' I think that translators can be helpful in those considerations, sometimes I would just give up, and ask the opinion of the translator, because it's hard to figure out all of the different issues.

On the other hand, because the linguistic resources are not usually in place at local levels, neither inmates nor lawyers can usually benefit from translators' experience. These already criminalized individuals thus find themselves in jail, and up for deportation, because they get trapped, in a range of different ways – as the same interviewee explains:

> I remember a very sad case we had recently of a guy, a Colombian fellow who just had a little gardening business. In Nashville, you may have noticed that most of the gardeners are Mexican. This fellow was actually Colombian but he was distributing his little cards, his business cards for his nursery on a street where the FBI had set up surveillance on a house where they knew some drug deals were taking place. Because he looked Hispanic and he was putting his little cards out, he got caught on video tape, and they went and picked him up and found out that he was here illegally. If they find you in this country illegally once, and deport you, it is a misdemeanor. But, if it is the second time, it becomes a felony, even if there has been no crime. This guy had been deported previously, and so now he is in jail with felony charges, because of this surveillance. He did not have anything to do with drugs, he was just a gardener.

This example raises another key issue; law enforcement officials have no interest in developing contentious relations with local populations, since it makes their job far more difficult and dangerous. For this reason, police forces around the country have openly disregarded immigration laws, which in some ways is

---

[4] A public defender is a lawyer provided by the state at no cost for eligible persons.

ideal, but since this simply leads to some very unfair discretionary practices, we need to attack the problem more directly, and this example suggests two more radical pathways. First, since this 'war on drugs' has entrapped so many people and led to such a monstrous level of incarceration in the US (more than 2,000,000 inmates, a huge number for drug-related offenses), it needs to be abandoned as a clear failure, and second, to address previous issues, interpreters need to line up as the 'experts' in forms of advocacy that promote multilingualism in the Americas. Finally, and most obviously, the borders need to come down between countries through the Americas, to eliminate the category of the 'illegal' altogether.

4.   Short-term goals

These are, or should be, long-term objectives. But in the interim, if the translator can be encouraged to act as an interpreter, to actively intervene, then the situations that lead to arrests or incarceration could be mitigated. This is however contingent upon other factors relating to the interpreters' own objectives, objectives which are suggested by Mason (2006:365):

> [T]he interpreter, like any real-time user and involved participant, has to do inferencing in order to cope with underdeterminacy: it is simply inescapable. At the same time, interpreters and translators, like any other communicator, have their own perlocutionary purposes and any attempt at accounting for interpreter behaviour independently of these is bound to be inadequate. Thus, an individual move by an interpreter may certainly be consistent with the principle of relevance, i.e. it may seek to achieve greatest contextual effect in exchange for minimum processing cost.

This however requires the interpreter to consider that being personally engaged in the case would be in their best interests, and it is in this sense that it would require a positive activism, because such actions "will be constrained by pretext, including the interpreter's conception of her own role, her personal motivations, and so on" (*ibid.*). There could thus be a range of incentives offered for such behaviour, that is, interpreters could be rewarded when it is clear that the 'message', and not simply the linguistic elements, have been both conveyed and understood in the interpreting setting; this would be akin to paying medical doctors when their patient's health improves, rather than the contrary.

For any of this to occur, the training of the interpreter would have to include some sensitization to the issues confronting the immigrant, particularly, of course, in cross-linguistic and cross-cultural exchanges. Cross-cultural or cross-linguistic translation would have to include interpreting legal rights across linguistic and cultural boundaries, and, *pace* Mason, this translation would have to be judged on its efficacy – not in its having communicated (solely) what is said; we would need to shift criteria, to focus on what is meant, what is understood, and what needs to be understood. A lawyer I interviewed provides us with as sense of what this might entail:

> The cop is supposed to have to tell the person that he can refuse to have his car searched. But if you pull some guy over that doesn't speak any English, how the hell do you explain to him that he doesn't have to consent? I had a federal case where they got permission to search the house. They brought a jailor out who speaks Spanish. She read him the rights in Spanish, and asked if the people in the house understood. So I said, tell me in Spanish what you told them. What she told them was, "you have a right not to use your rights." I said, "come on judge, that's not an explanation of rights!" It passed muster for that day in court. The evidence wasn't suppressed, and this kind of thing happens all the time.

This is a crucial point; for an officer in the United States (or Canada, although in the latter case rights are less clearly defined) to search a car, he or she must have probable cause. If there isn't any, then whatever is found in the course of that search is eligible for suppression. Another lawyer I interviewed clarifies this point:

> Consent has to be knowing, intelligent and voluntary, and for that, language is critically important, as is age, educational background, there are a number of factors to be considered. This is something we can challenge, and the way to do it is get a Spanish speaking expert witness who will watch the tape and say "this officer said 'Do you want eggs with your toast?' or something that was not 'Can I search the car?' We have had some success with this, but a lot of times courts bypass those requirements and find other reasons to justify the search after the fact, because when there are four or five kilos of cocaine found in the car, the courts are inclined to say 'listen, these cops had a hunch, and they acted on the hunch.' There are many more cases where I think that we should have been successful, than cases when we really were successful.

In the current system, however, whatever the officer says, the immigrant will be deemed to have consented, as a public defender made clear:

> The ways in which Spanish speaking clients – and we see it with consent to search issues when Spanish speaking clients are pulled over, – even if they don't understand what the officer is saying, there seems to be this desire to appease or consent, and I think that we see that sometimes with our clients, they consent without understanding. I

don't know if it's a reflection of the way that the justice system works
in Mexico, or if it's more tied to the culture.

But here is another way in which the system works against the foreign
born, because if there is abuse in this form, deportation itself can trump the
legal remedy, as one lawyer explains:

> So even if the immigrant technically has constitutional rights, the trump
> card of deportation ensures that she cannot use them, which leads to
> the truism that although these individuals may have a better shot at
> justice at higher level courts, they're unlikely to go much further than
> the point-of-entry to our legal system, the people doing the arrests, the
> bookings, and the original decision-making in the jails. And with these
> individuals, the handicap of not speaking English is paramount.

5.   Concluding remarks

The activism I have advocated here is, in my sense, justified on the basis of
an accurate presentation of the facts; immigrants are mistreated, particularly if
they do not have proper status, and this is clearly demonstrable by examining
the contextual facts surrounding immigrant arrests and incarceration. I have
suggested that another level of understanding is offered with reference to some
of Ian Mason's work, because he demonstrates methods of finding examples
of interpreter intervention in actual translations in settings such as immigration hearings. A careful examination of these translations and interpretations
offers us evidence for conclusions I have drawn from the texts themselves,
the kind of pragmatics work that is valuable for making the case for activist
translation to authorities or skeptics, among others. In this respect, the 'close
reading' Mason advocates and engages with, with reference to other work in
the realms of discourse analysis and pragmatics, is a particularly fruitful approach to translation studies for reasons he himself sets out (2006:366):

> Recognizing Carston's (2002) underdeterminacy hypothesis as valid,
> we have suggested that a way forward in analyzing the pragmatics
> of dialogue interpreting might lie in using the evidence of actual
> responses (and responses to responses) to trace the communication
> of meanings *beyond what is said*. In order to do this we need to in-
> corporate into our notion of context, in addition to a 'broad', framing
> context of situational and ethnographic information, a 'narrow' local
> element whereby user assumptions are negotiated and re-negotiated
> continuously.

I have focused in my examples upon the earlier stages of inquiry and arrest,
because this is often where the most egregious translation and representation

errors occur. At later stages in the process, when the immigrant finds him or herself facing an actual judge who will determine the consequences of the actions leading up to the sentencing, things seem to be a bit better, if only because there is a formal apparatus for determining the facts of the case, and a set of interpretation and translation norms in effect in the courtroom. And yet, even here discretion sets in; this unbelievable-but-true description from a lawyer I interviewed is emblematic of the whole situation:

> I was in Dayton County, where they had the historic monkey trial at the historic court house. I was on the side of this Hispanic kid who was charged with vehicular homicide; while on his way to work he fell asleep, crossed the center line, hit someone, and killed him. I went down there to represent him. As I'm sitting there, and there are lots of Hispanic folks because it's farm country. They were looking for someone to translate, and so someone says "Go get Paco, somebody said Paco is around." Paco had done eight months in jail and had become the darling of the sheriff and the judge, so they went to go get Paco. I'm not saying anything, I'm just from out of town, visiting, I'm going to hang out here to see what's happening. So I go up and stand next to him while he's translating, and I'm just saying "don't mind me, I'm just standing here." So the judge says to Paco, "You understand son, you have the right to go to trial." Paco translated this as: "You don't want to go to trial, you'll get more time." The judge says "You have a right to have a lawyer with you today." Paco says, "You can have a lawyer, but that means that they are going to continue it, and you don't want to do that, best thing you can do is plead guilty." So I finally got the judge's attention and said, "Ah, pardon me judge, I'm not so sure Paco is doing a real good job translating!" It may be a problem, it may not be a problem, but that was what was passing for translation. And I don't think it has changed, even though there are new rules, where you have to have someone certified. But the rule is, if you don't have a certified translator, then you have to have a registered translator. And if you don't have a registered translator, you can have uncle Joe. And if you don't have uncle Joe, you can have Paco. It just keeps coming down until Paco gets right back into court.

The image here is one where bad faith can prevail and destroy a life, and the life of the family to which the person is connected. But even when there is good faith, things can go awry because the criminalization of the population includes people who could help out in certain cases, as one lawyer in my data recalls:

> We cannot bring those witnesses because they have no documents and you don't want to expose them. I'm not going to go testify in court if I have no papers is the approach. And sometimes immigration is

there. It's not that I think they are just going to take them, but you just don't want to take the risk, and they don't want to take the risk. Those are really big challenges with this population, the ones that are here illegally. I always try to find out who in their family, as we say, has papers. And that would be the person that will come testify on their behalf and to show the judges that this is not just one person but this is a person with a family and children and paint a little bit of a different picture. Even the judges themselves, they have no idea. I had an experience with a judge and I can not believe it. He insisted that these people speak English because they can say "Thank you", or "Yes", or "My name is..." I was in a court room sitting with a client's relative that was considering testifying, at that point we didn't know if he was going to testify or not, or even if there was going to be a hearing. The guy on trial didn't speak any English whatsoever. So, it didn't matter if he stayed in the room or not because he wasn't going to understand anyway. But in general, you go out if you are a witness and you might need to testify. Somebody said "Hey, this person might need to testify', so I elbowed him and I said 'you've got to get out. You've got to go out.' So, the lawyer said, 'yes, your honor, he could leave, but he doesn't speak any English'. So the judge said: 'Sir, you need to leave the room', and he left. But I had already told him that he needed to go; and then he left. And she said, it was a female judge: "You see? He understood! He knows English." So those are the things you have to deal with. This office spends quite a bit of money having documents translated for our clients that don't speak English. To begin with, English itself is a hard language, and English speaking people have no idea what it takes. You can only imagine what somebody who doesn't speak English and has a very low level of education. I rarely get people who have completed high school. Rarely. And I have had one or two that have completed college.

A cautionary note is needed at this point. Efforts at improving the current system which attempt to induce or introduce 'caring' and subjectivity may not be of much help unless there is an appropriate institutional apparatus behind the proposed amendment, and some formal and recognizable set of norms that apply across the board. This is another area in which Mason's work has been valuable, because he has brought to bear an understanding of institutional constraints as well as institutional norms which operate in any given translation situation. His own conclusions to his work on accessing mutual cultural assumptions are helpful in this regard (2006:371):

> The institutional frame within which such events take place may, however, exert a higher-order contextual pressure and sequences have a tendency to return to original goals while individual implicatures are defeasible by the contextual frame. Thus, elsewhere in the data, "For

how long did you come here?" offers the implicature 'How long did you *intend to* stay here?' but is responded to (in the framing context of establishing what was declared on entry to the UK) as implicating 'How long did you *say* you would stay?'. Mutual accessibility of contextual assumptions does not seem to be preserved by many of these moves yet the 'speech-exchange system' (Schegloff, 1999) of dialogue interpreting proceeds undisturbed and this, together with the institutional setting, ensures that institutional goals are served.

This is where Mason's work on "actual responses" (*ibid.*:372) can provide powerful evidence for strong claims. And because our accessing such evidence requires the system to be open to the investigations of third parties (like translation researchers), such an approach may also help pry open the oft-closed doors of much needed inquiry – needed to show the workings of a system that is harmful to those caught in its grasp.

And so, consistent with the 'activist' agenda I have developed elsewhere, and aided by some of the implications of Mason's work, I would like to reiterate, by way of conclusions, some concrete ways to improve approaches to communication, interpretation and translation in such settings.

First, multilingualism needs to be actively promoted, particularly in the United States, where it is considered by many as an un-American activity – witness current debates on 'English only', particularly in the South. This effort would need to be spearheaded by (activist) interpreters and translators who need to present the virtues of multiple language competency in a range of settings.

Second, and to actualize the first, we need to fund multilingual training in schools, corporations and government offices; further, translation studies need to be promoted in institutions of higher learning.

Third, we need to look beyond our borders and form links to governments of nations from which our immigrants come; specifically, we need to promote ties between consulates, embassies, international agencies, NGOs, even international corporations, and we need to lobby them to get involved with the citizens of their countries who are now residing elsewhere.

Fourth, those who are in the translation area need to drop the façade of 'impartiality' when they are faced with clear and obvious abuses of power. This does not have to happen every day, it does not have to implicate everyone in this realm, but it should be discussed, particularly when we are dealing with vulnerable populations.

Fifth, given that more than 2,000,000 people sit inside US prisons on any given day, we need to advocate language instruction and provide materials to incarcerated people. The longer- term goal ought to be to liberate the vast majority of these people and to re-think how we punish non-violent or mentally ill individuals.

These efforts, which would impose few burdens upon current budgets and may in fact have the effect of creating valuable employment, are a bare minimum if we hope to advance the cause of equal rights and fairness in our societies. And efforts like this one, in which Ian Mason's hard work is recalled and studied, help us appreciate the extent to which his work – engaged, solid, serious – has consequences that we are only now beginning to realize.

References

Barsky, Robert F. (1994) 'The Interpreter and the Canadian Convention Refugee Hearing: Crossing the Potentially Life-threatening Boundaries between 'coccode-e-eh,' 'cluck-cluck,' and 'cot-cot-cot'', *TTR* 6(2): 131-56.

------ (1996) 'The Interpreter as Intercultural Agent in Convention Refugee Hearings', *The Translator* 2(1): 45-63.

------ (2001) *Arguing and Justifying: Assessing the Convention Refugee Choice of Moment, Motive and Host Country*, Aldershot: Ashgate.

------ (2006) 'From Discretion to Fictional Law', *SubStance* 35(1): 116-46.

------ (2007) 'Activist Translation in an Era of Fictional Law', in Sherry Simon (ed.) *Translation and Social Activism*, Special Issue of *TTR* 18(2): 17-48.

------ (2009) *Immigrant Incarceration*, Report for the Tennessee Department of Corrections.

Bourdieu, Pierre (1990) *Language and Symbolic Power*, edited by John Thomson, trans. by Gino Raymond and Matthew Adamson, Cambridge, MA: Harvard University Press.

Carston, Robyn (2002) *Thoughts and Utterances: the Pragmatics of Explicit Communication*, Blackwell, Oxford.

Fish, Stanley (1990) *Doing What Comes Naturally: Change, Rhetoric, and the Practice of Theory in Literary and Legal Studies*, Durham, NC: Duke University Press.

Mason, Ian (2006) 'On Mutual Accessibility of Contextual Assumptions in Dialogue Interpreting', *Journal of Pragmatics* 38(3): 359-73.

Sperber, Dan and Deidre Wilson (1986/1995) *Relevance: Communication and Cognition*, Oxford: Blackwell.

The Expanding World
Translation, Mobility and Global Futures

MICHAEL CRONIN
Dublin City University, Ireland

Abstract. *This essay examines the implications for translation of changing experiences of space and time in the contemporary world. It argues for a decisive shift from macro-modernity to micro-modernity in the late modern period and investigates how the perspective of micro-modernity illuminates actual and future practices of translation in the areas of new technology, migration and urbanization. The essay challenges particular 'culturalist' readings of translation and makes a case instead for a more agonistic conceptualization of what translators do in their work. The notion of the city as 'translation zone' is explored in the context of debates around multiculturalism and social cohesion and it is suggested that reflecting on translation is a way of thinking about what might constitute a notion of sustainability for cultures and societies.*

Manuel Esposito is not particularly enamoured of translation. In Roberto Bolaño's novel *2666* we learn that, though he ended up as the Spanish translator of the German writer Benno von Archimboldi, his initial attraction was to the work of Ernst Jünger. The narrator notes:

> Meanwhile, many of his acquaintances weren't just Jünger devotees; some of them were the author's translators, too, which was something Espinoza cared little about, since the glory he coveted was that of the writer, not the translator. (Bolaño 2009:6)

Esposito wants the coveted originality of the writer, not the secondary lustre of the translator. He loses interest in Jünger, however, discovers a passion for Benno von Archimboldi and finds, if not glory, a least a modicum of success as translator and expositor of the work of Archimboldi. What translation provides for Archimboldi is a kind of symbolic passport. Not only does his work offer the writings of the German author a passage into the world of Spanish speakers but Esposito's work as translator and commentator brings him into continuous contact with translators and commentators in other European languages. The novel charts in dizzying detail the wanderings of the translator-nomads. What I want to explore in this essay is how the linguistic restlessness of the translator and the spatial and cultural flux of late modernity are linked in important ways and how translation offers a way into thinking about what might constitute a notion of sustainability for cultures and societies.

Anthony Giddens famously, if not particularly memorably, defined globalization almost two decades ago as "the intensification of worldwide social relations which link distant localities in such a way that local happenings are shaped by events occurring many miles away and vice versa" (1990:64). It has become customary to speak of time-space compression in accounts of the contemporary world, where the time taken to travel distances was greatly reduced in the 20th century. The emergence of international institutions (IMF, World Bank, World Trade Organization (WTO)), the spread of global brands (McDonalds, Starbucks), heightened environmental awareness (Chernobyl, the Brundtland report (1987), UN reports on climate change), worldwide protest movements (Vietnam, anti-globalization protests) are seen as both causes and symptoms of the 'intensification of worldwide social relations'. Time-space convergence at a national level in the 19th century and the first half of the 20th century is facilitated notably through the construction of railways and road networks. Time-space convergence at a global level in the second half of the 20th century is enabled through the exponential growth in air travel and the proliferation of IT and telecommunications networks.

The last two centuries might be termed the era of *macro-modernity*, where the emphasis has been on assembling the overarching infrastructures which allow time-space compression to become a reality. So the most commonly invoked paradigm of our age is the planet as 'a shrinking world'. The collapse of Soviet communism and economic reforms in China further added to the sense of the rise of a global market-centred system (Fukuyama 1992). From this perspective not only is the world smaller but the earth is flatter, to borrow Thomas Friedman's coinage, where the world is conceived of as a level playing field, with all parties competing for the spoils of free trade (Friedman 2006).

The advent of globalization and globalizing processes is not always or inevitably seen as a benign development. From the rise of the anti-globalization movement in the 1990s to the meltdown of financial markets at the end of the first decade of the 21st century, globalization has become a synonym for a plethora of ills (Klein 2007). One constant is the contention that what it entails is an irretrievable loss of innocence, a death sentence for diversity and the spread of what I have called elsewhere 'clonialism', the viral spread of corporate, hegemonic sameness (Cronin 2003:128). As the world shrinks, so do our possibilities for exploring, preserving and promoting difference. The global villages begin to resemble each other in dispiritingly predictable ways, carbon copy model towns presided over by brand uniformity. There is, however, another way in which contemporary experience can be approached, and this is through the prism of what we might term *micro-modernity*. By this

I mean that, starting our analysis from the standpoint of the local, the nearby, the proximate, the micro, we can conceive of the local not as a point of arrival, the parachute drop for global forces, but as a point of departure, an opening out rather than a closing down, a way of re-enchanting a world grown weary of the jeremiads of cultural entropists. In advocating this shift of perspective, I wish to suggest that it is possible to situate translation in a new *politics of introversion* which seeks to expand possibilities, not reduce them, and which reconfigures fundamentals of space and time in the new century with attendant socio-political and cultural consequences. Three privileged sites of micro-modernity are mobility, digital worlds and urbanization. I will explore each of these sites in turn, incorporating specific translational perspectives where appropriate.

1. Mobility

When Italo Calvino's Mr Palomar enters a cheese shop in Paris he is enchanted by what he finds:

> Behind every cheese there is a pasture of different green under a different sky: meadows caked with the salt that the tides of Normandy deposit every evening; meadows scented with aromas in the windy sunlight of Provence; there are different flocks with their stablings and their transhumances; there are secret processes handed down over centuries. This shop is a museum: Mr Palomar visiting it, feels, as he does in the Louvre, behind every displayed object the presence of the civilization that has given it form and takes form from it. (Calvino 1986:66)

A random visit to a Parisian shop becomes a dramatic journey through space and time. A local shop becomes a secular stargate, a portal into the geography and history of an entire nation. Palomar's epiphany gives vivid expression to a distinction set up by the French travel theorist Jean-Didier Urbain between exotic travel and endotic travel (Urbain 1998:217-32). Exotic travel is the more conventional mode of thinking about travel, where travel is seen to involve leaving the prosaic world of the proximate everyday for a distant place, even if the notion of 'distance' can vary through time. Exotic travel implies leaving familiar surroundings for a place which is generally situated at some remove from the routine world of the traveller. From the perspective of macro-modernity, because far becomes nearer, it becomes all the more commonplace to equate travel with going far. Endotic travel, on the other hand, is an exercise in staying close by, not leaving the familiar and travelling interstitially through a world we thought we knew. Endotic travel is the mobile site of micro-modernity.

There are three different strands informing the practice of endotic travel. The first strand is the exploration of what Georges Perec has called the 'infra-ordinary' (Perec 1989). Perec explores the teeming detail of confined spaces in works such as *Espèces d'Espaces* (1974), *Tentative d'épuisement d'un lieu parisien* (1982) and *L'Infra-Ordinaire* (1989). In *Espèces d'espaces*, the narrative focus moves from the bed to the bedroom to the apartment to the building to the street to the town and space itself. In this reverse Google map, the cursor of the writerly eye pulls back from spatial minutiae to a picture which is constructed on a larger and larger scale. However, as is evident in *Tentative d'épuisement d'un lieu parisien*, where the narrator compulsorily lists all the goings on in and around the Café de la Mairie beside the Saint Sulpice church in Paris, the primary aim of Perec's method is to make evident the sheer scale of the 'infra-ordinary', the encyclopedic density of things going on in our immediate surroundings which generally pass unnoticed.

The second strand is an ethnology of proximity expressed in a tradition of writing which goes from Montesquieu's *Lettres Persanes* (1721/1964) to Marc Augé's *La Traversée du Luxembourg* (1985) and *Un Ethnologue dans le métro* (1986). In this ethnographic practice, the usual poles of enquiry are reversed so that it is the domestic not the foreign which becomes the focus of analytic enquiry. In Montesquieu's famous conceit, it is to treat French society and mores as purportedly observed from the viewpoint of Persian visitors. The familiar is exoticized through this foreignizing practice and along the way the French writer points up the disturbing shortcomings of a putatively 'civilized' society. Marc Augé, for his part, treats the Parisian underground as if it were an unknown and hitherto unexplored ethnographic terrain.

The third strand contributing to endotic travel practices is internal travel writing. Internal travel writing makes its point of departure, in a sense, its point of arrival. One of the earliest examples is Xavier de Maistre's *Voyage autour de ma chambre* (1794/1959). In this account de Maistre treats his bedroom in Paris as if it were a vast, uncharted and perilous territory, where moving from his bed to a chair has all the adventure of an expedition on the high seas. A more recent example is François Maspero's *Les Passagers du Roissy Express* (1990). In this travel account Maspero spends two months with the photographer Anaïk Frantz doing a journey that normally takes forty-five minutes. They stop off at each of the stations on the way to central Paris and what are revealed are whole other worlds normally invisible to the traveller hurtling through seemingly featureless spaces on the way from the airport to the city.

What these different strands share is that they are all strategies of defamiliarization. They compel the reader to look afresh, to call into question the taken for granted, to take on board the infinitely receding complexity of the putatively routine or prosaic. They suggest that shrinkage is not a matter of scale but of vision. A narrowing of focus, a reduction in scale can lead to an expansion of insight, an unleashing of interpretive and imaginative possibilities often smothered by the large-scale, long-range hubris of the macro-modern.

2. Endotic perspectives

There are two levels at which the notion of the endotic has implications for translation, the textual and the social. A common misconception among apprentice translators or external observers of translation practices is to assume that translation is first and foremost about foreign languages and their acquisition. In other words, translation is assumed to be primarily an exotic travelling practice, taking the translator to foreign languages, cultures and places. It goes without saying that this view is not wholly mistaken as not knowing a source language would be a poor qualification for a translator, even if this does not stop a great deal of poets in the English speaking world from 'translating' poets from languages wholly unknown to them (the fig leaf in this instance is the coy synonym, 'version'). However, what students of translation soon learn is that it is the endotic dimension to their travels in language which becomes paramount as they realize that they scarcely know the language they had hitherto taken for granted. Translation defamiliarizes the language of the proximate, of the everyday. The student translator becomes increasingly aware of the uncharted territories and the unsuspected complexities of the familiar tongue. They begin to explore domains of usage, webs of intertextual reference, differences of register, shifts in historical meaning which had previously remained under the radar of native language awareness. It is indeed the development of this endotic sensibility at a textual level which accounts for the significant and repeated contributions of translators to the construction and development of national languages.

The endotic manifestation at a social level is best captured in Stuart Hall's notion of 'vernacular cosmopolitanism' (Hall 2002:30). Hall argues that the most notable shift in societies in many parts of the globe in the latter half of the 20th century has been the rapid, internal differentiation of communities. In other words, whereas formerly, the foreign, the exotic, the other, was held to be over the border or beyond the mountains or over the sea, now the other is next door, or across the street or in the same office. Globalized patterns of migration and the creation of supra-national structures like the European Union have meant that a great many places – in particular, but not only, cities – are host to peoples with many different linguistic and cultural backgrounds. This, indeed, is one of the most salient features in Maspero's decelerated odyssey through the stations of the Roissy Express. He comes into contact with migrants speaking a plurality of languages and bringing with them a variety of spoken and unspoken histories. They are bearers of what James Clifford has called 'travel stories', which he distinguishes from "travel literature in the bourgeois sense" (Clifford 1992:110).

The stories are unlikely to be listened to, however, if there is no language in which they can be understood. This is where the endotic dimension of translation comes into play at a social level. What community interpreting most notably does is to open up the communication channels in an era of vernacular cosmopolitanism. As the neighbourhoods of global cities become more densely invested with the linguistic diversity of migrant populations, it is translators and interpreters who are crucially involved in making sure that voices are heard and that the attendant richness of multilingualism and polylingualism becomes something more than an incomprehensible soundtrack to visual paeans to multicultural diversity.

3.   Digital worlds

There is more than one way of making voices heard, however, and crucial to how we conceive of a sustainable future for humanity is the role of machine-human interaction. One of the most notable developments in the last two decades has been the shift from stand-alone PCs, located at fixed work stations, to the spread of distributed computing in the form of laptops, wireless PDAs, mobile phones with internet connectivity and so on. It is not only humans but their machines which are on the move. As Dennis and Urry express it:

> This trend in distributed computing is developing towards a shift to ubiquitous computing where associations between people, place/space, and time are embedded within a systemic relationship between a person and their kinetic environment. (Dennis and Urry 2007:13)

Ubiquitous computing, sometimes referred to as the 'third wave of computing', is one "whose cross-over point with personal computing will be around 2005-2020" and which may become "embedded in walls, chairs, clothing, light switches, cars – in everything" (Weiser and Brown 1996). Greenfield has talked of 'everyware' where information processing is embedded in the objects and surfaces of everyday life (Greenfield 2006:18). The probable social impact of everyware can be compared to electricity which passes invisibly through the walls of every home, office and car. The transition from fixed locations of access to increased wireless presence, coupled with the exponential growth of internet capability, means that greatly augmented information flows become part of an information-immersive environment.

A consequence of the emergence of ubiquitous computing is that computing capacity dissolves into the physical surroundings, architectures and infrastructures. Marcos Novak (2009) has developed the term 'transArchitecture' to signify "a liquid architecture that is transmitted across the global information networks; within physical space it exists as an invisible electronic double superimposed on our material world". William Mitchell in the 1990s had already spoken of a 'city of bits' where the combination of physical structures in urban spaces with the electronic spaces and telematics would be known as 'recombinant architectures' (Mitchell 1995:46-105). Although the multilingual has not appeared, somewhat predictably, in the literature so far, it is difficult to conceive of the trans-architectural in contemporary urban spaces without factoring in the multilingual. That is to say, part of the thinking about next-generation localization is precisely the role that translation will play in the era of distributed, ubiquitous computing.

It is possible to conceive of buildings – government offices, university halls of residence, transport hubs – which would be multilingually enabled. A hand-held device such as a mobile phone would allow the user to access relevant information in the language of his or her choice. Thus, rather than the static and serial presentation of information in a limited number of languages, such a development would allow for a customized interaction with the language user, with the possibility for continuous expansion in languages offered and information offered.

Advances in peer-to-peer computing and the semantic web further favour the transition from a notion of translation provision as available in parallel series to translation as part of a networked system, a potentially integrated nexus. In other words, rather than content being rolled out in a static, sequential manner (e.g. separate language information leaflets at tourist attractions), translated material would be personalized, user-driven and integrated into a dynamic system of ubiquitous delivery. Such developments are in line with the four dominant ideas for the future as articulated by the UK Foresight Report: Personal Mobility; Cyberspace; Smart Flows; and Urban Environment (Sharpe and Hodgson 2006). More specifically, the trans-architectural dimension to the practice of translation not only adds another dimension to the endotic experience of the social but it also invites larger considerations about how we might think about the 'Urban Environment'.

4.   Urbanization

A positive construction of language otherness in urban settings is to see linguistic otherness as an area of genuine possibility, bringing with it new perspectives, energies, traditions and forms of expression into a society. This, of course, begs the question as to how this positive view of alterity might be realized, in view of the sheer language diversity of contemporary migration. Here again translation has a crucial role to play, and nowhere more obviously than in urban planning. Richard Sennett claims, for example, that the major contemporary problem for urbanists committed to a cosmopolitan perspective is "how do you intensify rather than localize social interaction?" (Sennett 2002:47). One way of doing this is to see multilingual, multi-ethnic urban space first and foremost as a *translation zone*. In other words, if translation is primarily about a form of interaction with another language and culture (which in turn modifies one's own), then it is surely to translation that we must look if we want to think about how global neighbourhoods are to become something other than the regime of non-interactive indifference decried by Sennett.

China, for example, intends to move 400 million people, which is roughly half of the country's rural population, into urban centres by 2030 (Dennis and Urry 2007:10). The urbanization of the population is the rule rather than the exception in contemporary demographic developments, and indeed the nature and extent of urbanization has exercised many commentators, from Jacobs to Sassen (Jacobs 1962, Sassen 2006). Town planners ritually concern themselves with problems of traffic management, the state of public utilities, the availability of green spaces, the viability of urban communities, the sustainability of waste practices, and so on, but it seems inexplicable that the multilingual composition of cities across the planet is wholly ignored. The lacuna is all the more surprising in that language difference is the most immediate, audible and practical sign of the presence of others. More worryingly, the failure to address the question of multilingualism from an informed translation perspective allows the emergence of unhealthy alliances between stereotype and rejectionist purism. For example, the European Commission against Racism and Intolerance noted in its *Third Report on the Netherlands* that it had "received an increasing number of reports according to which racial profiling (i.e. the use, with no objective and reasonable justification of grounds such as race, colour, language, religion, nationality or national or ethnic origin in control, surveillance and other similar law enforcement activities) is not uncommon in the Netherlands" (European Commission against Racism and Intolerance 2007:12). Given that language tests are now a central and public part of citizenship requirements in countries such as the Netherlands, Denmark and the United Kingdom, it is hardly surprising that racial profiling should find an alibi in a systematic distrust of language difference. Indeed, translation itself has been identified by certain commentators in the United Kingdom as a dangerous abettor of civic disloyalty:

> It's a shocking figure: more than £100m was spent in the past year on translating and interpreting for British residents who don't speak English. In the name of multiculturalism, one Home Office-funded centre alone provides these services in 76 languages ... The financial cost is bad enough, but there is a wider problem about the confused signals we are sending to immigrant communities. We are telling them they don't have to learn English, let alone integrate. Worse by isolating them linguistically, we have created communities that are now incubators for islamo-fascism. (Rahman 2006)

There is a translation paradigm underlying these comments, an assimilationist paradigm which sees all newcomers and residents as translated into the dominant language of the host community. It is a unidirectional, binary conception of translation which adjudges the nature of translation to be *either* one thing *or* the other. Either everybody speaks the target language or everyone is condemned to the fractured solipsism of source languages. Such a translation scenario is ultimately grounded in the worldview of monoglossia which can only conceive of difference as oppositional. In other words, if the target language is to be dominant, then the very existence of source languages is a threat to the hegemony of the One. Arjun Appadurai, in his exploration of large-scale violence against minorities in Eastern Europe, Rwanda and India in the 1990s, speaks of the "anxiety of incompleteness" (Appadurai 2006:8). His argument is that numerical majorities can become violent, even genocidal towards "small numbers" when minorities remind majorities of the "small gap which lies between their conditions as majorities and the horizon of an unsullied national whole, a pure and untainted national ethos" (*ibid.*). Such movements become particularly prevalent in times of rapid change where national economies and welfare systems are made fragile by the globalization of financial and market relationships:

> The virtually complete loss of even the fiction of a national economy, which had some evidence for its existence in the eras of strong socialist states and central planning now leaves the cultural field as the main one in which fantasies of purity, authenticity, borders, and security can be enacted. (*ibid.*:22-23)

States which are invited to open themselves to the flows of Western capital and the ministrations of transnational corporations compensate by acting out dramas of national sovereignty in the cultural arena. Hence, the prevalence of moral panic around foreign migrants, foreign customs, foreign beliefs and foreign languages.

In positing the city as translation zone I am arguing for a different paradigmatic representation of translation and language. The fundamental move is to see translation as an analog, *both/and* praxis which allows for both the instrumental utility of target language translation and the pragmatic and cultural necessity of mother-tongue maintenance. In other words, translation can obviously be used to allow for the circulation of meaning between a dominant host community and different minority language groups (translation into the target language), but it can also be used as a means of legitimizing language alterity and social accommodation (provision of translating and interpreting services in minority or community languages). To take just one example, integration is not all about either English or nothing else. As the evidence of countless countries throughout the world attests, it is perfectly possible for human beings to operate in more than one language at any number of different levels (Edwards 1995). In this respect, paying due attention to the practice of translation and the encouragement of linguistic diversity in societies is to do nothing that is exceptional in global terms but is to perform a service which is deeply enriching in local contexts. What is more, authoritative research has shown that the surest way to enhance second-language acquisition is to pay careful attention to mother-tongue maintenance (Baker 2000, Cummins 2000, Skutnabb-Kangas 2000).

Crucial to the availability of translation is a conviction that language should not be seen as 'barrier' or an 'obstacle' but as an opportunity. Implicit in this conception is polyglossia rather than monoglossia. If multilingualism suggests a serial image of discrete units, polylingualism implies a more open, networked form of language relationships. Translators are, by definition, polylinguals, but in the repeated representations of cities as sites of serial monolingualism the role of polylinguals is minimized or forgotten. The reformulation of public space in urban centres as primarily a translation zone has the potential to promote a model of social cohesion which encourages the inclusion not the elimination of difference. So in everything, from small local theatres presenting translations of plays from different migrant languages to new voice recognition and speech synthesis technology producing discrete translations in wireless environments, to systematic client education for community interpreting, to translation workshops as part of diversity management courses in the workplace, the possibilities for a more dynamic and less hegemonic conception of urban centres from a translation perspective are numerous.

If cohesion is a watchword of civic viability, sustainability is the mantra of ecological survival. The Scottish theorist Alastair McIntosh describes a 'cycle of belonging' which he sees as integral to any notion of the sustainable (McIntosh 2008:235). The cycle has four elements which follow on from each other, a sense of place (grounding) which gives rise to a sense of identity (ego/head) that carries with it a sense of values (soul/heart) which generates in turn a sense of responsibility (action/hand) (*ibid.*). In emphasizing the role of place, McIntosh is trying to formulate a basis for collective togetherness and responsibility which has an inclusive civic basis rather than an exclusive ethnic basis. The focus on place has equally pressing pragmatic concerns which have to do with the sustainability of human communities. For humans to live like the average Indian, half a planet would be needed, to live like an average European, three would be needed, and to live like the average American, seven planets would be required. McIntosh concludes that "[i]t is only if we can find fulfilment in close proximity to one another and local place that we can hope to stop sucking what we need from all over the world" (*ibid.*:71-72).

It is the disconnection from place where agricultural land is drained, rivers are straightened and concrete is poured over ground that once served as a vital sponge which leads to the catastrophic flooding in various parts of the world, aggravated by increased rainfall due to climate change. But fundamental to any ethics of sustainability or cycle of belonging must be an understanding of place, not only as an object in space but as a phenomenon in time. By this I mean that there is a further dimension to the city as translation zone which resides not only in the social (community interpreting) or the technological (ubiquitous computing) but in the historical. The historical dimension fundamentally relates to the role of translation history in re-presenting histories of place. In this respect, translation history has much in common with contemporary 'global history' which crosses national frontiers, takes a long-term perspective, is comparative in spirit, draws on several disciplines and is particularly interested in questions of contact, exchange, hybridity and migration (Testot 2009:7-8).

In tracing histories of contact and exchange in urban settings, cultural historians, such as Sherry Simon, show that any proper or fuller understanding of place involves bringing to light the multiple, embedded stories of how language communities have negotiated their relationships through translation down through the centuries (Simon 2006). In other words, what is made apparent is that places have a multiplicity of origins and what contemporary migratory developments bring to the fore is the buried multiple histories of specific places. For example, Timothy Brook in *Vermeer's Hat: The 17th Century and the Dawn of the Global World* draws on the material objects found in Vermeer's paintings (a beaver fur hat, a china bowl) to chart the relationship between Dutch cities and forms of proto-globalization (Brook 2008). The objects are used as evidence to show how local lives were intensely connected with and affected by currents of migration, exchange and influence. None of these connections would have been possible were it not for the existence of translators and translation moments. In a sense, what is being suggested is an endotic form of translation history which explores the local place for its connections outwards, its inter-dependence on other languages, cultures, places. Allowing for this approach invests place with a form of fractal complexity which is appropriate to the model of micro-modernity mentioned at the outset of the essay. Highlighting the historical dimension has the added advantage of providing a historical 'home' to newcomers, in that they are made aware of the fact that many places have been places of passage and interchange and that their very 'newness' is part of a long tradition of arrival and settlement.

5.   Cultural translation

One common way of discussing both historical and contemporary developments in the context of urbanization and globalization is to speak about 'cultural translation'. In discussing cultural translation, part of the difficulty lies with the way in which culture itself has assumed a foundational role in contemporary society. If, in previous ages, God or Nature was seen as the ground on which all else rested for its meaning, in the post-modern age it is Culture which is summoned to the basement of epistemic and ontological coherence. The sense that culture goes all the way down satisfies the essentialists who see culture as a set of immutable attributes passed from one generation to the next. Conversely, the notion that anything can be understood as a cultural construction cheers the relativists who can disassemble the handiwork of national chauvinists. The primary difficulty is that both camps explicitly or implicitly subscribe to culturalist readings of social and historical phenomena, which has the signal disadvantage of marginalizing structural questions in political discourse and analysis. In other words, whereas formerly racial or class difference was invoked to justify exclusion and inequality, it is now culture which is recruited to justify surveillance and marginalization. 'They' are not like 'Us' because they eat differently or dress differently or speak differently. The differentialist racism of societies becomes culturalized.

This is one of the reasons why a common response to the highly mediated and mythologized 'crisis' of multiculturalism ('ghettoes' as the sleeper cells of terror) is to focus on the cultural shibboleths of integration, notably the language and citizenship tests mentioned earlier, designed to elicit appropriate cultural knowledge. However, the point about citizenship tests is not that most British or German or Danish or Dutch citizens would fail them. That is not what they are there for. The purpose is explicitly performative. The aim is to subject migrants to the public gaze, where the State can be seen to exact a particular form of linguistic or epistemic tribute. However, what is crucial to note is that 'integration', which is held up as the telos of the tests, is not a static but a dynamic category, which can be indefinitely reframed depending on the exigencies of the moment. That is to say, if the other becomes too well 'integrated', too well 'translated', if they enthusiastically embrace the language, institutions, the habitus of the host society, they become equally suspect as the 'fifth column', the 'enemy within', that dissimulate treachery through feigned assimilation.

The murderous forensics of anti-semitism in European history fed off precisely the highly volatile reconfiguration of what it meant to be 'integrated.' Therefore, the question which might be asked is whether the very term 'cultural' translation is not complicit in the de-politicization of the public sphere. As the social theorist Alana Lentin has noted:

> Many theorists, artists, musicians and writers have emphasised the fluidity of cultural identities. But without challenging the underlying reason for why culture dominates our understandings it is unlikely that this will have a significant impact in the realm of politics and policy making. Thinking culturally about difference is the default for not talking about "race", thereby avoiding the charge of racism. But the need for such a substitute obscures the fact that the hierarchy put in place by racism has been maintained. (2004:99)

When migrants are being asked to translate themselves into the dominant language and value system of the host community, they do so from a vantage point which is almost invariably structurally defined by categories of class and race, yet these structural conditions or contexts for the translation process (whose telos, the successful 'translation', is often indefinitely postponed) are rarely made explicit as such.

Translation historians have detailed the co-option of translation for the process of nation building and the manner in which linguistics in certain manifestations has posited a reified notion of what might constitute a speech community (Delisle and Woodsworth 1995). It is possible to argue, however, that the notion of cultural translation highlights an even more fundamental feature of contemporary societies than the oft-repeated lingering hegemony of nation-states, namely, an intolerance of conflict.

6. Conflict

A substantial section of bookshops in many richer countries is given over to self-help manuals. Implicit in these manuals is the notion that there is an ideal self which is somewhat out of kilter because it lacks confidence, vitamin B, the X factor or has failed to dejunk its life. 'I am not myself today' implies that there is a unitary, consensual self which is the desirable default value for the good life. This psychologised consensualism finds its correlative at a political level in the notion that representative democracy consists of a collection of points of view which are all equally valid. The point of view of the workers' representative where 2,000 jobs have been delocalized is as valid as that of the corporate vice-president who has engineered the 'rationalization'. So everybody gets to have their say. But what they are saying is that real conflict is no longer acceptable. In other words, in reality, points of view are irreducible, as speakers are situated very differently, both materially and structurally, but the false symmetrization of the mediasphere conceals the very genuine conflict of interests through the irenic fiction of the representative soundbite.

In another version of the tyranny of compliance, when social movements oppose government measures, such as penalizing public sector workers for the financial irresponsibility of the private sector, government spokespersons and stockbroker economists talk about a 'communications deficit'. If only the people understood what we were doing, they would realize it was ultimately for their own good. Opposition can only be conceived of as cussedness or stupidity. No allowance is made for the fact that there are grounded material interests and structural conditions which make opposition not only inevitable but vital. It is in this context that translation can be of value to us in proposing a way of thinking about the ontological necessity of conflict.

As even the most rudimentary translation exercise soon reveals, translation is above all an initiation into unsuspected complexity. The simplest of texts turns out to be not as straightforward as we thought. Putting what we find in one text into another language and text and culture throws up unsettling questions about our sense of our own language and makes the familiar alien. What this schooling in complexity reveals is the radical insufficiency of cultural shorthand. That is to say, the cultural categorization of society as made of recognizable types designated by labels – 'dyslexic', 'epileptic', 'Paddy', 'Gay', 'Muslim' – reduces the multi-dimensional complexity of humans to one defining trait. Once someone is described using one of these labels, that is all you need to know about them. They become transparent. What gay rights activists and the womens' movement in various parts of the globe and at different times have attempted to do is to restore multi-dimensionality and complexity to the lives of human beings who were deemed to be instantly intelligible as 'gay' or 'woman', gender or sexual orientation revealing all.

Transparency, of course, is a kind of invisibility, and this is conventionally how translation is perceived, as an unproblematic transcoding process. The practice is predictably different and translators must of necessity engage with the multi-dimensionality of texts, languages and cultures. Nothing can be taken for granted (novices take a lot for granted, hence the culture shock of translation). Words are not what they seem and cultures are maddeningly plural. But there is particular quality to the agonistic basis of translation. In the classic binaries of translation theory – SL and TL, source and target culture, author and translator, translator and reader – we find the binary logic of specular confrontation. Entities with fixed identities face up to each other in a zero sum of binary opposition. But translation as conflict is not confrontation, it is conflict as engagement with the multidimensionality of texts, languages and cultures. It contests the culturalist versions of contemporary biopower which denies translation and interpreting rights to internal minorities in the name of avoiding a 'clash of civilizations' where all conflict is presented as confrontation through the binary stereotyping of Us and Them.

An agonistic conception of translation, which runs directly counter to the beatific visions of universal understanding underlying many public pronouncements on the subject, takes as a basic premise the incomprehensibility of the other. That is to say, translation is not simply the revelation of what is already there. If that were the case, the statistical chances of a relatively large number of students, for example, producing identical translations would be high, whereas in reality this almost never holds true. The reason is that in translation we have the creation of some form of shared sense, some degree of commonality, which gives substance to the idea of translation as not the uncovering of a universal substrate, waiting to be revealed, but the contingent construction of bottom-up commonality. It is in this conflicted sense that translation can provide a way of thinking about contemporary multilingual and multicultural societies in a way that moves beyond revealed universalism and schismatic relativism. Christopher Prendergast, drawing on the work of Victor Segalen, claimed that we "are never 'closer' to another culture (and hence liberated from the raps of ethnocentrism) than when we fail to understand it, when confronted with the points of blockage to interpretive mastery" (Prendergast 2004:xi). If translation is about the eternally deferred, asymptotic attempts to get close to another culture, it also brings into sharp relief the material, social and historical situatedness of peoples, their languages and their texts.

A recurrent concern of the writings of Ian Mason has been an attention to what is actually there in translation and how the materiality of language engages the translator at many different levels. So Esposito need not have despaired. Translation in the current age is at the heart of what matters and offers us a way, both practical and conceptual, of envisioning sustainable communities in a period of great flux. The 'glory' however is not about power, but more humbly, survival.

References

Appadurai, Arjun (2006) *Fear of Small Numbers: An Essay on the Geography of Anger*, Durham NC: Duke University Press.

Augé, Marc (1985) *La Traversée du Luxembourg*, Paris: Hachette.

------ (1986) *Un ethnologue dans le métro*, Paris: Hachette.

Baker, Colin (2000) *A Parents' and Teachers' Guide to Bilingualism*, second edition, Clevedon: Multilingual Matters.

Bolaño, Roberto (2009) *2666*, trans. Natasha Wimmer, London: Picador.

Brook, Timothy (2008) *Vermeer's Hat: The 17th Century and the Dawn of the Global World*, London: Profile.

Calvino, Italo (1986) *Mr. Palomar*, tr. William Weaver, London: Picador.

Clifford, James (1992) 'Travelling Cultures', in Lawrence Grossberg, Cary Nelson and Paula A. Treichler (eds) *Cultural Studies*, London: Routledge, 96-111.

Cronin, Michael (2003) *Translation and Globalization*, London: Routledge.

Cummins, Jim (2000) *Language, Power and Pedagogy: Bilingual Children in the Crossfire*, Clevedon: Multlingual Matters.

Delisle, Jean and Judith Woodsworth (eds) (1995) *Translators through History*, Amsterdam: John Benjamins.

De Maistre, Xavier (1794/1959) *Voyage autour de ma chambre*, Paris: Laffont.

Dennis, Kingsley and John Urry (2007) *The Digital Nexus of Post-Automobility*, Lancaster: Department of Sociology, Lancaster University.

Edwards, John (1995) *Multilingualism*, London: Penguin.

European Commission against Racism and Intolerance (2007) *Third Report on the Netherlands*. Available at http://hudoc.ecri.coe.int/XMLEcri/ENGLISH/Cycle_03/03_CbC_eng/NLD-CbC-III-2008-3-ENG.pdf (accessed 12 March 2009).

Friedman, Thomas (2006) *The World is Flat: The Globalized World in the Twenty-First Century*, London: Penguin.

Fukuyama, Francis (1992) *The End of History and the Last Man*, London: Hamish Hamilton.

Giddens, Anthony (1990) *The Consequences of Modernity*, Stanford, CA: Stanford University Press.

Greenfield, Adam (2006) *Everyware: The Dawning Age of Ubiquitous Computing*, Berkeley, CA: New Riders.

Hall, Stuart (2002) 'Political Belonging in a World of Multiple Identities', in

Stephen Vertovec and Robin Cohen (eds) *Conceiving Cosmopolitanism: Theory, Context, Practice*, Oxford: Oxford University Press, 25-31.

Jacobs, Jane (1962/2000) *The Death and Life of Great American Cities*, London: Pimlico.

Klein, Naomi (2007) *The Shock Doctrine: The Rise of Disaster Capitalism*, London: Penguin.

Lentin, Alana (2004) 'The Problem of Culture and Human Rights in the Response to Racism', in Gavan Titley (ed.) *Resituating Culture*, Strasbourg: Council of Europe, 95-103.

Maspero, François (1990) *Les Passagers du Roissy Express*, Paris: Seuil.

McIntosh, Alastair (2008) *Hell and High Water: Climate Change, Hope and the Human Condition*, Edinburgh: Birlinn.

Mitchell, William (1995) *City of Bits: Space, Place and the Infobahn*, Cambridge, MA: MIT Press.

Montesquieu, Charles-Louis (1724/1964) *Lettres Persanes*, Paris: Garnier-Flammarion.

Novak, Marcos (2009) 'Transarchitecture'. Available at http://framework.v2.nl/archive/archive/node/notion/.xslt/nodenr-127479 (accessed 30 January 2009).

Perec, Georges (1974) *Espèces d'espaces*, Paris: Galilée.

------ (1982) *Tentative d'épuisement d'un lieu parisien*, Paris: Bourgois.

------ (1989) *L'infra-ordinaire*, Paris: Seuil.

Prendergast, Christopher (2004) 'Introduction', in Christopher Prendergast (ed.) *Debating World Literature*, London: Verso, vii-xiii.

Rahman, Zia Haider (2006) 'Hope of Escape Lost in Translation', *The Sunday Times*, 17 December.

Sassen, Saskia (2006) *Cities in a World Economy*, third edition, London: Sage.

Sennett, Richard (2002) 'Cosmopolitanism and the Social Experience of Cities', in Stephen Vertovec and Robin Cohen (eds) *Conceiving Cosmopolitanism: Theory, Context, Practice*, Oxford: Oxford University Press, 42-47.

Sharpe, Bill and Tony Hodgson (2006) *Towards a Cyber-Urban Ecology*, London: Foresight.

Simon, Sherry (2006) *Translating Montreal: Episodes in the Life of a Divided City*, Montreal & Kingston: McGill-Queen's University Press.

Skutnabb-Kangas, Tove (2000) *Linguistic Genocide in Education – or Worldwide Diversity and Human Rights?*, Mahwah, NJ: Lawrence Erlbaum.

Testot, Laurent (2009) 'La naissance d'une histoire-monde', *Sciences humaines* 200: 7-8.

Urbain, Jean-Didier (1998) *Secrets de voyage: menteurs, imposteurs et autres voyageurs immédiats*, Paris: Payot.

Weiser Mark and John S. Brown (1996) 'The Coming Age of Calm Technology'. Available at http://www.ubiq.com/hypertext/weiser/acmfuture2endnote.htm (accessed 1 March 2009).

Notes on Editors and Contributors

Editors

Mona Baker is Professor of Translation Studies at the Centre for Translation and Intercultural Studies, University of Manchester, UK. She is author of *In Other Words: A Coursebook on Translation* and *Translation and Conflict: A Narrative Account*; editor of the *Routledge Encyclopedia of Translation Studies* and *Critical Readings in Translation Studies*; founding editor of *The Translator: Studies in Intercultural Communication*; and founding Vice-President of the International Association for Translation & Intercultural Studies (IATIS).

Maeve Olohan is Senior Lecturer in Translation Studies at the Centre for Translation and Intercultural Studies, University of Manchester, UK. She is author of *Introducing Corpora in Translation Studies*; editor of *Intercultural Faultlines: Research Models in Translation Studies I*, and co-editor (with Myriam Salama-Carr) of *Science in Translation* (Special issue of *The Translator,* forthcoming). Her current research, and the subject of her forthcoming monograph, focuses on the translation of science.

María Calzada Pérez is Professor of Translation Studies at the Universitat Jaume I, Castellón de la Plana, Spain. She is author of *Transitivity in Translating. The Interdependence of Texture and Context, La aventura de la traducción. Dos monólogos de Alan Bennett* and *El espejo traductológico. Teorías y didácticas para la formación del traductor*; and editor of *Apropos of Ideology. Translation on Ideology – Ideologies in Translation Studies* and *Translation and Corpus Linguistics* (Special issue of the *International Journal of Translation*).

Contributors

Ali Aldahesh gained his PhD from the University of Western Sydney for a study on phrasal verbs in English and Arabic. He worked as a research assistant at UWS, making a significant contribution to the data collection methodology of the article published here. He is now a Lecturer in Arabic Language and Literature at the Centre for Arabic and Islamic Studies, Australian National University.

Alya' Al-Rubai'i is a former Professor at Al-Mustansiriyya University in Iraq (Translation Department, College of Arts), from where she gained a PhD in Linguistics and Translation in 1996, and currently teaches at Duhok University, also in Iraq. Her monograph, *Translation Criticism*, appeared in the Durham Modern Language Series/Arabic Series in 2005.

Robert Barsky's work has focused on language studies from a range of perspectives, generally related to studying power relations and the representation of the (oppressed) self in vicarious situations. He is author of *Constructing a Productive Other: Discourse Theory and the Convention Refugee Hearing* (1995) and *Arguing and Justifying: Assessing the Convention Refugee Choice of Moment, Motive and Host Country* (2001). He has also written a trilogy of works on Noam Chomsky: *Noam Chomsky: A Life of Dissent* (1997), *The Chomsky Effect: A Radical Works Beyond the Ivory Tower* (2007), and *From American Linguistics to Socialist Zionism: Zellig Harris's Radical Approach to Language Studies and Politics* (in press). He is currently working on a film and a new book on a radical Zionist organization called Avukah.

Morven Beaton-Thome is Lecturer in Interpreting and Translation Studies, University of Manchester, UK. From 2000 to 2007, she taught German- to-English conference interpreting and interpreting studies at Saarland University, Germany. Her PhD, *Intertextuality and Ideology in Interpreter-mediated Communication. The Case of the European Parliament*, was completed in 2007 under the supervision of Ian Mason and Colin B. Grant at Heriot-Watt University, Edinburgh. She has published in international peer-reviewed journals such as *The Translator*, with research interests continuing to revolve around the ideological role of conference interpreting in institutional settings and the issue of individual and collective interpreter agency.

Stuart Campbell is Professor and Pro Vice Chancellor (Learning & Teaching) at the University of Western Sydney, Australia. His research and publications focus on the issue of translation competence, especially of translators working into English as a second language. He has a special interest in Arabic, and much of his empirical work on translation competence draws on data from Arabic speakers. He has an additional research interest in the influence of Arabic on Indonesian and Malay, and has published in this field.

Raymond Chakhachiro holds a PhD in translation. He is a lecturer in interpreting and translation at the University of Western Sydney, Australia, and a professional interpreter and translator. His research interests include contrastive discourse analysis, comparative stylistics, translation criticism, contrastive pragmatics and conversation analysis.

Martha P.Y. Cheung is Chair Professor in Translation and Associate Vice-President of Hong Kong Baptist University. She has translated many works of Chinese Literature into English, including the works of Han Shaogong and

Liu Sola, and Hong Kong poets such as Leung Ping Kwan. Her most recent publications are *An Anthology of Chinese Discourse on Translation, Volume One: From Earliest Times to the Buddhist Project* (2006) and a guest-edited special issue of *The Translator* entitled *Chinese Discourses on Translation*. Her research interests include literary translation, translation history and translation theory. She is currently working on volume two of *An Anthology of Chinese Discourse on Translation*.

Michael Cronin holds a Personal Chair in the Faculty of Humanities and Social Sciences at Dublin City University, Ireland. He is author of *Translating Ireland* (1996), *Across the Lines* (2000), *Translation and Globalization* (2003), *Time Tracks: Scenes from the Irish Everyday* (2003), *Irish in the New Century/An Ghaeilge san Aois Nua* (2005), *Translation and Identity* (2006), *The Barrytown Trilogy* (2007) and *Translation Goes to the Movies* (2009); and co-editor of *Tourism in Ireland: A Critical Analysis* (1993), *Anthologie de nouvelles irlandaises* (1997), *Unity in Diversity?* (1998), *Reinventing Ireland* (2002), *Irish Tourism* (2003), *The Languages of Ireland* (2003) and *Transforming Ireland* (2009). He is an Honorary Member of the Irish Translators and Interpreters Association.

Theo Hermans is Professor of Dutch and Comparative Literature and Director of the Centre for Intercultural Studies at University College London (UCL). His research interests concern the theory and history of translation. His monographs include *The Structure of Modernist Poetry* (1982), *Translation in Systems* (1999) and *The Conference of the Tongues* (2007). He is the editor of, among others, *Crosscultural Transgressions* (2002), *Translating Others* (2006) and *A Literary History of the Low Countries* (2009).

Ji-Hae Kang is Associate Professor of Translation in the Department of English Language and Literature at Ajou University, Suwon, Republic of Korea. Her main research interests include translation in institutional settings, news media translation, and ideology in translating and interpreting.

Kaisa Koskinen is Acting Professor of English Translation at the University of Tampere, Finland. Her research interests include translation theories and methodology in translation studies, retranslation, EU translation and the ethics of translation. Her main publications are *Beyond Ambivalence. Postmodernity and the Ethics of Translation* (2000) and *Translating Institutions: An Ethnographic Study of EU Translation* (St. Jerome, 2008).

Matthew Maltby has recently completed a PhD at the University of Manchester, UK. His thesis addressed relations between interpreting policy in the asylum application context and wider issues such as discourses on immigration, the multiculturalist agenda and language policy.

Brian Mossop has been a translator, reviser and trainer in the Canadian federal government's Translation Bureau since 1974. He is the author of a textbook entitled *Revising and Editing for Translators* (2nd edition, St. Jerome, 2007) and has led workshops on revision for professional translators, both in Canada and abroad. He has also been a part-time instructor in specialized translation and translation theory at the York University School of Translation in Toronto for the past 30 years, and has published some 40 articles on translation in various translation studies journals.

Jeremy Munday is Senior Lecturer in Spanish Studies and Translation at the University of Leeds, UK. His research interests include translation theory, discourse and text analysis applied to translation, and the application of corpus-based tools to the contrastive analysis of language. His publications include *Introducing Translation Studies* (2001, second edition 2008), *Style and Ideology in Translation: Latin American Writing in English* (2008), *The Routledge Companion to Translation Studies* (2009) and, as co-author with Basil Hatim, *Translation: An Advanced Resource Book* (2004). He is Chair of the Publications Committee of the International Association for Translation and Intercultural Studies (IATIS), editor of *Translation as Intervention* (Continuum and IATIS, 2007) and co-editor, with Sonia Cunico, of the special issue of *The Translator* on Ideology and Translation (2007). He is also a qualified and published translator from Spanish and French to English.

Luis Pérez González is Senior Lecturer in Translation Studies at the Centre for Translation and Intercultural Studies, University of Manchester, where he teaches screen translation, translating for international organizations and interpreting. He has published in the fields of audiovisual translation, systemic functional linguistics and forensic linguistics and supervises doctoral research on audiovisual translation, multimodal communication and interpreting studies. He is Features Editor of *The Interpreter and Translator Trainer* and is currently guest-editing a special issue of the *Journal of Language and Politics* entitled *Translation and the Genealogy of Conflict*. A freelance translator for international organizations since 1995, he has recently acted as a consultant for the European Agency for Reconstruction on the development of translation and interpreter training programmes and translation certification mechanisms in Eastern Europe.

Rebecca Tipton is Lecturer in French at the University of Salford. She is a graduate of the University of Bradford MA in Translation and Interpreting and was a freelance translator, conference and public service interpreter before joining the University of Salford in 2003. Her research interests are in the sociology of the interpreter's workplace, interpreter neutrality and the politics of language services provision.

Cecilia Wadensjö is Professor in Translation Studies at the Institute of Interpretation and Translation Studies, Stockholm University, Sweden. She has published extensively on interpreting as a linguistic and social phenomenon, including a monograph entitled *Interpreting as Interaction* (Longmans, 1998), several articles in translation studies journals, and the co-edited volume *The Critical Link 4* (John Benjamins, 2007). She holds a PhD in Communication Studies from Linköping University, Sweden and a University Diploma in Interpreting (Swedish-Russian) from Stockholm University.

Berta Wakim is a PhD candidate in Linguistics and Translation at the University of Western Sydney. Her PhD explores the assessment of translation within a psycholinguistic theory of second language acquisition. She has worked as research assistant at UWS in the areas of translation processing, psycholinguistics and second language acquisition, as well as in the collection and processing of data from a joint project between UWS and Beijing Foreign Studies University. She is co-author, with Stuart Campbell, of 'Methodological Questions about Translation Research' (*Target*, 2007).

Author Index

Subject Index